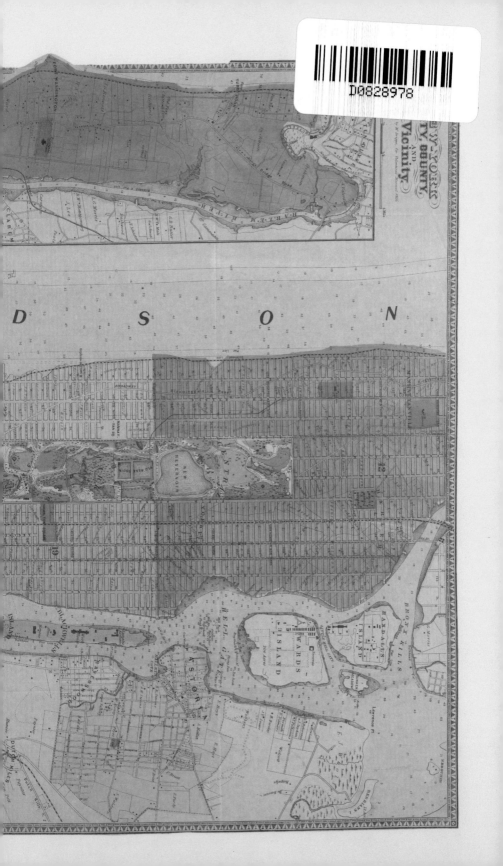

Scenes from the Life of a City

Scenes from the Life of a City

Corruption and Conscience in Old New York

Eric Homberger

Yale University Press · New Haven & London 1994

Set in Sabon by Best-set Typesetter Ltd., Hong Kong
Printed and bound in the United States of America by Edwards Brothers, Inc., Ann Arbor, Michigan

Library of Congress Cataloging-in-Publication Data

Homberger, Eric.
 Scenes from the life of a city: corruption and conscience in old New York/ Eric Homberger.
  p. cm.
 Includes bibliographical references and index.
 ISBN 0-300-06041-6
 1. New York (N.Y.)—History. 2. New York (N.Y.)—Social conditions.
I. Title.
F, 28. 44. H755 1994
974.7' 1—dc20   94-3334
                                                                                                    CIP

A catalogue record for this book is available from the British Library.

Frontispiece: A New York tenement house: "It follows, therefore, that a correction of the physical, will tend to abate the moral, evils of the community" (Dr. John H. Griscom, *The Sanitary Condition of the Laboring Population of New York*, 1844). The struggle to reform the tenement emerged out of the larger mid-century vision of a reformed, cleansed, sober community.

For Judy

Contents

Acknowledgements

T he support of my colleagues at the University of East Anglia in Norwich, England, and their material help in the form of study leave and grants towards research visits to America, have made this book possible.

I would also like to acknowledge the help during the writing of this book of Professor Daniel Aaron; Bill Albert; Professor Elizabeth Blackmar; Mrs. Sarah Cocke; the staff of the Rare Book Room, Countway Library of Medicine, Harvard University; my colleagues at the University of East Anglia: Richard Crockatt, Howard Temperley and Patricia Hollis; Professor Michael DePorte; Mr. John Dorsey, Research Library Office, Boston Public Library; Richard Hendrix; Margaret Homberger; Professor James Mushkat; Professor Jack Salzman and the Center of American Culture Studies, Columbia University; Scott Sanders; Donald and Meg Steiner; and George Abbott White of Brookline, MA. Robert Baldock's belief in this book kept it alive at certain moments when the way forward seemed unclear.

Particular debts of gratitude are owed to Robert Hamburger, William and Weslie Janeway, and George Kraus and Barbara Reno for their kind hospitality in New York.

It was only after the manuscript of this book was substantially complete that I encountered Claude Mançeron's heroic *Les Hommes de la Liberté*, in a compelling five-volume translation by Patricia Wolf (volume one) and Nancy Amphoux (the subsequent volumes), published by Alfred A. Knopf and Simon & Schuster, 1977–89. Before knowing about Mançeron's work, I had found my own way towards something of his method of intersecting biographies.

Early versions of material from chapter two on Madame Restell formed the basis for a lecture at the conference of the European Association for American Studies in London, in April 1990, subsequently published in the *Times Higher Education Supplement* in July 1990; material from chapter four was delivered as a lecture on the creation of Central Park at the University of New Hampshire in 1993.

Being married to a New Yorker has saved me from certain kinds of naiveté common to occasional visitors to the city. Judy Jones Homberger has more than shared my involvement with the lives of Restell, "Slippery Dick" and the others, and it is overwhelmingly to her that I owe the good years in which this book was written.

Introduction

This is a book about the problems posed by an alien, threatening underclass; about abortion; about corrupt politicians; and about the struggle, in a divided and fearful society, to create public space available to both rich and poor. To write about New York as it was, and is, and to call it "history" is a privilege which this book has allowed me. What unites these topics is a pervasive sense in New York that the spirit of community was being lost. The things which bound people to each other, and to the community where they lived, were perceived as having weakened.[1] This book is not specifically about the great "crisis of community" of the Civil War; nor does it address the violent draft riots of the summer of 1863. My subject is a smaller, domestic struggle within New York City over who was to control the community, and over the consequences of rapid urbanization and the perceived breakdown of values that accompanied the frantic growth of the city. Contemporaries viewed such things without the benefit of our sociological and political wisdom. Social conflicts were thus seen largely in "premodern" moral terms as a struggle between good men and bad. The respectable men and women who sought to reform New York retained a vision of community which was, above all, orderly, in which citizens accepted responsibility for themselves and for the civic order. Such people talked about the city and its problems in a language of "sunlight" and "gaslight"; they believed that simple and traditional morality was the best and perhaps only solution for the city's complex problems. They saw their campaigns typologically as incidents, chapters, in a larger struggle. New York was the battlefield, but the survival of the republic, of the Christian community itself, was the ultimate issue.

In a manner of speaking, the forces of reform and "virtue" could proudly point to their triumphs. Abortion was criminalized in the great struggle against Madame Restell. In the course of her career, the public's lax attitude towards abortion was drastically changed, and a harshly repressive public policy was established which criminalized abortion, a policy which persisted for more than a century. (This was, ironically, perceived to be a great *victory* for reform.) The sanitary reformers won their battles against corruption in the city government and continued their campaign against the worst consequences of a widespread public indifference to the causes of so much unnecessary mortality and illness. The Metropolitan Board of Health of 1865 was given powerful tools with which to fight the many problems caused by the explosive growth of polluting industry in the city, and overcrowded urban tenements. Nonetheless, theirs was a struggle in which there were no victories, only local successes. That most effective and corrupt Tweed "Ring" was driven out of power in 1871. Despite many social fears that it would be turned into a drunken beer garden, Central Park was a triumphant success. The agents of this process of transformation found that when they acted the issues were seldom as simple as they believed and their efforts were sometimes discouragingly ineffective. The ambitions of reformers were not modest, and their hopes for a restored community run through the following narratives like a leitmotif. It was not an age of diminished expectations, and each campaign was buoyed along by the hope that *this* reform would, at last, restore the true sense of community to New York.

The idea for this book probably began with a particular smell, a fetid odor noted by Matthew Hale Smith on a visit to a tenement in the Five Points:

> Drunken men, debased women, young girls, helpless children, are packed together in a filthy, under-ground room, destitute of light or ventilation, reeking with filth, and surrounded with a poisoned atmosphere. The decencies of life are abandoned, and blasphemy and ribald talk fill the place.[2]

Or it may have begun with a sentence spoken by the ex-mayor William F. Havemeyer. At the height of the crisis in September 1871 following the revelations of the frauds perpetrated by the Tweed Ring, Havemeyer secretly met with the comptroller, Richard Barrett Connolly—a key figure in the frauds—who was being set up as scapegoat by Tweed and the other Ring principals. A journalist from the New York *World* noted Havemeyer's words after the meeting: "I found him sick and almost ready to give way under the pressure. He said it was crucifying him."[3] It may even have begun with the plea of

Madame Restell facing the prospect of going to prison again at the age of sixty-five. She implored Judge Orlando L. Stewart to act in her defense: "Oh, don't refuse me! Take my case. I am able to pay you well and willing to pay liberally. Do not refuse me! Do not send me away!"[4]

Degradation, punishment, remorse: these were the wages of sin, indeed. New Yorkers expected nothing less. Contemporary sermons and the popular literature of moral instruction contain many such moments of painful recognition of sin, punishment and the hope for redemption. While attempting to unravel what led Connolly and Restell to their moments of anguish, it soon became clear that their stories did not quite fit the contemporary moral stereotypes. Connolly deftly absconded to Europe with millions of dollars of stolen money. Throughout a long career, indeed until the last days of her life, Restell neither felt guilt nor repentance at her trade. The "objects" of reform have a disconcerting capacity to resist or revise the agendas of reform. The "blasphemy and ribald talk" which filled the suffocating cellar, noted almost in passing by Smith, reveal something about the inhabitants which was largely inaudible to outsiders. When Rev. Peter Stryker visited tenements and slums in 1866, his presence aroused little interest. Such visits had become commonplace. As he prepared to leave one dark room, a group of "depraved" children mockingly called out "The miseries of New York!"[5] Their sarcastic voices have been submerged beneath the dominant discourses of society.

Smith's guide in the Five Points was Samuel B. Halliday, agent for the American Female Reform Society in their home mission in the New York slums. Halliday's account of his own activities, published in *The Lost and Found; or Life Among the Poor* (1859), makes instructive reading. He tells of an encounter with a starving woman and her four children, several of whom were showing symptoms of illness caused by the diseases consequent upon prostitution (the euphemism used was "dissipation"). The aims of the American Female Guardian Society, as it was subsequently renamed, were to prevent the corruption of the young by removing them from the sources of evil. When the woman refused to give her youngest daughter into the care of the society, Halliday refused all help to the family. He subsequently arranged for a friendly policeman (not so friendly to the poor) to arrest them as vagrants, after which the youngest daughter was committed to the care of the society by a magistrate. Another case, proudly recounted by Halliday, concerned "Tommy Mack," a young boy who was found on his own in the streets of New York in tattered clothes. Homeless children, temporarily abandoned by their parents, touched a particularly sensitive nerve in the moral concerns of New York. They were to be encountered in every tenement district, wandering the streets or playing in the alleys. It was the growth in the number of homeless children, estimated by the city's chief of police to be several thousand, which led to the formation in 1853 of Brace's Children's Aid Society. Halliday's response, described as though it was nothing out of the ordinary, was to take Tommy to be photographed. He then took the boy to The Tombs, New York's prison, where Tommy's mother was found. She was serving a thirty-day sentence for theft. The woman begged to have her son remain with her in prison, but Halliday was adamant and took the boy before a magistrate who committed him to the care of the society. Implicit is Halliday's belief that institutional care was preferable to that offered by a degraded family. The story of Tommy Mack has a denouement which helps to explain why home missionaries were sometimes attacked and reviled, and why their efforts were regarded suspiciously by tenement-dwellers. When the mother was released from The Tombs, both parents tried to obtain their child from the care of the society. Their writ of habeas corpus was rejected. Further legal maneuvers, including a writ of certiorari, proved equally unsuccessful. In a hearing before Judge James I. Roosevelt, the Supreme Court judge who will play a crucial role in the legal disputes over Central Park in chapter four, the parents argued that they were respectable and passionately cared for their son. At that moment the society's lawyer produced the photograph taken when Halliday first encountered Tommy Mack. Judge Roosevelt confirmed the order placing the child with the society. Repeated legal attempts to regain their son were all unsuccessful.[6]

Halliday regarded the story of Tommy Mack as a small victory for the forces of "sunlight" in the darkening gloom of the New York slums. He was quietly delighted at this salutary defeat of the brutal, intemperate slum-dwellers, but failed to ask what the parents' sustained and expensive legal battle for their son meant. It does not accord with Halliday's belief in their improvidence. As Nathaniel Hawthorne once slyly observed, motherhood in the slums was "strangely identical" to what we have known of it in the "happiest [of] homes".[7] The family may have only been broken up temporarily; (one can imagine the circumstances: the father seeking work outside the city, the mother, arrested and taken directly to prison, leaving the child on his own). The subsequent actions of the parents suggest that Tommy had not been callously abandoned or mistreated. Convinced that such people were "lost to all moral feeling, and to all sense of shame," Halliday could conceive of no alternative way to understand the condition of Tommy Mack.

We might easily construct another narrative, revising Halliday's understanding of the slum family. But that is not likely to produce a happier outcome for anyone involved, as a similar narrative, published by the American Female Guardian Society in 1859, makes clear. It describes two young girls, Susan and Ida, abandoned by their widowed mother and placed by charity workers with families in the country. The girls were reclaimed by their mother five years later in a fashion which raised the same problems of understanding. The veritable "phrenzy" of the mother's struggle to reclaim the girls, her "mother's conscience," seemed "strange" to the charity women. How was it that someone ". . . who had heretofore shown so much apathy toward her offspring, could now suffer so much on their account." Indeed, "[i]t was revolting to our sense of humanity and justice" to remove the girls from a home where "elevating and saving influences" abounded. Later contact with the girls strengthened their belief that parental instincts, and a substantial but confused public opinion, could not be trusted to provide an adequate guide. The mother and two girls sank into illness and the lowest depths of poverty, and it was only out of a Christian sense of loyalty that the younger girl, Ida, remained to look after her ill mother. They pleaded with Ida to accept their help. Perhaps she did; perhaps not; the outcome is left uncertain at the end. Within a Christian perspective, the child's faith had triumphed. Though wrecked, she was "divinely *rescued*." That too was a "victory" of sorts in the slums, but the story of Susan and Ida has about it a tinge of a deeper failure, a disturbing, tinny taste of complacency and evasive piety in the face of human disaster.[8]

Halliday (and his photographs) and the well-meaning ladies of the Female Guardian Society employ the instruments of a new kind of social power introduced into the lives of the slum family, in Halliday's case punishing it and breaking it apart. To make any headway in the slums, men and women like Halliday needed rigid certainties and the belief in the virtue of their own purposes. We perhaps understand with greater clarity the arrogance of his good intentions, and the ambiguity of the stories he recounts.

Abortionists, crooked politicians, and "the poor" were among the objects of reform in nineteenth-century New York, and we largely see such people through the accounts of those like Halliday who would reform them. The contemporary accounts of Restell are written by medical reformers, an Episcopal bishop, a physician, and a chief of police, each outspoken in his hostility to abortion and contempt for Restell. Virtually everything on Connolly comes heavily laden with the bitter anger of the campaign waged to destroy the Ring. Later scholars follow suit. This is thus a book in part about reformers, their self-characterization, rhetoric and tactics, and about the objects of their reforms. I have not offered here a comprehensive account of reform, but rather have sought to suggest something of its process in four narratives attending closely to the outcome of reform as revealed in the lives of specific individuals. Our understanding of the stated and perhaps latent objectives of reform has been shaped by the debate about whether reformers were dedicated to progress, improvement and the liberation of the individual, or whether their actions were class-bound, and reflected an upper-class and evangelical push for social control.[9] Social divisions within reform, and especially the divide between the elite boards of managers or trustees, the professional agents (like Halliday) and those, like Robert Hartley, who largely managed the day-to-day affairs of the societies, and the individuals of humbler origin who belonged to local churches, ward societies and who made up the foot-soldiers of such movements as temperance reform, suggest that the range of motives was diverse. There were, as Lewis Pease discovered, rich opportunities for disagreement between the Methodist patrons of his work in the Five Points and his own conclusions about what needed to be done. Few mechanics or artisans played leadership roles in reform movements, and fewer still from the elite had contact with the clients. (Charles Loring Brace was one of the few whose charitable work gave him entrée to the city's social elite while regularly bringing him into contact with the city's submerged life. He thus spoke with great authority across the city's social divisions.) Common commitment to a social end did not lessen the hierarchical nature of the social relations within reform organizations. For my part I have sought to read between the lines of reform and to ask what vision of community infused the efforts of specific individuals.

Dr. John H. Griscom's Society for the Reformation of Juvenile Delinquents, Halliday and the American Female Guardian Society, Caroline Kirkland's Home for Discharged Female Convicts, Rev. Lewis Morris Pease's Five Points House of Industry, Charles Loring Brace's Children's Aid Society, Robert M. Hartley's Association for Improving the Condition of the Poor, the Committee of Seventy, the Citizens' Association, physicians who manned the city's dispensaries as well as the well-intentioned and idealistic clergymen and prosperous New Yorkers who supported their efforts, represent the "sunshine" in the ethical scheme of mid-century New York. These people acted for the betterment of the community as they understood it while others did nothing. The silence of so many respectable people was a source of continued frustration for reformers, and of simmering outrage to those, like Theodore Roosevelt, who looked back with admiration at the generation of his father (a leading figure in commercial life who was a member of the Union League Club during the Civil War) and his uncle Robert Barnwell Roosevelt (lifelong Democrat, congressman and member of the Committee of Seventy which orchestrated the defeat of the Tweed Ring). He wrote of the antebellum elite:

> In the summer they all went to Saratoga or to Europe; in winter they came back to New York. Fifth Avenue was becoming the fashionable street, and on it they built their brownstone-front houses, all alike outside, and all furnished in the same style within,—heavy furniture, gilding, mirrors, glittering chandeliers. If a man was very rich he had a few feet more frontage, and more gilding, more mirrors, and more chandeliers. There was one incessant round of gaiety, but it possessed no variety whatsoever, and little interest.[10]

Roosevelt believed such people owed something more to society, and also to their class. The conservative activism which he so powerfully unleashed after the turn of the century drew more than we have suspected from the struggles of his father's and uncle's generation, and from the widespread belief that the disappearance of the elite from public life in mid-century was a major source of the many ills of the politics of New York. What unites the diverse efforts at reform discussed here is the concern to restore that elite to its former place at the heart of public affairs. The effort to reconstruct an aristocracy was also an attempt to redefine the role of the elite in a society whose democratic process had so far gone out of control that cynical, dishonest men dominated the city government. The revulsion that men of integrity felt at the very mention of the "government" of the city of New York was the first obstacle to comprehensive reform.

A related theme concerns the halting recognition that community itself would have to be salvaged from the false values that threatened to wreck society. Alienation (a term unknown to New Yorkers in this period, though they were remarkably acute in describing its symptoms), and not a full-hearted belief in community, seemed to be the condition of urban life. The breakdown of values and norms threatened everyone with "lawless social anarchy."[11] Ever boastful of the size, wealth and ceaseless energy of their city, New Yorkers knew that community had been lost, that the rich and poor lived in increasingly remote worlds; no one knew what to do about it. It was also clear that some did not wish to heal this breach and were determined to erect between themselves and the swirling slums an ever higher social and economic barrier.

These themes came together in the 1850s over the question of the creation of a large park in New York. The park idea demonstrated two things: that an elite could function effectively for the civic betterment, and that there could be an environment in which rich and poor met in informal conditions, without exacerbating social fears. Inevitably, the park had been interpreted as a vehicle for social control. Underlying the debates over the construction of Central Park were the class anxieties of the wealthy, and their deep-seated fear of social disorder. The park thus showed that government could create an environment where the sober lessons of community could be taught. It was also seen as a remarkably successful democratic experiment. Every day which passed without outbreaks of drunkenness or social disorder in the park was a striking vindication of the community's power to endure. "Who is not proud that, in a day of swindling in politics, and of cast-iron in building, such grand works can be achieved in rugged honesty and solid stone? It silences forever the clatter of skeptics of the democratic principle as inimical to vast public works."[12]

In the midst of an alienating urban environment, the park, and the efforts of its central designer and manager, Frederick Law Olmsted, represented a reconciliation of the aristocratic hope to reconstruct a role for an elite (newly invigorated by devotion to civic betterment) with the search for new forms of community in a democracy. With his Whiggish aristocratic sympathies and his democratic impulses, Olmsted is our representative man.[13] In his conservative belief in the need for institutions, and his personal inability to function within institutions controlled by others, he no less squarely embodies the contradictions of mid-century reform. He proudly defended the free labor of the northern economy in his books about the "Cotton Kingdom" in the 1850s and was wedded to individualism. Olmsted was no less aware that the needs of the community could no longer be left to individual benevolence. Indeed, the lessons of his important work with the Sanitary Commission during the Civil War showed that benevolence would have to be organized and directed. When the commissioners of the Central Park sought to direct and channel his own activities, he grew irritable, protested and eventually resigned. His ambivalent desire to reconstruct an aristocracy, and his belief in the democratic ability of the people to reconstruct community, were projected outward on to Central Park. The park itself is the most enduring monument we have to the hopes of mid-century reformers; of their ambivalences—and our own.

Eric Homberger
Norwich
New Year's Day, 1994

"... *New York is the* materialist *place in our country* ..."
Charles Loring Brace to John Hull Olmsted, 6 February 1851

"... *we may call New-York the* head *of the United States—if
not the entire head, it's certainly the largest developed organ
in the phrenological chart* ..."
  Glimpses of New-York City by a South Carolinian, 1852

"*The Metropolis is a symbol, an intensification of the country.*"

Junius Henri Browne,
The Great Metropolis: A Mirror of New York, 1869

"*Our slums express our civilization, ... and our rubbish heaps
tell sermons that our stones conceal.*"

Lewis Mumford,
Sticks and Stones, 1924

CHAPTER ONE

The lower depths

Take physick, pomp;
Expose thyself to feel what wretches feel . . .
King Lear

". . . look, and pass"

In late January 1840 Henry Longfellow willingly interrupted his round of academic tasks at Harvard to travel to New York City. He had been invited to lecture on literary topics at the New York Mercantile Library Association, and chose to give two talks on Dante and one on Jean Paul Richter, thus effectively combining his great enthusiasms for "Christian" Dante and "Romantic" German culture. Both writers led Longfellow away from the mundane and disappointing quotidian life of Boston, Cambridge and Harvard and suggested realms and aspirations that were sad, lofty, otherworldly and rich with the promise of spiritual kinship. Dante increasingly offered Longfellow spiritual consolation and emotional nourishment: "I know of no book so fearfully expressive of human passions as this," he wrote of the *Divine Comedy* in his journal on 9 January 1840.[1] George Ticknor, his predecessor at Harvard, had offered a course on the *Divine Comedy* during his term as teacher there between 1819–35. Ticknor's interests were historical and linguistic rather than literary, and he published nothing on Dante. Longfellow customarily read the poem aloud to his students, translating as he went, pausing to comment on particular episodes or matters which required explication. The allegorical structure of the *Divine Comedy*, and its figurative and symbolic meaning, seemed less important to Longfellow than a Romantic immediacy of response and a deep reverence. He translated Schelling's essay "Dante and the Divine Comedy" in 1848, and read it to his class. "It must have been darkness deep to them," he wrote in his diary, and afterwards confined his commentaries to the interpretation of the text's verbal complexities.[2] His celebrated translation of Dante, so often resumed and then put aside, eventually was published in 1867. James Russell Lowell, who helped Longfellow with the translation and eventually took over his friend's course in the 1870s, conducted Dante classes at Harvard in which the poem's aesthetic and ethical values were gravely noted. Barrett Wendell recalled a class with Lowell in 1876–7:

> "Here before us was a great poem—a lasting impression of what human life had meant to a human being, dead and gone these five centuries. Let us try, as best we might, to see what life had meant to this man; let us see what relation his experience, great and small, bore to ours; and, now and then, let us pause for a moment to notice how wonderfully beautiful his expression of this experience was. Let us read, as sympathetically as we could make ourselves read, the words of one who was as much a man as we; only vastly greater in his knowledge of wisdom and beauty." That was the spirit of Mr. Lowell's teaching.[3]

Americans in the nineteenth century read Dante largely as Lowell suggested; but for those closer to the problems of the city, Dante's descent into Hell lent itself to widespread use as a metaphor for social investigation.[4]

The key passage came in Canto III of the *Inferno*. Longfellow's translation describes the poet's visit to "the people dolorous." On hearing "sighs, complaints, and ululations loud," the poet began to weep:

> Languages diverse, horrible dialects,
> Accents of anger, words of agony,
> And voices high and hoarse, with sound of hands,
> Made up a tumult that goes whirling on
> Forever in that air forever black,
> Even as the sand doth, when the whirlwind breathes.[5]

The scene in *Inferno* III is a commentary upon other visits to the underworld, the nekuia in the *Iliad*, and Dante's model, *Aeneid* VI, in which Aeneas asked the Sibyl the meaning of the crowd which "came streaming to the banks" of the Acheron, and stood "begging to be first across/And reached out longing hands to the far shore."[6] The Sibyl explained that they were the souls of the unburied who had been denied permission to cross the Acheron until their bones were buried or they had wandered for one hundred years. Aeneas stopped "and stood/In pity for the souls' hard lot" (VI, 449–50). His old helmsman the drowned Palinurus was among the unburied and begged deliverance, but the Sibyl intervened before Aeneas could reply. Such a request was improper, she said; hope sustained by prayer was of no value. Only when the people, "induced by portents," built a tomb and made offerings could Palinurus' spirit be released. Salvation, in other words, was to come through the piety and virtue of the people. In *Inferno* III, Dante was shocked by the cries and whirling tumult and begged an explanation from Virgil. The reply he received carried none of the Sibyl's measured promise of hope, no hint of alleviation for souls stranded on the bank.

> I will tell thee very briefly.
> These people have not any hope of death;
> And this blind life of theirs is so debased,
> They envious are of every other fate.
> No fame of them the world permits to be;
> Misericord and Justice both disdain them.
> Let us not speak of them, but look, and pass. (III, 45–51)

The Sibyl held out some hope to Palinurus, though not of immediate redemption. The pleas for help and cries of pain and rage in the *Inferno* left the stern-faced Virgil unmoved. Punishment was just. The sufferers were not *deserving*, and Dante was advised to drop the subject.

Redemption and the shameful life

It is hardly surprising that such passages in Dante were read in the light of contemporary concerns. New York, and indeed every substantial city, was swarming with beggars. It seemed to some visitors that hands were held out everywhere, beseeching help:

> . . . beggars penetrate every quarter and corner of the town. You dare not leave your front door open, lest they enter your library or private chamber with a face that would curdle milk. They steal into every hotel drawing-room, in spite of porters and servants, and show you their lacerated forms. They come between you and your friends in Broadway whom you have not seen since boyhood, and thrust their sickening rags into your very face.[7]

In the slums the cries of the poor competed with the sounds of drunken revelry in the brothels, saloons and dance halls. A young theology student attending the destitute and sick on Blackwell's Island wrote to his sister: "You can have no idea, Emma, what an immense vat of misery and crime and filth much of this great city is!

I realize it more and more. Think of *ten thousand children* growing up almost sure to be prostitutes and rogues!"[8] "In New York poverty is simply a living death," wrote James D. McCabe, Jr. "The city is full of suffering and misery."[9]

Dante suggested a way to see, if not necessarily to understand, the most pressing and intractable problems of the day. In a sermon in New York on the "Shameful Life," Rev. Edwin Hubbell Chapin, explicating 8 John 10–11, argued:

> ... Christ gave the woman a chance to go and sin no more, and to recover the standard of virtue. This is what society should do now; for if God pardons, who shall refuse? If God takes up these poor, abandoned ones, who shall reject them? Yet this is just what we do. Society makes a Dante's hell of that state of Shameful Life; closes its doors, and inscribes over them, *"No hope."*[10]

The fate of young country girls, drawn into prostitution in New York, was described by Matthew Hale Smith in a passage which concluded with the same oft-quoted line from the *Inferno*:

> The vicious arms of New York stretch themselves hundreds of miles away into the country. In picnics, large gatherings, private academies, and on commencement occasions, victims are secured. Once in New York, the horror and remorse, the sickness and suffering of the new life, break on the victim. Tears of blood are shed without avail. The motto over bad New York is the startling words, "Whoso entereth here leaves hope behind."[11]

"As I moved through this place," remembered Rev. T. De Witt Talmage of the Five Points, "I said, 'This is the home of lost souls.' It was a Dante's Inferno; nothing to stir the mirth, but many things to fill the eyes with tears of pity."[12] The women to be found in the "basement brothels" of lower Manhattan were similarly described by the lawyers Howe and Hummel with a conventional allusion: "Their bloated forms, pimpled features and bloodshot eyes are suggestive of an Inferno, while their tawdry dresses, brazen leer, and disgusting assumption of an air of gay abandon, emphasizes their hideousness and renders it more repulsive."[13] The sexual and social logic behind these allusions to Dante connects a certain perception of the sin with an understanding of the nature of the woman as sinner. Reformers found many prostitutes unresponsive to their sermons and pleas to repent. Brazenly pleased with their lives, they were living proof that women were uniquely vulnerable to a complete, desolating corruption; the lost were truly lost. The prevalence of whoring in New York, and the role it played in the city's system

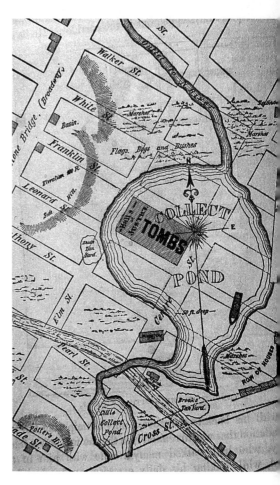

Right and facing page The Tombs was located on swampy land occupied by the city's tanners before the revolution. The Collect Pond was drained in 1808, and on this site the Halls of Justice (universally known as The Tombs) was completed in 1838. Designed for 200 prisoners, it often held twice that number.

of corruption, crime and the intricate web of vice, made it seem a one-way road to degradation and death. "After a woman once enter a house of prostitution and leads the life of all who dwell there, *it i too late*," wrote George G. Foster in 1850, strongly echoing th "abandon all hope" theme. "The woman is transformed to a devi and there is no hope for her."[14]

It was in The Tombs, New York's great prison, where the organi zational logic of the *Inferno* was applied: a hierarchy of crimes wa reflected in the ordering of cells. The Tombs was a prison within prison. The Egyptian-style outer building enclosed a large courtyar in which there stood a separate department reserved for male pris oners. A "Bridge of Sighs" connected the two buildings, above whic was the inscription: "Abandon Hope Ye Who Enter Here." In th courtyard, beneath the bridge, the prison gallows would be erecte on hanging days. The women's department and the police court wer

An account of The Tombs in 1846 noted that "dampness pervades the entire structure, and it is not an uncommon thing for the cells to be overflowed with the water which is forced back through the drain pipes..." (*A Picture of New York in 1846*, New York: Homans & Ellis, 1846).

in the outer building. Six comfortable cells, reserved for the wealthier class of accused criminals who were able to pay for superior accommodation, looked out at the passing scene of Center Street. On the fourth floor, closest to the skylight at the top of the inner building, which was its only source of ventilation, were those charged with assault and battery. On the third floor, were those held on charges of petty larceny. On the dank and gloomy second floor were those who had been accused of grand larceny and burglary, more serious crimes against property. Prison cells at The Tombs were like spacious coffins: just $6\frac{1}{2}$ feet wide by $12\frac{1}{2}$ deep and had no windows. Daylight filtered into the cells through a narrow aperture cut obliquely into the wall. No more than two men were placed in such a cell, though the "five-day" prisoners, convicted of lesser offenses, were kept in cells twice that size. There was a large "Bummers' Cell" for Saturday night drunks. Once a day prisoners were allowed out of their cells to walk around the railed balcony on each floor. There was a denominational rota of clergymen who preached, standing on a little platform, to the assembled Bummers. Prisoners in the cells could not see the preacher, but could listen to the sermon if the spirit moved them.

In the female department, containing about eighty prisoners, three-fourths were imprisoned for crimes resulting from habitual drunkenness. Mothers were allowed to keep their young children with them in The Tombs. Of the female prisoners it was estimated that no more than one out of twelve could either read or write. Half of the male prisoners were illiterate and uneducated. "Never before," wrote a reporter after visiting The Tombs, "did we look upon so many depraved and sunken specimens of human wretchedness as met our eye in this prison." A shower bath and bathing room were on the first floor. A fitting location: for it was in the shower room where the serious disciplinary measures were enforced. At that lowest circle of The Tombs prisoners were "disciplined" by mechanical devices, and also by water. From the first floor condemned prisoners were taken into the yard to be hung. It was a heart of darkness, of sorts, but one which so little bothered the authorities that engravings portraying tortures at the worst state facility at Auburn appeared several years later in *Harper's Weekly*. If the nearby Five Points House of Industry and the many benevolent institutions represented the aspirations of the reforming conscience of New York, for the poor The Tombs was the reality awaiting many on the wrong side of the Two Nations.[15]

Two Nations

The social order was changing, and contemporaries found many signs around them that the distance between classes was growing ever more pronounced. It was hard even for the most level-headed citizen to understand the strange new forms of life in American cities. Pierre Glendinning in Melville's *Pierre, or, The Ambiguities* (1852) arrives at the watch-house of an unnamed ward in New York to find a scene of "indescribable disorder":

> ... frantic, diseased-looking men and women of all colors, and in all imaginable flaunting, immodest, grotesque, and shattered dresses, were leaping, yelling, and cursing around him. The torn Madras handkerchiefs of negresses, and the red gowns of yellow girls, hanging in tatters from their naked bosoms, mixed with the rent dresses of deep-rouged

A punitive shower bath.

white women, and the split coats, checkered vests, and protruding shirts of pale, or whiskered, or haggard, or mustached fellows of all nations, some of whom seemed scared from their beds, and others seemingly arrested in the midst of some crazy and wanton dance. On all sides, were heard drunken male and female voices, in English, French, Spanish, and Portuguese, interlarded now and then, with the foulest of all human lingoes, that dialect of sin and death, known as the Cant language, or the Flash.[16]

Glendinning is stunned by this scene, and concludes that "[t]the thieves'-quarter, and all the brothels, Lock-and-Sin hospitals for incurables, and infirmaries and infernoes of hell seemed to have made

The Bishop's Mitre.

one combined sortie, and poured out upon earth through the vile vomitory of some unmentionable cellar." The clergy, who saw themselves as the conscience of the community, should have been the one group in the city with a full sense of the deepening social divisions. They were regularly in contact with the problem of poverty, but even the most concerned wondered whether, as clergymen, they were somehow disabled from grasping the problem fully. The most sensitive clergy were wracked by self-doubt. "We do not fairly take the free and unobstructed pressure of all surrounding society," wrote Orville Dewey to Rev. Henry W. Bellows in 1852,

> We are hedged around with artificial barriers, built up by superstitious reverence and false respect. We are cased in peculiarity. We meet and mingle with trouble and sorrow, — enough of them, too much,— but our treatment of them gets hackneyed, worn, weary, and reluctant. We grapple with the world's strife and trial, but it is in armor. Our excision from the world's pleasure and free intercourse, I doubt, is not good for us. We are a sort of moral eunuchs.[17]

Charles Loring Brace complained that of the entire Protestant clergy in New York in 1853, ". . . [t]here are not half a dozen of the whole number who ever have even traversed the poorest streets of the city. They know scarcely anything about the masses. They are in comfortable, honored positions, and live with and preach to the rich . . . [and] do not lead in a single great enterprise of humanity . . ."[18]

In his *Annual Report* for the Children's Aid Society, Brace hammered home year after year what he regarded as a dangerous fracture in the fabric of the community: "Union Square or the Avenues know as little of Water Street or Cherry Street as if they were different cities. The poor and the rich are forming almost castes toward one another."[19] Nothing could be further removed from Brace's progressive social concern than the didactic fiction of Catherine Maria Sedgwick—*A New England Tale* (1822), *Redwood* (1824), *Hope Leslie* (1827) and especially *The Poor Rich Man and the Rich Poor Man* (1837)—which addresses the alarming signs of growing inequality of wealth and power in American society by denying that the divisions were to be blamed on the rich. Sedgwick's characters suggest that inequality was "the necessary result of the human condition" and she piously blames the poor for being the authors of their misfortunes: "The rich here can make no separating lines which the poor cannot pass. It is the poor who fence themselves in with ignorance and press themselves down with shiftlessness and vice." And again:

> "If we can't have things right in this world, we can have right feelings; let us kneel down and pray together, Susan."
> "Oh, yes, Lottie, that is always a comfort."[20]

The "two nations" idea, popularized by a string of English novels beginning with Disraeli's *Sybil, or The Two Nations*, published in 1845 and soon pirated in twenty-five-cent editions in Cincinnati and elsewhere, did not seem "foreign" to American observers in the

1850s. Rather, it reflected a common apprehension at the changes being produced by urbanization and industrialism.

The champions of benevolence, such as the American Female Guardian Society, found that the deepening social divisions in New York were producing a crisis of representation. The society frankly presented the problem in an internal meeting in September 1849:

> We may cite in our memorial statistical facts, representing the thousands of wretched children in our cities, who are attendants of no school upon the week day or the Sabbath, and who, if spared, will inevitably grow up in utter ignorance and vice, unless reached by more efficient legislation than the mere *permission* to attend a free school if they will. We may present the cruelty of the doom that allies so many in our cities to the sad inheritance of the drunkard's child—with no adequate redress provided, though sufferers from cold and hunger and nakedness and peril. We can depict what our eyes have seen and our hearts have felt in relation to the moral renovation effected in cases quite similar, and by all that is deplorable in vice and lovely in virtue, we can intreat [*sic*] them to act on this question for God and humanity.[21]

Citing statistics, recounting endless tales of cruelty and doom, descriptions—the traditional weaponry of appeals to conscience—seemed to fall upon deaf ears, blind eyes. "There are," wrote Rev. Chapin, "immensities of human degradation which require the eye-witness to apprehend."[22] It was sometimes necessary, as Dr. John Griscom found, to resort to direct comparisons to make the point about social distance:

> The Fifth-avenue, one of the most spacious, elevated, cleanly and sparsely inhabited thoroughfares of this or any city, claims you as a resident. That noble street, within a range of one mile and a half, contains about 300 inhabited dwellings, averaging perhaps, five inmates each. There all that ingenuity can devise, or wealth purchase, contributes to the comfort and health of the occupants of its palatial mansions. Whenever disease, however trivial, invades a household, there hasten to its removal the most learned and skilled of the medical profession. Probably every child of the proper age attends school where there is no over-crowding, and no danger of small pox, scarlet fever, or any other of the diseases so prevalent and fatal among the less fortunate of the people. There the death rate is of course at the very lowest figure in the scale, and there the sanitary officer may pass by without inquiry or investigation. Alas! how difficult it is for the denizen of such a precinct to realize the deplorable contrast with other localities. But, to demonstrate to you the wide difference between your home and that of some of your fellow-citizens, I summon

your attention to the following *analysis of a single block* in the Fourth Ward:

> Fifty nine miserable buildings, occupied by 382 families, in which are 812 Irish, 218 Germans, 186 Italians, 189 Polanders, 39 Negroes, and 10 *Americans.* Total, 1,520.
>
> Of the 614 children, but 166 attend any school. Of the 906 adults, 605 can neither read nor write!
>
> There are about 50 degraded women, but *not one of them an American.*
>
> In this block are 33 underground tenements, the most of which are from 8 to 10 feet below the sidewalk.
>
> There are *twenty grog-shops.* One Sabbath a gentleman counted, for five hours, the number of persons who went into but *two* of them. There were 450 men, 445 women, 82 boys, and 68 girls! Total, 1,054 persons.

Such a picture as this has probably never been presented to your sight or your imagination.[23]

The imagination of social reform in mid-century New York was structured by such sharp differences of condition, and by the alarming difficulty even the "denizens of such a precinct" as Fifth Avenue had in grasping the causes of difference.

The 1 December 1860 issue of *Harper's Weekly* carried a double-page allegorical engraving by Winslow Homer,[24] *The Two Great Classes of Society,* which represented the Two Nations in a series of paired scenes from high life and low. At the center of the engraving is a semi-circular panel in which a man sits at a table counting money. In its simplest allegorical representation, this was the heart, or at least the counting-room, of the republic. Wall Street, and the biggest and most aggressive American banks, are symbolically represented through their most widely acknowledged commercial activity. To the left are two scenes, both drawing on conventional representations of the life of upper-class New York women. One is of a young lady reading a letter while a maid does her hair. The other image is of opulently dressed ladies at the opera.

The Academy of Music was founded in 1853 by a small number of wealthy New Yorkers who, in the aftermath of the notorious Astor Place Riot of 1849, and the closure of the Astor Place Opera House three years later, wanted a place where the cultural ambitions of the elite could be realized in an environment which was above all safe and respectable, but also on a scale which flattered their own sense of self-importance.[25] Located at 14th Street and Irving Avenue, the Academy contained a main auditorium which seated 4,000. At that time it was the largest opera hall in the world. These images of

Two Nations: by 1860 the divisions between rich and poor in New York were more blatant, an[d] more troubling. Winslow Homer was twenty-four when he published this image of complacenc[e] and deprivation in *Harper's Weekly*.

upper-class life in the *Harper's Weekly* engraving are paired on the right with a drawing of a starving seamstress, and a mother and daughter hovering over a cradle. They are obviously distraught. The seamstress was among the most widely exploited of all city workers. Every issue of *Peterson's Monthly*, filled with adaptations of the latest Parisian fashions to be seen on Broadway, carried with it a reminder of an invisible army of blandly exploited seamstresses. A plain cotton shirt or flannel undershirt could be ordered for six cents (two or three a day being the maximum which could be made). Fine linen shirts required fifteen to eighteen hours to complete, and cost fifty cents each. The starving seamstresses driven into the streets were a living reproach to an aristocracy proud of their "civilization." George G. Foster estimated that there were 30,000 seamstresses in New York in 1848.[26] The pleasures of "culture" are available to the rich; heartbreak and starvation are the lot of the poor. Above the central panel of the money counter are a pair of representations of men: on the left, a fashionable gentleman reclines, reading a copy of *Harper's Weekly*; on the right, a man stands grasping a chicken by the neck: these are images of comfort and leisure paired with a desperate moment of theft. Beneath the central panel a rich profusion of fowl and game hang, recalling the recent Thanksgiving festivities and anticipating the glorious feast of Christmas. The fowl and game symbolically represent what separates the "two great classes": celebrations, well-being, comfort. (The text reads, from left to right: "Those who have more Dinners than appetites." "Those who have more appetite than Dinners.")

To the right of the game and fowl is the only unpaired image in the allegory: a schoolboy bringing home a loaf of bread. Is he rejoining the distraught mother and daughter or the starving seamstress? The schoolboy represents one of the gravest worries of reformers, who feared the consequences of a corrupted, vicious youth being bred in the slums. He also represented one of the most active objects of the social concern of the reformers, such as Brace and Halliday, who sought out the young in the slums. And, in the social fables of Horatio Alger, who translated Brace's activities with the Children's Aid Society into educational tales for young readers across the nation, the figure of the young schoolboy in the engraving represented the social hope of the mid-century reformers. The structural implication of the division between opera-going socialites and seamstresses, of the form of the engraving, is that nothing can be done (except expressing disapproval). The purposeful activity of the young boy alone is a consolation. Winslow Homer's was a complex vision, ultimately left open. Time will tell whether the young boy will fulfill his promise.

The "sunlight" and "shadow" or "gaslight" books by Matthew Hale Smith, George G. Foster and others relied on the same "two nations" structural comparison of high and low, virtue and vice. Facing the title page of Smith's *Sunshine and Shadow in New York* (1868) is an engraving of two buildings and street scenes. The "sunshine" building is a well-maintained stone structure of four stories, with graceful coaches in the well-drained street; before it are pavements upon which elegantly dressed people stroll. (It is the mansion of A. T. Stewart on Fifth Avenue at 34th Street.) The buildings from the "shadow" are of two and three stories, made of wood or stone, and already invoke a hierarchy of size, materials and social prominence. They are in obvious disrepair. A teamster whips a woebegone horse; people are fighting on the pavements; and in the midst of this decay is the sole source of hope: The Old Brewery, location of the Five Points Mission sponsored by the Ladies Home Mission Society.

Other ways of seeing the two nations drew upon the dichotomies between a "wretched home" (a dark, unclean room, unlit stove, empty bowl, with cracked plaster, ragged child, Father drunkenly

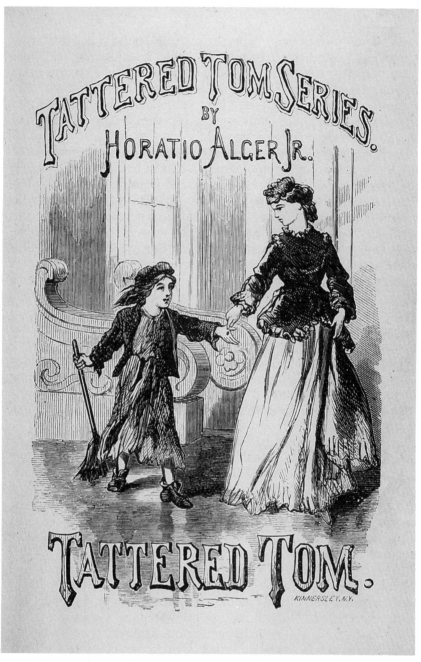

The blessings of charity: the frontispiece of the *Tattered Tom Series*, engraved by Kinnersley, published in Horatio Alger, Jr., *Phil the Fiddler; or, The Story of a Young Street Musician* (Boston: Loring, 1872).

sleeping at a table, upon which rests a bottle, while Mother stares moodily at him from bed, an infant in her arms) and the "happy home" (a room brightly lit with gas, with a crucifix upon the mantle, rich brocaded curtains at the windows, floral-patterned rugs on the floor; the older daughter is playing piano; the oldest boy looks at a specimen through a microscope, the middle boy is reading, the youngest talking to Mother; Father, meanwhile, sits, legs crossed, reading the paper.)[27] What did such images mean to New Yorkers? The representation of virtue, when not specifically rural, was highly charged with middle-class values and tastes. Wretchedness, deprivation, despair, and drunkenness, seemed to contemporaries the most likely outcome for those falling on the wrong side of the Two Nations: the choice was between domestic rectitude and contentment, or despair. Whatever middle ground was possible between the two was, for the purpose of making the point, completely excluded. Erupting into the "wretched" home is a policeman, with a billy club in one hand, and holding a lantern which sheds a faint light upon the scene. Winslow Homer envisaged the possibility of an outcome (the schoolboy) which would somehow emerge from the situation; for the wretched, the state alone can intervene, but its double meaning (club and faint illumination) left little likelihood of improving the family's plight.

After the Civil War half of the city population was born abroad. Old buildings were torn down and new, larger structures were built; empty blocks were filled in; streets were opened, widened, dug up for sewers; and there was a constant movement of people. The flood of immigrants was such that whole neighborhoods came to be seen as foreign cities where English was scarcely to be heard. In this world, increasingly alien to the white, Anglo-Saxon and Protestant Americans, the disease, filth and degradation were to be found which (in their darker imaginings) threatened the whole of civilized life. For those who wanted to strengthen the threatened lines of social communication, who wanted the slum-dwellers to live in decent, modest conditions and to have a better or at least a less unhealthy life, or who were moved by concerns no more elevated than the threats, social and sanitary, posed by the slums, the visits of Aeneas and Dante to the underworld suggested a metaphor, a trope, for the act of entering the new urban world and experiencing it. But where Dante's visit to the lower depths was to warn, to record the punishments of the wicked and sinful and to affirm the divine justice of their torment, nineteenth-century American reformers added another dimension: they wanted their readers to *understand* and even to *sympathize*. Their agenda was ameliorative, though they were seldom untouched by a swirling anger at the poor themselves, in all of their

Two Nations: A. T. Stewart's home on the northwest corner of Fifth Avenue at 34th Street (built in 1864 to the design of John Kellum) was the first of that street's mansions to break with the established pattern of brownstone residences.

Stewart built in white Carrara marble, and lavished staggering sums on every

...he rewards of "active benevolence."

swinish misery. "I passed yesterday on Blackwell's Island, and had forgotten that there were any but low-browed, ophthalmic, blotchy people in the world" (Catherine Maria Sedgwick, 1850).[28] The dialogue between concern and outrage, with all of its predictable class-based discomfiture, gave a particular shape to their approach to the problems of the very poorest.

Reformers knew in vivid detail that entrenched suspicions and fears among the comfortable would have to be challenged if the true conditions within the slums were to be understood; being of a pragmatic generation, they believed that if the problem was to be adequately understood it would have to be experienced, to be made available, in a way that was both comprehensible and effective. Despite an understandable reluctance to encourage the "most virtuous" from coming into contact with "pollution," voiced forcefully by Rev. Peter Stryker (who also thought it was a bad idea for his parishioners to read "minute accounts" of urban vice: "You will incur fearful risks in perusing the story of demoralization."[29]), pro-

(*caption continued*)

excessive detail. The Old Brewery in the Five Points was perhaps the worst slum in antebellum New York, housing hundreds of paupers, criminals, prostitutes and immigrants. The building was purchased by the Ladies' Home Missionary Society of the Methodist Episcopal church and on the site a modern mission was erected.

gressive clergy in New York sought to break down that separation of rich from poor through pleas for "active benevolence." But such pleas as that made by Rev. John M. Mason may have carried little expectation that his comfortable congregation would actually rise and seek out the impoverished.

> Go, with your opulence to the house of famine and the retreats of disease. Go, *deal thy bread to the hungry; when thou seest the naked, cover him; and hide thyself from thine own flesh.* Go and furnish means to rear the offspring of the poor; that they may at least have access to the word of your God. Go, and quicken the flight of the Angel, who has everlasting gospel to preach unto the nations.[30]

A generation later Chapin made the same demand: "You, yourself, must walk through those reeking labyrinths; must breathe that fetid air. . . ."[31] This seemed the only way to break through the widening gap between classes, and to soften the heartless indifference which characterized attitudes towards the poor among the middle class in New York. Rev. Orville Dewey, pastor of the Second Unitarian Church in New York, posed the problem directly to his parishioners:

> If I could take you one walk with me, beneath those over-shadowing tents of poverty, vice and misery; if I could show you how thousands and tens of thousands are living in the very midst of us, though seldom in our sight; if I could open to you all their miserable abodes—from the damp cellar, to the desolate garret—those gloomy tenements, without furniture, without food, without clothing, without one relic of earthly comfort of any sort; *if you could see* the besotted father, the haggard-looking mother, the loathsome features of sickness and heart-sinking wretchedness, that would glare upon you from many a dismal recess and untended cot; *if you could hear* the sighings of distress, the mutterings of anger, the sound of imprecations and curses, that measure out the hours of every day you live, and startle the ear of every midnight when you sleep, and which nothing but a strong police can hold in check; and oh! more than all—*could you behold* poor, pale, forlorn, innocent childhood in those scenes, shivering under reckless threats and blows, more even than from cold and nakedness; children— ah! sacred nurture of parental care, in which yours are reared up— children, unlike yours, trained to vice and beggary by the very first accents of lawful command that they ever hear; trained to falsehood and sin before they ever knew the voice of truth and purity; offered up in all their trusting simplicity a spectacle (God pity it!) to make a heart of adamant bleed—offered up, helpless, innocent victims, upon the altar of their parents' dissoluteness and misery; yes, my friends, if you could see and know all this, you would feel that something must be done in a case so awful and appalling.[32]

Dewey's formula ("if you could see and know all this, you would feel . . .") precisely captures the dilemma, and the strategy, of reform. The search for images of "grim want" to "disturb the slumbers of our wealthy who recline upon downy beds and luxuriate in spacious parlors" proceeded apace. "The crowded, filthy, badly ventilated, wretchedly contrived houses of this city are more than a disgrace to the community," angrily reminded Rev. Stryker:

> They are a standing reproach against our rich men, who ought, for the sake of humanity, to be using their surplus funds in erecting cheap and comfortable residences for the poor all over the island of Manhattan. . . . These men seem to be destitute of mind as well as soul. *Cannot they see* that our overflowing population is rapidly passing from poverty to crime, and the few dollars they are saving by their parsimony to leave to prodigal heirs, is converting thousands into beggars, thieves, prostitutes and murderers? *Are they so short sighted* that they cannot behold the pestilence and famine hovering like vultures around their anticipated victims, and threatening to depopulate us?[33]

Early in his work for the Children's Aid Society, Brace sought to bring "the women of New York who were awakening to a sense of their great responsibilities towards this class [of little girls begging in the area near Cherry, Water and Roosevelt Streets], to meet face to face the evils of which he was daily giving accounts in his addresses and writings." He found a number of "devoted women from the more fortunate classes" willing freely to give of their time, and few things cheered him more than their "self-sacrificing" example. Brace passionately believed in the need for "*personal visitation*": "It is not your gift, carelessly given; your charity bestowed publicly in mass, your food cast to the begging, which gladdens the squalid hovel and makes future penury easier borne. One word of sympathy, a look moistened with the heart's feelings, a laugh or a pleasant joke, *with* the judicious help, will go further in relieving poverty than many a cold and rich donation."[34] It was precisely the spirit of "practical benevolence" which alone (reformers believed) could break down the gulf which had opened between classes in New York. Stryker argued that "No man can afford to keep himself apart from human suffering. He needs the society of the beggar as much as he needs that of the rich. His heart must be put near to the heart of the great masses of mankind, or he loses that which is the greatest gain of human life,—human sympathy . . ."[35]

Dewey, Brace, Stryker and other reformers realistically knew that there was no possibility that substantial numbers of Americans would actually visit the slums, but the *imagination*[36] could conduct them into the lives of the poor, as they had been shown slavery in such works as Mrs. Stowe's *Uncle Tom's Cabin*. Facts and figures were inadequate for the fullest understanding of the problem. The weekly numbers of Henry Mayhew's *London Labour and the London Poor* (1851) were illustrated by woodcuts made from the daguerreotypes of Richard Beard. With the arrival of half-tone reproduction of photographic images in the 1880s, and the invention of magnesium flash powder which made indoor photography possible, the photograph became an indispensable tool in the hands of reformers. Jacob Riis, who had experienced the brutal, exhausting life of an impoverished immigrant in New York before he found work as a police reporter, began his celebrated slide talks on "The Other Half, How It Lives and Dies in New York" in 1888. (The "invitation" in photographs such as Riis's "Baxter Street Alley in Mulberry Bend" (1888) and similar work by Lewis Hine had a didactic and rhetorical aim: to invite the middle-class audience to contemplate "Gotham's crime and misery by night and day.")[37] The "sensation" literature which circulated in the workplaces and urban slums, and the dime novels, had a different readership in mind, though they too revealed the conditions prevalent in the city slums, while often conveying a moral message, warning of the wages of sin.[38] It became an essential project of reformers, and those hopping aboard the bandwagon of public concern, to find literary forms, the devices of culture, to overcome the increasing distance separating classes and races in American society.

The Virgilian invitation

In the Virgilian mode of social investigation—for this seems the most appropriate label—the guided tour of the underworld became one of the commonplace tropes of contemporary journalism. It was widely used by British reformers, and appears everywhere in the crusades of the Progressive era: in addition to his photographs, Riis introduced the slums and alleys below Chatham Street in *How the Other Half Lives* (1890) as though the reader was accompanying him upon a walk. "As we stroll from one narrow street to another..." he suggests to his reader-companion "Take a look into this Roosevelt Street alley..." Standing before a tenement, he asked:

> Suppose we look into one? No.—Cherry Street. Be a little careful, please! The hall is dark and you might stumble over the children pitching pennies back there. Not that it would hurt them; kicks and cuffs are their daily diet. They have little else. Here where the hall turns and dives into utter darkness is a step, and another, another. A flight of stairs. You can feel your way, if you cannot see it. Close? Yes! What would you

have? All the fresh air that ever enters these stairs comes from the hall-door that is forever slamming, and from the windows of dark bedrooms that in turn receive from the stairs their sole supply of the elements God meant to be free, but man deals out with such niggardly hand.[39]

By encouraging his readers to share the experience of the slums, he hoped that they would better understand the true nature of the problem. Not long after the publication of Riis's book, Commissioner Ballington Booth of the New York Salvation Army, accompanied by his wife and two other companions, appropriately disguised themselves and ventured forth at night into the Bowery and Five Points. (The intersection of Park, Worth and Baxter Streets, scarcely a ten-minute walk north of City Hall, was the heart of the worst slum in the city for most of the nineteenth century.) Their vivid account of what they saw was published in 1891 as *New York's Inferno: Scenes of pathos powerfully portrayed*. Sensation-seeking journalists prowled through the vice dens of the slums, and satirists found the editor's interest an irresistible target.[40]

The American interest in the slums of New York had, in the early decades of the century, no focus, no specific location which could give the Society for the Prevention of Pauperism, founded by John Griscom in 1817, and the New York Magdalen Society, devoted from the early 1830s to the rescue of fallen women, a physical and social symbol for their endeavors.[41] But there were, as Rev. John R. McDowall found, powerful inhibitions when it came to describing the vices and iniquities of the Five Points. McDowall's work in the Five Points, and his *Magdalen Journal* and *Magdalen Facts* (1832), brought him into conflict with his supporting society, the Female Benevolent Reform Society. Underlying the accusations of improper behavior, and financial disputes, there was an unmistakable reluctance on the part of the society to be associated with someone who not only dealt, day after day, with prostitutes, but who insisted on writing and talking about their plight and its causes. He was accused of spreading the *details* of sin, and thus, by a curious logic by no means unknown to later generations, of encouraging it. McDowall had repeatedly argued that the prostitutes were no worse, morally, than their patrons. By 1834, his lonely struggles in the Five Points had brought him to an important conclusion, one which made his break with the Presbyterian synod of New York inevitable:

He had labored with much solicitude to reclaim abandoned females for years, almost in vain. He had seen them promise well for weeks and months, and then "like a dog to his vomit, or a sow to her wallowing," return to their sins, until his hope in this department had perished. He had abandoned the idea that anything but temporarily and extremely limited advantages could be obtained from any measure short of reaching the public mind.[42]

This is an important moment in the creation of mid-nineteenth century reform. McDowall, who died in 1836 while charges were still pending against him from the Female Benevolent Society, grasped that modern reform is engaged in shaping consciousness, in making the public self-conscious. This is a point which Chapin made forcefully two decades later: "The civilization of our time is imperfect; involves many incongruities; perhaps creates some evil; but that it is an improved civilization, is evinced by the fact that it is *self-conscious*; for perception is the necessary antecedent of endeavor and success."[43]

The Five Points, long a site of decay, vice and corruption, remained to be discovered and made visible. That task was seized by Charles Dickens. On his celebrated American tour in 1842, he was accompanied by two policemen on a visit to the Five Points slum. "Ascend these pitch-dark stairs," he wrote, "heedful of a false footing on the trembling boards, and grope your way with me into this wolfish den, where neither ray of light nor breath of air, appears to come." A flickering match revealed "great mounds of dusty rags" which began to move. It was like a scene out of the *Inferno*. The floor was covered with "heaps of Negro women" shivering at the chilly and damp conditions. In the "housetop" or attic, Dickens found more sleeping people. It was a scene describable only in terms of last things, a ghastly parody of the moment of salvation and resurrection:

> They have a charcoal fire within; there is a smell of singeing clothes, or flesh, so close they gather round the brazier; and vapours issue forth that blind and suffocate. From every corner, as you glance about you in these dark retreats, some figure crawls half-awakened, as if the judgment-hour were near at hand, and every obscene grave were giving up its dead. Where dogs would howl to lie, women, and men and boys slink off to sleep, forcing the dislodged rats to move away in quest of better lodgings.[44]

The largest and most popular dance hall in the Five Points was Almack's, and Dickens noted that it was only to be ". . . approached by a descent. Shall we go it? It is but a moment."

Within a half-dozen years the Ladies' Home Missionary Society of the Methodist Episcopal church, strongly influenced by Phoebe Palmer's work as a tract distributor in the New York slums and her activities in a Methodist ministry at The Tombs in the 1840s, began their work at Five Points. The Ladies' Home Mission purchased the Old Brewery at Five Points for $16,000 and had it pulled down. In

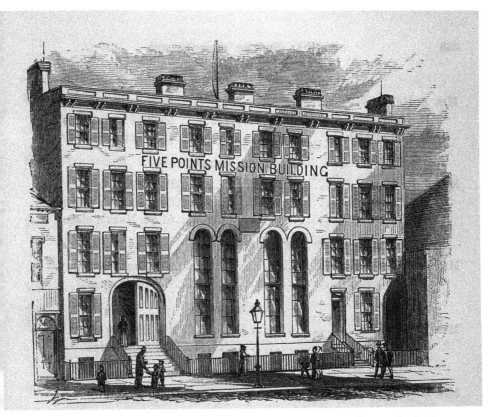

The Ladies Home Missionary Society physically embodied the resolve of evangelical reformers to carry their message into the heart of the city's slums.

its location they built a large, modern structure where they conducted missionary services, ran day and Sunday schools, and provided a free library. Where the contagious influences of intemperance and depravity once held sway, the "daylight" world of moral and educational improvement would do battle.[45] The missions in the Five Points were important touchstones of the city's struggle against hardship, poverty and vice. As early as 1846 guidebooks to the city provide lurid accounts of its inhabitants. Rev. Lewis Morris Pease, appointed by the Methodist Ladies to conduct the mission, had broken with them over matters of policy and in 1850 established the Five Points House of Industry, explicitly addressing the secular need to provide training and employment for the unemployed of the area.[46] The poet and traveler Bayard Taylor contributed an article to *The Nation* in 1866 (with an appropriately Dantean title, "A Descent into the Depths") describing a visit he made to the same Five Points slum on Centre Street which Dickens had visited. Accompanied by two friends, Taylor first went to the police station

Five Points House of Industry: the Rev. Lewis Pease argued for the secular needs of slu
dwellers.

on Mulberry Street, and then was taken by a detective to the Five Points. A knowledgeable guide, the Virgil-figure was essential to the strategy of the Virgilian mode, as was the description of the foul surroundings:

> I inhaled a last mouthful of fresh air, and plunged into a dim, dark, pestilential atmosphere. The walls were of bare stone, trickling with moisture; the floor boarded, indeed, but so covered with dirt as to be rather that than wood, and there was neither window, flue, nor hole of any kind to admit the air. Most of the space was taken up with berths of rough plank, built up in double tiers; the beds in them were either bundles of black rags or layers of foul straw. This was a lodging-house, made to contain twelve or more persons in a space fifteen feet square. The price of a bed is ten cents, and the rent paid by the lady proprietress of the den ten dollars a month.[47]

ne price of a bed is ten cents": Five Points Lodging House.

There was an implicit dramatic content to such narratives of exploration, one which Taylor has not exploited, but which sometimes played an important role. The visitor to the "Depths" was undergoing a shocking education, and inevitably his response became an equal competitor for the reader's attention. Taylor sought more to startle his readers and warn the public of the dangers of such pestilential conditions than to draw attention to his personal response to the Five Points. Nor did he attempt to evoke sympathy for the inhabitants of the cellars, who were described without excessive compassion:

> Everywhere the same crowd of unwashed humanity, the same rags and filth, the same stifling, stagnant atmosphere. The men were either abject, besotted, and reckless creatures, or criminals of a low and cowardly order; the women ... coarse, hard-featured, and having for the most part (as the Scotchman in [Charles Kingsley's] *Alton Locke* says) "their mouths full of vitriol and beastly words."

Six weeks after Taylor's article, Rev. Peter Stryker was invited by leading officers in the Metropolitan Police to visit "the most wretched haunts" of the city. Accompanied by several police officers as well as officers of his church, Stryker was taken to visit several inhabited cellars in the 4th ward. There were sixty such places in this ward, averaging ten inhabitants each. A night's lodging cost between six and fifteen cents.

> We went down into cellars dug deep in marshy ground, some of which were paved with cobble stones, and some roughly floored, all covered with filth, badly ventilated, and from which there met us as we entered, a damp, close, pestilential air, which cannot be described, but by one who has experienced it will be held in lasting remembrance. These subterranean caverns probably were never intended as places of abode. They are not fit to be used as storehouses. The very dogs and cats would, if unmolested, prefer the open street as an habitation.
>
> Yet here we found human beings—black and white, men, women and children, all huddled together. . . . One room we found in total darkness, except as the lantern of our guide threw a lurid glare upon the dismal scene. In another den a dirty tallow candle, consumed almost to the socket, served to show that the place was inhabited.[48]

Such scenes of degradation repeatedly appear in accounts of New York. Samuel B. Halliday, who was "Missionary" (i.e., agent) of the American Female Guardian Society, acted as guide taking Matthew Hale Smith into one of the worst tenements in the city:

> With a lantern and an officer, a visit to the cellars where the poor of New York sleep may be undertaken with safety. Fetid odors and pestiferous smells greet you as you descend. There bunks are built on the side of the room; beds filthier than can be imagined, and crowded with occupants. No regard is paid to age or sex. Men, women, and children are huddled together in one disgusting mass. Without a breath of air from without, these holes are hot-beds of pestilence. The landlord was asked, in one cellar, "How many can you lodge?" "We can lodge twenty-five; if we crowd, perhaps thirty."
>
> The lodgers in these filthy dens seem to be lost to all moral feeling, and to all sense of shame. They are not as decent as brutes. Drunken men, debased women, young girls, helpless children, are packed together in a filthy, under-ground room, destitute of light or ventilation, reeking of filth, and surrounded with a poisoned atmosphere. The decencies of life are abandoned, and blasphemy and ribald talk fill the place.[49]

The visit to the "lower depths" in the 1860s, and for many decades afterwards, readily assumed the Virgilian mode, either as a description of the writer's visit, or, as in Riis, a literary discourse which took the form of an invitation to accompany the writer. In both the presentation of the scene and the inhabitants, the personal feelings of the writer jostled with an attempt to record the conditions of slum life. Some writers assumed that the description of the conditions alone would produce a heightened response on the part of the reader; others, exploiting an elaborate and conventional rhetoric of social reform, sought to manipulate the reader's feelings more directly. The Virgilian mode was equally appropriate for a factual or an emotional approach; both shared the same didactic intention.

A writer using the Virgilian mode, in any of its forms, was committed to a certain relationship to an audience, and to the political process. The attempt to inform the public, to arouse its interest and concern, implied a wish to alter the climate in which legislators functioned. By summoning up an informed opinion, even if only within an influential stratum of the upper class, pressure from without was meant to counterbalance the forces of indifference, inertia and corruption which presided within the state. The description of squalor and neglect was designed to arouse public opinion, but the effectiveness of the strategy turned upon the extent to which public opinion could be mobilized, and was able to impose itself.

Urban poverty

In an article entitled "The Benevolent Institutions of New-York" in *Putnam's Monthly Magazine*, were listed twenty-two asylums, ninety societies, seventy-five secret and benevolent societies, eight hospitals and seven dispensaries active in the city in 1853. The successive volumes of *Valentine's Manual*, published annually from 1841 to 1870 by the common council as a record of the city's government and institutions (which was named after the long-serving clerk to the council David T. Valentine), devoted increasing space to such bodies: they were among the chief glories of the community. Nonetheless, as contemporaries reluctantly acknowledged, it was impossible to walk through the city without seeing beggars, malnourished children and the many distressing manifestations of poverty and unemployment. The uncoordinated efforts of diverse charities could not cope with the sheer scale of the problem, and unlike the efforts of similar bodies in the great urban centers in England, charities in New York functioned largely without the support of an enlightened public opinion. Time and time again in the 1840s and 1850s reformers sought to arouse public opinion and failed to do so. The absent philanthropist and armchair reformers were objects of scorn for the more intrepid explorers of the lower depths: "Reasoning in an armchair is very proper, and often very accurate, but the logic of starvation is too peremptory for syllogisms." Indeed, John Vose argued that "... if our philanthropists, our reformers, would but spend a few hours in visiting several hundred low and notorious 'holes,' to be found in Gotham, where they could, with their own eyes, obtain a slight view of the utter depravity, and sunken channels of vice, we are led to believe that it would nerve them on at once to cause a thorough reformation." Reports poured forth from the New York Association for Improving the Condition of the Poor (AICP), founded in 1842, and whose executive secretary for many years was Robert Hartley, but the activities of the volunteer "philanthropic laborers" and AICP's proposals for social reforms met with "a wall of indifference."[50]

Attitudes towards poverty, the poor, and the proper roles of charitable and state activities were shaped by Jacksonian individualism and a deeply ingrained belief that the poor, through weakness or viciousness, were largely responsible for their own fate. Urban poverty was thus blamed upon the poor themselves, whether due to their foreign origin, or innate defects of character. James Fenimore Cooper, writing in Paris in the 1820s, believed that misery and abject poverty were rare in New York and that the vice and idleness which were to be found had been caused by conditions elsewhere. The "poor of Europe" and not the native American were likely to be responsible. Catherine Maria Sedgwick, an incomparable source for the reassuring complacency of her age, proclaimed in *The Poor Rich Man and the Rich Poor Man* (1837) that "[i]n all our widespread country there is very little necessary poverty. In New England *none* that is not the result of vice or disease." Similar sentiments were expressed by a professor of English at Harvard: "I cannot recall much poverty or insignificance in this world which has not been fully and honestly earned." In a survey "Poor-Laws, and the Sources of Poverty Among Us," written in 1854, it was flatly asserted: "Necessary poverty is almost unknown." The author of this article continued:

> In the rear of the Astor House, in the city of New-York, the offal of that establishment is collected in barrels for removal. These are watched by middle-aged women, the most loathsome and the deepest-sunk in the scale of humanity of any beings we have ever seen. They bear hardly any vestige of womanhood in their countenances. Their cheeks are livid and bloated; their eyes are lustreless, like the eyes of swine; their teeth are discolored and decaying, and their hair is matted with dirt. Greasy hoods are upon their heads, and tattered shawls cover, but do not conceal, their exposed and unwashed bosoms. One—nose split in a quarrel; another has frequently a black eye; a third is cross-eyed, and a fourth has a deep scar upon her cheek. When an opportunity arrives, these wretched beings plunge their arms, up to their shoulders, if necess-

ary, into the exposed receptacles, which are filled with the refuse from the plates of the guests of the house, feathers, bits of fat, bones, and the entrails of fowls. What they gather, they put into their baskets, first satisfying their own hunger therefrom. We have seen one of these women plunge her arm into a moist and fast-corrupting mass of offal, and bringing out what seemed a ham-bone, tear off a morsel of meat therefrom, before she put it into her basket. They eat, and give their children to eat, of this food, and sell the fat and bones for liquor. We can look upon these creatures with some degree of composure, for they have lost nearly all resemblance to womankind; but we have had our hearts ache, at seeing little children accompanying or associating with these women. One, a friend once saw, ten or twelve years of age, pull her tattered frock, her only covering, high up to her arm-pits, and walk up and down before the hotel-gate, to the intense delight of the boys about, who shouted their ecstasies, while they threw sticks, and bits of dirt, at her. What a sight to see in a Christian land! We would be fain to hide our heads in confusion, were it not that these women and children are foreigners, every one.[51]

At first the problem was denied, and then it was blamed upon immigrants, especially the Irish; both responses are to be seen in the context of patriotism and civic pride and also of racism and xenophobia. Carroll-Smith Rosenberg suggests that anxieties about the impact of immigrants upon the quality of urban life cannot be dismissed ". . . as a self-serving oversimplification of a complex and threatening situation . . . [the] new arrivals had become New York's single most discordant social reality."[52] Americans of their generation did not want to believe that their country was marred by the social ills abundantly visible even in the greatest European states. When confronted by the crisis of overcrowded tenements and urban poverty, even the most enlightened New Yorkers sometimes responded with less than their usual large-mindedness. Miss Sedgwick, who followed her family into conversion to liberal Unitarianism, remained convinced that poverty was a moral failing. Hartley, whose roots were in Presbyterian evangelical piety, had been a leader in his church's house-to-house missionary work, an organizer of the New York City Tract Society and had worked for the Temperance Society. Believing that there was a connection between pure food, decent housing and the chances of leading a moral life, his attention to practical problems of relief were never far from a concern for moral values. Even though he started from such a different religious position, he shared Sedgwick's assumptions about the causes of the poverty.

Following the example of reformers like Thomas Chalmers in Glasgow and Joseph Tuckerman in Boston—who believed that benevolence which was neighborly and which was also based upon a comprehensive knowledge of local needs, had the best chance to exert the greatest Christian influence—Hartley and the AICP divided the city into sixteen districts, each controlled by an advisory committee which would appoint "visitors" who, in the spirit of missionaries, entered some of the worst slums in the city to study conditions and distribute relief. Their reports gave the AICP a unique insight into the conditions of the urban poor, and led to the establishment of two new medical dispensaries, and the creation of a model tenement. Indeed, the AICP under Hartley had "the most coherent and far-seeing public health program of any benevolent group" in New York.[53] By the late 1850s Hartley had come to the opinion that further sanitary and public health reforms were necessary. He urged the passage of municipal sanitary regulations and argued with private property developers that it was in their own interest to improve the design of their tenements. While the AICP identified many social wrongs, it did not strain the allegiance of its Protestant, middle-class merchants, bankers and professional men who largely made up the backbone of its supporters. Echoing Miss Sedgwick's thoughts on the problem of poverty, the 1868 *Annual Report* of the AICP defended the necessity of inequality:

> Want induces labor; without labor there could be no wealth; without wealth, the civilized world would become savage, and the kindly offices of charity be unknown. Hence, differences of condition are not only necessary to the highest degree of prosperity and happiness, but absolutely essential to the existence of a civilized state.[54]

The AICP interpretation of the origin of poverty closely reflected the moral values of middle-class America: there was work for any one who sought it, especially in the vast inner regions of the country. The inhabitants of the city tenements were therefore, as Hartley thought, self-made victims, largely responsible for their own poverty. They should not be cosseted. The distinction between the worthy and unworthy poor seemed equally self-evident. Opposing all random and private acts of charitableness, the AICP sought a system of personal relief for those who could best benefit from their efforts. The rest, the unworthy ones, were to be left to fester in their cellars and tenements. Implicit in his words was a message to the poor from the AICP: "go somewhere else."[55]

The Children's Aid Society, founded by Charles Loring Brace in 1853, argued that the solution to the problem of vagrant and criminal children was not expensive institutional care, but to send them to other communities, preferably rural. Groups of children from the streets of New York were sent to foster homes in the rural midwest.

he first theft: Charles Loring Brace sought the moral disinfection of the children of the slums.

(This is perhaps just the tip of an iceberg of such shipments of children: of 289 juvenile delinquents who were indentured by the Society for the Reformation of Juvenile Delinquents in 1853, fifty-five per cent, by far the largest single category, were sent to farmers. The percentage rose to sixty-five per cent in 1859.[56]) As many as 150,000 orphans were sent out of the big cities in the east by the CAS in a program which lasted until 1929. Brace distinguished the CAS from other Protestant benevolent societies by the conscious avoidance of missionary efforts. Nonetheless, the activities of his agents as well as those of Lewis Pease, Samuel Halliday, and others, were regarded with suspicion within the largely Catholic tenements. When a group of Catholics met in Buffalo in 1856 to discuss emigration from the slums, their deliberations were sharply rebuked by Archbishop Hughes of New York. Catholics feared that such emigration, assisted by a host of Protestant societies, was little more than a disguised form of proselytism. Until his death in 1864, Hughes blocked anything more than token Catholic emigration efforts from New York and the other large urban communities.[57]

Peter Cooper and Horace Greeley, alarmed at the plight of the immigrant unemployed in the city, organized the American and Foreign Emigrant Protective and Employment Society in the spring of 1854, to encourage the vast number of idle people in New York to find work on farms in the west. New Yorkers were highly indignant when they learned that poor law commissioners in Edinburgh were shipping their indigents to America, but the shipment elsewhere of the poor had obvious appeals for any group which had to deal with the problem. There was a similar internal trade in paupers, quietly mocking the vastly larger trade in slaves, within the United States. Trustees or responsible officials were empowered to auction paupers to the lowest bidders. In North Carolina, eight cents a day was the going rate in 1848. A decade later a bidder was found who promised to keep a pauper for a weekly sum of ninety-nine cents. In Barry County, Missouri, a pauper was "sold" for fifteen dollars a year.[58]

For those who refused to leave the city, the New York almshouse was located on a large crowded site shared with Bellevue Hospital between 25th and 29th Streets near the East River. The rapid expansion of the need for almshouse provision in the 1840s and 1850s led to repeated attempts by the Democrats, Whigs and American Republicans to relocate the almshouse to various sites proposed on Blackwell's and Randall's islands in the East River: this would have the advantage of isolating the inmates from deleterious contacts with the city around them, and would certainly improve discipline. The "virtuous poor" would thus be freed from the vices of pauperism, understood as an unwillingness to work and a preference for charity. The inexorable increase in the numbers of the poor, and the growth of city revenues directed towards the whole problem of relief, led to important administrative reforms. The office of Almshouse Commissioner was created in 1845, and a publicly elected board of almshouse governors was set up four years later. The almshouse was removed to a new site on Blackwell's Island in 1850, where the squalid, repressive harshness of conditions was soon a continuing source of concern. (Thoreau, willing as ever to play the fool to make an unwelcome point, saw in the experiences of the almshouse inmate in 1854 a potential source of hope: "You may perhaps have some pleasant, thrilling, glorious hours, even in a poorhouse. The setting sun is reflected from the windows of the almshouse as brightly as from the rich man's abode; the snow melts before its door as early in the spring. I do not see but a quiet mind may live as contentedly there, and have as cheering thoughts, as in a palace.") The Emigration Commission, established in 1847, made a contribution to the problem through a tax upon ships carrying immigrants; this money was available for the help of needy foreigners who had been in the United States for less than five years. The city dispensaries also played an important role in the lives of the poor. The dispensaries were organized throughout the city, with the work of the salaried resident physician supplemented by a staff of volunteer or "visiting" physicians. They were devoted, hard-working men, whose presence in the crowded tenements did much to relieve individual suffering. (In 1859, the five city dispensaries provided care for 134,418 patients. By 1866 that number rose to 184,000, approximately one sixth of whom were visited at home.)[59]

A representative dispensary physician was Job Smith, a Yale graduate who had studied under the famous clinician Austin Flint at the Buffalo Medical College. He received his medical degree from the College of Physicians and Surgeons in New York in 1853, and then entered private practice. For the next forty years, while holding professorships in pediatric medicine at Bellevue Hospital Medical School, Smith continued his voluntary work as a visiting physician in the dispensaries. Such men had great knowledge of the conditions in the slums and tenements. When the Citizens' Association organized a survey of housing and sanitary conditions in 1864, Dr. Job Smith served as a sanitary inspector and wrote the report on the 25th sanitary district, an area between 50th and 86th Streets on the West Side. Smith's older brother, the Bellevue surgeon and sanitary reformer Dr. Stephen Smith, was the principal organizer of the Citizens' Association report. Without civic-minded physicians like the Smith brothers, sanitary conditions in the city would undoubtedly have been worse. But the efforts of the city dispensaries,

Hartley's AICP, the CAS, Greeley and Cooper's Emigrant Protective and Employment Society, the YMCA, almshouse governors, the Emigration Commission, and the vast network of churches, tract societies, urban missionaries, temperance organizations, immigrant self-help societies and the *landsmannschaftn*, with divergent aspirations and contradictory messages for the poor, failed to do more than temper the worst excesses of the problem. The city inspector's department, and the eighteen health wardens charged with the detection and elimination of threatening nuisances, should have been playing a major role in the defense of the public health. There was virtually nothing being done by these gentlemen who were, with one exception, political hacks, ill-equipped to discharge their duties. Civic indifference was the rule. It was even argued that despite the vast sums spent on street cleaning and the health department, the provision of Croton water brought to reservoirs in the city by aqueduct and pipe from Westchester County from 1842, was "the only well-administered agency of sanitary protection which the government provides."[60]

Griscom as city inspector

The one exception, Dr. John H. Griscom, suggests the limitations of reform in the period before the Civil War.[61] Of Quaker background and Whig politics, he was educated at the prestigious medical school of the University of Pennsylvania. After several years' work at the New York Dispensary, Griscom was appointed city inspector in April 1842 by Robert H. Morris, Democratic mayor of New York. In "A Brief View of the Sanitary Condition of the City" (1842), Griscom argued that overcrowded housing was a major factor in the deteriorating health of the poor. The absence of ventilation in their dwellings made the spread of diseases virtually uncontrollable. If the city could impose restrictions on methods of construction to protect against the risk of fire, then similar powers should be taken to correct conditions which were no less dangerous to health. He followed Hartley's campaign, which identified the link between distillers and dairy farmers who flooded the city with contaminated and poor quality milk, and proposed that dairy owners be banned from feeding their cows on the swill from breweries. Both men suspected that "swill milk" was causing sickness and excess mortality among the children in the city. (Griscom and Hartley were allies in the AICP.)[62]

Conservative Democrats were unhappy when he urged that large sums be spent on preventive sanitary measures, such as sewers and the erection of public baths. Morris was a believer in small government, decentralization and Jacksonian individualism, and the city inspector's stream of reports and suggestions would have required the common council to interfere with the rights of property owners and the lives of the poor to an unprecedented extent. Griscom advocated a "health police" drawn from properly qualified members of the medical profession. He wanted a law passed to require "domiciliary cleanliness," enforceable by health inspectors. In effect he looked forward to a society in which doctors would have executive power over certain areas of public and private life. His concerns were more congenial to the Whigs and nativists, though they did precious little to address these problems when given the chance. When the Democrats regained control of the common council in April 1843, Griscom knew that the writing was on the wall:

> The chances of my remaining in office [he wrote to Lemuel Shattuck] are therefore slight—the only hope consisting in the efforts made for that purpose, by a few personal friends among the Locofocos, and in the credit I may have gained by the "Report." No previous officer has taking [*sic*] the stand I have, or labored so hard in the same direction. My work is unfinished, scarcely begun, and If I must go, the little good I may have done is likely to be lost. But hungry politicians care but little for those things, and I am prepared to walk out. If so, then I know of nothing to interfere with the prosecution of the Physiology [a book he had promised to write].[63]

A generation premature, Griscom was quickly replaced as city inspector by a less disturbing incumbent.

In his various communications to the common council, Griscom had sought to open the city's eyes to the conditions in the tenements. He noted that "few are aware of the dreadful extent of the disease and suffering" which existed among the poor. In *The Sanitary Condition of the Laboring Population of New York* (1845), which was consciously modeled upon Chadwick's *Report on the Sanitary Condition of the Labouring Population of Great Britain, and on the Means of its Improvement* (1842), Griscom included an invitation in the Virgilian mode to inspect conditions in the cellars:

> You must descend to them; you must feel the blast of foul air as it meets your face on opening the door; you must grope in the dark or hesitate until your eye becomes accustomed to the gloomy place, to enable you to find your way through the entry, over a broken floor, the boards of which are protected from your tread by a half-inch of hard dirt; you must inhale the suffocating vapor of the sitting and sleeping rooms; and in the dark, damp recess, endeavor to find the inmates by the sound of

their voices, or chance to see their figures moving between you and the flickering blaze of a shaving burning on the hearth, or the misty light of a window coated with dirt and festooned with cobwebs—or if in search of an invalid, take care that you do not fall full length upon the bed with her, by stumbling against the bundle of rags and straw, dignified by that name, lying on the floor, under the window, if window there is;—all this, and much more, beyond the reach of my pen, must be felt and seen, ere you can appreciate in its full force the mournful and disgusting condition, in which many thousands of the subjects of our government pass their lives.[64]

There were many contemporaries who believed that the squalor and diseases of the poor were in effect divine judgments. In response to the great cholera epidemic in 1832 the churches, following the example set by their British brethren, called for a national day of fasting and prayer to ward off the disease. The most advanced physicians of the age, however, believed that cholera and many other illnesses were caused by "miasma" produced by the city's filthy streets; it had been long observed that the clean and the temperate seemed nearly immune to the ravages of cholera. Cleanliness was regarded as being among the most powerful weapons in the fight against disease. Griscom went so far as to argue that "clean streets" were the remedy for many of the city's health problems. Through a careful examination of the mortality statistics, he demonstrated a relationship between the conditions in the crowded tenements and susceptibility to disease. He argued, as did his successors within the reforming medical community, that environment played a crucial role in health, and that living conditions could and should be regulated by the common council. Effectively reversing the widespread view of his contemporaries that moral failings and evil were expressed in poverty, uncleanliness and disease, Griscom argued that if the poor could only be taught, or compelled, to live cleanly and be more healthy, then the work of the tract societies, missionaries and schools "will have a redoubled effect, in mending their morals, and rendering them intelligent and happy."[65]

Of no less significance was his attention to the "troglodytes" or cave-dwellers as they were called, those who were so poor that they were forced to live in the worst conditions existing in New York, in the dank, unventilated cellars. The root of the problem was the system by which a property owner leased a building to a sub-landlord, who in turn subdivided the space to accommodate the largest possible number of tenants. As long as the owner received his rent, he ignored the property, and the agent or sub-landlord had no interest in maintenance or cleanliness, and indeed had a strong financial incentive to make maximum use possible of the property. The absence of regulations controlling such properties, the remote and indifferent owner, the voracious agent, combined to create conditions in which the "immense amount of sickness, physical disability and premature mortality" among the poor was due to preventable causes.

He noticed that the deteriorating conditions in the city were producing a previously unthinkable kind of scavenger population, the "chiffonier" or rag-picker. In doing so he naturally employed the Virgilian mode of invitation and description to draw his readers (at first instance, the common council, but it is obvious that he was addressing the whole community) into a fuller realization of the conditions in which such people lived:

> Let any one inspect closely the personal appearance of a "chiffonier," as he or she perseveringly overhauls a heap of street manure, or drags the gutter before his house, in search of "spoils"; let the living personification of uncleanness be thoroughly impressed upon his recollection, and then, if he will not visit it, let his imagination carry him to the home of the family, and see them drop in, successively with the proceeds of their daily labor, and deposit them in a corner, or under the tea-table, in the room, which is, at the same time, parlor, chamber, and kitchen, and find them in every part of the premises; will he wonder that . . . contagion should there assume its direst form?[66]

Griscom's many suggestions for social reform were ignored by the politicians, if not by his fellow physicians.[67] But his appeal to the public, through Virgilian invitation and description, suggested a tactic appropriate to a period in which the politicians largely rejected the reform agenda of physicians.

Dana at Five Points

Inevitably there were some who, out of curiosity or reforming zeal, took up the invitation to visit the slums made in Griscom's report. One such was a young lawyer and author from Boston, Richard Henry Dana, Jr. In New York in January 1843 to deliver a lecture, he completed his round of calls in the evening and, while walking down Broadway towards the home of his hosts, Mr. and Mrs. Robert Sedgwick, was possessed of "a sudden desire to see that sink of iniquity & filth, the 'Five Points.'" As he proceeded downtown, he observed that the buildings were "ruinous," the streets muddy and the sidewalks poorly lit. The sound of voices and the bustle of music and dancing accompanied him down the dark street. Dana saw a woman, amidst a profusion of drunken oaths and threats, being ejected from a house. Another woman, so drunk she could not walk unaided, loomed before him on the sidewalk. Groups of girls laughing and talking loudly ran from house to house. "Grog shops, oyster cellars & close, obscure & suspicious looking places of every description abounded," he wrote. A girl with a shawl draped over her head asked Dana where he was going. "I stopped & answered that I was only walking about a little to look round. She said 'I am doing the same.'" But when she tried to accompany the lawyer, he noted: "I hastened my pace & passed on." It was a surprisingly mild night, and women sitting in doorways or on steps called out to him, inviting him to "just sit down a minute." One such invitation, from a doorway set back from the street, caused Dana to pause. "I had a strong inclination to see the interior of such a house as they must live in, & finding that the room was lighted & seeing no men there & no signs of noise or company, I stopped in almost before I knew what I was doing." Inside in a room with a sanded floor there was a rough bar, and the younger of the two women invited him to "just step into the bed room: it was only the next room." Despite his fears that he might be robbed, in the spirit of "adventure" Dana entered a small, dark room which contained only a bed and a straw mattress:

> Taking for granted that I wished to use her for the purposes of her calling she asked me how much I would give. I said "What do you ask?" She hesitated a moment, & then answered hesitatingly, & evidently ready to lower her price if necessary, "half a dollar?" I was astonished at the mere pittance for which she would sell her wretched, worn out, prostituted body. I can hardly tell the disgust & pity I felt. I told her at once that I had no object but curiosity in coming into the house, yet gave her the money from fear lest, getting nothing, she might make a difficulty or try to have me plundered. She took the money & thanked me, but expressed no surprise at my curiosity or strangeness. Perhaps they are used to having visits of persons like myself from abroad & who wish to see the inside of such places.[68]

He was on the point of warning the prostitute of the moral dangers of her ways when he became uneasy. If anything should happen, if he was robbed or beaten, or if there was a police raid, he could "ill account" for his presence in such a place. He nervously reached down to make sure his gold watch was still securely attached to his waistcoat, and quickly departed. Returning back to Broadway, the lighted carriages and well dressed people on the street reassured him. At the Sedgwick's house on 9th Street he was admitted to the parlor by a servant: ". . . there, seated round a pleasant fire, sat a family solely of women, one the beautiful mother of five daughters, all of whom were yet to try the world & be tried by it, another a distinguished writer of moral stories & a firm believer in the general goodness & safety of her race [Catherine Maria Sedgwick], & two young girls, of fifteen or sixteen, just coming into womanhood;—I felt as though I was wandering in a dream, made up of strange extremes & unnatural contrast."[69] The dispersal of brothels to virtually all parts of the city after 1820 brought the "social evil" in sharp conjunction with scenes of domestic virtue. It was the "unnatural contrast" which so strongly impressed Dana.

Dana's experience of the slums was melodramatic and comical. The "sudden desire" which drew him towards the Five Points, and his "strong inclination" to enter the prostitute's rooms, were carefully noted in his journal. Like all great diarists he was attentive to details of appearance, and the sounds and smells of the streets; he recorded snatches of dialogue. The vivid life of Dana's description of the Five Points came from the author's reactions, those which he expressed and those which a more sophisticated age has learned to read into such self-revelation. He may have admitted to himself that he went to the slums out of curiosity, but his response was complex. When reformers like Robert M. Hartley, Charles Loring Brace and John H. Griscom issued their Virgilian invitations to the lower depths, they certainly did not have in mind experiences like Dana's. And that was the problem. In their eyes the slums represented a range of problems and challenges to those concerned with the welfare of the community. They would never admit to the many seductive charms of the slums to outsiders (its exotic remoteness from middle-class life in New York, and the sexual promise of an escape from conventions), and they failed to note that even for the destitute and those living in over-crowded tenement accommodation life on the margins offered entertainments, promises, satisfactions; that, for all their external signs of anarchy, the slums should be seen as communities, in which people—sometimes actively, sometimes as passive victims—responded to new forms of social life. Contemporaries vividly saw the horror of the slums, but had no conception that it might contain distinctive customs, standards, and forms of discourse. In *Our Old Home* (1863), reflecting back upon his years as American consul in Liverpool in the preceding decade, Hawthorne slyly noted of his occasional visits into the English urban slums that the feelings of maternal pride he observed were "strangely identical" to what was to be found in "the happiest homes." Indeed, among the foulest scenes he recognized the persistence of many a "womanly characteristic," and even "good breeding": "I am persuaded . . . that there were laws of intercourse which they never violated—a code of the cellar, the garret, the common staircase, the doorstep, the pavement, which perhaps had as deep a foundation in natural fitness as the code of the drawing room."[70] Two generations passed before sociologists like Charles H. Cooley (*Social Organization: A Study of the Larger Mind*, 1909) formulated the crucial importance of primary relations—the family and the neighborhood—in the sustenance of community, and Robert Park in a celebrated essay in 1915 ("The City: Suggestions for the Investigation of Human Behavior in the Urban Environment") argued that control based upon positive law was being replaced in the city by new forms of behavior rooted in the ethos and values of sub-communities. Reformers of the 1840s feared the slums, and wished to control them; they understood little of their energies, structures and sociality.

Dr. Smith discovers a typhus fever-nest

Dr. Stephen Smith, one of the great social reformers produced by New York in the nineteenth century, grew up on a farm near Skaneateles, Onondaga County, near Syracuse. The Smith family had settled in Connecticut in the seventeenth century, and his relations had served with distinction in the revolutionary army. Born in 1823, he attended local schools and at twenty was sent to study medicine under Dr. Caleb Green at the Cortland Academy in Homer, New York. He attended his first course of medical lectures in the Geneva [New York] Medical College in 1848, where he was a contemporary of the remarkable Elizabeth Blackwell, the first woman in the United States to study medicine at a recognized college. (Like most physicians of that generation, he was not persuaded of the fitness of women for the everyday duties of the profession.[71]) In 1848–9 Smith was a resident student in the hospital of the Sisters of Charity at Buffalo, and attended his second course of lectures at the Buffalo Medical College. His memories of the state of surgery in these years could be depended upon to chill the blood of later generations of medical students. He saw surgeons dressed in street clothes wearing bloody aprons operate upon unanaesthetized patients. In 1849 Smith attended his third course of lectures at the College of Physicians and Surgeons in New York City, where he finally graduated in the spring of 1850, and was successful in an application for an internship on the resident staff of Bellevue Hospital, three miles north of Wall Street on the East River.

Taking an appointment at Bellevue was a sign of social concern. The New York Hospital on Broadway was thought a more glamorous entrance to a medical career. The East Side, where the hospital

Dr. Stephen Smith, the Bellevue surgeon whose campaigning work as sanitary reformer led to the creation of the Metropolitan Board of Health.

filled a whole block between 26th and 27th Streets, from First Avenue to the river, was a district of tenements, groggeries and factories which constituted the eastern portion of the 21st ward, the bailiwick of Richard Barrett Connolly in the 1860s. The patients at Bellevue were the poorest of the poor. Sharing the site with a medical college and the city morgue, the hospital was located in a granite building without luxuries, surrounded by a high brick wall. A pesthouse had first been located on Bellevue Farm on Kipps Bay as a temporary measure during the yellow fever epidemic in 1795, with a view to turning it into a hospital when the fever abated. The large stone structure on the site, constructed by the common council as a prison, almshouse and hospital after 1811, contained separate wings for white and "colored" patients, as well as schoolrooms, carpentry shops, cells for the insane and forty-one rooms reserved for paupers.

The chief visiting surgeon was the fashionable physician Dr. David Hosack. The hospital's main concern was not with Hosack's society patients but with the plagues of smallpox, typhus and yellow fever which devastated New York every summer in the 1820s. Eventually it was decided to remove the prisoners to Bedloe's Island in the East River, and the women and insane to other establishments, leaving Bellevue as the city's main hospital during the cholera epidemic in 1832. When Smith arrived in 1850 the institution had fallen prey to political partisanship. The resident physician had become a political appointment, with a tenure of one year only; there was no discernible system of treatment, no organization, and patients were regularly left in filthy bedding. Even greater neglect prevailed in the "colored" wing. The sorry performance of Bellevue during the plague of 1847 led to a final separation of the almshouse from the hospital, and the installation of a new regime led by the city's most eminent medical men. The surgeon Valentine Mott and Hosack's pupil, Dr. J. W. Francis, who willingly treated the poor, led new members to the board of the quality of Willard Parker, William H. Van Buren and Alonzo Clark. Clark brought to Bellevue an iconoclastic conviction, based upon his studies in pathology, that fresh air and cleanliness were the first line of defense against illness. He insisted that hospital windows should be left open, patients kept clean, and as little medicine as possible be given to them. When Smith arrived to take up his internship, convalescent patients (the men smoking their pipes, the women sewing or reading) occupied benches on the lawn which ran down to the river, where a wharf awaited the arrival of the small steamer which came several times a week to collect the plain coffins of paupers to be buried in Potter's Field. White horse-drawn ambulances made a constant clatter on the nearby streets.

Clark had taught Smith at the College of Physicians and Surgeons, and welcomed him as an intern at Bellevue. While walking rounds with the legendary Alonzo Clark, Stephen Smith learned invaluable lessons about simplicity of treatment, and of the importance of painstaking preparation. His work as assistant surgeon under Clark led him to observe his chief's unheard-of treatment for puerperal peritonitis. The instructions he gave Smith were to dose his patients with opium "to within an inch of their lives." Clark's mixture of intuition and the dramatic gesture made him a hero to the younger medical staff at Bellevue, and to Smith in particular. One of Smith's first cases involved an externally caused rupture of the bladder, a fairly unusual problem about which doubt had been expressed in court as to whether it was in fact possible. He made an exhaustive search of the medical literature and was able to identify seventy-eight similar cases of rupture caused externally. This "remarkable piece of painstaking work" appeared in a medical journal in 1851, and was translated into several European languages. Smith also wrote reports on medical and surgical cases treated at Bellevue for the *New York Journal of Medicine*.[72]

Smith was soon showing an even more remarkable inventiveness and determination. After completing his two-year internship at Bellevue, the Charity Commissioners put him in charge of a group of typhus tents on Blackwell's Island, filled with immigrants suffering from "Spotted Fever". On examining the patients' records he noticed that many of them had lived in a single building on East 22nd Street. As he told the story in later years, Smith visited the house and found it in a state of utter dilapidation:

> ... the doors and windows were broken; the cellar was partly filled with filthy sewage; the floors were littered with decomposing straw, which the occupants used for bedding; every available place, from cellar to garret, was crowded with immigrants—men, women and children. The whole establishment was reeking with filth and the atmosphere was heavy with the sickening odor of the deadly typhus, which reigned supreme in every room.[73]

When he inquired of the residents who was responsible for the condition of the building, he was told that no rent was being collected. The building had virtually been abandoned. Someone in the neighborhood identified the agent, but when questioned this gentleman indignantly refused to do anything about the appalling conditions. Why should he spend good money to improve conditions for dirty immigrants? He refused to give Smith the name and address of the owner. It was hard to see what else could be done. Smith had friends in the police force, but they explained to the young surgeon that there was no ordinance applicable to the house on East 22nd Street. A quick check of the tax lists revealed the owner's name and address. He decided to make a direct appeal to the man's conscience. As far as the owner was concerned, if the property yielded no income, there was no question of wasting money on improvements. Smith was angrily told that the building was none of his concern.

The agent, the police and the owner would or could do nothing. In desperation he turned to the editor of the *Evening Post*, William Cullen Bryant, who supported the efforts of the sanitation reformers. Bryant heard the doctor out and suggested a polite form of black-mail. If Smith could persuade his friend in the police to issue a summons for a violation of a law which did not exist, Bryant would

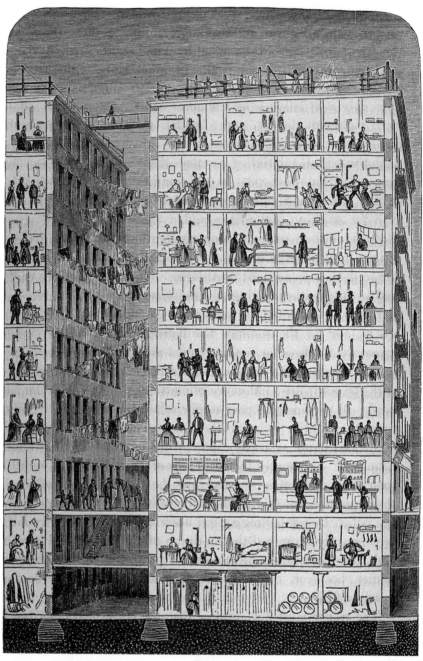

"Every available place . . . was crowded": a cut-away view of a New York tenement. A low bar on the first floor (note the child placing an order), an arrest by police on the third, and a domestic fight on the sixth floor, confirmed popular stereotypes of the poor.

have a reporter present at court and threaten the landowner with unpleasant publicity. On the morning when the summons was returnable at the Jefferson Market Police Court, the indignant owner was coolly apprised of Bryant's interest in the "fever-nest" on East 22nd Street. He hastily promised to make the needed improvements and, it is said, thanked Smith for calling the problem to his attention.[74]

Brought to a successful conclusion, this episode opened Smith's eyes to the power of publicity. The police and the *Evening Post* could not be expected to deal with thousands of separate properties throughout the city which were dangerous to health. Indeed, his own time for such a campaign was severely limited. But this experience helped him to see the potential power of an aroused public opinion. The public was ignorant of medical hazards and uninterested in spending money on improvements, but "public opinion" could be manipulated by those with the requisite power and intelligence. The immediate concern of physicians was the elimination of man-made fever-nests; beyond that, as the policies advocated by Dr. Griscom in the 1840s suggested, the most forward-looking physicians wanted executive power to improve sanitary conditions throughout the whole city. Such a reform might be aided by Virgilian appeals addressed to the dozing consciences of the middle class, but Smith's experience suggested that the use of the press, the creation and manipulation of a sympathetic public opinion, and drawing together the intelligent professional men of the city into a solid and respectable phalanx for reform, like that which existed in the great cities of England, were more likely to succeed. He unhesitatingly availed himself of the Virgilian invitation when addressing politicians and the public:

> As you look into these abodes of wretchedness, filth and disease, the inmates manifest the same lethargic habits as animals, burrowing in the ground. They are, indeed, half-narcotized by the constant inhalation of the emanations of their own bodies, and by a prolonged absence of light and fresh air. Here we never find sound health, while the constant sickness rate ranges from 75 to 90 per cent.[75]

He understood that action as well as appeals for sympathy were required; "[t]he first task of the doctor is ... political: the struggle against disease must begin with a war against bad government."[76]

Throughout the 1850s, when Smith was co-editor and then editor of the *New York Journal of Medicine*, reformers made repeated efforts to bring the inadequacies of the city's sanitary condition to the attention of the public and the state legislature. Without exception the reformers were defeated in Albany, the state capital, the veritable slough of Despond for progressive measures of any sort. They believed that reforms largely failed due to corruption in the city health department, which was the source of the bribes which blocked their efforts at Albany. Smith's editorials kept the issues squarely before his readership. The reforms of that decade emerged largely out of the medical profession's growing consciousness of their role as stewards of the public well-being. The medical campaign against abortion, which was remarkably successful in changing public attitudes, was already underway in the 1850s. The attempt to reform public health administration began, as did the campaign against abortion, in the face of an apathetic public opinion. (Griscom observed that "There is no denial that the mortality of this city is much greater than that of many others of far inferior advantage for salubrity and longevity, and yet the trumpet of the archangel sounds in their ears in vain.")[77] The horrors of insanitary housing and disease were easier to discuss in public than abortion, but were a more difficult political target. The huge task of cleansing the city's streets had become an important part of the system of urban patronage and corruption, and the health wardens who were responsible for attending to threats to public health were, without exception, unqualified men appointed for political services. The filthy state of the city's streets was further proof of official corruption:

> . . . this town, that should be so clean,
> Is the dirtiest city that was ever seen.
> From end to end of each filthy street
> Nothing is pure and nothing is sweet,
> And the mire our rolling wheels that clogs
> Is foul with the bodies of cats and dogs,
> And the offal of cleaner brutes than they
> Who leave our streets in so vile a way
> In spite of all the money we pay.[78]

Sanitary reformers confronted a wide array of vested interests which the enemies of abortion did not face. There were many more landlords than abortionists in New York. The public largely seems to have blamed the tenants and not the landlords for the conditions in the slums. The tenants were a highly visible social problem, while landlords often lived elsewhere and kept their identity a secret from the tenants and the public. It was easier to drive abortionists out of business than to deal with complicated problems of overcrowding, illness and disease. Abortion was a highly visible target, and, as the story of Madame Restell makes clear, moral reformers and doctors found it easier to arouse the public to the wickedness of abortion than to move the city and state governments into enacting public health reforms.[79] Their struggle to reform sanitary conditions expressed the conscience of a profession, but the implications of what they demanded cut deeply into the valuable patronage available to local politicians. It became clear that the medical profession alone, and acting in its own name, was no match for Tammany (the political club which dominated Democratic Party politics for most of the century) and corruption.[80]

A decade of struggle

John H. Griscom, chairman of the public health committee of the New York Academy of Medicine, issued a report in 1852 which called upon the city to reform its own administration. The AICP published a report in the same year which sought to alert the public to the deteriorating conditions in the city slums. In 1854, the AICP launched a study of the deteriorating mortality figures. The differences between wards were startling. In 1855 the association had a "model" tenement built on the corner of Mott and Elizabeth streets. The rapid deterioration of this tenement, which soon became a notorious slum, did much to discredit the cause of housing reform.[81] The campaigns of the 1850s led to the creation of a legislative committee in Albany which visited New York in March 1855. Farsighted reforms were once again suggested, but the legislature remained indifferent. In 1856, the Academy of Medicine submitted a memorial of the problem to the legislature. Griscom's efforts were sympathetically received by Republicans such as Henry J. Raymond in the *New York Times*, and other papers hostile to the Democrats, but the medical profession was divided over the public health issue and "paid agents and corrupt officials" succeeded in destroying the measure.[82] Further memorials were submitted to the legislature in 1858, with the same result. The legislators took no initiatives on such matters unless there were strong reasons to do so, and the reformers firmly believed that bribery and corruption, originating in the city inspector's department, prevented all hope of reform. In April 1858 the board of supervisors of New York County requested the state senate appoint a select committee to investigate the health department of the city. The Academy of Medicine, divided for the moment between Griscom's allies and critics, no longer spoke with a single voice. Sensing that there was a risk of losing impetus, the leading physicians in favor of public health formed the New York Sanitary Association in January 1859. Griscom became the first vice-president, and Stephen Smith was a member of the council. The Sanitary

Association supported research into public hygiene, conducted public meetings, issued propaganda, and provided expert witnesses for select committees.[83] Naturally its voice was the strongest among those supporting a reform bill in the Senate. But once again the measure failed to receive a two-thirds majority in the assembly when a key supporter unexpectedly withdrew his support. There was nothing for the Sanitary Association to do but try again. In 1860, leading merchants endorsed a reform bill, memorials were sent to Albany, the AICP again pledged its support, and the *Times*, praising the new bill as "the most popular and important measure before the Legislature," reached deep within its Gladstone bag of emotional rhetoric to shock the public:

> Supposing, as we go for our places of business some pleasant morning, Death should exhibit his victims of the twenty-four preceding hours in the City Hall Park—*twenty-seven corpses of men, women and children*—some disfigured with that most disgusting of all diseases, small-pox—a disease which should never be known in a civilized community; others ghastly from the death-struggle with the nameless afflictions which riot among our poor unchecked by any remedial measures? What horror would thrill this entire community! How eager would be the inquiry, What measures can instantly be adopted to prevent a repetition of this dreadful spectacle? But is it any the less dreadful that, instead of displaying his victim to the public gaze, Death, with stealthy tread, steals them from the obscure homes of the poor, and silently consigns them to the depositories of the dead around our City? The terrible truth still remains, that of the sixty-four deaths which daily occur in this City, twenty-seven are from diseases which might have been prevented. Though the bodies of these twenty-seven murdered citizens are not every morning exhibited in the City Park, yet their names and residences are every day recorded in the City Inspector's office, and the grand total for the year is 9,600![84]

And yet the bill was again foiled in Albany. The reformers were bitter, not least because they believed that they had been defeated by corrupt influences. "It is averred that about $30,000 was raised in this city, among the office-holders, and expended to defeat the Health Bill of last Winter."[85]

> ... all good influences [wrote Stephen Smith] were impotent when opposed by log-rolling corruption, gridiron railroads' prizes, and the tempting gold that had been accumulated by depleting assessments upon the over-paid attachés of the so-called Health Department with its hundred and twenty-five thousand dollars of unearned salaries.[86]

When the city inspector's annual report for 1860 appeared, Smith seemed subdued. New York had "the highest death-rate of any civilized city in the world," but despite passionate reiteration this fact seemed to make little impact.[87] The reformers had nothing to show for more than a decade's work. Griscom addressed the Sanitary Association in the tones of a defeated though still defiant military leader:

> Though seven times defeated in their efforts to stay the progress of disease and death, their hearts fail not, nor is their determination abated. Nor though seventy times seven should the enemies of this holy cause succeed, by bribery and corruption, in postponing the day for the inauguration of the most valuable of all the reforms known amongst men, will its votaries lay aside their armor to contend for the faith which animates them with the assurance of final success.[88]

What was to be done, they asked, and like bemused Russian intelligentsia they looked to history to redeem their crusade. History duly obliged. The outbreak of the Civil War in April 1861 drew some of the most effective reformers away from purely local concerns. Dr. Elisha Harris, a prominent member of the Sanitary Association, journeyed to Washington with a group of sanitary reformers soon after the war began in the hope of persuading a reluctant administration of the usefulness of a body of volunteers, drawn from the leaders of the medical and business community, to advise the medical department of the Union Army. They advocated the creation of a United States Sanitary Commission. Harris and Frederick Law Olmsted examined the condition of army camps in the Washington area, and submitted a report which revealed a disheartening mismanagement and slovenliness: virtually none of the camps had a proper system of drainage ditches, latrines were too near the camp and generally consisted of an unfenced open ditch, and the soldiers' clothing was filthy and the men lousy. There was much here for the cleanliness campaigners to do. While inspecting Massachusetts troops, Samuel Gridley Howe, best known for his pioneering work with the education of the blind and mentally retarded, advocated "Soap! Soap! Soap!"[89] The principal objective of the Sanitary Commission was the reduction of preventable deaths in the Union Army. Implicit also was the larger project of "the best men" taking power from the hands of ineffectual and corrupt politicians: this was the dream of reformers in the second half of the century.[90]

As war-fever swept New York, almost the entire staff of Bellevue volunteered for duty with the army or the New York Sanitary

Association. Smith offered his services to the Emergency Corps of Surgeons, and he visited military hospitals in several cities.[91] He also worked at a tent hospital set up in Central Park. His experiences operating on war wounds led him to devise a technique in amputations that would eliminate soreness caused by the rubbing of the stump against an artificial limb. (He found that a long front flap of skin and a short rear flap created a better pad for the stump.) Smith drew upon these experiences in his manual for the use of field surgeons, *A Handbook of Surgical Operations* (1862), which went through twenty editions and became the standard medical text. He also wrote a brief guide on the technique of amputations which was circulated to surgeons through the army and collected in *Military Medical and Surgical Essays*, a volume prepared in 1864 for the United States Sanitary Commission and edited by the Surgeon-General. Smith compared Syme's and Progoff's methods for amputation at the ankle bone and gave a practical, detailed account of the technique of amputation and post-operative treatment.

The campaign for health reform was kept alive during the early days of the war by Griscom. In 1861, he persuaded the Academy of Medicine to appoint a committee to work with the Sanitary Association on the reform of public health laws—the first attempt to apply to public health reforms which emerged out of the war.[92] Yet another Metropolitan health bill was submitted to the legislature in 1862 by the Academy of Medicine, the Sanitary Association and similar professional societies from King's and Richmond counties. Two other bills were also being circulated, one from the police, largely giving them control of the enforcement of health laws; and a third emerged from the city inspector's office calculated to spoil the chances of the other two. Writing in the *American Medical Times* when the doctors' bill was introduced, Smith could hardly conceal his anger:

> It seems incredible that an intelligent and Christian city could witness the annual decimation of its people by preventable diseases without putting forth every honorable exertion to apply the remedy . . . The hearts of the people are wrung with anguish when a score or two of lives are sacrificed on an ill-conceived battle-field; the commanding officer is suspended from command; a military commission inquires into the minute details of his plans, and if it proves him incompetent he is dismissed from service. But New York, calmly indifferent, witnesses the annual slaughter of more of her citizens than occurs in a hundred destructive battles; no official is hurled with popular indignation from power; no searching inquiry is made for the causes of this costly sacrifice to official incompetency and neglect . . .[93]

Two enemies of reform

The war was the health reformers' darkest period. The 1862 health bill was defeated, and at last Stephen Smith was able to identify those who contributed to its downfall. A statement issued by the Republican mayor George Opdyke called for amendments to the bill which would give the mayor decisive power on the Metropolitan Board of Health. Without political control, he felt the measure should not be passed: it was a matter of democracy, of the rights of the people. The reformers were astounded by Opdyke's intervention. Before his election in 1861 as a bipartisan People's Union candidate—Richard B. Connolly was re-elected to the state senate on the same platform—he had been a leader of the "radical" anti-Weed faction on the "Democratic" wing of the Republican Party. He had been praised by Bryant (in a letter to Abraham Lincoln) as "a man who has made finance the subject of long and profound study, and whom no possible temptation could move from his integrity." The "radicals" were the strongest supporters for reforming health legislation. Smith concluded that Opdyke had in effect "joined the 'Ring' that by corruption, falsehood, political intrigues, and every unseemly device, annually unites in unholy bonds to defeat this most righteous measure."[94] Frustrated by their inability to turn public support into legislative action at Albany, Smith and his allies were bitterly disappointed by the actions of the mayor which blocked health reform. Opdyke's appointment of F. I. A. "Frank" Boole as city inspector in June 1863 was the last straw. Their warning about the consequences of corruption and civic neglect of the slums was powerfully underlined in July when the city was shaken by draft riots, in which a mob poured out of the slums and lynched African-Americans, drove the police off the streets and wrecked property worth millions of dollars. Mayor Opdyke's house on Fifth Avenue was attacked, and a vigilante force of fifty men, armed with swords, carbines and pistols, was required to prevent it being looted and burnt. After watching the way the unfortunate Opdyke was overwhelmed by the draft riots in July 1863, the editor of *The Nation*, E. L. Godkin, came to the same conclusion as had Smith: "Opdyke is, I consider a consummate rascal, to whom politics is a branch of his trade, and nothing more."[95]

Embittered at Opdyke's betrayal, reformers took their revenge in 1863 when the New York Union Party nominated a conservative as its candidate for mayor.[96] Some sanitarians decided that the cause was hopeless and further agitation a waste of time. In the gloomy aftermath of defeat Smith tried to rally the legions of reform. In doing so he restated the case for their "righteous measure":

We should not . . . lose sight of the fact that we are striving to accomplish a reform which in importance and in magnitude rises superior to all civil, social, religious, or political questions of the times. It aims to incorporate the higher elements of a Christian civilization in the administration of our civil affairs. . . . [The proposed] health reforms tend to develop a strong and healthy generation of citizens. They provide well-ventilated dwellings, they remove all local influences which debilitate and deteriorate, or which stifle the growth of the young, finally they protect the unsuspecting against adulterated and improper foods and drinks. Thirdly, all health reforms add largely to the sum of human happiness. They make happy homes, and from this springs that greatest of all public virtues, domestic contentment. In this estimate we should take into consideration the innumerable blessings, social, civil, and religious, which flow from a home where ruddy health glows upon every cheek. The cheerful and social family circle adds to the community citizens having correct and intelligent views of their civil and religious obligations, with a conscientious determination to fulfill them.[97]

Happy homes and domestic contentment were the "family values" most widely cherished in nineteenth-century New York. When he returned to the home of Mrs. Robert Sedgwick after his expedition to the Five Points in 1843, Dana was heartened by a "cheerful light coming from behind curtained parlor windows, where [there] were happy, affectionate & virtuous people connected by the ties of blood & friendship & enjoying the charities & honors of life."[98] Few Americans wrote more passionately than Catherine Maria Sedgwick of the home as refuge and touchstone:

—and—seem to me to have the true idea of a home—a place guaranteed against all foreign intervention; a sanctuary of domestic rights and freedom; a temple with open doors, but never to be entered by the profane; a missionary station, whence light is to go forth to the heathen around them; a life-school; an insurance office for the next generation; a fortress of religion and morality; a guarded passage to the holy land for them, tended by their two little angels. Such securities for the permanence of our institutions, carried wherever they go, will defend us against swarms of Irish, and Irish priests and German radicals.[99]

The idea of home, the ideal of domesticity and "the family circle," were potent symbols for Americans in mid-century. Horace Bushnell's *Christian Nurture* (1847) did much to persuade contemporaries that family life and the home were engaged in the sacred work of shaping the Christian child.[100] "Home" for Rev. Chapin was a powerful force for good in social life. There was, as well, an ethical dimension to the romantic architectural styles advocated by Andrew Jackson Downing in his writing on landscape gardening and cottage architecture. The house was both a school and a church, and the gothic revival styles advocated by Downing employed a range of symbols (especially the cross) which were daily reminders of the duty of "Christian nurture." Downing argued that the rightly designed home, and the beautiful garden, would serve as "an unfailing barrier against vice, immorality and bad habits."[101] What made the slums so terrible was that they deprived the children of the poor of the inoculating benefits of "home."

> In many of these hot-beds of disease were found infants perishing for want of food which famishing mothers could not furnish; while on every hand were to be seen *that* poverty, squalor, sickness and despair, which render the homes of the poor wretched beyond description. Again, many boys were found whose memories failed to reach back to the time when they enjoyed the luxuries of a bed, who never in all their sad lives remember to have slept under a roof, utter strangers to a mother's care or a father's advice. In their brief vocabularies the word "home" so dear to most of us is wholly without meaning.[102]

However uncomfortable and poorly decorated the American home was, and however stilted relations between men and women became, the word "home" itself brought forth passionate and sentimental effusions: "Oh, may your home and mine," wrote Charles Loring Brace to his closest (male) friend,

> be something different from—I must say—the majority in our country. May there be a warmth and light about it, such as cheers at once even the stranger who enters. May we deny ourselves, for years, sensuality and display, rather than that there ever should be a want of time and of means to make our home happy and cheerful. May even our love within it be so little selfish, that no one can leave our company without a happier heart.[103]

(For John Ruskin in *Sesame and Lilies* (1865), the home was ". . . a sacred place, a vestal temple, a temple of the hearth.") Dr. Smith shared the commonplace of "home" and "domestic contentment" expressed by Dana, Sedgwick and Brace. It had become a "redemptive counterpart", as Nancy Cott has suggested, to the many evils of the world. To Smith and many reformers of his generation, the Metropolitan Board of Health was part of a larger crusade for virtue and purity within the community, of which the home and family circle were the universally acknowledged models of relationships and duties.[104]

To Dr. Smith, Mayor Opdyke had a corrupt colleague in the conspiracy against sanitary reform—Boole—the city inspector who was notorious even among thieves for his greed and unscrupulous corruption:

> An' there's Boole! Oh, bejabbers! the scoundhrelly Blue-nose
> Has brought all his brothers to share in the swag;
> He has houses, seven-thirties, and green-backs, and few knows
> The size of the "stale" he has tied in his bag.
>   "An' the moment," he says, "that they shtop him from thievin,
> He'll to Canady carry his bones and his purse.
> May the divil go wid him our counthry when leavin—
> On the black British spy be the Irishman's curse."[105]

He was a Tammany man. In the long and complex history of New York city politics, Tammany Hall was a unique institution: long-lived, corrupt, and effective, and Boole was heart and soul a loyalist of the hall. A ship-builder by trade, he was elected as a Democrat to the common council in 1856 and held his seat in two successive elections. Despite an involvement in a fraudulent claim of expenses, described in the *Herald* as "one of the grossest swindles ever perpetrated by the Corporation," he was elected as alderman for the 12th district in 1858 and again in 1859. He became chairman of the committee on streets and railroads, an office full of lucrative possibilities.[106] Boole sought the Tammany nomination for comptroller in 1862, but in a straight fight between Matthew T. Brennan he was forced to give way. As recompense, perhaps, he was appointed city inspector by Opdyke in June 1863. At the time of his appointment Frank Boole was forty-two. With the city inspector's large budget in hand, he sought the Democratic nomination for mayor. He was able to secure, or perhaps to purchase, the backing of ex-mayor Fernando Wood's breakaway political club, Mozart Hall. His main rival for the Tammany nomination was the wealthy fur dealer, C. Godfrey Gunther, who was a Peace Democrat, outspoken in his support for the South. If Boss Tweed, the leader of Tammany Hall, failed to support him, Gunther threatened to run as an independent.[107] Boole was an old crony of Tweed's, but the Draft Riots earlier that year had temporarily given supporters of the war an upper hand in both Tammany and Mozart Hall. Peter B. Sweeny and the new leadership preferred Boole, a "War Democrat," who had a good record on the war and appeared a likely winner.

Although Boole came from a working-class background, and was forced to invest the whole of his personal wealth into the campaign, he had the resources of the city inspector's office at his disposal: he hired 250 new men immediately before the election (and fired

150 immediately afterwards).[108] Gunther, embraced by the "Peace" faction of the Democracy led by the lawyer John McKeon, came out with a violent anti-black platform. When Boole declined to follow suit, he appeared at an election meeting of black voters held at the Metropolitan Assembly Rooms, and openly asked for their support. Promising to seek the end of the excluding of blacks from the Eighth Avenue streetcars, he was branded by political opponents as a "nigger lover." Reformers, very far from being of one mind on the question of black suffrage, saw in this aspect of Boole's campaign simply a demagogic ploy. They generally considered him to be "as nauseating a type of politician as Tammany could bring forth."[109] The contest between Boole and Gunther in the mayoral election of 3 December 1864 was thus marked by racial bigotry, in addition to the usual mixture of distrust, plotting and betrayal. In the end Boole's friends secretly threw their support behind Gunther, who won with forty per cent of the total votes cast.[110] Reformers applauded the embarrassment of Tammany, saluted Gunther's victory as a hopeful portent, and confidently expected that they had seen the last of Boole. If it was a choice between the lesser of two evils, the reformers believed that the racist Gunther was more likely to acquiesce in the agenda of reform than the notoriously corrupt Boole. Within Tammany Hall, news of Boole's defeat was received with calm. Tammany hearts were with the "Peace" faction.[111]

> The terrible defeat Boole suffered in the Mayoralty contest . . . [recalled a Tammany annalist] impoverished him and rendered him extremely poor, as everything he had in the world was staked on the issue of the election. After this he was known but little in our local politics, driven as he was from the City Inspectorship by the passage by the Legislature of the "Health Bill" establishing the Department of Public Health. At the many misfortunes that overtook him, his mind became shattered and the light of his reason passed away, and he died, some years ago, a miserable and an almost forgotten man, in a lunatic asylum in the interior of the State. The fate of Frank Boole was more than he deserved. While he was ambitious, he was true and generous to his friends, many of whom soon forget him in his poverty and distress, when they found he could be of service to them no longer.[112]

This sentimental account of Boole gives a thoroughly misleading picture of the events which followed the 1863 election. Far from being a shattered man, he remained city inspector and single-handedly engaged and for three years repelled the massed forces of reform in New York.

The case against Boole emerged in the immediate aftermath of his unsuccessful bid for mayor. He and his friends prevented a grand jury from hearing the allegations, which were then submitted directly to governor Horatio Seymour. There were two clear and highly damaging complaints: that Boole as city inspector had ignored an offer by Garrit E. Winants to collect and remove (without cost to the city) all ashes which Winants planned to use as landfill on property he owned in Jersey City; the second allegation concerned the padding of the city inspector's payroll in the period immediately before the election. Affidavits from Winants and others painted a picture of Boole as a devious and deceitful thief who ought to have been removed from office.[113] The offer from Winants would have deprived Boole of his share, reputed to be between twenty-five and fifty per cent of the total expenditure for the removal of ashes. Mayor Gunther unsuccessfully ordered his suspension. Investigations into Boole's conduct of his department soon revealed some interesting practices. A man named Daniel B. Badger testified before a state senate committee that in 1864 he had put in a bid for $300,000 for the contract to clean the city's streets. When it was opened, Boole announced that Badger's bid was for $500,000 and proceeded to give the contract elsewhere. The cost of cleaning the streets was $800,000 in 1864. There were many witnesses who claimed that they had paid Boole various sums, around $200 each, for positions in his department—only to be suddenly dismissed later.[114] The reformers' exasperating struggle to rid the city of Boole's incompetence and corruption persuaded many that the root of the problem lay in democracy itself. In a sermon delivered on the Fourth of July, 1869, entitled the "Moral Theory of Civil Liberty," Henry Ward Beecher offered a comparison of Paris under the Second Empire of Louis Napoleon with New York and its democratic institutions:

> There may not be many nations in which the people are freer, and in which life and property are safer, than in ours; but there are few cities on the globe where life is so unsafe, and where property is so unsafe—where so much is stolen by direct brutality, and so much more by judicial brutality—as in New-York. And probably there is no place on the earth where life and property are safer, and justice better executed than in Paris. In certain respects, there is more liberty in that city than in perhaps any other. So [we see] that despotism may flourish under republican institutions, and liberty may thrive under monarchical institutions. It illustrates the fact that the nature of civil liberty, and the nature of personal liberty, are to be determined more from the condition of the individuals, than from the importation of names and forms and customs.[115]

(Beecher's parishioners were approximately balanced between artisans and skilled laborers on the one hand and merchants on the other: his audience was perhaps representative of newer, upwardly mobile elements within the Brooklyn social mix. About a quarter of Beecher's parish commuted into New York City to work. They would certainly have had strong reasons to fear the unbridled sway of corruption in New York.) Radical Republicans came to think increasingly that democratic institutions, as they then functioned, were no protection against despotism. The position of city inspector could no longer be entrusted to the democratic choice of the city. The city inspector should be appointed by the state legislature, not elected within the city. In the end it was decided to remove altogether from the city inspector's department responsibility for street cleaning.[116] Reform took the shape of eliminating health and cleanliness from the malign abuses of democracy. Indeed, reform in mid-century often explicitly rejected the idea that politics (or democracy) had anything to do with the running of a great metropolis.[117] Ever contemptuous of the reformers, Tweed again tried to give Boole the mayoral nomination in 1865, but the public outcry at the city inspector's blatant corruption forced him to pull back and replace him with the equally pliant John T. Hoffman, who served the two-year term beginning early in 1866.

The Citizens' Association conducts a sanitary survey

Neither the Academy of Medicine nor the Sanitary Association had succeeded in loosening the legislative blockade of reform; on their own and in combination they were too easily condemned as special interest organizations, inadequate for the larger purposes of reform. But with the election of Gunther as mayor in 1863, new initiatives for reform were soon made. A small group of medical reformers (including Willard Parker, Elisha Harris, and Stephen Smith) met with the mayor in December. An invitation was issued in January 1864 to a wider circle of civic-minded men to join the new association, and in July and August invitations were issued to workers and foremen in the iron and book trades to attend public meetings on the state of the city government. Thus the Citizens' Association "for purposes of public usefulness" was founded. Upwards of 100 figures from the financial and commercial elite of New York, including William B. Astor, who was succeeded as the association's president by the banker James Brown (who had been one of the founders of the AICP), Peter Cooper, Hamilton Fish, the banker and politician August Belmont, John Jacob Astor, Jr., the distinguished lawyer

Charles O'Conor and congressman Robert B. Roosevelt were publicly associated with the Citizens' Association. The moving spirit behind the new body was Nathaniel Sands, formerly a member of the New York Sanitary Association, who strengthened ties between the physicians and the political reformers.[118]

The friends of sanitary reform sought through the Citizens' Association the legislative changes which they had tried and failed to achieve for more than a decade on their own. The political aspirations of the sanitarians and lay reformers coincided with the need to pursue changes in the city inspector's department. It was in itself a highly desirable reform, made more urgent by the threat of violence posed by the slums-dwellers. One of the members of the association, the lawyer Dorman B. Eaton, suggested the tactics for a new campaign.[119] The association should establish two specialist councils, one on law and one on hygiene, and leading medical experts should be invited to join the latter. They would help to identify the nature and extent of the threats to public health represented by the slums. Eaton proposed that a major survey of housing conditions be undertaken. The other council would prepare a bill for the legislature which would be modeled upon the work of Chadwick and his followers in Britain. In February 1864, the association issued an appeal to doctors. The leading sanitarians in the city, including Elisha Harris and Stephen Smith, joined the executive committee of the Council of Hygiene and Public Health.

In the meantime a delegation was sent by the association to Albany to make a fresh assessment of the attitudes of legislators towards sanitary reform. They found both Republicans and Democrats, for somewhat different reasons, less interested in reform than at any time in the past decade. The Republicans feared that an unpopular measure in the nation's largest city might hurt President Lincoln's chances for re-election, while the Tammany Democrats recognized that the creation of a nonpolitical Metropolitan health board would hurt themselves most of all.

After its organization in April 1864, the Council of Hygiene and Public Health lobbied enthusiastically for the passage of legislation. Despite the ineffectiveness of these efforts, the growing threat of another cholera outbreak was discussed at a public meeting of the reformers on 8 November, where it was decided to raise $50,000 to make house-to-house visits. From this project came the request to Dr. Stephen Smith to conduct a sanitary survey of the city. With a speed perhaps unthinkable before the medical profession's experience with the United States Sanitary Commission, Smith recruited twenty-nine sanitary inspectors, largely from the physicians who had worked in the city dispensaries or on the commission, and the support staff able to provide maps, diagrams and statistical tables. The design of the survey and the recruiting of its personnel were complete by July. The survey proper was rapidly finished by early December. *The Report of the Council of Hygiene of the Citizens' Association of New York upon the Sanitary Condition of the City* was intended to accompany the submission to the state legislature of a Metropolitan health bill, drawn up by Dorman B. Eaton's Council of Law of the Citizens' Association.[120] The full reports of the sanitary inspectors filled many volumes. Elisha Harris, secretary of the Council of Hygiene, prepared a 500-page single-volume version of the report for wider circulation, generally referred to as *The Sanitary Condition of New York*. "The effect of this report was electrical," recalled Dr. Charles F. Chandler; "it was a revelation; the public awoke and demanded reform."[121] A brilliant professor of chemistry at Columbia University and a close colleague of Stephen Smith's, Chandler was recalling events some forty-six years distant when he spoke. There was no immediate public awakening to the cause of sanitary reform, and political opposition was certainly not swept aside. But there is no doubt that *The Sanitary Condition of New York* made a substantial impact. It is a remarkable document, as interesting when read for its picture of the community, as a community, as it is an account of the physical environment and sanitary condition of the city's inhabitants.

The volume is divided into two parts. The first, some 130 pages, consists of a general survey of the problem and a presentation of the suggested remedies. The second part, consisting of summaries of the sanitary inspectors' reports for each of the twenty-nine districts in the city, provides specific details about a range of problems, from sewers to street paving, housing, and the character of the inhabitants.

To read the volume is to understand what the breakdown of community entailed for New York. The meaning of "community" is indeed the subtext of *The Sanitary Condition of New York*. At one point in the introduction, addressing the widespread assumption that New York was a divided society of "Two Nations," Smith argued that "[t]he inhabitants of a densely populated town may be regarded as a single family, living in contiguous or narrowly separated apartments, any one of which may be as certainly as speedily rendered infectious as the cells of a prison."[122] A report from a sanitary inspector who followed the story of a man in the 11th ward who had died of typhus fever touched the heart of the matter. A few days later, the man's daughter, who lived in the 17th ward, was attacked by the same fever after visiting her father and soon died. Another sister who lived in Brooklyn, who had also visited her father's sick room, contracted the disease and died. A third sister, living on Avenue A, contracted the fever when she attended her father and sisters. After visiting one of the sick daughters, another relative brought the fever to her home on 11th Street. Each successive distribution of the disease created new centers of infection and dreadful risks for husbands, wives, children, friends and neighbors (lvii). The illness of one was a threat to the whole community. The competitive individualism of New Yorkers was so deeply entrenched that, as the former city inspector Dr. John H. Griscom had repeatedly discovered, the language of "community" and "public interest" struggled for a hearing. Dr. John Bell argued in 1860 that there was, or should be, a community of interest binding rich and poor together:

> The rich man, in his spacious mansion, has a direct personal interest in the health and domestic comfort of his poor neighbor; and the more secluded and shut out from the world, in a dark court or alley, is this neighbor, the greater is this interest. His open windows will give entrance, not only to the refreshing breeze, but also to the poisoned air emanating from congregated beings in the confined lodgings, and from the unremoved refuse or offal adjacent. It is thus that Typhus Fever, beginning in the hovels of the poor, finds its way into the luxurious abodes of the rich.[123]

The social contract ultimately comes down to this: you will infect me, I will infect you, unless we both recognize the danger and act, as a community, to save ourselves. New York clergymen such as Chapin believed passionately that the recognition of community was irresistible:

> "Am I my brothers' keeper?" *you* ask, perhaps, with a tone of surprise, or scorn. *You* ask O! respectable gentleman or lady; O! man in the thick of business; O! self-indulgent Epicurean;—and the answer comes to you not from the ground merely, but from the universal air—the answer of kindred pulses, of confluent sympathies, of an inseparable humanity— though it swarms in rags, and riots in shame, and seems far off from you in its hell of debasement and despair.[124]

Infection, and not the heightened moral sense, seemed the most likely product of the degraded urban environment in the eyes of the sanitary reformers. To overcome the ingrained individualism, selfishness, and social divisions in New York, sanitary reformers found that the family was the most traditional metaphor for community. It provided them with a comprehensible warning: a threat to one family was ultimately a threat to the whole community.

Things which could endanger public health were seldom reported; there seemed to be no one to report them to. The introduction to the *Report* noted the experience of a member of the Council of

Hygiene, who visited five homes within fifty yards of one of the largest wholesalers of dry goods in the city in which he found smallpox. Since the discovery of vaccination by Jenner in 1798, smallpox was a preventable disease, yet here it was, threatening a succession of unsuspecting tenants, visitors to nearby shops, and workers in offices and businesses (lv). A "great commercial city" puts into jeopardy "the prosperity of trade" if it leaves such abuses unattended (lxi).

The inspectors were careful to point out that even the "most favored" and wealthiest districts of the city were threatened by potential sources of infection and by foul smells. Many "squares" within the city were of "mixed sanitary condition":

> In them, the child of wealthy parents may hear from his comfortable bed the cries of his unfortunate brother, in the dampness and darkness of the tenant-house. The air of such a neighborhood is infected, and occupants of the better class houses are living in a state of constant exposure to some of those contagious diseases so often prevalent in tenant-dwellings. It is not only the poor but the rich who should be interested in the sanitary condition of the city, for diseases are often raging within a stone's toss of their houses . . . (131)

Disease was no respecter of social rank. Although epidemics inflicted the "immoral and degraded classes" first, they were easily capable of leaping over "all barriers physical and social" (218). Indeed, the inspector in this district warned that even the air of New York carried its threat promiscuously to the rich and the poor. The city streets were freely strewn with garbage which in time became desiccated and was converted into dust by the summer sun.

> And now every horse that passes stirs it up, every vehicle leaves a cloud of it behind; it is lifted into the air with every wind and carried in every direction. Those who are directly responsible for this state of things suffer no more than the cleanly and thrifty who are so unfortunate as to live anywhere the wind, blowing from this quarter, reaches them. . . . As we pass by our mouths become full of it, we draw it in with our breath, it is swallowed into the stomach, it penetrates our dress and clings to, until it has covered, our perspiring skin. (208)

Visitors to the city found the streets almost incomprehensibly filthy. "The mire was ankle-deep in Broadway," wrote the editor of *Chambers' Journal* from Edinburgh,

> and the more narrow business streets were barely passable. The thing was really droll. All along the foot-pavements there stood, night and day, as if fixtures, boxes, buckets, lidless flour-barrels, baskets, decayed

tea-chests, rusty iron pans, and earthenware jars full of coal-ashes. There they rested, some close to the houses, some leaning over into the gutter, some on the door-steps, some knocked over and spilt, and to get forward you required to take constant care not to fall over them. . . . Passing up Broadway on this occasion, and looking into a side-street, the scene of confused débris was of a kind not to be easily forgotten—ashes, vegetable refuse, old hats without crowns, worn-out shoes, and other household wreck, lay scattered about as a field of agreeable inquiry for a number of long-legged and industrious pigs.[125]

William Chambers' good temperament should not disguise the significance of this description: why do New Yorkers tolerate these conditions? Does anyone care? Who is responsible? The sanitary reform movement had been hammering away at the problem of the city's streets. It seemed to be the link between the political problem (an ineffective and corrupt city inspector's office) and the sanitary problem. "Little attention is now paid to garbage boxes," they had argued in the 1863 meeting with mayor Gunther, "but all the refuse of the dwellings is thrown promiscuously into the streets, from which it is, apparently, never to be removed. Here it lies, the hot summer through, sending forth its disease-generating emanations, which fill, with disgusting odors, all the air, and permeate every habitable recess."[126]

Even newly built houses were not immune from threats to health. The inspector for the 25th district noted that there was a ten-dollar charge for connecting a new house to the city sewer system. This, plus the actual cost of constructing the drain, encouraged builders to connect five or six houses to the sewer with a single drain, and with the cheapest materials available. The odors which emanated were a frequent source of complaint and a threat to health (287). There were certain moments in the *Report* when the sanitary inspectors addressed the wealthy directly, hoping to shake their assumption that they were secure from the many threats to public health: "Let the wealthy resident upon Fifth Avenue walk along 17th Street from First Avenue to the East River, and examine the houses and look at their population as he pursues his way; and if he can read certain results in their causes, he will see enough to diminish his sense of security in his own house" (220).

The many authors of the *Report* presented a picture of mutually uncomprehending and hostile groups, each in their own way rejecting any obligation to the community at large. Indeed, the concept of "community" was simply absent from the observed lives of the people of the city. Although the sanitary reformers did not offer an analysis of the different groups within the city, and worked with assumptions about class which were largely intuitive and commonsensical, they assumed a society already deeply divided between "capitalists" and laborers or the poor. Like reformers of the progressive era, the doctors offered themselves as a group standing above and outside the conflict they described. Their own role was to call attention to the way both the rich and the poor ignored the threats to public health, and thus created a situation in which medically trained people were needed to preserve the public interest.

The doctors, perhaps with a little encouragement from Stephen Smith, were unsparing in their comments upon the speculators, landlords and "capitalists" who owned the tenant-houses in New York. The term "tenant-house" was used to describe dwellings which were occupied by three or more families, and for which rent was charged by the month. Originally private houses of the commercial classes, the former owners having sold out or moved uptown as the intensity of business in the lower wards increased, the generous rooms in Colonial and Federal houses were partitioned, making space for several families where one had previously lived, and these crowded accommodations were in turn "packed" by the admission of boarders. The first building in New York specifically constructed as a tenant-house was erected in 1835. Perhaps half of the inspectors blamed the landlords for their "criminal selfishness and indifference" (lxxix). They were "avaricious and unscrupulous speculators" (lxxx), moved only by "cupidity" (99). The inspector in the 4th district, Dr. Ezra R. Pulling, a veteran of the United States Sanitary Commission, explained how the system of tenant-houses worked in New York:

> They are, in many instances, owned by large capitalists, by whom they are farmed out to a class of factors who make this their especial business. These men pay to the owners of the property a sum which is considered a fair return on the capital invested, and rely for their profits (which are often enormous) on the additional amount which they can extort from the wretched tenants whose homes frequently become almost untenantable for want of repairs, which the "agent" deems it to his interest to withhold. These men contrive to absorb most of the scanty surplus which remains to the tenants after paying for their miserable food, shelter, and raiment. They are, in many instances, proprietors of low groceries, liquor stores, and "policy shops" connected with such premises . . . (56, 58)

One of the central features of the *Report* was the attempt to prove, beyond reasonable doubt, that overcrowding and unsanitary conditions in tenant-houses were responsible for much of the preventable sickness and disease in the city. One inspector after another noted evidence that the landlords were solely interested in the income they received from their investments and callously disregarded the conditions their tenants lived in. No inspector wrote more passionately than Dr. H. M. Field, describing the 18th district:

> Every expenditure of money, which the law does not force them to, is refused; and blinds half swung and ready to fall and crush with the first strong wind; doors long off their hinges, which open and shut by being taken up bodily and put out of or in the way; chimneys as apt to conduct the smoke into the room as out of it; stagnant, seething, overflowing privies, left uncleansed through the hot months of summer, though pestilence itself should breed from them . . . and all this day after day, month after month, year in and year out, now a little better, and now worse again. (219)

In 1864 there were 15,511 tenant-houses in New York. More than half of the city's inhabitants—half a million people—lived in such environments (349). A vocal minority of the contributors were driven to speak out against this "oppression of the poor" and followed Dr. Field as he asked fundamental questions of the unfettered rights of property:

> No man has moral right to build a house, leaving out all the modern appliances and conveniences, even to ventilation, because they cost a little money, and then to crowd twenty families into it. Yet there are hundreds of such houses in our city, and many more are being built. No landlord has a right to refuse all the most obvious and necessary repairs to a house, until it is in such a state of ruin that nails and spikes must be driven in to keep it together. Nor has he a right to withhold all sanitary care and inspection until the contents of the vaults [of the privies] are more than even with the surface of the ground, and have become a constant nuisance and cause of disease and death. (220)

The *Report* was no less scathing about the tenant-house dwellers, whose filthy habits and ignorance of the basic principles of sanitation made already deplorable conditions worse. Inspectors who complained of the failure of the health department to cleanse the city streets pointed out that it had become customary to throw refuse of all kinds into the streets and alleys. "The tenants of the houses without house-drainage generally throw their house-slops indiscriminately anywhere into the streets, alleys, courts, yards, and sometimes into cellars and passages" (151). People answered "calls of nature" in every alley, backyard and warehouse wall, creating a "disgusting stench" (105). The contents of chamber pots were often thrown out of windows, or deposited on the roof (290). Inhabitants of the 14th district were described as "uncleanly in their persons and habits, and grossly addicted to intemperance, that fertile source of vice, misery and crime" (166). Many tenant-house dwellers in the 5th district were "of careless and filthy habits," wrote the inspector,

> taking no concern for the general comfort or neatness of their apartments; sleeping and eating together in their ill-ventilated and crowded apartments; disposing of their slops and garbage so as to save themselves from personal exertion, as much as possible, with very few facilities to aid them; employing their ill-trained, ill-conditioned children in these household labors of carrying water and slops through the dark passage-ways, and up and down rickety stairs. (68)

The inspector in the 20th district commented upon the bed clothing of the poor, "which has the appearance of rarely being washed or changed, and is consequently saturated with the secretions from the bodies of their occupants" (245). The 22nd district was in an even more appalling state: "The offensive odor from these coverings is sometimes exceedingly disgusting and persistent, so much so that when handled the hands become so permeated with the odor that notwithstanding all efforts in cleansing they are rendered positively disgusting for one or two days after" (273).

Among those alert to the dangers, there was universal recognition of the need for changes in the personal habits of the poor. Medical missionaries and health wardens had an immense task of education before them. (Some iconoclastic spirits like Dr. John Acheson suggested that "it is almost impossible to instill good habits, intelligence, and morality into people who live in the contracted and unventilated apartments of overcrowded and closely-packed houses, filled with the noisome odors arising from streets reeking with filth, or from neglected privies and court-yards" [113].) Inspectors were able to point to the existence of clean and respectable tenant-houses, invariably occupied by German and not Irish immigrants, and to certain parts of the city where the old custom survived of the owner or occupant (or their servants) sweeping the street in front of their residence. But the stable New York dominated by merchants and artisans living in their own homes and maintaining some responsibility for the condition of the environment seemed irretrievably lost. By the 1880s, such memories belonged to "Old New York" and to an age when "[o]ur streets were kept cleaner . . . since every one was responsible for a space in front of his building extending to the middle of the street . . ."[127] Between the indifference of the landlord, who lived elsewhere, and the carelessness of the tenant, the environment of the city as a place to live deteriorated year by year: ". . . for twenty-five years past the rate of mortality in this city has been increasing, and . . . it has fluctuated from the ratio of 1 death to every

39 of the population, to as great an increase as 1 death to every 27, and even to every 22½ of the living" (xliv). There was a general refusal of responsibility. People in the 12th district showed "a great comparative indifference to contagious maladies . . . and much carelessness as to prophylactic measures on the part of the landlord" (139). In the 20th landlords blamed the tenants for rubbish accumulated in cellars, while the tenants declared their innocence and blamed their predecessors. "It seemed to be no one's business to remove this dirt . . ." (243).

The *Report* refers several times to the draft riots of July 1863. "The terrible elements of society we saw brought to the surface during a great popular outbreak, are equally in existence at the present moment; nay, more, they are increasing year by year. The tocsin which next summons them from their dark and noisome haunts may be the prelude to a scene of universal pillage, slaughter, and destruction" (65). For most of the sanitary inspectors the desire to dampen social discontent was a motive, among many, in their work. Yet the description of the poor in the *Report* was far removed from the scenes of 1863. What at one level of commentary was "carelessness" and "indifference" on the part of the poor seemed to others a syndrome rather inelegantly referred to as "Tenant-House Rot."[128] The unwell often exhibited a lack of energy and a dispirited manner while others, with no obvious maladies, seemed "idle, listless, and look like prisoners in a cell that have now some one to visit and look at them" (102). Poor quality food, and all the other features of tenant-house life, seemed to produce "a generally-impaired vitality" (212) which rendered the inhabitants especially vulnerable to diseases and illnesses. Even those who developed signs of "apparent immunity" to the characteristic maladies of the tenant-house often exhibited "a degree of both mental and physical degeneration" (246). The inspector of the 4th district quoted from a report entitled "Gotham Court" on Cherry Street which he prepared for the New York Dispensary in 1859:

The eye becomes bleared, the senses blunted, the limbs shrunken and tremulous, the secretions exceedingly offensive.

There is a state of premature decay. In this condition of life the ties of nature seem to be unloosed. Maternal instinct and filial affection seem to participate in the general decay of soul and body. A kind Providence, whose hand is visible even here, mercifully provides that the almost inevitable decay and death which man's criminal neglect entails on the offspring of the unfortunates who dwell in these dreary mansions, shall elicit comparatively feeble pangs of parental anguish. (64)

Another inspector compared the effect of demoralization upon tenant-house dwellers to the "subtle, insidious" action of lead upon the human organism:

> A man gradually loses ambition and hope; concern for the well-being of himself and his family, by slow degrees, lose their hold upon him. He becomes what cannot be better expressed than by the term *nil admirari.* Loss of physical vigor attends this corresponding condition of the mind, until at length lassitude and depression of spirits and constant ennui get such control over him that no power or effort of the will can shake them off. (221)

Read with sufficient care, the *Report* does much to explain why, despite the chaotic and appalling conditions in the tenant-houses, there had been only sporadic outbreaks of serious social disorder. The environment in which the poor lived sapped their energy, destroyed their physical strength, crushed their self-respect and surrounded them with the "avaricious" and the indifferent. The physicians of New York, or at least those actively pursuing sanitary reform, were the only group in the city which seemed to promise some relief for tenant-house dwellers as a class.

The Metropolitan health bill

While Stephen Smith prepared the sanitary survey, Dorman B. Eaton and the Council of Law prepared legislation to establish the Metropolitan health board. The central feature of their proposal was to abolish the city health department and replace it by a body representing a larger area co-extensive with the recently reformed Metropolitan Police. The council believed that reform was only possible if control could be wrested from the urban corruptionists. Eaton incorporated certain features in the bill which had appeared in British health legislation, but which were unprecedented in the United States: namely, that the board should be able to function without the possibility of delay by injunction. Stephen Smith described the unique powers of the board: "What it declares to be a nuisance—dangerous to life and detrimental to health—no one should call in question. When it orders a nuisance to be abated within a given fixed time no mandamus should avail to stay its action or the enforcement of its decree. A Board of Health, in his [Eaton's] opinion, should make its own laws, execute its own laws and sit in judgment on its own acts. It must be an *imperium in imperio.*"[129]

It was an autocratic power, disguised in opaque legal language on the reasonable presumption that the legislature would have gutted the bill if the implied powers of the board had been made explicit. In any event, the elections in December 1864 resulted in a wartime Republican triumph, and the mood in Albany was receptive to anything which might harry and embarrass the city Democrats. On the suggestion of the Republican senator from Onondaga County, Andrew Dickson White, Republicans directed their attention to the health department, and the city inspector Frank Boole. The Metropolitan health bill was introduced in January 1865 and referred to the committee on cities and villages, where it made rapid progress, buoyed up by widespread press support. When the city health wardens were examined, they revealed something of the nature of Boole's administration:

> Mr. Health Officer, have you any "highjinnicks" in your district?
> Yes, sir.
> Much?
> Yes, sir, quite a good deal.
> Have you done anything in regard to them?
> Yes, sir; I have done all that I could.
> Witness, now on your oath, do you know what the word "highjinnicks" means?
> Yes, sir.
> What does it mean?
> It means the bad smells that arise from standing water.[130]

Reformers, physicians and clergymen revealed in their testimony a greater knowledge of the problems of the city than the health department and were able to show the legislators the ineffectual work of the city inspector's department. Eaton made a "brilliant and exhaustive" speech upon the nature of sanitary legislation and the value to cities of adequate health laws.[131]

Smith was called to testify before a joint committee of both houses on 13 February. With Frank Boole and several health wardens sitting uncomfortably nearby as he spoke, Smith portrayed a community in the midst of a terrible social tragedy. Half the population of New

(facing page)
Gotham Court, 37–9 Cherry Street, erected as a model tenement in 1850, was soon among the most notorious buildings in the city. It consisted of two rows of back-to-back five-story houses, 234 feet long by thirty-four feet wide, entered through narrow alleys which ran the length of the building. The 1865 sanitary inspection recorded that "Of the entire number of tenements, four only were found in a condition approaching cleanliness. It need scarcely be said that the entire establishment swarms with vermin." Demolished 1895.

York had a death rate typical of a healthy country town. In the 17th ward (which ran northward from Rivington Street to 14th Street, bounded on the east by Avenue B and Clinton Street and on the west by the Bowery and Fourth Avenue, an area which was inhabited by Irish and German immigrants living in tenements which averaged nearly thirty inhabitants per house) there were seventeen deaths per 1,000 inhabitants. In the 4th ward (site of the notorious Gotham Court in Cherry Street, a tenement which housed 500 persons, with an infant-mortality rate of forty-four per cent) and the 6th ward, which ran from Chatham Street and Park Row north to Canal Street, between Broadway and the Bowery, inhabited by the poor, death rates varied from thirty-six to forty per 1,000.[132] Tens of thousands of people lived in conditions of utter vileness, filth and degradation (63). At a time when the ratio of deaths per 1,000 in the United States was twenty-three, Smith estimated that fully half of the city's mortality rate was preventable. He quoted liberally from the graphic and detailed notes and reports of the sanitary inspectors, some of which were not included in the *Report* when it appeared in June, to illustrate housing conditions and the state of the city's streets. Refuting the notion that the poor health conditions in New York were due to immigrants, he argued that they were caused by half a million people being "submerged in filth, and half-stifled in an atmosphere charged with all the elements of death" (128). Smith particularly stressed the effects of such terrible conditions upon the tenant-house dwellers, and issued an invitation in the Virgilian mode to the legislators to attend to the "living reality" of the slums. "It is only by personal inspection that one can learn to what depths of social and physical degradation human beings can descend" (89–90). The "inmates" of "these abodes of wretchedness, filth and disease" exhibited "the same lethargic habits as animals, burrowing in the ground. They are, indeed, half-narcotized by the constant inhalation of the emanations of their own bodies, and by a prolonged absence of light and fresh air" (88). His account of conditions in the worst slums emphasized the moral disaster experienced by the "inmates":

Here [in overcrowded accommodation] they eat, drink, sleep, work, dress and undress without the possibility of that privacy which an innate modesty imperatively demands. In sickness and in health it is the same.

What is the consequence? The sense of shame—the greatest, surest safeguard of virtue, except the grace of God—is gradually blunted, ruined, and finally destroyed. New scenes are witnessed and participated in, with a countenance of brass, the very thought of which, once, would have filled the sensitive heart of modesty with pain, a[n]d covered its cheeks with burning blushes. The mind of one thus brought in daily and nightly contact with such scenes must become greatly debased, and its fall, before the assaults of vice, rendered almost certain. (94, 97)

He referred to the experience of missionaries, preachers and others bringing the gospel into the slums who had begun to question whether their efforts should be abandoned until physical conditions were improved. "Their intellects are so blunted," he argued, "and their perceptions so perverted by the noxious atmosphere which they breathe, and the all-pervading filth in which they live, move, and have their being, that they are not susceptible to moral or religious influence" (101).

His language was pessimistic and brutal. It had perhaps never occurred to Smith that he was, in a sense, brutalizing the "inmates" by writing about them in such a fashion. To Smith these people *were* brutalized—by conditions, by their ignorance, by those who preyed on them. Those who were concerned with their plight saw, above all, victims, who had no time for dignity or self-respect. It is hard to feel that reformers *chose* to ignore the existential and psychological integrity of the subjects of their activities, but they were confronted with conditions so horrific, so inhuman, that sympathy and outrage seem to have greatly preceded recognition of a shared humanity. Before we repudiate the forms of their concern, we must recall that they were virtually alone in speaking out. Elsewhere the plight of those in the lower depths was greeted with indifference or fear.

Smith's comments upon the city inspector's department were in the vein of his many editorials in the *American Medical Times*: hard-hitting and extreme. He claimed that New York was "a city without any sanitary government." Although the city employed forty-five health wardens, they were, without exception, "grossly ignorant" liquor dealers; the whole of Boole's department was "a gigantic imposture" (144–5). What was needed was that the city keep its streets clean, and its tenant-houses be placed in good sanitary condition. Smith urged that it was the duty of the municipal government, and, failing that, the state legislature, to enable the "poor and humblest citizen" to escape the "reign of filth" (131). Landlords must be compelled to keep their properties in good order. He did not use the more radical arguments in the *Report* about the cupidity of landlords, or repeat the many challenges to their property rights. The reforms proposed in the Metropolitan health bill were sweeping enough. The new health body should be independent of political control, composed of men with business and medical experience, and staffed by skilled medical officers working in close alliance with the police. Smith's testimony was virtually unanswerable, and in March, the measure proceded to a vote in the senate. A month after Smith's testimony was delivered in Albany, the text of his address appeared on the front page of the *New York Times*, an indication perhaps that those who knew the ways of politics were concerned at the progress of the legislation.[133]

It was late in the session, and the city inspector availed himself of every delaying tactic imaginable in the hope that the measure would be talked out. There were many facts to be examined, claims to be tested. Disagreement within the Republican majority, rooted in a struggle between the newly ascendant Radicals and the old Whiggish conservative forces in the party, led to an amendment (it was virtually an alternative bill) being offered by Dr. Lewis A. Sayre, the resident physician and agent of the board of health, which would have eliminated the role of the police on the health board and given the governor and his political friends control over the substantial health and street-cleaning budget. (The obviously useful Dr. Sayre's salary was doubled to $2,500 in the board of health estimates as of 31 December 1864.)[134]

Stephen Smith accepted that this would result in a more efficient body. The senate passed the revised measure, but in the assembly the Republicans were divided and could not agree on the precise shape of the reformed department. Cynics, such as the versifier "Miles O'Reilly" (Charles G. Halpine), saw other, less-worthy motives playing a role in the Republican deliberations:

> "The Health Bill"
> *A talk between two Repubs at Albany*
>
> "Shall we pass this great bill for the public health?"
> "Why, that is no longer the question;
> But shall endless sources of power and wealth,
> And unlimited chances of public stealth—
> On the cholera-plea and the public health—
> Be secured for our party's digestion?"
>
> "And if to our party this power is glide,
> And these chances of wealth be won for us?"
> "Why, the next question, then, we have got to decide
> Is this: shall we make it 'an equal divide'
> Betwixt the Weed-Seward and the Radical side,
> Or give all to Lord Thurlow or Horace?"
>
> "The Senate thinks Weed should be given the whole,
> And the Board of Police therefore packed on;
> But the bully Assembly's as black as a coal,
> And the Radical rascals say 'Thurlow's control

Is already too great for the good of his soul,'
And they're down like Old Scratch on Tom Acton."

"So between them the Health Bill is dragged either way,
And all kinds of fools' errands is sent on?"
"Why, yes; but you'll find they'll agree some fine day
Not to lose such rich chances for pickings and pay;
And the Health Bill — at least so I heard Lyman say—
Will be given to Lord Horace through Fenton."[135]

The Radicals commanded a majority of those present in the assembly, but not, as required to pass the bill, a majority of the total number of electors. The measure was defeated for 1865, but the story was swallowed up in the all-consuming grief which followed the assassination of President Lincoln. Sanitary reformers believed that once again Boole's bribery had been responsible for the defeat in the assembly. In early April, Horace Greeley wildly attacked the venality of the legislature in the *Tribune*.

Frank Boole took advantage of his reprieve at Albany to make a highly publicized tour of the streets of New York. Godkin admitted that he had "no very sanguine expectations" that reform of the health department would succeed.[136] Despite Boss Tweed's half-hearted support, the allegations of corruption against Boole and the unmistakable state of the city's streets put paid to his hopes for higher office. His nomination was withdrawn and John T. Hoffman led the Tammany campaign in the autumn to a narrow victory, defeating his Republican opponent by 1,000 votes. Basking in the victory over the Confederacy, Republicans elsewhere made sweeping gains in the state legislature and greatly strengthened the ranks of the supporters of the Metropolitan health bill. Reformers had done what they could; events now swept them to victory.

Within weeks of the bill's defeat at Albany in April 1865, New York newspapers carried reports of an outbreak of cholera in eastern Europe and followed the story throughout the summer as the disease spread across the Continent. The Council of Hygiene *Report*, which was published in June, forcefully reminded the public of the magnitude of the threat posed by housing conditions in the city. Virtually on the eve of the election in October the *Atalanta* arrived in New York harbor with sixty-five cases of cholera on board. Other ships were certainly bringing the contagion from Europe. "No quarantine precautions against this disease will prevail," noted George Templeton Strong on 5 November. "What we need is practical sanitary reformation of back streets, tenement houses, and pestiferous bone-boiling establishments. Thereby, and by nothing else, can the inevitable epidemic be mitigated. The city government will not do this, or any other good work, honestly and thoroughly, for it is rotten to the core." Substantially before there was a scientific understanding of cholera, the commonsense ethical-cum-scientific notions of bourgeois reformers had identified the likely method of the transmission of the disease. "Cholera is a consequence of unwashed hands."[137]

The *Evening Post* dramatically invited the United States Sanitary Commission to rescue the city from the threatening epidemic, but such a civilian task was far outside its mandate, and in any event the commission was in the midst of a rapid demobilization.[138] The new mayor, Tweed's man John T. Hoffman, was firmly opposed to the Metropolitan health bill, but the renewed threat of cholera, the agitation of the Citizens' Association, the powerful advocacy of reform in the *Report*, Stephen Smith's remarkable testimony in Albany, and the Republican triumph in the 1865 election in New York, combined to sweep aside resistance to reform.

The new act became law on 26 February 1866, creating a board of health composed of nine members, four commissioners appointed by the governor with the consent of the senate (three had to be physicians), the health official of the port, and the four Metropolitan police commissioners.[139] By the spring the new board of health was in place. Stalwarts of the long struggle for sanitary reform were elected to leading positions on the first board of health: Jackson S. Schultz was elected president; Dr. Elisha Harris, corresponding secretary of the New York Sanitary Association, became registrar of records; and Dorman B. Eaton was elected counsel of the board.[140] Dr. Smith became chairman of the sanitary committee of the Board of Health. Reform had put them all into power.

An unusually severe winter slowed transmission of the disease, enabling New York to escape a cholera epidemic that year. The board's sweeping powers promised vigorous action to enforce sanitary regulations, but there was little acceptance of the exercise of such executive powers and the board acted circumspectly, as though as concerned to preserve its own existence in a hostile political environment as it was anxious to effect sanitary reforms. In a sweeping survey of the first *Annual Report of the Metropolitan Board of Health* in 1868, Edward B. Dalton, M.D., who had been appointed sanitary superintendent at the meeting in March 1866 when the Metropolitan Board of Health was first organized, spoke with authority when he spelled out the logic of institutional caution:

> A people long accustomed to order their lives, each individual in his own way, without reference to those about him, cannot all at once be brought to see the benefit of a measure which shall subordinate personal advantage to the general good.

To any measure of this sort the people must be educated. They must be led by their own observation to believe in it. They must be given time, from step to step, to see in what direction the work is tending, and to discern that each individual will in the end enjoy far greater benefits when all shall so live as to contribute to the public welfare.[141]

The utopian hopes of the reformers had achieved much. (The Metropolitan Board, in its first six months of life, received 28,330 complaints, and among the board's actions were the removal of 38,314 loads of night soil from the city, the clearing of 103 dead horses, 3,865 dead dogs and cats, the disposal of 20,045 pounds of unsound veal, 155,520 pounds of unsound fish, and 92,260 barrels of offal. By the standards of New York over the past two decades, these were heroic figures.[142]) Boole was at last vanquished. But it was abundantly clear that sanitary reform had not transformed the city. Tweed, Connolly and their friends remained in power. The prospects, which lay at the heart of their campaigns, for that deeper reform of social values and the emergence of a different and more responsible sense of community, were no closer than they had ever been. After decades of passionate advocacy of the need to educate the poor, there remained the problem of the rich. "It can hardly be that in any heathen country men of wealth, influence, power," wrote Frederick Law Olmsted,

have been more thoroughly licentious, selfish, conscienceless than those who occupy the most important public stations in this community of New York—who are the leaders, in a large way, of Society here. Every young man knows, knows by personal observation if he is rich & weak & depraved enough—that the greatest wealth, consideration, power, luxury is given by Society as the reward for the most unscrupulous, cruel & reckless gambling & speculation and the most unbridled & beastly licentiousness.[143]

CHAPTER TWO

"The heart sickens at such a narrative": Madame Restell

The invention of a celebrated female physician

H er story began like a sentimental novel about the misfortunes of an immigrant in New York. It ended with a
scene from a gothic horror story or a grim, didactic melodrama.
A journeyman English tailor, Harry Somers, his wife, and their
daughter Caroline, one-and-a-half-years old, arrived in New York
early in 1832. They took two rooms at 27 Chatham Street. Mrs.
Somers, born Caroline Ann Trow in the village of Painswick in
Gloucestershire, soon found work in the neighborhood as a seamstress and dressmaker. Her father, John Trow, had been a poor
laborer, and she had received virtually no education. Before her
marriage she had worked as a serving maid in a butcher's family.
Another story about her early years contended that she had worked
as a barmaid in a London gin-shop, or that she had been a serving
maid in a London butcher shop. Her English birth was unknown to
some of those who wrote about her in later years. There is even some
disagreement about whether Harry Somers died before or after he
was thought to have come to New York, or whether it was her
husband or an elderly mother who accompanied her. Most sources
agree that her husband did not long survive the voyage, dying of
fever. Mrs. Somers was a young widow with a child to support who
had no relatives in America. Her family in Gloucestershire was too
poor and too distant to be of help. There is no record of her character
in those years. To survive at all required strength and resilience, but
what little we know of her early years was largely compiled by Mrs.
Somers's many enemies. It was said that she met a pill compounder

and vendor who lived in an adjacent house on Chatham Street who taught certain secrets of the trade to the young widow. Mrs. Somers soon tried her hand at concocting pills for various common ailments of the lung, liver and stomach, and acquired a local reputation for her remedies. She told her neighbors and customers that she had obtained her "receipts" from an aunt or grandmother in England who was the professional successor of her good uncle, Dr. Restell, whose pills were renowned with ladies. She fancifully claimed to have recrossed the Atlantic to visit her aunt, and to have returned with a supply of "Monthly" pills to remove obstructions. There were even more wonderful powders for sale at five dollars a packet which prevented conception. As the demand for her pills and potions grew, Mrs. Somers abandoned her work as dressmaker to attend to the medical needs of her lady customers.

She met Charles Lohman, a Russian of German descent, and they married in 1836 or 1837. He had emigrated to New York in 1829 and at the time they met was working as a compositor on the newly founded *New York Herald*. A freethinker, he was also a manufacturer of quack medicines under the professional name "Dr. A. M. Mauriceau."[1] In addition to selling pills and potions, he was a quack popularizer of medical knowledge. A. M. Mauriceau's *Married Women's Private Medical Companion*, published in 1847 and frequently reprinted, was in effect a sustained advertisement for the Portuguese Pills and other goods ("Desomeaux's Preventive to Conception" at ten dollars for several packages, "French Secret Coverings" at five dollars for a dozen) which he sold by mail order. He claimed to have learned of their emmenagogic and abortifacient qualities while living in France.[2] Mauriceau's recipe for "tonic bitters," recommended for women suffering from a retention of the menses, was particularly memorable: "Take prickly ash bark, two ounces; wild cherry tree bark, two ounces; Seneca snake-root, one ounce; tanzy [*sic*], one ounce; gum socotrine aloes, half an ounce; devil's bit, two ounces: pulverize; to every two ounces of the powder add half a pint of boiling water and one quart of Holland gin, and half a wine-glassful taken three or four times a day."[3] The *Companion* was partially plagiarized from Robert Dale Owen's *Moral Physiology* (1832), the first book on contraception to be published in the United States.[4]

Seizing the opportunity suggested by his wife's potions, amidst the advertisements for animal magnetism, phrenology, mesmerism, Dr. Moffat's Vegetable Life Pills, the "Matchless Sanative" (an acclaimed German discovery which turned out to be colored water), Ayer's Cherry Pectoral, Dr. Moore's Essence of Life (for coughs), and Dr. Morehead's magnetic belts, braces and plasters, he placed adver-

THE MARRIED WOMAN'S
PRIVATE MEDICAL COMPANION,

EMBRACING THE TREATMENT OF

MENSTRUATION, OR MONTHLY TURNS,

DURING THEIR

STOPPAGE, IRREGULARITY, OR ENTIRE SUPPRESSION

PREGNANCY,

AND

HOW IT MAY BE DETERMINED;
WITH THE TREATMENT OF ITS VARIOUS DISEASES.

DISCOVERY TO

PREVENT PREGNANCY;

THE GREAT AND IMPORTANT NECESSITY WHERE

MALFORMATION OR INABILITY EXISTS
TO GIVE BIRTH.

TO PREVENT MISCARRIAGE OR ABORTION.

WHEN PROPER AND NECESSARY

TO EFFECT MISCARRIAGE.

WHEN ATTENDED WITH ENTIRE SAFETY.

CAUSES AND MODE OF CURE OF BARRENNESS,
OR STERILITY.

bY DR. A. M. MAURICEAU,

Professor of Diseases of Women

Office, 129 Liberty street.

NEW YORK
1850.

Charles Lohman, as "Dr. A. M. Mauriceau," offered advice and sold pills to pregnant women.

tisements for the services and products of Madame Restell, the celebrated female physician, who was to be found at 148 Greenwich Street. Lohman was said to have borrowed money to place her first advertisement in the *Sun*. Notices for his own enterprises and for those of his wife soon became a regular feature of the *Sun*, *Herald*, and elsewhere in the New York press, which greatly added to the visibility of their joint business ventures. He maintained separate offices at 129 Liberty Street, describing himself in newspaper advertisements as a "Professor of Diseases of Women." Lohman's understanding that abortion and contraception needed a modern marketing campaign placed him in the vanguard of business thought in the 1840s.[5] His advertisements made Madame Restell rich and notorious, though she was only one of dozens offering similar services in the press. Most advertisements for abortionists were brief and to the point:

> A LADIES' PHYSICIAN. DR. ——, PROFESSOR OF Midwifery, over 20 years' successful practice in this city, guarantees certain relief to ladies, with or without medicine, at one interview. Unfortunates please call. Relief certain. Residence ——. Elegant rooms for ladies requiring nursing.

Lohman's touch in the *Herald* was altogether on a different scale:

> Important to married females—Madame Restell's Preventive Powders. These valuable powders have been universally adopted in Europe, but France in particular, for upwards of thirty years, as well as by thousands in this country as being the only mild, safe and efficacious remedy for married ladies whose health forbids a too rapid increase of family. Madame Restell, as is well known, was for thirty years Female Physician in the two principal female hospitals in Europe—those of Vienna and Paris—where, favored by her great experience and opportunities, she attained that celebrity in those great discoveries in medical science so specially adapted to the female frame for which her medicines now stand unrivaled, as well in this country as in Europe. Her acquaintance with the physiology and anatomy of the female frame enabled her— by tracing the decline and ill health of married females scarce in the meridian of life, and the consequent rapid and often apparently inexplicable causes which consign many a fond mother to a premature grave, to their true source—to arrive at a knowledge of the primary cause of female indisposition—especially of married females—which in 1808 led to the discovery of her celebrated Preventive Powders. Their adoption has been the means of preserving not only the health but even the life of many an affectionate wife and fond mother. Is it not wise and virtuous to prevent evils to which we are subject by simple and healthy

means within our control? Every dispassionate, virtuous and enlightened mind will unhesitatingly answer in the affirmative. This is all that Madame Restell recommends, or ever recommended. Price five dollars a package, accompanied with full and particular directions.[6]

Lohman's rhetoric was undoubtedly effective. The bogus nature of the powders on offer, an equally fictional career in Vienna and Paris, and the decades of experience which he lavished upon his wife (who was born four years after she was reputed to have discovered "the primary cause of female indisposition" in 1808) suggest that the couple were engaged upon a simple confidence trick.

Abortion: economics and etiquette

The demand for abortion at all levels of American society was no fiction. Colonial society knew little of abortion, and birthrates approached the biological maximum.[7] From about 1810, the birthrate began to decline, due to improved standards of living, better medical care, and changes in the role which women were beginning to play within society. Knowledge of contraceptive techniques, from *coitus interruptus* to sheaths made from goats' bladders, and diaphragms made of hollowed halves of lemons, spread more widely among women who wished to restrict the size of their families. These techniques were unreliable, however, and many women were forced to turn to abortion to control their fertility. Freethinkers like Robert Dale Owen and Charles Knowlton, author of *Fruits of Philosophy; or, The Private Companion of Young Married People* (1832), took the lead in placing birth control on the agenda of public debate. Most contemporary observers noted a growth in demand for abortions, and there was a dramatic increase in the visibility of people like Mauriceau and Restell who promised effective solutions to female problems in the 1840s. It is likely that in the early part of the century some knowledge of manual techniques for abortion, from knitting needles to whalebone probes, was part of the oral culture of women in America. Traditional folk wisdom recommended vigorous physical activity, such as jumping or horseback-riding, as being sometimes effective in producing miscarriages.[8] For those who declined long rides in the country or jumps off wood piles, there was a host of potions, some new, some of hoary antiquity, which were believed to cause abortions. Dozens of abortifacients—"female pills" or "lunar pills"—guaranteed to remove "strictures" and "monthly obstructions" were sold at mid-century either through the mails or by physicians.[9] Many substances were believed to have the properties of abortifacients, and some were easily available: aloes, ferrous sulfate, savin, pennyroyal, tansy, cottonseed oil, motherwort, quinine, and ergot of rye (taken with gin, honey and cayenne pepper in various mixtures and combinations) were used to produce violent contractions of the uterus and induce abortion. An abortion pill chemically analyzed in the 1870s was found to contain the sour combination of ergot, oil of savin and aloes.[10]

The pharmacopoeia of abortion in the the early years of the nineteenth century crossed the boundaries which the "regular" physicians were trying to erect between their work and that of the "irregulars." The medical profession in the 1830s was at a low ebb of public esteem and seemed to offer only what was described as "heroic" or "sanguinary" therapy, which involved extremes of bleeding and purging.[11] The "regulars" administered calomel (a therapeutically useless chloride of mercury), tartrate of antinomy, or jalap, and other cathartics which had an immediate, violent and debilitating effect upon unwell patients.

Drugs and medications had little scientific basis, and most existing medical procedures seemed ineffective or positively dangerous to health.[12] The many failings of the profession encouraged an explosion of quackery, self-dosing and medical sectarianism. "Regulars" bitterly denounced the dangers of self-medication, and succeeded in passing a law in New York State which made the unregulated profession of medicine to be a petty crime. Public opinion in Jacksonian America was deeply suspicious of the claims of professional men to a monopoly of their trade and welcomed the great extension in the choice of medical treatments available in the 1830s. Excluded from the training and medical societies of the regular profession, homeopaths created their own parallel colleges, medical journals and societies. They advocated a wide variety of mild herbal cures. The eclectics, botanicals and Thomsonians were at one in their rejection of the excesses of bleeding and purging, and their diverse enthusiasts jostled with the advocates of hydropathy (water cure), mesmerism, faith-cure and other even more obscure sects for the clients which the "regulars" regarded as rightly their own.[13] So astute an observer as E. L. Godkin, editor of *The Nation*, wondered whether medical men, in despair at the excesses of their profession, any longer believed it was possible to do more than ". . . simply plac[e] the patient in the most favorable natural conditions, giving him good food and drink and plenty of fresh air when he is weak, prescribing abstinence when he is overfed, exercise when he is too sedentary, rest when he is jaded."[14] In the face of the devastating effects of "heroic" medicine, this clinical nihilism had an undoubted appeal.

In addition to the confused divisions between practitioners of different kinds of medicine, and their preferred forms of treatment, there were powerful cultural inhibitions upon the conduct of mid-wifery. Despite the prudery which surrounded the idea of intimate physical examinations of women by men, male physicians had largely supplanted female midwives for well-to-do American women by the 1820s. Speculum examinations were regarded as *socially* unsuitable: "No practitioner, whose mind is properly constituted, will propose the examination unless he conceives it absolutely necess-ary; and, when proposed, if executed in the way recommended by Dr. Warrington . . . the most fastidious would scarcely object."[15] An elaborate ritual surrounded pre-natal examinations, which were conducted with the female fully dressed, and the doctor carefully averting his eyes. Etiquette prescribed certain topics of conversation during the examination, and a delicacy of hand movements and precise and carefully regulated forms of physical contact which were designed to avoid embarrassment. Everyone, including the obligatory older female present throughout, pretended that nothing out of the ordinary was occurring. Visual examination of a patient's pelvic region was under no circumstances allowed, and "demonstrative" midwifery at American medical schools was only permitted through the use of diagrams and mannequins made of buckskin. Physicians trained in Europe worked with wax models which often had long hair and realistic features made by Italian craftsmen. The abdomens could be tilted up to reveal reproductive organs and a fetus. Attempts to have students in American medical schools examine pregnant women met with stern and highly public rebukes.[16]

Since pregnancy could not be proven until "quickening," when physical movement of the fetus could be felt, early abortion was only a misdemeanor, not heavily penalized in law, and few convictions for criminal abortion could be secured. (Buried in this usage of "quickening" was an allusion to the state of spiritual quickening which haunted the evangelical revivalism of the 1830s.) Indeed, the difference between a "formed" fetus and one that was "unformed," and thus not yet "ensouled" (believed to occur within a forty-to eighty-day period, in which the rational soul was developed out of its vegetable state), entered Catholic moral teaching in the twelfth and thirteenth centuries, a distinction which was the basis for the argument made by influential theologians that while abortion was a sin against the commandment not to kill, it was not a homicide to abort an "unformed" fetus. But a series of papal bulls, culminating in Pope Pius IX's *Apostolicae Sedis* (1869) sharply changed church law by eliminating the Aristotelian distinction between formed and unformed fetus. Abortion in any circumstances, except those of

"An elaborate ritual . . ."

ectopic pregnancy and cancer of the uterus, was declared a mortal sin.[17] Catholic contributions to the debate in New York were marginal, but the convergence of Protestant and Catholic attitudes is a phenomenon of interest.

Women obtained abortions as they thought necessary, and the public seems to have ignored the subject. There is no doubt that a large number of abortions were performed by "regular" physicians. But the growing scientific basis of medicine, traditional attitudes towards saving life, a powerful conservative sense of the role of women in society, and a recognition of the economic competition of the "irregulars" and abortionists—as James C. Mohr puts it, an opposition "partly ideological, partly scientific, partly moral, and partly practical"—made "regular" physicians the first group to seek to change Americans' generally passive attitude towards abortion. Despite the growing opposition of the medical profession, and some clergymen, contemporary observers agreed that the public did not regard abortion as a crime.[18]

For its opponents, abortion was a unique wrong. It was hard to avoid the stories in the press about practitioners and victims, and the advertisements, placards and leaflets offering yet another "remedy" for monthly problems. In response to this increased visibility, abortion was increasingly condemned from pulpits and in pamphlets and articles, sometimes in the same newspapers which carried Mauriceau's and Restell's advertisements. The earliest of these denunciations which specifically named Restell appeared in 1839, and expressed a concern which runs throughout the abortion debate during her lifetime. Restell's activities, and the very idea of abortion, were not merely repugnant; abortion was a criminal activity which undermined "the root of all social order," the family.[19] Abortion symbolized the deepening anxiety some Americans felt at the decay of the secure patriarchal and social construction of society. These denunciations were often marked by an underlying edge of hysteria at the idea that abortion was no longer only the resort of the poor, the unwed and the betrayed, but had become acceptable among the better-off, white, Protestant married women in America. A case from the 1870s illustrates the problem. A woman was found lying on the sidewalk in Brooklyn, suffering acutely. She was taken to hospital, diagnosed as having just had an abortion, and as being in such a state that "recovery [seemed] improbable." When visited in hospital by a Brooklyn policeman, she told a remarkable story. Her name was Louisa E. Arlington, wife of Gen. Frederick W. Arlington, who lived with her husband at a hotel in New York. Advised by a lady friend to seek an abortion, she was recommended to consult a doctor on Bleecker Street. Arrangements were rapidly made, and she was taken to the home of a "female practitioner" in Brooklyn. The woman, described as an elderly, harsh-featured German, caused Mrs. Arlington such pain that the man who accompanied her was forced to administer chloroform. When she woke up in great agony, she found herself lying on a street in Brooklyn, her expensive clothes having been replaced by cheaper, coarser clothing. The abortionist, quickly identified, was taken to Mrs. Arlington's bedside in the hospital and was identified by the dying woman. She had paid fifty dollars for the abortion, and pleaded with reporters not to mention her name in the paper. She feared that her husband would be ashamed. When the abortionist, Helena Kolls, appeared in court, she was described as being "richly dressed in silk and jewels."[20]

The triumphant advance of modern ways of thinking was encouraging, wrote Walt Whitman in *The Brooklyn Daily Times*, but not in matters of morality.

> "Progress" and "liberal Ideas" are good, in many things. But what may be good in material science may be evil continually when applied to moral questions. The sacredness, the divine institution of the marriage tie, lies at the root of the welfare, the safety, the very existence of every Christian nation. Palsied be the hand, blistered the tongue that would make one movement to defeat its holy purposes, or to weaken its binding nature by a single breath! When that goes, all goes—the domestic hearth—the dignity and virtue of woman—the sweetness of childhood—the manliness of manhood.[21]

Returning to the subject in 1858, Whitman reflected that it was the "educated and refined" ladies of fashion and social position (such as the unfortunate Mrs. Arlington) whose "moral sense" needed to be awakened. "[I]t is no uncommon thing for medical attendants to be as coolly and unconcernedly asked to produce abortion as a dentist would be to draw a tooth." He regarded abortion as a measure of the state of civilization itself: "Unless our boasted civilization is to sink to the level of Chinese barbarism, our women, of every class and degree, must be convinced that to deprive their inchoate offspring of life is to commit Murder, and that under circumstances of aggravation which make the foulest of crimes more atrocious."[22]

The attacks on middle-class women often took the form of accusations that they had abandoned the traditional role of mother for fashionable luxury and self-indulgence. A puritanical rhetoric was tightly wrapped around the denunciations of "luxury" and immorality. As late as 1872 a New York journalist lashed out, in notably aggressive and homophobic language, against the "fashionable" churches for their failure to denounce abortion as a sin. Abortion became a touchstone for understanding the divisions between conservatives and liberals within American Protestant churches:

> As a first step it is necessary to reform what is known as "fashionable" churches, where preachers who are outrageous burlesques of Him who preached the Sermon on the Mount, mince into their pulpits to smooth the primrose path to heaven, for hearers who are satires on the Christian faith. The time has fully come when we must do something if we would be saved, and that something must be done to restore purity to the homes of the people, and, above all, to the marriage tie. That can never be done

THE WOMEN OF NEW YORK; OR, THE UNDER WORLD OF THE GREAT CITY.

BY CHAS E. ELLINGTON,

NEW YORK
THE NEW YORK BOOK CO.
NO. 145 NASSAU STREET.
1869.

Enemies of abortion like Whitman rounded upon "educated and refined" ladies of fashion. Ellington and other journalists pandered to the intense public fascination with vice in New York.

so long as fashionable congregations, led by pastors false to their duty, fall down and worship gold, and that magnified, instead of "Christ and Him crucified."[23]

Dr. Stephen Smith found that the frequency of abortions in New York was thirteen times higher than in Boston, for which he blamed public indifference:

> It is not alone the ignorant and vicious that consider it no crime; the religious equally entertain the belief that abortions may be practiced without a shadow of guilt . . . the public mind to-day is inclined to regard abortion as a crime only under certain circumstances. The life that is sacrificed is regarded as unreal, and the convenience or comfort of the parents is alone consulted.[24]

The practice of abortion flourished in mid-century America, though it had few defenders. Even the most resolute advocates of feminine equality were unprepared to argue in public that a pregnant woman ought to be free to seek an abortion if she felt it was right. Restell's "Preventive Powders" could not prevent conception and her "Monthly" remedies could not, with any certainty, produce abortions; but the explosion of mail-order business suggests that there was an unsatisfied demand in the vast hinterland of rural America. Abortions occurred, whether caused by natural means or otherwise, and Restell's dubious pills and powders seemed to promise hope for the desperate.[25]

Mrs. Purdy, Mrs. M., Mary Rogers and the case of Eliza Ann Munson

Madame Restell conducted her business without concealment or at least no more than contemporary euphemisms required, which in any event concealed nothing. For ten years she prospered, confounding her commercial rivals and critics in the press. The pages of James Gordon Bennett's *Herald* were more jocularly critical of Restell's moralizing critics than of Restell herself. She offered accommodation for patients who sought her professional services, and sold medicines from her house at 148 Greenwich Street which she and Lohman rented in 1840. (Edgar Allan Poe lived nearby at 130 Greenwich Street in April 1844.) Restell's brother Joseph Trow came over from England and worked as an assistant and pill-maker for her business and her husband's. Their pills were being sold at several locations in the city and by an agent in New England.

Madame Restell's early notoriety was caused by the case of Mrs. Purdy. In June 1839, Mrs. Mary Ann Purdy, described as "a woman of ordinary intellect, of fickle disposition, not illiterate for her station, but easily influenced," appealed to Restell for drugs to produce an abortion. When the preparations had no effect, Mrs. Purdy returned to Greenwich Street and begged for a "manipular operation." She later blamed her unfortunate premature delivery upon "severe exertion in washing." Her health was never the same after the abortion, but it is highly unlikely that the case would have come to public notice had there not been a bitter row between Mrs. Purdy, her husband William and Restell over a watch, chain and rings given to the abortionist in lieu of payment. The consequent publicity was a two-edged sword for Restell: it undoubtedly brought her greater numbers of clients, but it also intensified the hostility to her activities on the part of the medical profession, preachers and politicians. The sums involved were small, merely a matter of six dollars which Restell received from a pawnbroker for Mrs. Purdy's jewelry. Later in her career it is inconceivable that such a damaging public argument would have been pursued for such a trifling amount. Mrs. Purdy sought the return of her jewelry, but Restell refused to turn over the pawnshop ticket until the full fee was paid: ". . . we have done it very low, much lower than we are in the habit of doing it, and I have given $5 of the $6 to the doctor. If you had gone your full time, it would have cost you a good deal more." When Mrs. Purdy threatened to tell her husband, Restell pointed out "Oh, you cannot do that, for it will be a State Prison offense for you as well as for me." William Purdy, an employee of the Harlem Railroad Company, denied in court that he wrote threatening letters to Restell to force the return of his property. When he began to air his complaints in public, and in newspaper offices, he was dismissed by his employers. Purdy believed it was due to the devious and blackmailing power of Restell; his employer told him that unfavorable publicity was hurting railroad revenues.

The case only came to court in March 1841, when Mrs. Purdy, by then near death, summoned a police clerk to her bedside and made a deposition that on 2 June and 22 July 1839 Restell had attempted to produce an abortion upon her. A warrant was issued, and Restell was brought to Purdy's home, where she was formally identified by the dying woman. The deposition was read to her, and Restell was given the opportunity to question Mrs. Purdy, who died four weeks later. She was held in lieu of bail at the Hall of Justice, universally known as "The Tombs," that "dismal-fronted pile of bastard Egyptian, like an enchanter's palace in a melodrama" as Dickens described it in his *American Notes*, for four months from

March until the case was heard at the Court of General Sessions in New York in July 1841.[26] Her attorneys succeeded in having bail reduced from $5,000 to $3,000, but so intense was the publicity given to the Purdy case that "respectable gentlemen" could not be found to act as sureties. Much of the trial was taken up with the specific circumstances of the death-bed deposition, and its legal validity in such a case. In the end the judge accepted Mrs. Purdy's deposition, and the jury needed only ten minutes to convict Restell of two counts of attempting to procure an abortion. But sentencing never took place, due to technical faults in the death-bed deposition. Restell's lawyer appealed to the State Supreme Court and the conviction was thrown out. In later years she boasted of having bribed her way out of trouble.[27]

In 1842 Dr. Gunning S. Bedford, Professor of Midwifery and the Diseases of Women and Children at New York University, was brought in to consult with two doctors over the case of Mrs. M., a mother of two children, who had been suffering for fourteen hours in a labor which seemed no farther advanced. Dr. Bedford examined the patient and found that the opening in the womb was sealed, as though it had been injured by instruments in previous deliveries. The patient was in the gravest danger from a ruptured womb. Her fetus, under constant pressure from the contractions of the uterus, was equally in a perilous state. No surgeon in the United States had ever successfully performed an operation to save a patient with such a problem. The doctor who had attended Mrs. M. on both previous confinements assured Dr. Bedford that she had had easy deliveries. On further questioning, the pregnant woman revealed that she had consulted Restell six weeks after becoming pregnant. She was given powders and instructions in their use, but found them ineffective and returned to Restell to ask if there was no other way to make her miscarry:

> "Yes," says Madame Restell, "I can probe you; but I must have my price for this operation." "What do you probe with?" "A piece of whalebone." "Well," thought the patient, but without expressing it, "I cannot afford to pay your price, and I will probe myself." She returned home and used the whalebone several times; it produced considerable pain, followed by a discharge of blood.[28]

Dr. Bedford successfully performed an operation to open the sealed uterus, allowing a vigorous and healthy child to be born. Mrs. M. soon recovered. When the doctor called on his patient ten weeks later, he learned that Restell had aborted her five times previously, each time by potions. In the course of conversation, the patient mentioned that she knew a great number of women who were in the habit of applying to Restell for the purpose of miscarrying, and that she scarcely ever failed in the attempt. She mentioned a woman who lived on Houston Street and who was five months' pregnant. Restell probed her and a fetus was delivered, which, to use her own words, "kicked several times after it was put into the bowl." "It . . . seems too monstrous that such gross violations of the laws, both of God and man, should be suffered in the very heart of a community professing to be Christian, and to be governed by law and good order."[29] Dr. Bedford described the case in a medical journal in the fervent hope "that the disclosures here may tend to the arrest of this woman, and the infliction of the severest penalty of the law." No such prosecution occurred in the case of Mrs. M., but when Restell was arrested later in the decade, Bedford gave damaging testimony for the prosecution which helped send her to prison.[30]

A second arrest of Restell, in 1845, occasioned a veritable storm of publicity, especially in the newly founded *National Police Gazette*, where once again the story of Mary Rogers, the murdered "Beautiful Seegar Girl" whose body was found in the Hudson River off Hoboken on 28 July 1841, was resurrected to boost circulation. The accusation was made several times that Restell was the phantom abortionist in the Rogers case. As early as 30 August 1841, a New York magazine had mentioned "the Restell school" as being involved. Edgar Allen Poe says nothing of this in "The Mystery of Marie Rogêt" as it appeared in *Snowden's Ladies Companion* in November and December 1842, and February 1843. When he came to revise his story for a collection of his tales in 1845, he accepted the "abortion" theory. Scholars have examined Poe's revision with great care, and in particular have fastened upon five blank weeks in Poe's life, between 19 November and 25 December 1842. If Poe had been conducting his own research upon the murder in this period, and if, when he came to live with his wife Virginia in a single room on Greenwich Street in April 1844, he had come across more information about his neighbor Restell, there is perhaps more than a little room for a little armchair sleuthing. The other abortionist named in the Rogers case was "Madame" Catherine Costello, who was practicing in Jersey City in the summer of 1841. It was claimed that she was an agent of Restell.[31]

In April 1844, Eliza Ann Munson of New Haven, Connecticut, died from medicines she had taken to induce a miscarriage. She was a seventeen-year-old who had been abandoned by her lover and sent out of town to Restell for an abortion. It was subsequently discovered that Munson had a second abortion performed by a Mrs. Bird. Restell was indicted in May for her initial abortion upon Munson, but the case was quietly dropped without public explanation. The Rogers case, to which Restell was tenuously linked, and the Munson prosecution suggest that as with the trade in slaves and the movement of paupers out of urban areas, there was developing a regional organization of the abortion trade. When the need arose, customers could be referred to a practitioner in an adjacent locality, or a remote one.

Her deftness in avoiding prosecution was attributed by many to bribery. Restell was building a formidable reputation as someone virtually beyond the reach of the law. She was living proof that it was all too easy to evade the existing laws on abortion in the 1840s.

Signs of the decay of contemporary morality

People who visited her house in Greenwich Street after reading about her in the newly founded *National Police Gazette* expected to find a "den of horrors." Instead, they found Restell living in a tastefully over-decorated house in the modern New York fashion:

> Her spacious parlors, with folding doors, are carpeted with the richest Brussels—the furniture is elegant—the mirror superb—the candelabra and ornamental bejouterie, splendid; the pictures which adorn the walls are gems of art, rare and costly, bespeaking the taste and wealth of the owner.

Nor was Madame a "female fiend":

> ... she is charming; her figure is admirable—her toilet is irreproachable. To wear her dresses with such an air, she must have seen the best society; and so she has—professionally. Her short sleeve exposes a round, plump arm, that looks remarkably white and enticing. Her low-neck dress shows to great advantage her round, handsome shoulders, and a bust of faultless development. Her head is well formed, her hair is admirably arranged, and her features show energy and intelligence.[32]

The effrontery of this "shameless" woman riding up Broadway in a carriage drawn by four horses and accompanied by a servant in a "neat and modest" livery was a daily insult to a righteous Christian city. She showed none of the physical symptoms of moral wickedness. A novelist in the late 1840s portrayed Restell as a positively regal figure. "The devil in her heart showed not his green eyes in her face, and it needed the eye to follow her to her palace, and to view the nonchalance of manner with which she administered pill after pill, and applied draught after draught, to realize the full extent of her depravity." One contemporary noted that she "turns up her pretty

eyes at the idea of her being a female hyena; and as for her commit-
ting any crime, she doesn't believe a word of it." Indeed, Restell
continued to claim that she was a "regular" physician, as much
entitled to practice her profession as the celebrated Dr. Carnochan or
Dr. Dixon.[33] As she saw her life, the furniture and decor of her home
on Greenwich Street, her dress and bearing, the coach and liveried
servants, the fashionable elegance of her establishment, were proof of
her high-minded devotion to the allaying of female fears, the removal
of agonies, the concealment of sorrows and misfortunes of those
abandoned to their fate by a harsh social order. Bystanders were
unable to read upon her features any evidence of sin or depravity.
Preachers were not slow to remind their congregations of the fearsome wages of sin, but, as the coach bearing Madame Restell proceeded up Broadway into the sparsely populated northern reaches of
Manhattan for a pleasant drive, the lesson imparted was that she saw
herself as a successful businesswoman and something of a public
benefactress, not as a miserable and wretched sinner.

Many of her clients were young girls, vulnerable and abandoned,
who were often seen by New Yorkers as weak-willed sinners, symbols of the decay of contemporary morality. Although she was
reviled as a vicious and depraved woman, the paradox is that in her
personal relations with the women who sought her help there was a
humane sympathy not always to be observed in the world of purity
crusaders. Would a pregnant unmarried shopgirl receive sympathetic
help, or sermons, from the New York Female Moral Reform Society,
founded in 1834, which proposed to station "companies of pious
males or females" outside brothels and to rescue and reform "fallen
women" wherever they may be found in the city's areas of vice
dance-halls?[34] Restell became a complex cultural icon for New
Yorkers in the 1840s. She was the conscious invention of Mrs.
Lohman, Mrs. Somers and the butcher's maid, Caroline Ann Trow.
In New York in the 1840s there were many such self-created individuals, flaunting their prosperity and newly adopted identities.
None was so extravagant or brazen in the eyes of respectable people
as Restell, but there was enough of the self-made woman about her
to tinge with complexity the moral condemnation of her activities.
She was certainly, to many New Yorkers, a quintessence of evil and
a portent of a new immoralism. However, to some of her customers,
at least, she became a "mother" who alone seemed willing and able
to help a girl in desperate trouble, providing that is she, or her lover,
had sufficient money. The public expected sinners in this, as in other
walks of life, to show an awareness of guilt. But in the 1840s she
seems not to have been bothered by feelings of remorse. "The sinner
is 'dead in trespass and sins,'" wrote John McDowell, D.D., "and he

must be made spiritually alive. He is destitute of holiness, and a principle of holiness must be formed within. This will be effected only by an Almighty power. The power that does effect this change is the Holy Spirit."[35] And if the sinner remained impervious to guilt, or to the promise of salvation, what then? Restell was thus an ominous sign of an emerging urban world in which sinners walked through the streets apparently unscathed by their sinfulness, and affected a blasé attitude towards moral certainties. She was a daily reminder of the breakdown of communal values. Other abortionists afforded more convenient sermons for the pulpit and press. A Boston abortionist, Mrs. Caswell, was reported to have become "possessed of a mania for giving to the poor, and sought to hide her many enormities from the public gaze, by sending presents of food, &c, to Massachusetts regiments at the seat of war."[36]

It is fanciful to see her as a reformer, a crusader who sought to alleviate the sum total of misery in the community. She was, rather, more akin to the sharp American business person of the 1840s, who saw her opportunities and took them. The attractive role of public benefactress was not wholly inappropriate, but, above all, abortion was a business. The whole subject of abortion was one which contemporaries found hard to discuss dispassionately, and it was even harder to base discussion upon confirmed facts. Even the total number of abortionists practicing in New York was subject to wild speculation. The use of multiple pseudonyms makes newspaper advertisements an unreliable measure of the trade. A certain proportion of those who offered abortion services were out and out frauds, preying upon vulnerable women. Some, but not all, vendors of pills and potions guaranteed to "relieve ladies without danger or chance of publicity" were equally frauds. And, since abortions were performed by physicians, midwives and others who were not practicing abortionists, the best we can do is to rely upon the estimate of Edward Crapsey in 1872, who thought that twenty, and not 200, abortionists were working in New York. The rates they charged, and the income such women earned, were subjects of considerable discussion. One of Restell's competitors in New York in the 1870s was said to have made an average profit of $2,000 per month. At the lower end of the market a fee of $10 was being widely charged for abortions. Madame Grindle, whose offices were on 26th Street between Sixth and Seventh Avenue, charged $300 for a week's stay and had a capacity to accommodate twenty patients at a time. There was an extra fee for medical attention and board if the stay was extended, and a $100-fee if the baby was to be adopted. Madame West, who with her husband conducted an abortion mill on West 40th Street near Broadway, charged $300 for an abortion with a guarantee of "no trouble." (During the Civil War a replacement or substitute for military service could be purchased for $300. Between 1869 and 1879 the average daily wage for an unskilled laborer fell from $1.91 to $1.29: even at $10 dollars an abortion was expensive for most Americans.) Like Restell, Grindle and West were aiming at the more lucrative end of the market. The interior of Grindle's establishment was furnished ". . . with taste and elegance. The parlors are spacious, and contain all the decorations, upholstery, cabinet-ware, piano, book-case, &c., that is found in a respectable home." The furnishing of Restell's successive offices was on an even more lavish scale, and reflected not only the rise in her income but the higher social level of her clientele. Advertisements appeared in the press announcing that Madame Restell had opened "branch offices" in Boston and Philadelphia.[37]

The demand for her help was seemingly without limit. Yet the climate was becoming increasingly hostile to her activities. In 1845 the New York legislature, in part responding to laws passed in Massachusetts and Maine earlier in the decade, and in part reacting against the notoriety of Madame Restell, made the death of a woman or fetus consequent upon abortion after quickening a manslaughter in the second degree, punishable as a felony. Commercial abortionists were a particular target of the law, which included a section aimed at anyone who administered, prescribed, advised or procured a criminal abortion, and for the first time included the woman having the abortion in the net. A term in prison or a fine up to $1,000 could result. Similar laws were passed in many states and territories, but legislators soon found that such measures were difficult to enforce: no matter how strong the suspicions, evidence was seldom sufficient to obtain convictions. The new laws of the 1840s did little to curb the practice but were a sign that the traditional public indifference to abortion was changing. Although no convictions were obtained under them, the new laws sharpened public awareness of the dramatic increase and visibility of abortion in the city. They were also a potent symbol of the anxieties society had been expressing about female sexuality, and of the claims for equality and suffrage which a significant minority of women were making for their sex. The ineffective abortion laws of the 1840s were a marker for the direction of social attitudes later in the century, and a police action in the ongoing war over sexuality as American prudery and puritanism experienced the multiple strains of rapid social change.[38]

As Madame Restell's business grew, wrote a "Physician of New York," "so did the hopes, the avarice and the audacity of the woman." Her relations with Charles Lohman were said to have been unhappy. They were both described as being inordinately greedy, and were said to have quarreled repeatedly over money. Despite periods of reconciliation, the impression strongly survives that they regarded each other with entrenched hostility. Despite her unhappiness at home, there was business to attend to and women who needed her help across the country.

Mary Applegate and Maria Bodine

One such woman was Mary Applegate, who had been living with Madame Restell for "treatment," and who swore out an affidavit before the Democratic Mayor William F. Havemeyer. Applegate claimed that her baby had been born alive but that Restell would not account for it. "I have been an inmate of Madame Restell's house for some time [she told Mayor Havemeyer]. I have been unfortunate, sir, as you may suppose, or I would not have been in such a place, but what I want is my baby. I don't know what she has done with it. Indeed I love it, sir, and I want it back. I believe she done something to it. Oh, your Honor, will you help me, and God will bless you?"[39]

Various accounts of Applegate's experiences are contradictory, and there is little evidence other than her own words. But they chillingly convey the nightmare world into which a young woman could fall in the 1840s. No account exists of Eliza Munson's experience, sent from New Haven to New York to have an abortion; Mary Applegate told her story repeatedly and with increasing desperation. She had worked in the home of Augustus Edwards, a Philadelphia stockbroker, with whom she had intercourse over a period of several years. When she became pregnant, he agreed under threat of exposure to pay for her to leave the city and have the baby. Writing as "Mr. St. Clair Mason," he sent funds to enable the child to be born at Restell's establishment on Greenwich Street. Applegate repeatedly refused Restell's request that the baby be adopted. After the child was born, Restell told her that Mr. Mason had written instructing the infant to be placed with a wet nurse. Applegate demanded to meet the woman and was introduced to a Catherine Rider, who said she was a mason's wife living in Harlem. Applegate agreed reluctantly to the arrangement; she never saw her child again. Edwards denied that he had instructed the child to be put out to nurse, and when he confronted the abortionist, ". . . Restell denied any knowledge of Deponent, and [said] that no female had been delivered of a child for several months past, in her house. Deponent has also made inquiries of Mrs. Restell, and she says, that she does not know where the nurse is who took the child, or in whose custody the child is."

Applegate's story moved Havemeyer, who advised her to swear an affidavit against Restell, upon which he would issue a warrant for the search of her house. (Abortionists were believed to murder callously any infants which they could not sell for adoption. The cost of an infant from a "baby farm" was twenty-five dollars.) But no infant was ever found. Nothing was as it seemed in such a world. The other women staying in Restell's Greenwich Street establishment disguised their own identities. "Restell," "Mason," and "Rider" used false names; the infant was taken by use of a false letter, and was given a new name. Only Applegate and her infant were real. To find oneself, at such a moment, in the hands of Madame Restell was very far from the consoling and supportive experience which other women had had as her client. Restell told Applegate that there were many men in New York who would be happy to keep such a good-looking woman. She would have to give up the baby and prostitute herself, but a good life, with fine clothes, was sure to follow if she listened to Madame Restell's words.[40] It was as though Applegate had entered the world of the novels of Sue, "Gaslight" Foster, Lippard and "Ned Buntline"; only her tears were real; and no infant was ever discovered.

In the wake of simultaneous attacks on Restell in the *New York Medical and Surgical Reporter* and the *National Police Gazette* on 21 February 1846, an old antagonist of Restell's named George Dixon seized the opportunity to issue a handbill calling for a protest meeting. Since the New York anti-abolition riots of 1834, the call for a "protest meeting" was understood in certain parts of the city to be a coded summons to mob action. On the morning of 23 February "a great crowd" gathered with the intention of mobbing the house. "Hand her out." "Where's Mary Applegate's child?" echoed before the empty dwelling. Having been warned of the trouble, Restell had gone elsewhere. Physical assaults and the destruction of property were a common feature of such attacks. Although the police were soon able to clear the street, she did not wait for a second demonstration of her neighbors' opinion of her activities. Madame Restell swiftly moved her business to 148 Chambers Street. (Brothels, which moved into "respectable" neighborhoods in this decade, were even more likely to be the object of mob violence. Chambers Street was the longstanding southern boundary of the West Broadway brothel area.) Defenders of traditional values were shocked by the *visibility* of urban vice, but in the 1840s law and community sentiment were less able, in a diverse and complex city, to control the activities of people like Restell. Mob action was often their only recourse.[41]

Her new neighbors on Chambers Street apparently tolerated her presence. Although no evidence was ever found of Applegate's baby,

Its enemies saw abortion as a crime transcendent in its evil, and struggled to find visual images to capture the force of their revulsion.

Restell was bound over by a magistrate for a year. It was widely believed that she had once again bribed herself out of trouble. When this accusation appeared in the *Tribune*, Restell boldly defended herself:

> How stand the facts in connection with "justice" being bought with "gold": a charge most infamous, outrageous and flagrant, as involving the highest, most esteemed and unblemished citizens in the land. The *only* trial [in] which I was involved that took place was on a charge of misdemeanor, some years since, in which, by the ruling of the Supreme Court, Chief Justice Nelson and Judges Cohen and Bronson, the *only* evidence upon which a verdict was obtained was pronounced "illegal and inadmissible in every view which the Court had been able to take." This decision I caused to be extensively published in full, with the view that the facts connected with the charge should be known. Will it be pretended that the Supreme Court sacrificed justice to gold? It is really too monstrous that such a silly epistle should have found room in your paper.

It would appear that the well established maxim that every person shall be deemed innocent until proved guilty is to be superseded by one which shall deem every one guilty until proved innocent.

I would ask, farther, whether there are any individual rights guaranteed to us? How far we are at liberty to indulge our individual tastes in our expenditures?—Whether we can use two horses or four (if an emergency occurs of long distance and heavy, bad roads) without being subjected to spiteful and malicious animadversions from every "sour grapes" through the medium of respectable papers? And how is one "defying public opinion," "scorning laws," and doing a variety of atrocious deeds by using more than two or "three bays (one, by-the-by, is a chestnut) and a gray?"

Surely it is not within the province of "public opinion" to say whether a person shall have a coat of blue, brown, or green. It is alleged, and with some force, that individual independence is already nearly crushed by the many-headed monster "public opinion" and would be completely tyrannized over if some people had their way. There is but little difference between one tyrant and another, except that the many-headed one is the greatest. In conclusion, Sir, I would leave it to every impartial, liberal, high-minded person, whether these uncalled for attacks partake not of the fell spirit of persecution, even if not of worse motives. Yours, &c.

MADAME RESTELL.[42]

She was not prepared to hide, or to accept the role of wicked woman which her enemies sought to give her. Whether they liked it or not, Restell knew the language of individual rights as well as any "impartial, liberal, high-minded" person. After fifteen years in New York, Caroline Ann Trow, Mrs. Harry Somers, Mrs. Charles Lohman and Madame Restell had mastered the rhetoric of privilege, and claimed the right to enjoy her wealth—like every other prosperous resident in the city.

In July 1846 she received a country girl, Maria Bodine, who had come to New York from Orange County, New Jersey. Bodine claimed that Restell had performed an operation upon her which resulted in a premature delivery. On her return home, in a weak physical condition, Bodine consulted a local physician who wrote a letter to William V. Brady, mayor of New York in 1847–8, who referred the matter to the police. Her story was all too typical. Employed as a housekeeper by Joseph P. Cook, owner of cotton mills at Ramapo, New Jersey, Bodine claimed that she had been seduced by Cook. When she became pregnant, she was persuaded by her employer to consult Restell for an abortion. Bodine was secretly brought to the city and was placed in a private boardinghouse to await the convening of the grand jury on 6 September. Her testimony resulted in bills of indictment for manslaughter in the second degree against Restell, Cook, and Cook's intermediary, John McCann. Armed with a bench warrant, a detective proceeded directly to Restell's house on Chambers Street. Her activities had been under police observation for two years. Callers at her house were followed to their residences and questioned. This, in view of the new legislation against abortion, seemed a perfect opportunity to move against "Madame Killer" as she came to be called. The detective was invited to wait in the parlor until Restell and her husband returned from their usual morning ride. He later described the scene when she returned:

> Being told by her servant that a gentleman was awaiting her in the parlor, she glided in, dressed in the most fashionable manner, but upon seeing me, hesitated and said "How do you do, Mr. B——?" and inquired what I desired. I informed her that my call was a professional one, and exhibiting my bench warrant told her I would be obliged to take her into custody and accompany her to the court, which was now in session at the Tombs.[43]

Charles Lohman expressed the hope that the detective "would not make any public exposure of his wife in the street" and requested permission that she be allowed to change her dress. To prevent an escape, the detective kept his foot carefully wedged in the door of Restell's room while she changed. He even agreed to follow them on the opposite side of the street on the route to The Tombs. Bail was set at $10,000 and, on 10 September, she was arraigned on a charge of manslaughter in the course of procuring an abortion on Maria Bodine. The court repeatedly rejected her bondsmen as being insufficient for the seriousness of the charge, and thus Restell was kept in The Tombs. The defense case was led by James T. Brady and David Graham, Jr., the prosecution by the District Attorney John McKeon and Ogden Hoffman. These were formidable men, indeed: McKeon served several terms in the New York State Assembly and was twice elected to Congress. He served as Public Prosecutor before succeeding Charles O'Conor as United States District Attorney. A determined Copperhead, McKeon was a maverick figure within the Democratic Party in the city and the organizer of a personal faction, the "McKeon Democracy," in 1862–3, whose candidate, C. Godfrey Gunther, blocked Fernando Wood's bid for a fourth term as mayor. McKeon was one of the "respectable" men who opposed "Boss" Tweed in the early period of his rise to power, and such are the ironies of the legal profession, he served as one of the panel of lawyers who represented "Slippery Dick" Connolly in 1872.[44]

Hoffman, the son of a Superior Court judge, had like McKeon served in Congress, had been United States District Attorney, and was reputed to be the greatest criminal trial lawyer of the age. His "exceptionally melodious voice" made a deep impression on juries, and was recalled in later years with awe.[45]

Restell's trial in the Court of General Sessions before recorder Scott and aldermen Feeks and Tappan lasted for eighteen days from 20 October 1847. After the Purdy case in 1841, and the Applegate agitation earlier in the year, there was intense public interest in the details of the Bodine abortion. The testimony was widely printed in newspapers. The assistant district attorney, Jonas Phillips, set the opening tone of the trial:

> The heart sickens at such a narrative. Nature is appalled, that woman, the last and loveliest of her works, could so unsex herself, as to perpetrate such fiend-like enormities.
>
> The gardener watches with jealous care the seed he cast into the fertile earth, until it germs, and buds, and blooms, in the consummated perfection of nature's loveliness. But this defendant destroys the germ of nature—she kills the unborn infant; endangers, if she does not destroy, the mother's life, ruins her health; and all for the sake of the base lucre . . .[46]

Nature is at once judge and victim of Restell's actions. Femininity is seen both as the "consummated perfection" of "nature's loveliness" as well as being the perpetrator of "fiend-like enormities." The prosecutor's language reflects an anxiety at a radical instability in the moral universe. If femininity could be so grossly perverted, that most entrenched of values, nature, was no less threatened. In the eyes of the prosecution, Restell was guilty of gender-crime, a transgression of the American Cult of the True Woman.[47] Such crimes against nature, and against the sexual identity of all women, deserved the most severe punishment.

The jury listened to Bodine, twenty-six years old but obviously in fragile health, with rapt attention. The prosecution focused on the costs of an abortion. Restell told Bodine that it would be a very expensive and complicated job because the fetus was quick. The initial physical examination by Madame Restell cost five dollars, and the operation a further $100. It is possible that the details which followed had never been imagined by God-fearing New Yorkers:

> "We went up stairs [Bodine explained]; Madame Restell took the pillows off the bed, and directed me to lay on the floor, right down; I did so; she said she wanted to make an examination, to see how far I was advanced; I lay down as directed, and for five or ten minutes with her

hands, she made an examination; she inserted her hand up my body, in the vagina; (in a whisper, but audible, and repeated by Phillips). She hurt me very much, and I made loud groans. The reason she was so long, she said was, that I was differently situated from any one else; she could not find the right direction; she turned her hand round in my body as if she was breaking something; the operation continued from five to near ten minutes; I had my courses while she was in the room, and I noticed it on her leaving . . ."

Bodine testified that she had taken the tablets given her by Restell for two days, but continued in great pain. Madame slept with her, through vomiting and a violently upset stomach. The miscarriage was finally obtained after Bodine was seated on an earthenware chamber which tapered to a narrow bottom: "Madame Restell again inserted her hand; she hurt me so, I hallooed out and gripped her hand; she told me to have patience, and I would call her 'mother' for it . . ."

After two days of nursing and recuperation, Restell gave Bodine money to pay for her passage home, and for refreshments on the journey. She took Bodine into the parlor and gave her a glass of wine. There were many things to say, much advice to be given. Restell showed Bodine how to relieve the distress in her breasts, which were painful and leaking milk. She offered to call out her coach if any police were snooping outside, and warned Bodine not to tell anyone what had happened. They shook hands, Restell gave her a kiss and warned her never to allow herself to be taken advantage of again.

Restell's lawyers attacked Bodine's testimony and, in the time-honored traditions of the legal profession, scathingly sought to discredit her before the jury. "This woman had for years, constantly and habitually, indulged in habits of prostitution . . ." argued Mr. Brady: "She is the felon, the instigator, the prompter." The aggressive attack on Bodine continued for two full days, interrupted by the witness's spells of fainting, and was followed by the testimony of Dr. Samuel C. Smith of Montgomery, Orange County, who was responsible for reporting the abortion to the authorities. Eminent figures from the New York medical community were called upon to provide expert testimony on pregnancy and abortion. Dr. Chandler Gilman explained the medical symptoms of pregnancy. Dr. Gunning Bedford, who had been Restell's bitter enemy since he first encountered one of her clients in 1842, was questioned on several precise anatomical topics by Ogden Hoffman and caused a sensation in court by the conclusions he offered:

Q. Would the facility of entering the vagina, or the womb, increase according to the advance in pregnancy?   A.   Certainly—but the danger would increase too. Q. Supposing the hand were introduced and worked round and round, so, as has been described, what would be the effects? A. The most horrible. Q. Could a wire be under the finger at the time of such an operation? A. Undoubtedly, that's the way the thing is done![48]

The transcript recorded a "great sensation throughout the court" at Dr. Bedford's revelations.

In the end, and in no small part due to a "torrent of eloquence" unleashed by Hoffman, Restell was acquitted of the manslaughter charge, but convicted, and sentenced to a year in prison on Blackwell's Island for the misdemeanor. Walt Whitman rejoiced in the *Brooklyn Daily Eagle* that the "child-murderess" and "she-wolf" had received her just desserts. In the world of gambling dens, groggeries and brothels, Restell's imprisonment was spoken of with awe. A writ of error was filed with the Supreme Court, requesting a review of proceedings, but Restell's lawyers failed to obtain bail and she was forced to wait in the Eldridge Street Jail for nearly a year. In late June 1848 she was sent to Blackwell's Island to serve her full term of imprisonment. She was not released until the autumn of 1849.[49]

The Bodine case confirmed Restell's notoriety. Novelists coyly alluded to her. Confronted by a pregnant lover in *The Mysteries and Miseries of New York*, a melodramatic tale by "Ned Buntline," a New York gentleman has an obvious solution:

"... I will preserve you from the danger of your present situation."

"Albert, do I understand you? Is not one of the risks at which you hint, the loss of my life? To comply, with that to which you allude, must I not be a murderer?"

"No. Use not such harsh terms, my dear. It is not murder! Mrs. Sitstill, to whom I would send you, is a kind woman, a very useful one to society. Many a girl from the highest grades of our aristocracy thanks her now, that her name is free from stain."[50]

Restell appeared in George Thompson's anonymous novel *The Countess, or, Memoirs of Women of Leisure* (1849) as one of the seven "Daughters of Venus," a secret society of wantons and prostitutes engaged in a conspiracy against the virtuous maidens of New York. George Lippard's Gothic tales of aristocratic wrongdoing in New York, *The Empire City; or, New York by Night and Day* (1850) and *New York: Its Upper Ten and Lower Million* (1853) contain descriptions of Restell as "Madam Resimer," a "fiend in human shape," as well as a lurid account of her "den" on Greenwich Street. "Restell is so notorious that she is more talked of and written about than even [the newspaperman Horace] Greeley or [the prominent store owner A.T.] Stewart," asserted Junius Henri Browne; but the trial did little to extend the terms of the public debate upon the issue of abortion.[51] It suited the defense as well as the prosecution to confine the trial to a narrow range of issues. Thanks to the scandal-mongering *National Police Gazette*, which printed copious extracts from the testimony given during the trial and published a sensational pamphlet (*Wonderful Trial of Caroline Lohman, Alias Restell*, 1847) afterwards, the public was afforded an account of shockingly intimate behavior.

Medical journals had regularly printed accounts of vaginal examinations, to the point where Dr. Stephen Smith rebuked a "mania" on the part of physicians for speculum investigations of the uterus. This was the moment which Foucault describes as the advent of the new medical technologies of sex and a dramatic expansion of concern with sex while the culture remained ever more prudish about what could be said about the activities of abortionists.[52] Bryant's *Evening Post* covered the trial in two paragraphs, never once mentioning the nature of Restell's manslaughter or the word abortion. It was common before the Civil War for the press to draw a veil of reticence across the details. In the process of powerfully affirming the sexual and moral codes of the community, the testimony given at the Bodine case transgressed the limits it was meant to uphold and for a brief moment allowed a glimpse into one of the most intimate areas of American life. Such details as provided by Maria Bodine were regarded by the respectable and the custodians of culture for many years as so deeply embarrassing as to be, literally, unmentionable. But the Bodine case, like so many other aspects of Restell's career, hints at a public increasingly hungry for such prurient matter, and for whom the proprieties no longer mattered. Restell's *fame*, in other words, was built upon a conspiracy of euphemisms.

Of the public discussions emerging out of the Bodine case, at least one sought to break out of the prosecution's rhetoric. A certain "Physician of New York" published a pamphlet (*Madame Restell: An Account of her Life and Horrible Practices*, 1847), in which he sought to shift public attention from the abortionist to those who sought abortions in the first place. This was Restellism, "a catering to the weakness and wickedness of human nature." The woman herself was the "hired instrument of a guilt" and should not, the "Physician" argued, be the sole object of public indignation. He actually sought to imagine how Restell might defend herself:

"Why, woman have you done this detestable deed—."

"You have heard the mother testify that the deed was done at her demand, and to save her daughter—you have heard the daughter

THIRD EDITION—PRICE 6½ CENTS.

WONDERFUL TRIAL

OF

CAROLINE LOHMAN, ALIAS RESTELL,

WITH SPEECHES OF COUNSEL, CHARGE OF COURT,

AND VERDICT OF JURY.

[REPORTED IN FULL FOR THE NATIONAL POLICE GAZETTE.]

PORTRAIT OF MADAME RESTELL,

Title-page of the *National Police Gazette* transcription of the trial of Restell for carrying out an abortion on Maria Bodine.

declare, that she had only this left to save her from suicide. If I have done evil, it was to prevent a much greater. Her life is saved—her reputation, dearer than life, is preserved."

"Infamous wretch," we answer, "the laws pronounce your act a felony. Society demands your punishment."

"Society first demanded the crime," persists this monster, "society compelled it; let society furnish the seducer, who caused its necessity; let society cease from punishing the mere frailties of our nature with its heaviest retributions, and we should not attempt to conceal them with crimes. . . ."[53]

The "Physician" passionately condemned the attempt to produce early miscarriages as an "outrage on nature," and an act "at once detestable and diabolical." The full significance of Restellism as it was perceived by her contemporaries transcended her personal guilt. "Madame Restell tells your daughter how she may defile her body and debase her mind without fear or hesitation."[54] This was a theme of many a New York sermon:

> Could all the dissolute escape disease and shame, and all the ambitious and proud and envious, escape disappointment and chagrin, and every negligent and wicked man, in fine, be freed from the proper consequences of his folly and sin, what would become of society? I say that its very bands would be dissolved, and the system of a moral, providential government would be at an end . . .[55]

A world in which evil had no consequence teetered on the verge of anarchy, universal corruption and the end of all morality.

As Madame Restell endured her term on Blackwell's Island she may have reflected bitterly upon the increasingly complex intertwining of hypocrisy and morality in American society.[56] Sergeant Taft of the Oak Street Police Station, who was then working as a carpenter on the island, received orders to fit up her cell, which had previously been used as a storeroom. He remembered that a large featherbed was installed, and that Restell was given charge of the women's sewing room, perhaps the easiest work available in the prison. (The warden, Jacob Acker, was discharged when the press revealed the full extent of the "villainous favoritism" which Restell had secured through bribery.[57]) She wore a prison dress which had been tastefully bleached and looked more like merino wool, over which she wore a black silk apron, which nearly reached to the floor, and a black silk hood. Her husband called every afternoon. "She was a large, handsome woman when she came there," Sergeant Taft recalled, "and seemed to feel her imprisonment greatly. She acted in a very ladylike way, but appeared very sad throughout her confinement. . . . She said when she quit Blackwell's Island [in June 1849] that she should never go there again."[58]

Joining the "Shoddy Aristocracy" of New York

Restell's experience of prison was a reminder that she remained vulnerable. The constant threat of arrest and the need for bribes and blackmail must have been as commonplace an experience as police surveillance and public condemnation. A resourceful woman, she had been able to arrange for special privileges while on Blackwell's Island. Bribery could, in most circumstances, keep the police at bay.[59] But even in New York bribery was not enough, and could offer no long-term security for the family. Only money and respectability could do that. The most dramatic resolve she brought back across the East River from Blackwell's Island was to become very rich. By the standards of most people in New York, Restell was already prosperous. One estimate put her personal wealth at this time at $100,000. But she had seen something of the really rich and committed herself to work unremittingly towards the security which only they enjoyed. How could an abortionist become respectable in New York? However gaily she asserted her moral innocence, Madame Restell could not but know that she was despised by the leaders of the community. She found that it was harder to be rich and respectable in New York than rich and scandalous.

The city had never been so openly flamboyant. Henry Ward Beecher, the impulsive preacher of stormy and pictorial vehemence, was summoned to Plymouth Church in Brooklyn in 1847. P. T. Barnum, whose American Museum on Broadway at Ann Street, was the greatest popular entertainment in the city, reached his peak when he presented Jenny Lind to audiences of 10,000 at Castle Garden in 1850. Political life was dominated by vivid demagogues like Fernando Wood, whose three terms as mayor entrenched corruption in city government. The streets were commanded by the likes of Captain Isaiah Rynders, political boss of the 6th ward and patron of the terrifying Dead Rabbits, a gang from the Five Points. John Morrissey, an ex-pugilist and political tough, became a powerful presence in Tammany Hall. In the 1850s Madame Restell sought, gradually, to change the way she was perceived by society. The lease on their residence on Greenwich Street was given up in 1848, and while Restell was on Blackwell's Island her husband had bought a house further to the north at 162 Chambers Street. The move uptown made good sense; it was the New York tradition.

Despite the new legal inhibitions, and the deepening hostility of some elements in the medical profession, the public attitude towards abortion seemed to be changing only gradually; the demand for abortion remained at a very high level. It is nonetheless true that Restell resumed her work as an abortionist when she returned home from prison. When an affidavit was filed in 1855 by one Fredericka Medinger alleging that a living infant delivered at Restell's Chambers Street establishment had subsequently disappeared, the plaintiff failed to appear in court. Such matters had best be dealt with quietly, and in a liberal financial spirit. Her immediate need was to avoid bad publicity, and the authorities seem to have been willing to allow the abortion trade to enter a period of "benign neglect."[60]

Though her husband was a freethinker, she began to attend an Episcopal church after she left prison. Her daughter Carrie Somers was an attractive young lady in her early twenties. Although she occasionally assisted her mother in attending to pregnant women, her attractiveness was taken to stand for everything that was the opposite of her mother. "Beautiful almost beyond conception," wrote George Thompson, "and lovely and amiable in her disposition as woman can be, she has many admirers who love her for herself, for even the man dyed in crime could not love a woman so utterly detested as her mother."[61] Restell deliberately sought to raise the social level of her clientele, in part by raising prices and by requiring new clients to provide "references" from those familiar to her. She tried to emulate the richest people in the city by doing business only with exclusive importers, auctioneers and the best jewelers, buying only the most luxurious things for her home, and dressing in fashionable elegance. Everything possible was done to show the public that Madame Restell was quality, and that her customers were among the wealthiest and most exclusive in the city. Without the arduous training in leisure required of women of the upper orders, "pecuniary emulation," in Thorstein Veblen's phrase, alone testified to her achievement and, indeed, respectability.[62] It was clear that a good match for Carrie Somers was needed.

Having prospered as quack pill merchants and abortionists, Madame Restell and her husband turned in the early 1850s to property speculation, a most traditional path to riches in New York. The rapid expansion of the population of the city, which grew from 312,710 in 1840 to 515,547 in 1850, and the impressive signs of commercial activity and trade, led to frenzied leaps in real estate values in the upper reaches of the island. A gridiron pattern, decided upon early in the century, which encouraged uniform-sized housing lots, made speculation particularly attractive. The Lohmans proved adept at buying cheap and selling when the market was at its highest. Their most famous purchase was ten lots fronting on the east side of Fifth Avenue between 52nd and 53rd Streets for $36,500. When the value of this property rose sufficiently, Lohman sold several lots and borrowed $27,000 from the Mutual Life Insurance Company to develop the site. When the identity of the owners became known, a group of respectable citizens anxious to preserve the character of the city's most aristocratic thoroughfare offered the Lohmans $5,000 to go elsewhere.[63] This smacked of "the fell spirit of persecution," and the notorious lady declared that "there was not money enough in New York" to prevent her building on Fifth Avenue. The site was probably worth $600,000 by the 1860s. Without the knowledge of her husband, Madame Restell bought up the mortgage on the Fifth Avenue property and then loaned her husband the enormous sum of $147,000 to build a handsome brownstone and a private residence and office on the remaining lots. The transaction said a great deal about the relationship between the two, and of the fundamental mistrust that must have prevailed between them. For the last ten years of his life, Lohman devoted himself to his real estate interests and was said "to have been one of the shrewdest operators in New York."[64] She too was a clever operator and protected herself financially in her transactions with her husband, though some contemporaries mistakenly believed that Lohman was her financier. Restell exercised a similar caution in relations with her daughter.[65]

The *New York Times* painted a different picture of Restell's property transactions. The couple were so notorious that the purchases of land on Fifth Avenue had to be undertaken secretly through an agent, and while the great house was being built the identity of the owner was kept a strict secret by the builder. The adjoining brownstone, the *Times* suggested, was for a "long time" an unproductive investment because the aversion to Madame Restell was so great. Even when rents were reduced by fifty per cent it proved difficult to find tenants, and in the end Lohman was forced to lease it as an apartment building. She was even obliged to mortgage it for $150,000.[66] The two accounts of their property transactions are not contradictory; it is likely that many of their transactions were conducted through agents. Secrecy in property speculation would hardly have been unusual. And the money Madame Restell covertly loaned her husband to build the "Osborne" may have been repaid later through a mortgage, if she had further purchases in mind. She would in effect have paid herself off, and have had a large sum in hand from the bank. The transaction suggests her shrewdness.

It was a truth universally assumed that abortionists engaged in blackmail. The confidences imparted would provide many opportunities, and a wealthy clientele like Restell's was an obvious target for the unscrupulous. James D. McCabe, Jr., suggested that she used the children born under her care as a means of extorting money from the parents.[67] Despite the many suggestions to the contrary, there is no evidence that she engaged in blackmail. It is not, admittedly, the kind of activity which either party would choose to publicize, but if she had been a blackmailer it is hard to believe that some word or detail of her activities would not have circulated in the city.

Her annual income from her "practice" was said to amount to $30,000 in 1869, probably a substantial understatement, and her total wealth, estimated nine years later, was said to have been between $850,000 and $1,000,000. One estimate placed it as high as $1,500,000.[68] The gap between income and wealth was too vast to have been made up by blackmail, for it would have been required on a prodigious scale and could not have avoided publicity. Her wealth, rather, came from clever property speculation and from money wisely invested in government bonds. Every bribe she paid to a policeman, detective, politician or judge, for which we again have no precise information, carried with it a further possibility of reverse blackmail. Restell sometimes liked to intimate that she had secret information concerning many eminent New Yorkers; these seemed to grow geometrically in eminence with the vagueness of her assertion.[69] No doubt many people feared the revelations she could make, but in the end she said nothing, and left no destructive testament. She worked in a climate well-suited to blackmail, but we have too little information to decide the question with confidence. She may have been a blackmailer; she was certainly the victim of blackmail throughout her career.

By the time they moved into their new home on Fifth Avenue in 1865, they had both changed. Lohman was a tall and, by contemporary accounts, a handsome man given to a fashionable stoutness in later years. He was easy with guests and impressed visitors with his polite manners and an affable good nature. Middle age was not so kind to Madame Restell. Junius Henri Browne, understating her age by several years, wrote in 1869:

> Once she was handsome, I understand; but now, in her fiftieth year, she is a gross, coarse, though not heartless-looking woman, with black eyes, black hair, barely touched with gray ... She would be mistaken for the proprietress of a bagnio, with her flaring colors, her glittering jewels, her tawdry carriage, for she is the embodiment of the principle of bad taste in all that belongs to her.[70]

George Ellington closely followed Browne in his account of "The Wickedest Woman in New York" in 1870:

Madame Restell, 1870: "Once she was handsome, but possesses now no traces of her former beauty. She looks like an upstart or 'shoddy' female, but not particularly wicked or heartless."

Madame —— is about fifty-five years of age, is a short, plump, vulgar-looking woman, with dark, piercing eyes and jet-black hair. Once she was handsome, but possesses now no traces of her former beauty. She looks like an upstart or "shoddy" female, but not particularly wicked or heartless.[71]

The insistence that Madame Restell was "the embodiment of bad taste" and a "shoddy" female, suggests that her determination to cultivate the upper classes in New York had met at least with some success. There would have been no need to insist upon her vulgarity if she had not succeeded in passing herself off as someone who had the right to offer hospitality to those of refinement. Her entertainment evenings were legendary in a city noted for extravagance and display. One visitor to her house described the scene:

Servants, wearing black garments and white neckties, were busy carrying refreshments around. Many persons, preferring the pleasures of eating to those of playing or dancing, were seated in another room at a table loaded with meats and delicacies. Next to this, another room, elegantly furnished, was crowded with young and old men, indulging in smoking.[72]

The house which they began to build at 657 Fifth Avenue (the northeast corner of 52nd Street and Fifth Avenue) in 1862 was known popularly as "the palace." It was constructed over three years and was said to have cost $200,000. Along with its stables and gardens, it was one of the finest private residences in the city. The "Physician of New York" greatly admired Restell's establishment on Greenwich Street, but her house on Fifth Avenue was on a more lavish scale altogether. No residence in New York in the 1860s could rival the parvenu ostentation of A. T. Stewart, who, in 1864, bought Dr. "Sarsparilla" Townsend's home on the northwest corner of Fifth Avenue at 34th Street. Stewart had the site razed, and erected a spectacular mansion of white Carrara marble which he proceeded to fill with the most expensive statuary, the most widely admired works of art, the finest carpeting, etc., costing between one and two million dollars. (In 1863, he paid income tax on an annual income of $1,843,637, making him the richest man in the country.)[73] An immigrant like Restell, Stewart was in the eyes of "society" little more than a successful shopkeeper. Like Stewart's grandiose home, Restell's "palace" was an important marker for the new standards of conspicuous consumption expected of the wealthy. The "Shoddy Aristocracy," made rich by the feverish speculation during the Civil War, differed from the wealthy of the previous generation, or at least were regarded as having inferior social breeding, less civic consciousness. The newly rich, like Jim Fisk, "Boss" Tweed and "Slippery Dick" Connolly, were no less conscious than "Madame Killer" that a display of riches and extravagance was the most significant statements available to a New Yorker. Without established family traditions in New York, such people were forced to invent a sign of their worth that could be universally understood. The Italianate mansions, French châteaux, and pseudo-gothic castles grew like mushrooms on Fifth Avenue, only to be torn down for even larger and more fantastical establishments later in the century. (It was only after Restell's death that the Vanderbilts began construction of their twin houses in the immediate vicinity of "the palace" on Fifth Avenue. They were reported to have spent $15,000,000 on the construction, decoration and furnishing of two houses.[74]) "Some of these rooms," reported "Asmodeus" [Ferdinand Longchamp], after a visit to Madame Restell's,

The magnificence of Restell's and Lohman's "Palace," in this colored lithograph by Hatch & Co. from 1875, attracted much comment. The window shades were said to have cost $1,000 each. The "Osborne" was built on the undeveloped lots above the "Palace" on Fifth Avenue.

were lined with fine brocatel, imported from France and Italy, China and Japan, the latter conspicuous for their fantastical drawings and patterns; others with Persian and Indian cloths; and the several pieces of furniture were of unexceptionable taste. Some were inlaid with gold, bronze, of China; some were made up of rosewood artistically carved. Gems of art and curiosities of every description were displayed upon tables; and through the house, made bright as day by hundreds of gaslights, one walked on soft, smooth carpets of the best manufactures of Europe. They alone were worth a fortune.[75]

Another visitor gave an even more detailed description of the glories of Madame Restell's house:

On the first floor are the grand hall of tessellated marble, lined with mirrors; the three immense dining-rooms, furnished in bronze and gold with yellow satin hangings, an enormous French mirror in mosaic gilding at every panel; ceilings in medallions and cornices; more parlors and reception rooms; butler's pantry lined with solid silver services;

dining-room with all imported furniture. ... The whole house is filled with statuettes, paintings, rare bronzes, ornamental and valuable clocks, candelabras, silver globes and articles of *virtu*, chosen with unexceptionable taste.[76]

There was a circular picture-gallery on the fourth floor, and a billiard-room, dancing hall with piano and pictures on the fifth, which commanded a fine view of Fifth Avenue. Two Italian craftsmen worked for twelve months on the frescoed ceilings, reportedly at a cost of $20,000. Nothing in the house attracted so much attention as the window shades, each hand-painted by leading artists in the city, which were said to cost $1,000 each. The house had thirty windows. Ellington thought they were "very vulgar": "No other house on Fifth Avenue or in New York possesses such shades, or indeed, would any one else in the city want to."[77] The term "vulgar" in New York was a weapon of class rebuke, an aristocratic placing of those ignorant of the nature of "taste." In the eyes of "old money," Madame Restell was invincibly vulgar and her attempts to gain admittance to the society of decent New Yorkers was yet another sign of the decay of the moral fiber of the age. Others saw in the luxury of Restell's establishment nothing less than a horror built upon horrors. For such people her "vulgarity" was utterly inconsequential: "Whenever I pass it, it seems to cast a deeper shadow than any other house, and a sense of chillness, such as comes from opened vaults in the graveyard, to steal from its grim doorways and windows hung with showy curtains, which shut in what few of us dare believe, and none of us care to see."[78] The metaphysical shudder caused by Restell's opulent mansion was particularly intense in the aftermath of her death:

> On all sides [of her mansion] are the richest furnishings imaginable. Pure white Carara [*sic*] marble, cut in delicate diamond tiles and tablets, line the floors of the hall passages and dining-room. Do not turn pale if the marble tablets, strangely enough, remind you of the tomb-stones. Tremble not if the thought occur to you that these tablets over which we are walking are leaves in the book of Fate which will be opened in the other world.[79]

Family life

Restell and Lohman had no children. The daughter of her first marriage, Caroline Somers, lived with her mother until she married a carpenter from Tarrytown named Isaac Purdy (no relation to the woman whose death brought Restell to court in the 1840s) in 1853, who was said to have been connected to the family of Hon. Ambrose Purdy, a member of the assembly for Westchester. Restell retained Assemblyman Purdy as her lawyer in 1878, but after her death he was quick to deny that there had been any family connection. As a sign of her growing social acceptability, Carrie and Isaac were married by Jacob A. Westervelt, the Democratic shipbuilder who was mayor of New York.[80] She gave the young couple $3,000 to spend on a trip to Europe, and on their return she bought them a house in Tarrytown. It was at the time of this marriage that Restell made her first will, which was deposited at the Surrogate's office. When Purdy was taken prisoner by the Confederates in 1864, Carrie and the surviving children (two had died – Frances Annie in 1859 and Florence Annie in March 1863) were brought to live at "the palace" with Restell and Lohman. Purdy died in the notorious prisoner of war camp at Andersonville, Georgia, in November 1864. After a brief widowhood, Mrs. Purdy formed a relationship with a policeman named Farrell, whom she secretly married ten months after the death of her husband. Learning of this deception, Restell virtually disowned her daughter, and never ceased to harbor the liveliest resentment towards her. The deaths of her grandchildren darkened Restell's life, if the monument she erected to their memory at the Tarrytown cemetery is a guide to feelings as well as a reflection of the intense mid-century sentimentalizing of children. On an ornamental pedestal of granite and marble was placed a frame of marble around sheets of plate glass, forming a glass case within which, reposing on a miniature mattress of pure marble, lay a sleeping child. It was said to have been modeled from one of the dead infants Madame Restell's order.[81] The surviving grandchildren (a boy named Charles Robert Purdy and a girl, Caroline Somers Purdy, also known as Carrie) were the objects of her deepest affection. She lavished upon them every luxury and attention, and when they were old enough she brought them to live with her on Fifth Avenue. For fourteen years until the events of 1878, Restell refused to receive Farrell in her home.

The "wickedest woman in New York" was by now a sternly formidable Victorian matron to her family. She ruled domestic affairs with an iron fist. But she chose, quietly, to temper her displeasure at her daughter's marriage by secretly supporting them through her grandchildren. Farrell, who had hoped for advantage through his connection with Restell, was forced to remain in the police force. He was eventually promoted to sergeant, but became addicted to drink, lost his position, and worked at odd jobs in the city. Farrell lived with his wife in a small house on Houston Street. As the children grew older their visits to their parents' home, in their grandmother's splendid carriage, became more frequent. In time a reconciliation was achieved, but Restell did not consent to the Farrells living under her roof. In 1877, she obtained a position for Farrell as a watchman at the Grand Central Depot, and rented a home for them on West 47th Street. She remained suspicious of her son-in-law, and early the next year quietly arranged for her lawyer to transfer some $6,000 to $8,000 in personal property to her grandson, explaining that she had "a desire to get the property out of the reach of certain of her relatives." She was similarly severe in her relations with her brother Joseph Trow. He had worked for Restell since the 1840s, but his choice of a bride in 1873 broke up their business relationship. Trow was forced to take Restell to court to recover bonds worth $10,000 which he claimed to have been given to him for three decades' faithful service. After his marriage, Restell stopped payment of income to Trow from these bonds and claimed that he had surrendered his interest in them for an unspecified consideration.[82] Displeasure at the behavior of her relatives was quickly expressed by Restell, and long remembered.

Charles Lohman revised his will in 1875, leaving his wife a life interest in his real estate and absolute ownership of their personal property. Lohman made a provision that on his wife's death half of the estate should go to his granddaughter Carrie, and at her death to Carrie's children. Restell provided similarly for Charles in her will. The only provision for her daughter Caroline Farrell was $3,000 annually, paid in such a way that Farrell could not anticipate payments or have any control of them. She left her considerable personal jewelry to her granddaughter Carrie: a diamond ring, one diamond bracelet, a pair of diamond earrings, a diamond bonnetpin, ten diamond rings, one rich gold bracelet with opal and diamond settings, a necklace consisting of three strings of pearls and diamond clasp, one necklace of five strings of pearls and diamond clasp, one all-pearl necklace, one pearl breastpin, one pearl bracelet, one pair of pearl earrings, one pearl ring, one opal ring set in eighteen diamonds "and also the parlor organ used by her, the grand action Steinway piano used by her, and the Bibles and Bible-stand, to have the same for and during her natural life."[83] Many a fine jeweler in New York must have viewed the denunciations of Restell with mixed feelings. There was nothing of the half-measure about her.

Lohman died early in 1876. The *National Police Gazette* printed an account of the death-room scene which more than hinted at skullduggery:

The "doctor" did not seem particularly ill when he took to his bed. While he had not been feeling right for some time, no grave apprehension was felt concerning his condition. Lohman raised himself in bed and said to a young man who had been visiting him every day: "Hand me the medicine-bottle from the bureau, will you?" The visitor looked around and seeing no bottle, replied: "What bottle? There is none here." "Why, it was there a few minutes ago," the invalid exclaimed. "Who could have taken it?" In a fit of angry impatience he rang the service bell. His wife appeared in answer to the summons, holding a medicine-bottle in her hand, and looking, so the eye-witness stated, strangely excited. "What the devil did you take my medicine for?" Lohman asked impetuously. "Well, I thought the bottle was getting empty," she replied, "and I had better replenish it." He was by no means reconciled with the explanation: "It was more than half full when I had it before and didn't need renewing." "Well, I thought it did," was the reply, and with that she deposited the bottle, which was now nearly full, on the bureau. That very night Lohman died.[84]

No clergyman was called, and early the next morning the body of Charles Lohman was carried to Tarrytown where he was buried. This seemed to the *Police Gazette* to point irresistibly towards foul play, and their suspicions were heightened by a report that there were relations in Prussia with a claim upon his estate. The conclusion was irresistible: Madame Restell murdered Lohman to secure her interest in his property. It was not likely that the husband of a woman guilty of so many unspeakable crimes could die a natural death. The script called for something much darker than that. But the death-bed scene as described, with an agitated and confused patient and a harried wife, belongs more to everyday life than to murderous melodrama.

A widow at the age of sixty-five, Restell lived increasingly for her grandchildren. Like any other ambitious New York matron, she sought to gain admission for them at the schools and social rounds designed for the children of the wealthy. When Carrie married a Mr. William Shannon, the young couple moved into "the palace." Her affection for her grandchildren was reciprocated, and Charles Purdy accompanied his grandmother on her court appearances in 1878. Above all, Restell dreaded the consequences of her own notoriety. Whenever she appeared in public, her carriage was followed by cries of the street children: "Yah! Your house is built on babies' skulls!"[85] Very few people knew that when she moved into the house on Fifth Avenue she had virtually ceased to perform abortions. She had quietly left behind what had made her so notorious, but the past reputation clung to her. Hints of this change appeared in the press. She told a reporter from the *New York Times* in 1871 that she had stopped taking "risks" when she moved into the grand house on Fifth Avenue: "We have had so much trouble about these matters we don't take any more risks. In all the six years that we have lived in this house there has never a stranger slept under the roof—none in fact but our own family."[86] When she sought to retain Judge Orlando L. Stewart as her lawyer in 1878, she was asked:

> "Madam, how old are you?" She said, "I am sixty-seven." I said: "You are a woman of advanced years and very ample fortune. Why do you continue this business?" She replied: "I have not done any business of this kind for twelve years. I have sold pills, but they were harmless. The other business, of producing abortions, I have not done in twelve years."[87]

Restell's son-in-law made the same point after her death: "There never has been a patient taken in this house, and all attempts [by Anthony Comstock] to prove it would have failed."[88] This point began to appear in published accounts of Restell, such as McCabe's in 1882: "She would never commit an abortion outright, but would safely deliver her patients, [and] take care of the children born in her house . . ."[89]

"This is a murderous age"

The campaign against corruption in public life was in reality a process that included many diverse reform constituencies and confronted some powerful and entrenched social and economic interests. Merchants, manufacturers and bankers, who had taken a leading role in supporting the YMCA movement when it was transplanted from England in the early 1850s, and who had for decades supported the Association for Improving the Condition of the Poor, were convinced that things were growing worse year by year.[90] Certain reforms had been enacted. The state legislature passed the first new anti-abortion laws in two decades, banning advertisements (like Restell's) which offered abortion services. In 1869, a law was passed which made the destruction of a fetus at any stage punishable as a second degree manslaughter. Over the wily objections of a corrupt city inspector, the Metropolitan Board of Health had been created in 1866, and a fearsome cholera epidemic averted. Tweed, "Slippery Dick" Connolly and their gang remained firmly in control of the city. But, as the sanitary survey conducted by the Citizens' Association in 1865 revealed, the festering slum fever-nests and tenements were owned by wealthy New York investors and speculators, who received an annual return of twenty-five per cent and more on their investments, and undoubtedly had powerful financial motives to ignore conditions in their properties:

> . . . those wealthy citizens should be held responsible who have had the means and influence to change the physical condition of the City, but who have seemed to be as unconscious of its material debasement as if they had inherited from their respectable ancestor, Diderick [*sic*] Knickerbocker, his marvelous capacity for obliviousness.[91]

Editorials in the *New York Times* extolled "The City of New-York— Its Growth and Destiny" but the reformers knew that New York was a community given to lax moral standards, and was besieged by temptations to wickedness. Child prostitution, assignation houses, saloons, taverns, grog-shops, dance-halls, gambling dens, to say nothing about the pornographers and abortionists, constituted highly visible aspects of daily life in the city. Every respectable theater-goer knew that if they cared to look up beyond the dress and family circles they would see the top gallery, or "third tier," which was given over to the exclusive use of prostitutes and their patrons.[92]

In 1866 the YMCA privately circulated a report, "A Memorandum Respecting New York as a Field for Moral and Christian Effort Among Young Men." Indeed, the city was a magnificent challenge for the men of the "sunlight." The police, courts and prisons, had to be urged, sometimes repeatedly, to enforce the laws. Bribery and a strong inclination to live and let live within the police force combined to make the enforcement of some existing laws problematic. When police did nothing, private individuals, spurred by the powerful motor of the individual conscience, were forced to act against wrong doing. When a concerted effort was made, the results could be dramatic. More than a hint of what was to come appeared in the speech of Judge Bedford in the Court of General Sessions in 1871, sentencing Michael A. Wolff to prison for performing an abortion upon a woman who subsequently died:

> Wolff, you are a well-known abortionist. But a few days ago, Judge Dowling inaugurated throughout this City an admirable system for the suppression of this rapidly-increasing crime. That system is now being faithfully carried out with telling effect by [Police] Superintendent Kelso. The people may rest assured that the District-Attorney, Recorder and myself will give, on all proper occasions, every assistance to crush out this monstrous crime, and to banish from our midst these traffickers in human life. In one word the authorities have declared war to the bitter end against the fraternity which you, today, so guiltily represent. Let every professional abortionist—male and female, rich and poor, in this

City—take warning, for on conviction their fate shall be the same as yours, namely, confinement in the State Prison for the period of seven years, the longest term allowed under the statute.[93]

The message for Restell was explicit. The judges may have shyed away from the manifest frauds and crimes of the Tweed Ring (which remained in power for another nine months), but abortion was to be treated unmercifully.

One of the leading figures in the purity crusade was Anthony Comstock who, while earning twenty-seven dollars per week as a salesman in a dry-goods establishment in 1871, had begun a personal campaign against immorality.[94] He reported to the police commissioner an officer who refused to close saloons illegally open on Sunday. Even Comstock probably knew that Sabbatarian laws were deeply unpopular in the city and were widely ignored, but he was a humorless, literal-minded man.[95] His early, single-handed activities against Sabbath-breakers and vendors of pornography won the backing of the YMCA in New York, which set up a Committee for the Suppression of Vice. Comstock was awarded a $500 purse for his efforts, and soon transformed the committee into an instrument for his personal crusade. When he attracted too much adverse publicity —it is worth emphasizing that there were many who doubted Comstock's methods and who attacked his motives—he severed the committee's link with the YMCA, changed its name into the Society for the Suppression of Vice, and continued largely as before.

In the two decades before his death in 1915, he had become at least for the younger generation of writers something of a laughing-stock. The modern movement in literature defined itself in large measure through its hostility to everything he stood for. Comstock was a ridiculous figure, an enemy of free expression and sexual candidness. H. L. Mencken conducted a sustained campaign in *The Smart Set* and the *American Mercury* against Comstock's activities and his legacy. (In one memorable essay he summed up the purity crusader's view of feminine purity: "A good woman, to him, was simply one who was efficiently policed.") Robert Minor's cartoon of a frantic, bloated, sword-wielding Comstock, fatally ensnared in the coils of female flesh, enlivened *The Masses* in 1915. So proverbial had Comstock's activities become that George Bernard Shaw invented a term, "comstockery," to describe officious censorship. Comstock was indeed the official bluenose of New York, and boasted of having had 160 tons of "obscene" literature destroyed. At first the rebels mocked and satirized; by the 1920s the very conceptual framework of comstockery was disintegrating in the withering light of the emerging social sciences.[96]

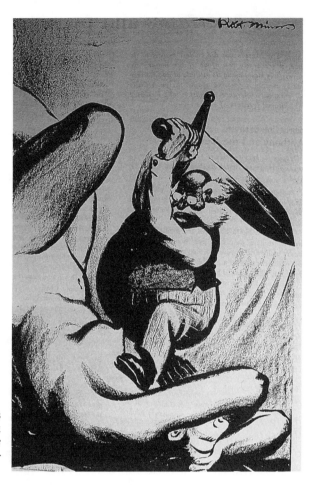

Robert Minor's cartoon of Comstock appeared in *The Masses*, October–November 1915.

A man moved by strong, simple moral dictates, and without the slightest hint of self-doubt, Comstock was uniquely effective as a purity reformer because of his determination to translate outrage into concrete action. He wanted to do *something* and never doubted the justness of his cause. A diary entry from 1871, the year in which the Tweed Ring was finally brought down, suggests the intensity of his indignation at public corruption:

> O how I loath the actions of corrupt officials in our city. This is a murderous age. Crime stalketh abroad by daylight and Public officers wink at it. Money can buy our judges and corrupt our juries. But God helping me, it shall never buy or sell me. I believe Jesus never would wink at any wrong nor would he countenance it.[97]

Comstock had a flair for publicity and understood the importance of educating and manipulating public opinion in the crusade for righteousness. In a sense he was the P. T. Barnum of social purity, and acted with a fine sense of the theatrical dimension of his cause. Early in his career he invited the *Tribune* to send a reporter to accompany his raids on Sabbath-breaking saloons. He chose to operate in the glare of publicity and to use the popular press as a weapon against the immoralists.[98] Newspapers condemned immorality, but when, like the *Herald*, they printed advertisements for abortionists such as Restell and Mauriceau, there was deep-seated ambivalence. By the time Comstock's career reached its apogee at the turn of the century, the climate of opinion had shifted firmly away from the laxity and ambivalence which he had exploited. In the aftermath of the fall of Tweed, the New York State legislature passed another anti-abortion bill in 1872 which made the death of a fetus or pregnant woman punishable by a long prison sentence. Abortifacients could no longer legally be manufactured, advertised or sold. The cases of "medical malpractice" which began to appear in the press showed the unmistakable signs of Comstock's activities. In August 1872, he reported to Captain Byrne of the 15th precinct that the residence of Charles W. Selden at 67 Amity Street contained "a quantity of obscene goods." Byrne had been keeping the house under observation, having been alerted by Selden's advertisements in the press offering help for "special diseases." A warrant was obtained, and Byrne searched the house. "Proceeding into the front parlor," began the press report,

> Capt. Byrne found a young girl in a semi-nude condition lying on a sofa. She was very much frightened, but on being reassured of her safety by the Captain, said that her name was Barbara Voss, seventeen years old, German by birth, and residing at No. 326 Second Street, Jersey City. She said that she worked in a silver-plating establishment at the corner of John-street and Broadway. Becoming pregnant six weeks she informed her mother, who advised her to accompany [a machinist, 52, from Jersey City named Cushing] Savage to a doctor's office in Amity-street. She consented, and on Sunday the 18th inst., Savage brought her to Selden's place. Selden then used an electric battery on her, and then performed an operation with instruments. Not finding any change, she again went to Selden four days after, when another operation was performed. No effect being noticeable, she went to Selden's yesterday evening to learn her actual condition. Selden, Savage and the woman [Jenny] Sharp [who was Selden's assistant] were locked up in Fifteenth Precinct Station-house. Selden is thirty-three years old, of good education, and gentlemanly appearance. Dr. Steele was called by Capt. Byrne, and the girl Voss described to him the method of using the electric battery, and the character of the instruments used by Selden while

performing the operations. The girl Voss was sent to the House of Detention. The prisoners will be arraigned at Jefferson Market [Police Court] today.[99]

The story of "the girl Voss" is far more desperate than anything Comstock was prepared to acknowledge. With the encouragement of her mother, accompanied by someone who may have been nothing more than a neighbor, she twice submitted to pain—what, in another context, would be monstrous torture—and suffered the indignity of the failure of the attempted abortion, and consignment to the House of Detention on Blackwell's Island. Her story, if anyone cared to listen to it, effectively begins the legacy of Comstock for American women.

Other bit-players in the opening scenes of this story were:

July 1872, Hackettstown, NJ: Dr. Simon Taft is arrested for performing an abortion.

August 1872: Mrs. Clara Smith, a nineteen-year-old married woman, fearful of the pain of childbirth, dies after an abortion. It may have been self-administered.

October 1872, Louisiana: Ella Hersland dies after an abortion. A man named Collins is indicted for murder. Hersland's mother and sister are indicted as accessories.

October 1872: Emma Bristol, thirty-two, native of England, employed at A. T. Stewart's store in New York, is seduced by George Tompkins, proprietor of a wholesale tea store. Tompkins uses an "iron instrument for a criminal purpose." "Her condition is extremely critical."

November 1872, Rochester, NY: Esther Cole dies three days after an attempted abortion. She is buried secretly in Canada. Dr. Paul Davis, a physician of Rochester, is arrested for murder after her corpse is exhumed.

December 1872, Boston: Dr. C. A. Hill, a physician, and an assistant, are arrested for causing an abortion upon Mary A. McDonald.

February 1873: a letter protesting his innocence and appealing for help appears in the *New York Times* from Rosenzweig, the abortionist who was convicted of murdering Alice Bowlsby.

April 1873: Dr. David Brown of Boston, sixty-six, after serving a ten-year sentence for abortion is arrested for "medical malpractice." Jumps bail. He is found practicing medicine in New York under the name Kingcade.

April 1873: after responding to a letter from Comstock requesting pills and instructions for producing abortions, Dr. Wright of New York is arrested. Comstock is the only witness at Dr. Wright's trial.

April 1873, Chicago: Mrs. Hall dies suddenly at the Grand Central Hotel.
It is discovered that she has just had an abortion.[100]

It was against this background that the denouement of Restell's story
was played out.

It was the press which brought Comstock into contact with
"Madame Killer." He used the extraordinary latitude of the newspaper advertising columns, which had helped to expand the market
for abortion and pornography, as a way to entrap and punish the
guilty. As in the case of Dr. Wright in 1873, he would write, often
from addresses outside the city and with a false name, to publishers
of obscene literature, ordering copies of their publications. When
they were received he obtained a warrant to arrest the publisher
and seize his stock. Thus he turned the commercial strategy of the
pornographers into their greatest vulnerability. In 1872 Comstock
journeyed to Washington, where he urged upon the Congress an
amendment to the Post Office Act of June of that year. The
"Comstock Law," as it soon came to be known, made illegal the
importing, mailing or interstate transport of items "designed or
intended for the prevention of conception or the procuring of abortion."[101] Advertisements for abortifacients were less in evidence
after this amendment was passed in 1873. Although changes in the
wording of advertisements enabled the terms of the law to be evaded,
by the late 1870s the era of commercial visibility for abortion was
drawing to an end. Between 1873 and 1877, he was responsible
for the prosecution of more abortionists than any other person in
the United States, but it was noted that his percentage of convictions
was lower here than in any other area of his activity.[102] It is quite
possible that the sale of contraceptive information and abortifacients
continued largely as before. The relative ineffectuality of the
"Comstock Law" led Comstock, now appointed a Special Agent of
the United States Post Office, to seek another way to end the trade.
One of the crusader's bitterest enemies, De Robigné M. Bennett, had
an alternative theory about why Comstock decided to move against
Restell:

The treasure of his "Society for the Suppression of Vice" had become
exhausted. The donations of the previous year had not been as generous
as in other years, and it began to be a matter of some solicitude with
him as to where the money was to come from to admit of his drawing
his annual salary of four thousand dollars. It was believed that if two
or three indictments could be obtained against that wealthy woman,
who had obtained her money in so questionable a manner, large sums
could be drawn from her in the name of decency, morality and
religion.[103]

He approached the onslaught on the notorious Restell with the same energy and tactical cunning which had proven so effective against pornographers. He wrote to her from outside the city pretending to be the friend of an unmarried woman who was pregnant and desperately in need of help. It was the kind of story Restell had repeatedly heard for four decades, and she did not fail to respond. On 28 January 1878, Comstock called upon Madame Restell in the basement office in her "palace" on Fifth Avenue. He had disguised himself sufficiently to escape discovery, for by the late 1870s his was a familiar face, portrayed in numerous cartoons. He called again on 7 February, seeking medicines and instruments which would produce an abortion, as well as requesting professional advice from Restell on what he should do. In court he testified that on the 28th she sold him a bottle containing white powder and a syringe, and on 7 February he bought from Restell for ten dollars a package consisting of "a bottle of dark-colored liquid, an envelope with some small sugar pills and a few directions." He then proceeded to obtain a warrant for her arrest and returned on Monday, 11 February, to search the house and arrest Madame Restell. If Comstock expected to find clients having abortions in Restell's house, he was disappointed. He did not even find any instruments or medicines until he insisted upon entering what was described as the wine room. Here a large seizure was made. Why was a woman as rich as Restell bothering with such petty transactions? The only really plausible explanation is that she continued to sell her potions, pills and instruments because she felt some sympathy for pregnant women.

He took her before Justice Kilbreth at the Jefferson Market Police Court, where she was arraigned on the appropriate charges. Bail was set at $10,000, but when Restell produced this sum in bonds, the judge refused them, agreeing only to accept deeds of property to that value. It was late in the day and nothing could be done at such short notice. She was held overnight in The Tombs. On Tuesday the judge once again refused to accept her lawyer's offer of money in lieu of securities and she was taken to The Tombs for another night. The memory of detention in The Tombs in 1847, when she had been repeatedly denied bail, must have come flooding back. "I know where I am," remarked Bartleby when he arrived at The Tombs in Melville's "Story of Wall-Street," and so did Madame Restell.[104] This was the nightmare come back again. In the early 1840s she had been able to escape from the courts with the payment of a strategic bribe, but the attitude of the judge suggested that the old laxity had finally changed.

Now that she was in jail, she found it desperately hard to get out. On Wednesday her lawyer persuaded Judge Donohue in the Supreme

Court Chambers to issue a writ of habeas corpus to examine the legality of her detention. After legal argument, the judge was satisfied at Kilbreth's actions and dissolved the writ. Later that afternoon the Justice again agreed to accept bail for Restell, but only on the condition that sureties to the value of $10,000 would appear before the court. Restell's lawyer pleaded that public disclosure of their names would inhibit respectable people from coming forward. The Justice refused to ban the publication of their names, or to question them in private. Every step was calculated to hinder Restell's efforts to be released from The Tombs. The first surety to be examined, Francis J. Graham, was a boot-and-shoe maker whose business was at Vesey and Greenwich Streets. He claimed to own the building, and estimated its worth between $40,000 and $50,000. He had paid nearly $1,000 in tax on it the year before. But when Justice Kilbreth looked his name up in the city directory, it was revealed that Graham's real first name was Joseph. He told the court "that he had sometimes passed in social pleasantries as Francis instead of Joseph Graham" but that he "had never signed any papers or done any business except under his real name." He was accepted as a surety, but Graham refused to have his correct name appear in the papers as Restell's bondsman and declined to sign his name to the bail bond until another bondsman was secured. A "solid-looking business man, about 50" was the next person to be examined. Equally reluctant to be named in the press, he said he had a wife and family of children growing up, and "if his name was published as her bondsman, people would say that the Madame had done something for him and now compelled him to reciprocate by bailing her out of The Tombs, and that would disgrace his family." Without an assurance of anonymity, the second potential bondsman withdrew. Justice Kilbreth would not accept $10,000 in cash, plus the bond of Graham, and once again Restell was returned to The Tombs. One of her lawyers was heard to remark on leaving court: "Money! We've plenty of that. But what good is it with the newspapers against us?"[105]

On the next day, 14 February, two qualified sureties appeared in court, James Gonoude and Jacob Schwartz. Restell was allowed home for the night, but had to appear in court the next morning for an examination of the charges, a legal procedure to enable the defendant to know the nature of the charges against her: a magistrate only needed probable cause that an offense had occurred to order a trial. Accompanied by her grandson Charles Purdy, and "plainly but richly dressed in a costume of black silk, a black velvet overgarment ornamented with beads, and a black bonnet with a bright red feather and trimmings," Restell appeared in court on the 15th only to find that a postponement was necessary due to Comstock having prior commitments out of town. One of her sureties, James Gonoude, relinquished his role as bondsman, and hurried out of court rather than answer any questions. "Oh, he wasn't paid enough," remarked one of Restell's lawyers. Jacob Schwartz, a German Jewish baker, remained willing to continue as bondsman, and explained the arrangement between himself and her lawyers:

> "I thought something this morning of withdrawing. I don't know this woman. I never saw her before. But she has secured me by depositing to my account in the Union Trust Company $10,000 in Government bonds in the event of her forfeiture of bail, and I have the bank's receipt in my pocket. I don't think she is quite as bad as some other people in this world. She has acted squarely with me in this business, and so far as I'm concerned I want her to have a fair show. So let my name remain."[106]

The third surety was John Lauritz, a saloon-keeper on 12th Street and Seventh Avenue, who was observed by a sharp-eyed reporter of the *New York Times* to have rushed out of the courtroom in the middle of the proceedings saying he was going to Restell's house to receive $300 promised to him as a bonus. When the sums being paid to obtain sureties became generally known, large numbers of men anxious to "turn an honest penny" appeared at court to offer their services. Estimates appeared in the press that the struggle to obtain bondsmen had cost Restell fully $3,000 for the week.

At the postponed examination on 24 February, Restell's lawyer pleaded with Justice Kilbreth to hold the examination in private. But the judge did not agree that the public recital of the evidence was likely to prejudice a potential jury. Charles Purdy claimed that he was himself a member of the Society for the Suppression of Vice, and, in another appeal to Kilbreth on the second day of the examination, put forward the argument that the public reporting of the evidence against Restell would encourage those who could not resist temptation into crime. Purdy, we need reminding, was the leading defense counsel. (But Restell had already decided to drop him from the case and had successfully pleaded with ex-Judge Orlando L. Stewart to represent her at the trial.) When on Friday, 1 March, the final and, one suspects, pro forma, request for dismissal of the charges was denied and Restell was committed for trail, she elected to be tried in the Court of General Sessions. Once again the question of bail was raised. Purdy applied to Judge Donohue for a writ of certiorari and of habeas corpus to obtain Restell's release. Brought before Judge Lawrence on 5 March, she heard her lawyer argue that there was no evidence in the case beyond her own statements to Comstock, and that no proof had been offered that the articles she sold him actually could cause an abortion. After spending another night in The Tombs Restell was remanded in custody, the writs having been dismissed. Her lawyers immediately went before Judge Sutherland in the Court of General Sessions in an unsuccessful attempt to have the bail reduced. After some negotiations, bail was set at a prisoner's bond of $5,000, a like amount in a surety, and $10,000 deposited with the District Attorney's office. These were soon provided, and on 8 March Restell returned home. She appeared in court on the 12th, to hear that the grand jury had found true bills on both counts, and, on the 29th, she formally entered a plea of not guilty.

Restell's state of mind throughout February and March was carefully concealed from the public. Night after night in The Tombs her spirits had been raised and then dashed by each legal maneuver to gain her bail. Bail bondsmen, unwilling to be associated with her case in public, though quite willing secretly to take her money, were a repeated source of bitterness. Constant court appearances, the drain upon her financial resources, and nervous tension, all took their toll. The brave insouciance with which she walked onto Blackwell's Island in the 1840s was gone. The pressure of hostile public opinion, and a press which hounded her every step, mattered far more to her family now than it had done years ago. She had spent two decades and more trying in her own way to make sure that this would never happen to her again, and she could now see that she had failed. On 23 March, she deposited a new will at the office of the Surrogate, and requested that her previous will of 1875 be returned to her.

In court she was neatly dressed, calm, attentive and seemingly unconcerned at the course of the proceedings. She was wearing a dark plain dress, with an embroidered red cloak "that had had hard usage," a somber black velvet bonnet (with a black feather for decoration) and black kid gloves. The only hints of her wealth were the costly camel's hair shawl which she wore and a pair of diamond earrings. She was watched carefully for signs of remorse, or indeed of any hint of how she was coping with her ordeal. She appeared "haggard and drawn" to one journalist in court, who noted that her eyes were restless. In public she gave an appearance of dignified forbearance. She seemed to be determined to "carry it off," and slip out of the legal snares; New York had no respect for piteousness. An indication of what lay behind the façade came in early March when she decided to replace her attorney. Judge Stewart later said that when she called at his offices she seemed "much excited and nervous" and that she had thrown herself upon her knees and implored him to accept her as his client: "Oh, don't refuse me! Take my case. I am able to pay you well and willing to pay liberally. Do not refuse me! Do not send me away!"[107] He admitted some surprise at the "terror and anxiety" which the forthcoming trial had for Restell. He would have expected greater equanimity from someone so notorious, who had, even though decades ago, already been imprisoned. On subsequent visits she appeared more "calm and self-contained" and he thought nothing more about her fears. Word that the District Attorney had transferred the case to the Court of Oyer and Terminer, and had been put on the calendar for Monday, 1 April (when a date for trial would be set) only reached Stewart on Saturday, 30 March. Worried that Restell might hear of this sudden change of plans from her bail bondsmen, he hurried to "the palace" where he found her "in a state of great nervous anxiety." For years she had boldly denied feelings of guilt about abortion, but the news from her lawyer threw Restell into a state of panic. Were new, more serious charges to be filed against her? Dread of the forthcoming ordeal, and anxiety about its effects upon her family, robbed Restell of her composure and resilience. What she could not face was the public humiliation of her grandchildren. It was unthinkable. "She did not care for herself, but she could not endure to have them exposed to the disgrace of her public trial. She talked in an excited manner, cried, and made the most earnest and piteous appeals to me to stand by her and do what I could do for her. I staid by her and calmed her down until she seemed quite quiet."[108]

Members of her family recalled that Restell spent most of Sunday, 31 March walking through the house, talking to herself in a distraught manner. She repeatedly said that she could not endure a public trial, that she did not know why she had been put in such a position as she had never harmed anyone, and that she did not know why people were so bitter. Her granddaughter Carrie recalled later that Restell had several times said that "If I could only get sick and die. I wish I were dead, as it would then end all." She retired at nine o'clock, earlier than usual, and seemed a little calmer to her granddaughter.

At seven o'clock the next morning, the chambermaid, Maggie McGrath, noted that the bathroom door on the second floor was open, and that there was a nightdress thrown over the chair. After finishing her breakfast the maid knocked on the door of her mistress's bedroom. When there was no reply she entered the bathroom, where she found the folding wooden doors of the tub partly closed. Opening the doors she "uncovered a spectacle that curdled her blood and sent her screaming with horror from the room." The tub was filled with warm, pale red water and in it lay the naked body of Madame Restell with one hand extended slightly out of the water, the other dropped at her side. The chambermaid's screams alerted the household. One of the servants saw an eight-inch carving knife in bottom of the tub.

A servant was sent to fetch Judge Stewart, who notified the coroner and the court where Restell was due to appear later that morning. Coroner Woltman and Deputy Coroner Cushman arrived in mid-morning and examined the body which they found still in the tub. There was a deep incised wound across the throat of the dead woman, extending from ear to ear. They also noted that two attempts had been made with the knife before the final cut. Depositions were taken from everyone in the household, while the undertaker packed the body in ice and moved it to the floor of the parlor. The coroner returned later that evening with his jury which quickly reached a verdict of suicide. To avoid further scandal the family decided on a private burial the next day. The casket was sealed and carried in a hearse to Grand Central Depot where it was placed on the 11:03 train for Tarrytown. Madame Restell was buried beside her husband in the picturesque Sleepy Hollow Cemetery, in a plot which sloped gently towards the banks of the Hudson. Hers was the largest and most ostentatious monument in that part of the cemetery. No doubt those who knew something of the activities of Ann Lohman viewed the carved figure of a sleeping infant on the monument with mixed emotions.

Wild stories continued to circulate in the city for weeks after her shocking death. It was said that Restell had escaped to Europe (the bolt-hole of choice of the Tweed Ring), or to Canada, and that the woman found in the bathtub was actually the corpse of a patient who had died at her hands, and that neither the coroner nor his deputy nor anyone in the jury knew her well enough to make a proper identification. Another story which briefly circulated was that she had been murdered by wealthy people to prevent the disclosure of their names in a trial. One of her bondsmen, John Lauritz, claimed to have received a telegram from Restell in Paris. "Dot vas a bum corpse," he was heard to claim. In the eyes of the *New York Times*, she had led a "criminal life" and Comstock boasted that she was the fifteenth person who had been driven to suicide by his purity crusade.[109] Whitman's cheers soon ceased. The postmaster in Boston, who often took a lead in such matters, proposed to exclude copies of Whitman's *Leaves of Grass* from the United States mail under a provision of the "Comstock Law."[110]

"Boss" Tweed died in Ludlow Street Prison less than two weeks after Restell's suicide. John Morrissey, pugilist and opponent of Tweed in the Democratic Party, died on May Day. William Cullen Bryant, for so long the soul of the New York Democracy, died less than two weeks later. On the 19th, Washington Vermilye, member of

"Hers was the largest...": Sleepy Hollow Cemetery, Tarrytown, NY.

the Committee of Seventy, died. Later in the summer Evert Duyckinck, man of letters and friend of Herman Melville, died; a day later, on 14 August, he was followed by John Van Buren, the son of the ex-President and a powerful force in the Democratic Party. In mid-October Ambrose Kingsland, sperm-oil merchant and the proposer of Central Park during his term as mayor died.[111] It was a time for funerals, and, in some cases, for heartfelt mourning. In a bare six months Restell, Tweed and the rest had been swept from the scene.

CHAPTER THREE

"Slippery Dick"

On the art of rising in the city

T he son of an Irish village schoolteacher, Richard Barrett
Connolly emigrated to America in 1826.

> So adieu, my dear father, adieu, my dear mother,
> Farewell to my sister, farewell to my brother;
> I am bound for America, my fortune to try . . .
> > "The Streams of Bunclody" (ballad)[1]

He was sixteen and joined an older brother already in America.
Another version has it that he came to New York when "very young"
and that he was educated in public schools in the city.[2] A third
Connolly boy remained in Ireland and was said to have become a
wealthy man. No "Ragged Dick," he was a model young immigrant,
reputed to have impressed his teachers as "a bright and apt scholar,
excelling especially in mathematics, of which he was peculiarly
fond." Without a large, supportive family to smooth his way forward
(nothing more is heard about his older brother), Connolly was
largely on his own. President Jackson was in the White House, and
young men like Connolly felt that the world was theirs for the taking.
He was not backward when opportunities came his way. He lived
for a time in Philadelphia, and only settled in New York "owing to
a low intrigue with a market-woman."[3] He was first employed by the
auctioneers John Heggarty & Sons, where he remained "about eight
years." He then worked for Simeon Draper, who had married
Heggarty's daughter and became one of the city's wealthiest and
most prestigious auctioneers. Draper was a prominent two-fisted

Warning the unwary of the notorious mock auctions held on Chatham Street, opposite the park.

Whig politician who led a Whig mob in the election riots in 1834.[4] Working for years in the respectable end of the auction business would have been quite an education in the ways of the business world. New York was notorious for its "mock" auctions, and there was much for a bright, quick-eyed young man to learn—about the false bidders, the nearby "respectable" merchants who willingly affirmed the genuineness of fake gems or jewelry, subtle switches of goods after the auction, and the mixing of lower-value goods with the higher quality material offered at the auction. Above all, let us assume that Connolly, not yet "Slippery Dick," observed, and learned the many uses of a carefully constructed façade of earnestness and sincerity which was necessary for the successful operation of a mock auction.[5] In 1866, the *Manual of the Corporation* included an engraving of a group of decrepit two-story houses on Chatham Street, opposite the park. A figure stands in the street holding a placard, "Beware of Mock Auctions," while various figures point. It is an enigmatic image, perhaps included in the *Manual* as a hint that such practices were part of the city's past, that reform and publicity had rid the city of such frauds. That was far from the truth. Connolly was elected comptroller in 1866, and his greatest and most persuasive performance was about to begin.

During this early period in Connolly's life, he resided in the 7th ward, a low area of docks, warehouses and over-crowded housing bounded by Catherine Street, East Broadway and Gouverneur Street on the East River. Connolly entered Democratic Party politics as a young man, and soon became "an adroit manager of ward meetings and primaries" and was appointed secretary of the ward Central Committee. There are few contemporary records to mark his rise up the ladder of politics, but rumors about Connolly long persisted: "It was said that, while his neat penmanship was much admired, he could not be trusted to count votes correctly," wrote M. R. Werner in 1928. Werner's source for this story was Charles F. Wingate, writing in 1874: "Though his neat penmanship was admired, he could not be trusted even to count votes after a ballot." Counting votes "correctly" in the ward elections in the 1830s did not always mean what reformers forty years later wanted it to mean. The *Irish Citizen* sardonically asked: "What does a political address mean when it asks for honest men? Why it means men of our party."[6]

The myth of success in America, the "poor-boy-makes-good" saga, takes on a particularly interesting twist with Connolly. In 1868, at a time when he was approaching the apogee of his political career in New York, *Ragged Dick or Street Life in New York* was published by Horatio Alger, Jr. By then, Connolly had long been nicknamed "Slippery Dick." His contemporaries, or at least those on the inside at Tammany Hall, regarded him as untrustworthy, dishonest, and in every respect the antithesis of the "frank, straight-forward" and above all honest hero of Alger's moral fables for adolescents. Yet he was perhaps the truer child of the myth of success than "Ragged Dick." He, too, was "an enterprising young man" who, when he saw a chance for a speculation, was "determined to avail himself of it."[7] "Slippery Dick" did not invest in Erie rail shares, as "Ragged Dick" teasingly suggested he regularly did. Rather, he was part of the machinery, led by Jay Gould and Jim Fisk, which bilked the Erie shareholders out of their wealth. "Ragged Dick's" bankbook was stolen by Jim Travis, a fellow-resident of their boarding house. Far, far better to be the one who as comptroller steals the bank altogether.[8] Travis was sentenced as a petty thief to nine months on Blackwell's Island. "Slippery Dick" slipped through the hands of the law and spent his last years comfortably in European exile.

Scarcely anyone who knew "Slippery Dick," and few people since then, have thought him worth defending. Other members of the Ring—the political milking-machine orchestrated by "Boss" Tweed, which also included the mayor Oakey Hall, and Peter B. ("Brains" or "Bismarck") Sweeny—have had their partisans. After all, even though they stole a lot of money, they did some good for the city in the process. One historian has described their regime as a nascent welfare state.[9] Connolly was the comptroller, the treasurer, of New York City from 1867 to 1871; but he cut and ran, some saying that he got away with as much as six million dollars. In his European exile Connolly became the scapegoat for the Ring. Tweed died in prison; although disgraced, Sweeny and Hall remained in the city. Ironically, "Slippery Dick" was himself betrayed by the reformers, led by the priggish, self-righteous Democrat Samuel J. Tilden, who rose to national prominence through his attacks upon the urban corruptionists. But when it came to betrayal, they were all experts. His fellow conspirators, encouraged by Tweed, tried to throw all the blame on Connolly. Damned on all sides as "Slippery Dick," it is as though he, and not the carnival of treachery and ambition which was New York politics in the 1860s and 1870s, was the real villain of the piece.

Connolly was a vivid and easily recognizable figure. His double chin and expansive body were, like Tweed's diamond stickpin, evidence for the prosecution. Even in an age in which male portliness was admired, Connolly was a bloated figure. (No slouch himself, Tweed regularly threatened to top 300 lb.) Although he was more than a dozen years older than Tweed, the cartoonists who portrayed Connolly gave no hint of the man's age, or of the qualities noted in the *New York Herald* in 1871, late in Connolly's public career: "The Comptroller stood consulting with County Auditor Lynes, and although looking somewhat anxious was nevertheless quite pleasant. His profile resembled that of Washington perhaps more than ever, and he carried himself with a nonchalance most extraordinary in view of the exciting and troublous incidents connected with the situation."[10] Admittedly, the *Herald* was not a newspaper in the vanguard of opposition to the Ring; but to make such a comparison, at a moment when accusations of theft and fraud were repeatedly being heard, suggests that the character of Connolly is as much an issue as his actions. Connolly's decision to put the comptroller's office at the disposal of the reformers opened the first massive crack in the seemingly impregnable Ring. Few remembered that Connolly, now fallen from power, had once seemed a dignified man, or that the *New York Times* had praised him in 1859 as someone who "almost alone stands forth untainted by the breath of distrust." When Connolly ran for comptroller in 1866, he had been endorsed by the *Herald* in fulsome terms: "Richard B. Connolly is the only candidate in the field who is really properly qualified to discharge the duties of the office. He is a shrewd man, a good financier and wholly independent of all cliques and factions."[11] The men of standing who brought the Ring down in 1871 were quick to blacken the character of Tweed, Connolly and their associates.

The line on Connolly was firmly established during his lifetime. Abram Genung, writing in 1871 while Connolly was still in office, said that "the facility with which he made and broke promises was his most marked characteristic." Genung also affirmed that Connolly was nothing less than "the most unmitigated liar in the community." Charles Wingate portrayed the ex-comptroller in 1874 as "cold, crafty, and cowardly, with a smooth, oily, insinuating manner." Theodore P. Cook recalled Connolly in 1876 as "a timid man, but greedy" who contributed to the Ring "an abundance of low cunning." After his death, these characterizations were readily repeated. Matthew Breen described Connolly in 1899 as "mean and crafty." John D. Townsend remembered him in 1901 as "the coldest and most unfeeling one of the gang." Virtually everyone who has written about the Tweed Ring has followed suit: to Albert Bigelow Paine in 1904 Connolly was "without an honest bone in his body." De Alva Stanwood Alexander described him in 1909 as "mean and crafty." Although he seemed to be "the most respectable of the three [Ring] figures in appearance," Allan Nevins argued in 1922 that Connolly was "an ignorant Irish-born bookkeeper" who brought "low cunning, the product of a mixture of cowardice and greed" to the public life of the city. M. R. Werner concluded in 1928 that Connolly was "crafty, insinuating, but somewhat cowardly." So firmly entrenched were these judgments that they were repeated by Oakey Hall's biographer, Croswell Bowen, in 1956 ("an unctuous, Uriah Heep-type book keeper") and by Seymour J. Mandelbaum, in a judicious assessment of Tweed in 1965 ("an obsequious man").[12] He may have been all of these things—mean, crafty and unctuous— but it is hard not to feel that the denunciations of Connolly essentially derive from the highly partisan views of the reformers who were his enemies and who drove him out of public life.

After the fall of the Ring, a new narrative was written about public life in American cities. The leading parts were once again to be assigned to men of probity. The old script, the old corrupt fiction, was at last to be exposed and driven out of circulation. But the corruptionists, and their pictures of city life, were deeply entrenched and artfully contrived. In August 1870, the board of aldermen of the city of New York directed John Hardy, clerk of the common council, to compile and publish a *Manual of the Corporation of the City of New York* for that year. The corporation *Manuals* had been published since 1841, becoming progressively larger and more expensive. They contain a cornucopia of historical information about the public life of the city, including descriptions of virtually every institution,

"A cornucopia of information about the city . . . the *Manual* . . . is also one of the most extravagant fictions produced in New York in the nineteenth century." The symbolism of the design, drawing upon the seal granted to New Amsterdam, alludes to the sources of the community's early wealth, the beaver pelt. The windmill and public or private, and the names of governing bodies, trustees and officers. A complete list appears of the occupants of the venerable public offices of the city corporation, and the state of New York, as does the vote, ward by ward, for the mayoralty from 1834 to 1869. The *Manual* contains ancient street plans, charts of the harbor, and a miscellany of reprinted historical documents relating to the colonial city. In addition to its role as gazetteer, a great deal of current financial information is included, from the funded debt to city appropriations and expenditures. There are hundreds of graceful engravings of buildings and street scenes, suggesting an orderly community, with well-maintained streets, handsome houses and dignified public buildings. The *Manual* of the corporation is an extremely useful reference book; it is also one of the most extravagant fictions produced in New York in the nineteenth century.

The *Manual* contains no entry for Tammany Hall, the political body which for most of the century dominated the Democratic Party in the city. Nor is there a portrait of Tammany's leader, William M. Tweed. Yet Tammany and Tweed were by far the most important facts about New York in 1870. As it saw itself and was perceived by most Americans, New York scarcely appears in the *Manual*. For a sense of the city as its inhabitants experienced it, we should probably turn to any of a dozen guides to the pleasures and vices of the city. People wanted to read about New York and its scandals. Alger's *Ragged Dick*, when it was not actively engaged in reforming morals, was a well-informed guide book to the sights and scenes of the city, and a dossier of scams and urban trickery, such as the notorious drop-game and the bogus check swindle.[13] Matthew Hale Smith's *Sunshine and Shadow in New York* (1868), written for an adult audience, was a compilation of gossip, anecdote and inside information about the city's lowlife and its great institutions. He takes his readers into Harry Hill's Dance-House, and analyzes the failures and successes of popular showman P. T. Barnum. There are accounts of the grand hotels and shops, sketches of the lives of the rich (John Jacob Astor, Cornelius Vanderbilt, August Belmont) and portraits of eminent figures of the legal establishment, the churches and the press. Smith includes detailed accounts of city beggars, tramps, prostitutes, gambling-houses, con-men, street-walkers, and houses of assignation

(*caption continued*)
barrel recall the flour-milling monopoly granted to the city in 1678. It is not the mock auctions, low saloons, stinking tenements, political corruption and gangs like the Dead Rabbits which stand for the city, but a nobler vision of communication, trade, learning, medicine and the intrepidity of an Indian sachem which constitute the heritage of city, as viewed by the common council in 1870.

Tammany Hall was a place—a large hall and hotel on East 14th Street—and a band of political confederates who donned ceremonial gear, bestowed honorific Indian titles upon each other, and ruthlessly dominated the Democratic Party in New York City for virtually the whole of the nineteenth century.

and explains the ways of New York swindlers and blackmailers. Put beside the elaborate artifice of the *Manual* of the corporation, *Ragged Dick* and *Sunshine and Shadow in New York* portray a world dominated by the extremes of implausible virtue and tempting vice. The *Manual* exhibits the face which Tweed and his administration sought to present to the world. To the Union League Club, it represented little more than ". . . a miscellaneous collection of useless trash . . .", published at a larcenously high cost.[14] Smith's guide, and the many similar books which contain roughly the same material and from the same point of view, presents the form of contemporary concern about the city, juxtaposing stories about crimes and urban vice with accounts of the successful and virtuous. The sheer act of conjunction gave a powerful hint about the way the city itself was understood.[15] Was the "Shadow" to prevail, and the prostitutes and criminals left to corrupt the entire nation? Or were the philanthropists, churchmen and virtuous men in commerce and the law to lead the community to bask in the "Sunshine" of morality and good works? The events which resulted in the downfall of the Tweed Ring in 1871 were further proof, if anyone doubted, that the city, and especially New York City, was the supreme battlefield of the age upon which virtue struggled against vice.

The story of the destruction of the Ring was repeatedly told in the aftermath of 1871, and many historians in our own time have accepted judgments made in the heat of the battle, promulgated by the victorious side. One of the most conspicuous victims of the way this story has been told was "Slippery Dick."

Connolly felt himself to be the odd man out in Tweed's Ring, for he was an Irishman, born in County Cork in 1810. (Was "Brains" Sweeny, the son of an Irishman who kept a saloon in Park Row, any less *Irish* than Connolly? Hardly.) Being an Irishman in New York was not an unmixed blessing. The distinguished lawyer Charles O'Conor, whose family had been in America for two generations (his father Thomas had edited *The Shamrock*, the first paper in New York specifically for Irish and Catholic readers), claimed that he had suffered professionally and politically because he was Irish and Roman Catholic. O'Conor, a renowned lawyer and pro-slavery Democrat, insisted that "his supposed nationality and his faith had always obstructed his path."[16] In the struggle against the Tweed gang, the reformers turned to O'Conor for advice, and appointed him Special State Attorney General to pursue the vast sums stolen by Tweed's associates. O'Conor's professional reputation overcame the disadvantage of his Irishness; but in the popular mind the "popular" prejudices about the Irish reigned largely unchallenged. At mid-century the Irish were seen as rowdy ne'er-do-wells, impulsive, quarrelsome, drunken and threadbare. Thomas Nast's drawings of simian, pipe-smoking Irish proletarians, and his fierce anti-Catholic cartoons, were from the same pen which so devastatingly portrayed Tweed and the Ring.[17] The Irish, and immigrants in general, were blamed for urban vice.

In a climate increasingly hostile to Roman Catholicism and the Irish, Connolly found that it was easier to accept and use Irishness than to transcend it, as Charles O'Conor had done. The willingness to *use* Irishness masks an ambivalence in Connolly. He was a skeptic in matters of religion and chose not to marry within the immigrant community at a time when Catholic-Protestant intermarriages were exceedingly rare. Though in time he became recognized as an expert on all matters Irish in the eyes of his Tammany colleagues, there is some reason to doubt whether he ever won the complete confidence of the Irish community, or at least of certain elements within it. There was more to Connolly than the identities of professional Irishman and New York Irish politician. After (white) manhood suffrage was extended in New York in the late 1820s, the Democratic Party and Tammany Hall had its uses for young Irish-American politicians like

Connolly, whose task was to bring the Irish working class to the voting stations on behalf of Tammany Democrats. He rose to power on the brimming Irish vote, and was one of the first generation of ethnic politicians who consolidated the Democratic Party's hold upon the big city immigrant population. In turn Tammany offered Connolly a vehicle for his personal ambitions in a city whose Protestant population and commercial elite were largely determined to exclude the Irish from political power.

In the fragmentary and sometimes self-serving accounts of Connolly's early years we see the outline of a career, a path followed by many ambitious young Irishmen in America. While working at the auctioneers he began to attend local ward meetings of the Democratic Party. In time he was made secretary of the committee of management. In a political culture of fanatical partisanship, Connolly was a noted partisan, one of the "Hooray Boys."[18] At first through minor tasks, and then perhaps with particular services to powerful men in the party, he began to be noticed. In 1836 he served as a delegate to the nominating convention for the 11th ward. A year later, at the age of twenty-seven, he married Maria ("Mary") Schenck Townsend, twenty-one, who was described in the *New York Times* as "the daughter of an old New Yorker." The ceremony took place at the Orchard Street Universalist Church. (The clergyman who officiated at their marriage survived to address Mrs. Connolly's funeral at the Fourth Universalist Church at 45th Street and Fifth Avenue in 1879.) Marriage in a liberal Protestant church immediately marked Connolly out as an unusual Irish New Yorker. His public career seems not to have directly suffered as a result; rather, it may have made his relations with financiers and bankers somewhat easier. Mary Connolly, who had been a member of the board of trustees of the New York Medical College of Women, was affectionately remembered for her charitable works.

Continuing to work for auctioneers in the city, he increasingly devoted himself to political matters. He was elected to the Tammany Society on 21 October 1839, and that year served as secretary to the Tammany Young Man's General Committee, which, under the chairmanship of Fernando Wood, had moved the party's moderates decisively towards Locofocoism and anti-monopolyism. The Tammany Old Guard, who generally supported Andrew Jackson but who represented substantial financial interests threatened by an excessively vigorous anti-monopoly policy (and thus were known as Bank Democrats) were in the way, and Wood, with Connolly a pace or two behind, led the revision of alignments which promised to drive them out of the party.[19]

Two years his junior, Wood was a high-flyer, already aiming at a congressional seat and even greater things. Having been a Quaker, clerk, grocer, cigar-roller and "the keeper of a low groggery," he represented a decisive break with the gentlemen merchants who had previously held power in New York. (To his opponents, Wood was "[t]he king of the Dead Rabbits, that indomitable knave and demagogue . . .".)[20] Elected to Congress at the age of twenty-eight in 1840, he was "the people's candidate . . . a Democrat of the Democrats, the standard bearer of the Bowery Boys, the Fourth Warders, and of the Bloody Sixth."[21] During his term in Washington, Fernando Wood was a good Jacksonian Democrat who opposed the establishment of a national bank, opposed tariffs to aid domestic manufactures, and, in the name of the "simple republicanism" of his constituents, opposed the financial estimates which would create "a powerful and splendid navy, with all its paraphernalia of pomp and tyranny." Wood supported states' rights and regularly voted with pro-slavery Southern Democrats. Indeed, of the forty-one-strong New York congressional delegation, he "was easily the most pro-Southern."[22] His election as mayor in 1854 shook the younger generation of Tammany "Braves," such coming men as "Honest John" Kelly, Peter B. Sweeny and William M. Tweed. The most prolonged battles of their political careers were aimed at preventing Wood from completely dominating Tammany during his three terms as mayor (1854–8, 1860–62). Connolly played an important role in the struggle, for it was widely believed that he alone could challenge Wood's control of the Irish vote.[23] But by all accounts, Connolly and Wood worked harmoniously together on the Young Men's General Committee, which was responsible for staging mass meetings, printing and distributing posters and leaflets, and no doubt in providing fists and stout shoulders on behalf of Tammany candidates during elections.

With a young and growing family, the Connollys moved frequently in the early 1840s. At first they lived at 172 East Broadway, then at 175 Henry Street and then at 26 Gouverneur Street.[24] Their world was remote from the New York of the brownstone houses and the elegance of Fifth Avenue, that placid and uneventful scene which Edith Wharton recalled in her memoirs, "along which genteel landaus, broughams and victorias, and more countrified vehicles of the 'carry-all' and 'surrey' type moved up and down at decent intervals and a decorous pace." Connolly was a politician in an age in which respectable New Yorkers were coming to regard politics with the same haughty contempt which they felt towards those engaged in "trade." ("No retail dealer," recalled Edith Wharton with grim relish, "no matter how palatial his shop-front or how tempting his millions, was received in New York society until long after I was grown up.")[25] Wealthy men accounted for two-thirds of the aldermen in New York in 1826. By 1837, that figure was down to three-eighths, and the proportion was reduced to one-quarter by the middle of the century. Merchants and lawyers made up nearly half of the membership of the city council between 1825 and 1837. Over the next dozen years they only represented a quarter of the membership.[26] The organs of respectable opinion repeatedly called this state of affairs to the attention of their readers, alternately blaming the phenomenon of the vanishing elite on the political system itself, or upon the excesses of democracy. This was one of the most salient of the "unforeseen tendencies" of democracy itself.[27] A typical note was sounded in the *North American Review* in October 1866:

> That the government of the city of New York has had, for several years past, an exceedingly bad name in the world, is probably known to all our readers. It has fallen into complete contempt. It is a dishonor to belong to it. Persons of good repute do not willingly associate with the rulers of the city, unless they are known to be of the small number who hold their offices for the purpose of frustrating iniquitous schemes.[28]

The withdrawal of the social and financial elites from politics was the central feature of city life as Connolly's generation experienced it. The politics of the federal period were cited by older residents, who nostalgically recalled a New York in which corruption was uncommon. (They had perhaps forgotten the acrimonious debates about the spoils system which had played such a major part in the politics of the early decades of the century.) The belief was widespread that the decay of public morality was but a generation old. "Twenty-five years ago, the best, the most intelligent, the most active men of the city, of all classes and vocations, did not hesitate to devote hours, and days, and nights of their time, without hope or desire of remuneration, to the affairs of the city."[29] It was every bit as universally believed that the withdrawal of the gentry from public life had left a vacuum into which the unscrupulous rushed. "Probably there never was a time before in New-York when citizens with such perfect unanimity looked *away* from the City Fathers, as if from *them* none were so verdant as to expect help."[30]

Patronage

Connolly's future in New York politics was decided in the course of a dispute over the patronage exercised by the new Democratic president, James K. Polk. After his election in November 1845, he was urged by rival factions in the New York Democratic Party to get rid of the incumbent collector of the port, Cornelius Van Ness, whose vigorous removal of subordinates in 1844 marked him as among the most pliant supporters of President John Tyler. It was an important position, perhaps the most important patronage position at the disposal of the President. The collector was the highest paid official in the federal government; his formal duties consisted of receiving and recording manifests of and documents relating to ships arriving in the port of New York, and receiving all duties paid. His equally important responsibilities were political: his every activity was intended to strengthen the administration in the most populous city of the largest state. The collector's office was in an imposing Greek Revival pile, the New Custom House, located at the corner of Wall and Nassau Streets.[31] Desperate to retain his job, Van Ness placed most of the collector's powers of patronage in the hands of a faction of the Democratic Party, the conservative Hunkers led by ex-governor William Marcy. In return for their support, Van Ness agreed to remove from office all of their radical opponents, followers of ex-President Van Buren contemptuously known as the Barnburners. Van Ness was a friend of Senator John Calhoun and his maintenance in office was a daily reminder, in the eyes of the Van Burenites, of Polk's submission to the southern wing of the party. In May 1845 Polk decided to keep Van Ness in office while appeasing the Van Burenites with other appointments. The maneuver did not work. Van Ness's attempts to gain influence within Tammany backfired when the Barnburners secured a working majority at the society's spring nominating convention (where William Havemeyer, the sugar merchant and supporter of Van Buren, was nominated for mayor). In conversation with Samuel J. Tilden, the New York lawyer active in Democratic politics, Polk "complained bitterly of the attempts to intimidate and coerce him" on the subject of Van Ness. It seemed as though he could please no one whether Van Ness stayed or went.[32] The Hunkers demanded that the president keep Van Ness, but, surprisingly, were the only ones who were satisfied when Polk decided to replace the collector with Cornelius W. Lawrence, a banker who had been Democratic mayor of New York for three terms in 1834–7. One of the most important sources of political patronage was now safely in the hands of the conservative wing of the Democratic Party.[33]

Connolly was appointed by Van Ness to a clerkship in the Custom House, and so highly did the new collector appreciate Connolly's abilities that he was made chief of the statistical bureau. Connolly's obituary in the *Herald* explains that Lawrence used his influence with the secretary of the Treasury, Robert J. Walker, to secure for Connolly a role in the revision of the tariff of 1846. The

"Walker Tariff" was one of the lowest the country had known, and was obviously to the taste of most New York Democrats. Connolly, the man who was accused of dishonesty and incompetence, demonstrated in the Custom House a high degree of professional skill.

The account of these events in Connolly's *New York Times* obituary in 1880 differs in almost every detail and interpretation. As they tell it, Connolly's first political office came in 1847, "the last year of President Tyler's term." But Tyler left office in 1845. The obituary states that Connolly was appointed by Cornelius Van Ness, and, although he was soon promoted and given an increased salary, he was busy forming a ring to control patronage in the auditor's office:

> His scheme contemplated the removal of the Auditor, but that officer discovered the plot and frustrated it by having Connolly ousted from his department. He was retained in Government employ, however, all through the term of Collector Lawrence, who succeeded Van Ness, but he was transferred to the "Statistical Bureau," where a clerkship was provided for him. When Collector [Hugh] Maxwell assumed control at the Custom House [in 1849], Connolly's friends lost their power and his services were dispensed with.

The *New York Times* story was based upon a letter published in that newspaper on 17 September 1871, which appeared at the height of a sustained effort by reformers to discredit Connolly. It was, in other words, a highly partisan source. It is conceivable that Connolly, a well-known Democratic loyalist, might have received preferment from Van Ness, who sought to please Democrats in New York. But even Charles Francis Adams, Jr., whose articles appeared under Wingate's name, and who seldom failed to repeat an unfavorable story about Connolly, said nothing about any skullduggery in the auditor's office. Without independent corroboration, the episode must be relegated to the myths and lies circulated by Connolly's enemies.

When Zachary Taylor was elected President on the Whig ticket in 1848, Nathaniel Hawthorne lost his post as surveyor of the revenue in the Salem Custom House.[34] He described himself as having been beheaded by the partisans of the incoming administration. "The moment when a man's head drops off is seldom or never, I am inclined to think, precisely the most agreeable of his life," he mused, in the first chapter of *The Scarlet Letter* (1850). The whole of the "Custom-House" chapter in his novel was a subtle and decidedly "posthumous" revenge against those who engineered his expulsion from office, and the similar fate suffered by hundreds of Democratic

Party supporters across the country—among whose number was Richard B. Connolly. After being expelled from the Custom House in New York, he moved to the post of discount clerk in the Bank of North America, where he remained from 1849 to 1852. The former mayor William F. Havemeyer became president of the bank in 1851. Asked years later about Connolly's work, he affirmed that he "performed all his duties faithfully, in spite of his City Hall tendencies."[35] Havemeyer noted that Connolly "did not evince any great financial abilities," but the *New York Times* claimed that he had given "excellent satisfaction" to his employers.

Connolly won the Tammany Hall nomination for county clerk in 1852. Resigning from the bank upon his election, he served in that office until the end of the decade. Havemeyer recalled, in a scene worthy of the later career of Richard Hunter, Esq., formerly "Ragged Dick," having offered his discount clerk some sensible advice upon his return to public life:

> "Now, Dick Connolly, as long as you remain in office, remain a poor man; it will save you endless worry and trouble. If you save $500 or $1,000, buy a house and say nothing about it. When you retire from office you will have one or two houses half paid for, you will not have been bothered by importunate borrowers of money, and you will have saved your reputation as an honest man."[36]

With what expression did Connolly listen to these sentiments from his employer, who ranked among the wealthiest men in New York?[37] The *New York Times* primly recalled that during Connolly's two terms as county clerk "no charges other than those of a political nature were made against him, and in general he fulfilled his duties in a manner creditable to himself and satisfactory to the tax-payer." Ironically, it was the very same newspaper which extravagantly praised Connolly a few days before his successful bid for re-election in 1855. It was a sentence the editors of the *Times* preferred to forget: "Mr. Connolly's friends have much reason to feel proud of their nominee, for amid all the storm, and whirlwind of public suspicion, the crop of indictments for corruption, and the complaints for inefficiency against public officers, he, almost alone, stands forth untainted by the breath of distrust—the idol and the nominee of every branch of the great Democratic family."[38]

The "political" complaints, and "City Hall tendencies" recalled by Havemeyer are virtually all that survive to record Connolly's political activities in the early 1850s. (He had written to President Franklin Pierce in 1853 on behalf of an "active, energetic working Democrat" named Turner who was seeking a post in the new administration. Connolly said nothing of Turner's abilities, but emphasized the applicant's "many valuable services towards the success of his party in this and other states." That was the way politics worked.)[39] In the office of county clerk his opportunities for political intrigue were limitless, but outside Tammany Hall he remained invisible. He had no place in high "society." Of his private life in these years, his relations with his family and children, nothing is known. He was one of those hungry, effective men who swept into politics in the wake of the "better persons" who were steadily moving uptown and removing themselves from the hurly-burly of public life. Havemeyer's sententious advice came as though from another planet.

The struggle against the mayor

The disappearance of the Whigs after 1852 removed an influential party from city politics and encouraged insurgency within the ranks of the Democrats. "Workerist" demands for relief intensified in the depression in the middle of the decade and national political issues were reflected in the disputes between "Free-Soil" Democrats and their conservative enemies, the pro-Southern Hunkers who were accusing the "Free-Soils" of being abolitionists and Barnburners.[40] The leader of Tammany Hall was the demagogic Fernando Wood, failed Democratic candidate for mayor in 1850 and victor in a four-cornered election for mayor in November 1854.

Opposed to Wood were the great array of reformers, conservative Democrats, ex-Whigs, nativists and an ambitious and opportunistic group of young politicians on the make led by ex-congressman Tweed, county clerk Connolly, and Peter B. Sweeny, who was instructed by Connolly in the fine art of political oratory. Connolly appears as a schemer and a Tammany insider in the early 1850s. Recognizing that their internal disputes threatened to keep them from the sinecures of city and state office in the aftermath of the defeat of Wood by the Whig sperm-oil dealer Ambrose Kingsland in the 1850 mayoral election, the council of sachems formed a "unity" committee of Barnburner and Hunker sachems—Elijah Purdy, Daniel Delavan and Connolly—to persuade various national politicians of the party's commitment to lofty, patriotic sentiments. A year later he was a member of the committee of arrangements for the traditional Tammany Fourth of July festivities. In 1853, Connolly was deeply involved in internecine warfare between "Hards" and "Softs," factions which coalesced in the late 1840s. Personal ambition first, and attitudes towards the Missouri Compromise of 1850 (supported by the Hards) and the Fugitive Slave Law (opposed by the Softs, whose ranks included advocates of "popular" or squatter sovereignty as well as former Free Soilers) defined the fluid pattern of allegiances. Fernando Wood was a Soft. Connolly aligned himself with the Hards, and went down to defeat in the April 1853 elections for sachems which was swept by the Softs, led by Elijah Purdy and Isaac V. Fowler. The men who had formed the notorious Tweed Ring sized each other up in the struggle to deny Wood the nomination for mayor. Connolly's activities in the Young Men's Democratic Union Club brought him into contact with some interesting people; along with Isaac H. Bailey, the wealthy tanner Jackson S. Schultz and Henry G. Stebbins (who were to play major roles in the fall of the Tweed Ring in 1871), Connolly was elected a vice-president of a mass meeting held in the City Hall Park in support of the amended city charter of 1853 which was designed to throw out the "Forty Thieves."[41]

Presenting himself as a moderate healer of the divisions between Hards and Softs, Wood ignored contentious national issues in his successful campaign for mayor in 1854, offering instead a vision of an honest and efficiently managed city government. His moves to assert the mayor's nonpartisan control over the ramshackle New York police force alarmed conservatives, who denounced his "one-man rule." Vigorous actions to improve street cleaning and other reforms met with mixed success. Even those who supported the idea of a large park in the city were unhappy when Wood took control of the project in 1856. It was noted that Wood owned properties adjacent to the park, and such an enterprise left in his hands seemed to his enemies a classic example of graft and corruption masquerading as a desirable public improvement. The prospect of important new sources of employment had undoubtedly strengthened Wood's standing with the working class during his first term as mayor. He was re-elected in 1856, and amidst repeated accusations of fraud and dishonesty, when the opportunity presented itself in 1857, Republican legislators in Albany removed control of the park from the mayor and vested it in a nonpartisan commission and an advisory committee that included Washington Irving, George Bancroft and the *Tribune* journalist Charles A. Dana. (See chapter four for the role of this advisory committee.) By September of that year Frederick Law Olmsted had been appointed superintendent of the construction of Central Park, thus completely removing an important source of patronage from the city's mayor.

The Metropolitan Police Act of 11 April 1857, and the Excise Act, passed a week later, effectively completed the Republican reorganization of the government of the city. State appointed commissions, like that administering Central Park, controlled the city's wharves, piers, pilots and administered the construction of new public buildings.[42] The control of patronage assured by these reforms did much to strengthen the Republicans. Wood's theme as mayor was the need to reassemble and concentrate the powers of city government which had been dispersed through successive constitutional reforms. He was also prepared, in the Locofoco tradition, to address the victims of the economic recession of October 1857:

> Labor was never so depressed as now. . . .
> This is the time to remember the poor!
> Do we not owe industry every thing? It is its products that has [sic] built up this great city.
> Do not let us be ungrateful as well as inhuman. Do not let it be said that labor, which produces everything, gets nothing, and dies of hunger in our midst, whilst capital, which produces nothing, gets every thing, and pampers in luxury and plenty.[43]

He was felt to be too sympathetic towards workingmen's demands, and the conservative element in the Democratic Party, led by the *Evening Post*, denounced his support for the "monstrous doctrines" of providing work and food for the city unemployed.[44] Aristocratic New York regarded Wood, and his supporters, with undisguised contempt: "On our way home [from the Broadway Theater, wrote George Templeton Strong in November 1857], we met a procession of the *demos* marching down from the Academy of Music, where Fernando Wood has been assembling his blackguard backers. The procession was strong in numbers; 'Sons of Belial flushed with insolence' and bad liquor, but, considering that Fernando Wood is the regular Democratic nominee, perhaps not larger than was to be expected."[45]

The revised charter forced Wood to stand for re-election in December 1857, one year after his re-election to a two-year term. The desire to get rid of Wood proved sufficiently strong for many of the most prominent Tammany men to hold discussions among the various anti-Wood factions of the Democracy (which Connolly participated in), with Republicans and Know-Nothings. These negotiations led to the nonpartisan nomination of the German-American paint manufacturer and former Free Soiler Daniel Tiemann, who succeeded in winning a significant proportion of Wood's coalition of labor and ethnic support. The ex-mayor's fortunes seemed on the wane. He failed to win control of the Tammany Society in the internal elections in April 1858, and equally failed in his attempt to control President Buchanan's patronage in New York.[46]

Out of power, Wood began to meet with his supporters at Mozart Hall, at the corner of Broadway and Bond Street. ("Its name," noted George Templeton Strong, "is rather suggestive of lager-beer saloons and lust-gartens, but it is a respectable room for concerts and meetings. . . .")[47] Proclaiming his strict party loyalty and belief that his followers constituted the true regular Democracy of New York, for a decade Wood challenged Tammany for control of the party. Described in the *New York Times* as a person who ". . . prostituted every particle of his official power to the grossest partisanship, and the most shameless advancement of his selfish aims," nonetheless as the Mozart Hall candidate in the mayoral election of 1 December 1859, Wood stunned the city by defeating both the Tammany candidate, Havemeyer, and the Republican George Opdyke.[48] His return to power outraged bystanders, such as the unitarian pastor, Rev. Orville Dewey, who blamed the indifference of the upper class for Wood's success. "I wish he would take out some of your rich, stupid, arms-folded, purse-clutching millionaires in Washington Square and flay them alive. Something of the sort must be done, before our infatuated city upper classes will come to their senses." To regular Democrats like Tilden, the tragedy of Wood's re-election in 1859 was that by working with the outsiders, he had divided the huge natural strength of the party.[49] Virtually all municipal departments remained in the hands of Wood's political enemies. The Republicans controlled the Custom House. Even the alms houses were administered by a state-appointed commissioner. There were lessons to be learned from Wood's manipulation of the party, and his assiduous work with outsiders.[50]

A Hard along with Tweed and Sweeny, Connolly's main contribution in the 1857 and 1859 elections lay in the Irish saloons and ward associations, where he moved—all smiles and laughter and backslapping—seeking to deny Wood a plurality of Irish votes. It was one of the wonders of Wood's career that he passed through the violently anti-Catholic Know-Nothings in the mid-1850s without suffering the loss of Irish immigrant support. Wood was hard to tar with his own grievous crimes: corruption was always so intricately intermingled with his own distinctive brand of demagoguery that he was almost untouchable by reformers. And, naturally, historians have little to get their teeth into.[51]

Although only a supervisor, out of the struggle against Wood, Tweed emerged as a formidable power within the Democratic Party. Wood was a demagogue and corruptionist, but his activities paled before the diligent labors of Tweed who formed a corrupt ring in 1857 within the board of supervisors. A Republican supervisor was paid $2,500 to stay away from the meeting at which inspectors of elections were appointed. Tweed never looked back.[52] As county clerk with an office in City Hall, Connolly was in an excellent position to know what was being stolen by Tweed and his henchmen.

The great political issues of the day, the burning debates over John Brown's raid, and of slavery and secession, meant less to the politicians of New York than the local fruits of power. There was much earnest talk in Concord and Boston (where Emerson lectured on 8 November on "Courage" and described Brown's fate on the gallows as a glorious, saintly martyrdom) about "the sad Harper's Ferry business." John Brown's coffin lay temporarily stored in a railroad shed in New York on 3 December, on its journey north from his disaster at Harper's Ferry, while the assembled legions of the Democracy met at the Cooper Union in support of the mayoral candidacy of that old, respectable warhorse, Havemeyer. The Democracy had nothing to say about Brown, but when Abraham Lincoln spoke at the Cooper Union two months later he courageously addressed the challenge Brown made to the survival of slavery in the union while deftly marginalizing Brown as a self-righteous monomaniac, a Guy Fawkes. There were reasons for Lincoln's caution, for anti-slavery Republicans feared being associated with the traitor and "madman."[53] On the 6th Fernando Wood, outspoken in his sympathies for the south, was now elected mayor of New York for the third time. Beyond the policy debates within the Democracy in the 1850s, what was at stake in Tweed's and Connolly's struggle against Fernando Wood was power pursued on all sides with unsleeping determination.

"War Democrats"

Connolly easily won election as state senator from the 7th district in 1859. Once again the august *New York Times* approved of his candidature, noting that Connolly had received the endorsement of all groups within the notoriously fractious Democratic Party. He served on the standing committees on canals, privileges, elections and public buildings in both the sessions of 1860 and 1861. On 19 February 1861, and again on 15 April, three days after the bombardment of Fort Sumter, Connolly was passionate in his defense of the Union: "Four times, Sir, have I been honored by the Democracy of the city and county of New York, by being elected to responsible and honorable positions, and, therefore, four times, at least, have I sworn to support the Constitution of the United States and that bold flag. Sir, I shall support it now. (Great applause.)"[54]

Such speeches gave Connolly a reputation as a patriot, but they were not calculated to win the favor of his political allies in the New York Democracy. Sympathy for the South had been widespread in the city, where many jobs and businesses depended upon the cotton trade. Nativist and racist sentiments ran deeply and had been encouraged by Wood.[55] His brother Ben, editor of the *New York Daily News*, urged that all of the Southern political and constitutional demands be accepted. Described by E. L. Godkin as "a dealer in lottery tickets, of unknown or doubtful antecedents, and very limited education, representing in Congress a district in this city inhabited almost exclusively by low Irish, and constituting the New York Whitechapel," Ben Wood was the spokesman for the Democrats in the saloons and tenements of New York who opposed coercion of the slaveholders.[56] He was also the only politician during the Civil War to write a novel, a Copperhead romance of the Civil War entitled *Fort Lafayette; or, Love and Secession* (1862).

New York Democrats, with long standing political and financial ties to the south, called for compromise, for a resuscitation of the Missouri Compromise; they were against any physical steps to prevent the secession of the southern states. At a dinner at Astor House in late February 1861, the London *Times* correspondent William Howard Russell heard Democrats such as Samuel J. Tilden and George Bancroft argue that they ". . . could not bring themselves to allow their old opponents, the Republicans now in power, to dispose of the armed forces of the Union against their brother democrats in the Southern states."[57] Weighty arguments were heard across the main mercantile streets of the city that coercion was unconstitutional.

Nonetheless, when the South Carolinians opened fire on Fort Sumter on April 12, New Yorkers responded with indignation. The 6th Massachusetts Regiment marched through the city on the 17th, the first of a seemingly endless procession on its way to defend Washington. Marching with bayonets raised before a silent crowd along Broadway and Fulton Street, the regimental band struck up "Yankee Doodle" and was greeted by ringing cheers. Walt Whitman was thrilled by the scene:

Arm'd regiments arrive every day, pass through the city, and embark from the wharves,
(How good they look as they tramp down the river, sweaty, with their guns on their shoulders!
How I love them! how I could hug them, with their brown faces and their clothes and knapsacks cover'd with dust!)
The blood of the city up—arm'd! arm'd! the cry everywhere

The flags flung out from the steeples of churches and from all the public buildings and stores . . .[58]

"Immense crowd; immense cheering," noted an astonished George Templeton Strong. "My eyes filled with tears, and I was half choked in sympathy with the contagious excitement. God be praised for the unity of feeling here!" (This same regiment was attacked by pro-Southern mobs as they marched through Baltimore several days later, which resulted in the deaths of four Union soldiers.)

On the 19th, the 7th New York Regiment, darlings of the city's elite, made a triumphal march down a Broadway festooned with banners, flags and pennants, through an immense crowd. Hotels and stores competed to display red, white and blue bunting and banners. (No less significant, at the Chamber of Commerce that morning patriotic merchants, led by Samuel Ruggles, formed a committee to ensure that the remaining $9 million of the government war loan was taken up.) The relief expressed by Strong was readily echoed in conservative circles. Rev. Henry W. Bellows wrote on the same day to his son Russell who was studying at Harvard:

Last Saturday & Sunday [13–14 April] were blue days. We did nt [*sic*] know where the national spirit was, or how it would act. But Monday morning, generous breath of enthusiasm began to clear the atmosphere & by this time, doubt, disaffection, division[,] party jealousy, every thing hostile to unity & the government, has been blown below the horizon, if not out of existence. The most generous, free & consecrated determination exists to vindicate the flag, maintain the Government & hold together the Union. The commercial film has ceased to tarnish our patriotic fervor.[59]

On the 20th perhaps the largest crowd New York had ever seen, some half-million people, turned out for an immense Union parade and meeting in Union Square. The three and one half acres of the park were jammed with fervent patriots; bands were cheered; songs rang across the square; buildings were festooned with flags and banners. The heroes of the hour were Maj. Robert Anderson and the gallant defenders of Fort Sumter. The fervor was all the more intense because of its unexpectedness. The politicians and civic leaders on the platform, whose speeches inevitably went on a bit, were strong Union men, Democrat or Republican, entitled to their moment of glory; the crowd, which had dabbled with disunion in the past, now enjoyed the unexpected glow of civic unity. The city, a little stunned at this change of heart, boasted of its significance, and carried on (for a time) as if New York had always been a bastion of Unionist sentiment. The official business of the meeting was to form a Union

Defense Committee, composed of a blue-chip assemblage of the city's mercantile and financial leaders. And what of the political figures who shortly before had defended states' rights and slavery? They jumped on the bandwagon, led by the agile Fernando Wood, who had proposed that New York City secede from the Union in January 1861. Quick to read the popular mood, Wood announced his support for the Constitution and the Union.[60]

On the 22nd the common council voted to raise $1,000,000 to equip and train volunteers for the army. Blue-ribbon women's organizations, led by some of the city's most prominent social figures (Mesdames Astor, Cooper, Bellows, Aspinwall, Fish, Dix) formed the Women's Central Association for Relief. Between 17 April and 29 June 1861, over 50,000 soldiers departed through New York, each regiment parading through the city accompanied by bands and showered with public acclaim. (The city was to see nothing like it again until 1917.) Anti-secession mobs appeared and a police guard was placed around mayor Wood's home. Pro-southern newspapers like Ben Wood's *Daily News* were threatened with violence if they failed to display the flag. Nearly two years later, draft rioters cheered before the offices of the *Daily Caucasian* and Ben Wood's paper, and threatened to lynch Horace Greeley, the abolitionist editor of the *Tribune*.[61]

With the war effort of the city's elites in full gear, others scrambled to join the procession. In his address to the great rally of 20 April, Fernando Wood called for the creation of a "Mozart Regiment." Mindful of its reputation as a hotbed of appeasement towards the slaveholders, several weeks later Tammany formed the "Jackson Guard."[62] At the end of the month some 900 men of the Tammany regiment were mustered for inspection and sent forward to the front in July. The 40th Regiment (Mozart) New York State Volunteers, and the 71st (Jackson) fought respectably in the war. After consolidations with other, smaller regiments, the 40th reported 936 war losses from an initial muster of 1,000 men. Of the Jackson, it was written: "In bayonet charges, in hand to hand conflicts, in valor on the field and in privations and sufferings in trenches and in marches, this Regiment . . . has a history of the highest honor."[63] They joined the 8th (Blenker's Regiment, composed of German émigrés), the 39th (composed of the Garibaldi Guard, the Italian Legion, the Netherlands Legion, the Polish Legion and the First Foreign Rifles), the 69th (Irish Roman Catholic), and the 79th (the Cameron Rifle Highlanders, in plaid pantaloons) as part of the city's undisciplined, exotically uniformed multi-cultural contribution to the war effort.

The onset of the Civil War intensified the divisions in the Democratic Party in New York.[64] "War Democrats," as they came to be

FERNANDO WOOD,

IN HIS FAMOUS RÔLE OF OLIVER CROMWELL.

"WE MUST DISSOLVE THIS ABOLITION CONGRESS, AND IT IS TO BE DONE AFTER THE MANNER OF OLIVER CROMWELL, BY WALKING INTO—" ETC., ETC.
(*Vide Reports of Speech at Cooper Institute.*)

"Fernando Wood called . . .": Wood and his followers in Tammany Hall and then in Mozart Hall may have dreamed of his becoming the Cromwell of Congress. To his enemies, he was the epitome of Copperhead treacherousness and political corruption.

described, supported the war but feared any move to lower the city Democrats' guard against the Republicans. Their complex maneuvering seemed at times aimed more at enemies within Tammany Hall than at the rebellion. Tweed, Connolly and Alderman Henry "Prince Hal" Genet prepared a slate of candidates for the fall nominating convention in 1861 which put them in opposition to the regular Tammany nominees. Tweed ran for sheriff, Genet for county clerk. In the end both were successful, and the insurgents and regulars united behind Tammany for the election. But the continued perception that the Democrats were not wholeheartedly behind the war effort hurt Tweed's candidacy, and Fernando Wood's man, James Lynch, succeeded in beating Tweed and decisively winning election as sheriff.[65]

Peace Democrats were formed from various factions on the conservative wing of the party. Traditional Jacksonian doctrines of defending personal liberties and state sovereignty had a continued appeal in New York. The conservatives also voiced party anxieties that the war would do nothing but political harm to the Democrats. Following the battle of Bull Run in July 1861, they blocked attempts by the Republican State Committee to join with the Democratic State Committee to create an uncontested Union ticket. They also insisted on a platform which rejected censorship of the "peace" press, and restoration of habeas corpus—both of which were profoundly objectionable, even treasonable, to the War Democrats, who organized a "People's Convention" which came out unequivocally for the war. The "Union" ticket proved irresistible at the polls in November 1861, and the Republicans captured control of the legislature. Connolly had made his position clear when he delivered a speech in the senate clearly in sympathy with the Union:

> I feel that an emergency so vast, a ruin so terrible as that now pending over the land of my adoption and most grateful love, demands at the hands of every patriotic man, whether Republican or Democrat, the sacrifice of his personal asperities, prejudices or opinions of a partisan nature, in order to save, reconstruct and perpetuate that Union to which we are all indebted for the unexampled prosperity of this country in all its material relations, and the public recognition of our glorious though infant flag among the proudest nationalities of the earth.[66]

For these courageous sentiments Connolly was promptly dropped by Tammany Hall and denied re-nomination as a Democrat. He declined to go quietly. Oliver Charlick (who had been an alderman in the 1840s) received the joint nomination of Tammany and Wood's Mozart Hall. Perhaps anticipating such a moment when he called for support for the war which transcended party loyalties, he now shrugged off a lifetime's political loyalty and ran for a second term in the state senate as a Republican and People's Union candidate in the 7th senatorial district. Connolly was elected in the November poll.[67]

Opdyke was a former Democratic Barnburner who had made a fortune selling cheap clothing for southern cotton hands, and who had written *A Treatise on Political Economy* (1851) in which he argued that slavery was a great misfortune for the south. Now turned Republican candidate for mayor in 1861, he narrowly defeated the German Democrat Gunther and drove Fernando Wood into third place. (Oakey Hall, with the support of Mozart Hall, was elected District Attorney.) The switch of party allegiance showed that Connolly had superb political instincts, and was fast on his feet. At the end of 1861, Tweed and Wood were temporarily in eclipse, the Democratic Party had lost power in the city and the state, while the patriotic Connolly's career was flying high.

His only son, James Townsend Connolly, enlisted in the Union Army and was taken a prisoner of war and held in squalid conditions in Libby Prison in Richmond.[68] State Senator Connolly's commitment to the Union, at a time when the New York Democratic Party was rife with Copperhead sentiment and "Peace Democrats" who were actively opposing the war, defending slavery and seeking the defeat of Lincoln, brought him friends and no little political influence among Republicans. His major legislative effort in 1862 concerned the repeal of nativist measures which placed Catholic church property—owned by the church and not, as was the case for Protestants, by the congregation—on a disadvantageous basis. His speech in the senate, designed to shore up support within the Irish constituency, put special emphasis upon the contributions loyal Catholics were making to the war effort.[69]

Within the city the conflict between the supporters of Fernando Wood's Mozart Hall and Tweed and Genet's Tammany Hall nearly destroyed Connolly's career. Despite a convincing re-election, early in 1862 he reformed his former alliance with Genet in an attempt to dislodge Purdy and the older sachems of the Tammany General Committee. He hoped to achieve this by restoring Mozart Hall to the Tammany fold. Together with Genet and ex-Mayor Wood, he would thus isolate and destroy the growing power of Tweed.[70] If Tammany and Mozart Hall held common primaries they could subtly maneuver the defeat of Tweed's nominees. Connolly persuaded his Tammany colleagues that the disasters of the November and December 1861 elections would be repeated, and warned that unless the split with Mozart Hall were healed, they would again face electoral defeat. He headed a Tammany delegation which met with Wood on 9 October, at which it was decided that both factions would seek to unite behind a common list of candidates.[71] Aware of the inner agenda of Connolly's negotiations, Tweed spotted its weak link, the ambition of the plotters. He succeeded in isolating Connolly from his erstwhile allies by switching support to Genet, while persuading dissident elements within Mozart Hall to endorse Matthew Brennan, leader of the 4th ward (a traditional Tammany stronghold), who was Connolly's rival for the comptrollership. Thinking that he might repeat his success of 1861 when he defeated the Tammany candidate for the state senate, Connolly issued "flaming posters" announcing his intention to run as an independent. But the People's Union supported the incumbent Republican for comptroller, and Connolly, "sore spirited and heart grieved," found himself the loser in this complicated and muddled plotting.[72] He appealed at the last moment to Tweed for Tammany support, but, in truth, had little to offer in return and came away empty handed. He addressed the nomination meeting at the Cooper Union on 28 November 1862, burying the hatchet with Tammany, but he was said to have been bitter and unforgiving at Brennan's role in his defeat and quietly hoped to work against a Tammany electoral victory.[73] In the December election he watched Brennan defeat the Republican candidate for comptroller by nearly 14,000 votes.

Plots and counter-plots

At the age of fifty-two Connolly returned again to private life. The former "Hooray Boy" and political schemer had risen to the stature of a patriot and an alliance-maker. Defeat by Tweed and loss of office left Connolly in an uncomfortable no man's land, where he joined the ranks of other ghosts who had been dislodged from positions of power in Tammany by Wood or Tweed, and who tried, as manfully as possible, to regard defeat at the hands of such men as a sign of political integrity. Connolly, who had excellent connections with the banking and financial interests of the city and was perhaps one of the few Irish immigrants who did so, soon obtained employment at the Central National Bank. His salary of $2,500 per annum, which constituted great riches in the eyes of nine New Yorkers out of ten, must have seemed a noose to ambition. On $2,500 a man could live comfortably; but boredom and ambition combined to disrupt any arcadian thoughts he may have had about leading a quiet life with Mary away from the tumult of East 14th Street and Tammany Hall. Connolly once again began to explore the chances of defeating Tweed's candidates for the Tammany Council in 1864.[74] It was a smaller and less ambitious plot than the one with "Prince Hal" Genet in 1862, but the object was the same: the dislodgment of Tweed. Among the other plotters was the mayor, C. Godfrey Gunther, a strange bedfellow for such a passionate supporter of the Union as Connolly. Gunther had narrowly lost the 1861 mayoral election. Despite his victory over F. I. A. Boole in 1864, his term in office as mayor (1864–5) left him with few friends. The other plotters were an assortment of disgruntled has-beens, including the former Grand Sachem Nelson Waterbury, who was defeated by Oakey Hall as District Attorney of New York County in 1862 and deposed by Tweed from his exalted position in Tammany when Tweed came to power in 1863.[75] Also among the plotters was the former recording secretary of the Loco-Foco Party, Fitzwilliam Byrdsall, who by the 1860s was the leader of the anti-abolitionist States Rights Association. Gunther, Waterbury and Byrdsall had each been opposed or outmaneuvered by Tweed in the past and were now thirsting for revenge.[76] Unknown to his co-conspirators, Connolly was secretly relaying details of their plans to Tweed. "Slippery Dick" indeed! The destruction of the plot of Gunther, Waterbury and Byrdsall by Connolly as agent provocateur was the price he had to pay to re-enter the game. In 1865 the "Boss" took his political revenge: Gunther could attract less than 7,000 votes for a second term as mayor, running a poor fourth to Tweed's hand-picked candidate, John T. Hoffman.[77]

Connolly did not find it easy to collect the political debt which he now believed was owed him by Tweed. He was elected Sachem of Tammany Hall in April 1863, in partial acknowledgment of political services to Tweed. At the annual Fourth of July celebrations that year, Tweed, Sweeny, Oakey Hall and Connolly were seated at the ceremonial high table. During the remaining years of the Civil War Tweed reigned supreme. Elijah Purdy was Grand Sachem of Tammany Hall until 1866, and was followed by John T. Hoffman before Tweed's power was perfected. It was clear that he controlled the city Democratic Party. Tweed was the first man simultaneously to be chairman of the Tammany General Committee and chairman of the Tammany Society.

Once again, Connolly's fate was intimately linked with the appointment of a new collector of the port of New York. In September 1864, President Lincoln appointed Simeon Draper to fill the vacancy caused by the resignation in August of Hiram Barney as collector. Draper had been Connolly's employer in the 1830s. Like so many Whigs of his generation, he had entered the Republican Party in the 1850s, and was a firm Lincoln man. Draper enforced greater political discipline in the Custom House, and helped Lincoln narrowly carry New York against the Democrats' native son candidate, General George McClellan, in 1864. After the assassination of Lincoln in April 1865, Andrew Johnson forced Draper out of office and replaced him with ex-Senator Preston King. King's nervous breakdown and suicide on 13 November triggered off one of the great symbolic struggles of Johnson's administration. There were three serious candidates whose rival sets of supporters in the city were vigorous in pursuit of the patronage. Joshua Bailey was backed by Sidney Gay of the *Tribune*, Parke Godwin of the *Evening Post*, George Opdyke and the financier Daniel Drew. Chauncey Depew had the backing of congressman Roscoe Conkling and twenty-four out of the twenty-seven Republican state senators. The third candidate, Henry A.

Smythe, had important backing from Jay Cooke and the commercial and financial community.[78] He had been a partner in a Boston manufacturing company which had opened an office in New York, and head of a dry-goods firm of Smythe, Sprague and Cooper. In the late 1850s he was principal organizer and president of the Central National Bank. In 1863 he was one of the six patriots who signed the forms of association that created the Union League Club. When the war ended, he strongly supported President Johnson's liberal policy toward the south.

Johnson's motives throughout have been variously interpreted. He had an interest in improving his ties with New York Democrats in the hope of blocking the congressional Republicans' plans for a radical reconstruction of the south. And so a figure like Connolly, a New York Irish Democrat, with a good patriotic record on the war was able to use his connections with the administration to secure the appointment of Henry Smythe, his former employer at the Central National Bank, as collector. His was by no means the only voice urging President Johnson to appoint Smythe. Clever Democrats like Samuel Tilden and Manton Marble of the *World* did their best to deepen the split in the Republican ranks by reporting to the President that the Seward-Weed Republicans in the state were opposed to the administration and could not be relied upon for support. The appointment of Smythe would command the respect of the whole people and would do much, they argued, to forge an alliance between an embattled President and the Democrats. Against the advice of his Secretary of War, Gideon Welles, who regarded Smythe as "a very indifferent officer as well as a useless politician," Johnson, perhaps recalling Tyler's troubles over the collectorship, accepted the advice of the Democrats and appointed Smythe. The *New York Times* approved of the appointment, noting that Smythe was ". . . perfectly independent and will act upon his own judgment and convictions. That he is sound and patriotic we are assured, and hence we cheerfully acquiesce in the appointment."[79] His support among the Democrats, and willingness to satisfy their hunger for a share of the collector's patronage, as well as Smythe's solid reputation, did much to ensure his confirmation. It was an important moment for Connolly, and it did much to revive his flagging political career. His role in the matter was appreciated by his fellow Democrats. It also proved an unexpected boon for Herman Melville. On hearing news of Smythe's appointment in November 1866, Melville wrote to him asking for a position. They had met in Switzerland in 1857. After years of fruitless office-seeking, Melville was appointed Customs Inspector No. 75, at a salary of four dollars per diem, a post which he held until his retirement in 1885.[80]

Smythe's performance in office was disappointing. The radical Republicans saw him as a catspaw of the Weed-Seward machine, and it was assumed that Smythe would use his powers to support conservative Republicans. These expectations were soon confirmed—in spades. Smythe removed 830 officials from positions within the Custom House (a new record for political ruthlessness). Nonetheless his performance in office was soon criticized. In particular, the conduct of "general order" business (the storage of unclaimed goods) involved him in some highly improper negotiations to privatize the transactions to a firm which promised to pay a kickback of $2,000 to Smythe's private secretary, $5,000 each to two prominent senators and to create a "political fund" of $10,000, administered by Smythe himself. He also added to the payroll and salary costs some $100,000 over the levels reached by his predecessors. A congressional committee called for Smythe's impeachment, but the Radicals narrowly failed to carry the vote. Smythe's reputation was besmirched and Radicals had little difficulty blocking his proposed nomination as ambassador to Austria. During the attempt to impeach President Johnson, Smythe led a group of businessmen who collected a purse of $100,000 to be given to the President if impeachment succeeded. In the event of an acquittal, they planned to pay $50,000 towards the costs of counsel.

Connolly was leader of the Democratic Party in the 21st ward, which ran from Fourth Avenue to the East River, between 26th and 39th Streets, which included the site of Bellevue Hospital. The street-level of all buildings which lined the avenues in this ward was occupied by stores, saloons and other commercial premises. West of Third Avenue there were streets with elegant townhouses and a wealthy population. East of Third were the slums and "tenant-houses" or tenements, inhabited by an overwhelmingly Irish immigrant population. Four slaughter-houses were located in the ward, but by far the greatest health hazard were the 1,026 tenements which housed 36,675 people in 1864. Only four wards out of the city's twenty-two had more tenement houses than the 21st, and only two—the notorious 11th and 17th in "Kleindeutschland"—had a higher total population of tenement-dwellers. Connolly strode the streets of the 21st as a dignified man of influence in the eyes of the Irish immigrants who made up the majority of the ward's population. He may also have stepped carefully to avoid the cows, goats and fowl that were kept in large numbers by the residents, and been wise to cross nimbly over the poorly maintained cobblestone streets, which were receptacles for household slops, decaying garbage and stagnant water. "He was a powerful man in his ward and district," Tweed, thinking of the large majority of votes which Hoffman and Hall had received from the 21st ward in 1867 and 1868, later said of

Connolly. "We could not get along without him, and annexed him for the vote he controlled." (Since its formation before the 1854 election, the 21st had been a closely fought district with little loyalty to Tammany Hall. Wood carried the 21st in 1856 and 1859; Republicans easily won during the Civil War; and it was not until Connolly's position was secure that the 21st was secure for the Ring. In 1869 it cast the second largest number of total votes in the city election.)[81]

In the relationship between the two men, Connolly's need was the more urgent; he now moved decisively within the orbit of the "Boss." There was also another matter. Connolly was broke. This inconvenient fact was brought out in a court case shortly before he became comptroller. Sued for debt by one Henry Felter, a Broadway liquor merchant, Connolly swore in court "that he owned no property at all." A discount clerk's salary was insufficient to the needs of even a modest establishment. Connolly expected to live in a style befitting his ambitions. Political expediency and the need for money drove him into Tweed's arms.[82]

Matthew T. Brennan, the comptroller since 1862, had been showing signs (in the eyes of Sweeny and Tweed) of unexpected and unwelcome probity. As the mayoral election of 1863 approached, the city inspector Frank Boole sent his brother to the comptroller's office with a warrant for the amount needed to meet his payroll. Suspecting that Boole was illegally inflating the sums, Brennan, like an honest man, refused to make further payments on Boole's warrant and assumed authority to pay workmen in the city inspector's department directly. Predictably, many of these "employees" failed to request their pay and thousands of dollars went uncollected. This fraud formed a central part of the accusations against Boole. Brennan also played an important role in the early stages of the legal dispute over a corrupt lease for offices in a property in Nassau Street which Fernando Wood bribed the common council to endorse. Suspecting that the lease was fraudulent, Brennan repeatedly and courageously blocked Wood's moves in 1866 to have the lease signed and paid. Increasingly annoyed by Brennan's honesty, Sweeny and Tweed decided to make him an example of what happened to those who did not go along. When his term ended in the autumn of 1866 they denied Brennan the re-nomination for comptroller. An incredulous Brennan heard from Sweeny that he had been dropped because he "won't make money yourself nor let others make any."[83] He had done what an honest man should do; and was abruptly punished for his integrity.

The comptrollership had taken on a distinctive new importance because the Republicans planned to strip the city government of much of its former authority. In the reconstructed government of

New York the comptroller was going to be a powerful figure. Brennan had many enemies in Tammany Hall, but a deal was crafted whereby Tammany would support the Mozart Hall candidate for register in the November elections, in turn for Mozart's backing of Brennan in December. This deal fell apart when "Miles O'Reilly" (Brig. Gen. Halpine) defeated his Mozart rival by nearly 20,000 votes in the first election. Could Brennan, or any Tammany incumbent be elected in the light of such a strong anti-Ring turnout? On 17 November, Brennan startled the community by announcing that he would not run for office again, attributing his decision to the failure of the reform elements in the business community, especially the Citizens' Association, to support his fight against corruption.[84] In the immediate aftermath of Brennan's letter of resignation, the street commissioner Charles G. Cornell also resigned. He was faced with an investigation of charges of fraud. Tweed was appointed by mayor Hoffman as acting commissioner, a post which became one of the cornerstones of his political power. With the race for comptroller wide open, and with Tammany appearing weakened and vulnerable, the idea of an outside candidate was widely discussed. The Police Justice Michael Connolly was highly regarded among reform Democratic organizations. With each boomlet of enthusiasm for a reformer, the chances improved that Tammany as well would turn to an outsider, untainted by the corruption of the recent past. "Slippery Dick" was such a man. He had the support of collector Smythe, the generous support of Bennett's *Herald*, and was clearly a qualified and experienced candidate. The nominating convention at Tammany Hall on 24 November was conducted in the traditional fashion. After the nomination was settled, a committee was formed of members from each ward in the city to seek out Connolly, inform him of the decision, and bring him to the convention floor. Connolly awaited the decision elsewhere in the building, and accepted the nomination with a graceful address in which he expressed his sense of gratitude to Tammany Hall for every political opportunity he had enjoyed (tactfully ignoring his campaigns against Tammany candidates earlier in the decade). He pledged himself to fulfill the duties of comptroller with strict regard to integrity, and to the satisfaction of the assembled Democratic Party. On 1 December, a rally was held for Connolly at the large hall of the Cooper Institute. On the flag-draped speaker's platform, before a large crowd, sat mayor John T. Hoffman, Judge Cardozo, James T. Brady, recorder Hackett, sheriff John Kelly and Oakey Hall. It was a strangely subdued meeting, with speaker after speaker noting the apathy towards the election that prevailed throughout the city.[85] "Slippery Dick" ran against Michael Connolly and Richard Kelly, nominated

A loyal Tammany Democrat and tool of Tweed, Hoffman served two terms as mayor of New York City (1865–8), and was twice elected governor of the state of New York (1869–73).

by the Republicans. In an unpredictable three-way race, with a demoralized Tammany Hall, and the mayhem caused by two candidates with the same name and the consequent dilution of his support in the Irish community, he was barely elected. Connolly failed to win the support of the *Irish American* and embarrassingly failed to carry his own 21st ward, but piled up a sufficient plurality of votes in the traditional Democratic wards in lower Manhattan to be assured victory.[86]

R. B. CONNOLLY.

GEO. W. McLEAN.

COMPTROLLER.

STREET COMMISSIONER.

HON. JNO. T. HOFFMAN.

THOS. STEPHENS.

MAYOR.

RICHARD O'GORMAN.

PRES. CROTON AQUEDUCT DEPART.

COUNSEL FOR THE CORPORATION.

HEADS OF EXECUTIVE DEPARTMENTS
CITY GOVERMENT.

The heads of the executive departments of the city of New York with Connolly, clean-shaven and honest, at the beginning of his career as comptroller.

Thus "Slippery Dick," the outside candidate, became comptroller. He took office on 7 January 1867, and was immediately embroiled in the legal battles over Wood's Nassau Street property. The attorney representing the common council, Isaiah Williams, served Connolly with a complaint on 8 January stating that there had been bribery and requiring that the lease should not be paid. Wood responded by extracting a writ of mandamus from Judge Leonard, demanding that Connolly pay the lease, or show good cause why he could not. At a hearing at the end of February, Judge Leonard swept aside Connolly's objections, and ordered the lease to be executed and delivered. Williams's case, damaged by disagreements between himself and the corporation counsel, Richard O'Gorman, failed because there had been no proof of corruption. This case, which dragged on until August 1868, was just one of many examples of corrupt practices and sharp-witted legal battles. It suggested to Connolly, and to others, that the forces of virtue (in this case the idealistic and honest lawyer Williams) were outgunned in the city. It gave heart to the corrupt, and loosened the ethical restraints of those who, like Connolly, in another context might have been willing to stand up to corruption. The fate of his predecessor, dumped by Tweed, was warning enough.

Comptroller for the "Ring"

Tweed's "confession," published in 1877, indicated that payments to Connolly began even before he was elected comptroller, in September 1866. That year he gave Connolly $27,484, and in successive years until December 1870 his share of the loot amounted to $165,726.[87] Such payments actually constituted a small proportion of the money that came into Connolly's hands. The vast majority of Ring proceeds were handled by the agents of the four principals. Tweed's were looked after by Elbert A. Woodward, deputy clerk of the board of supervisors, and sometimes by other functionaries. Connolly used an official from his office, the city auditor James Watson.[88] The mayor, Oakey Hall, received his share through either Hugh Smith or James Sweeny. Peter B. Sweeny, city chamberlain, used his brother James, or Charles H. Green, as his agent. Cash payments to the Ring were made to the bagmen (Woodward, Smith, Sweeny, Green or Watson) and shared out, on a prearranged formula, among the principals. The agents were the only ones who really knew what the Ring was doing.

The "Boss": during Connolly's tenure as comptroller Tweed was unquestionably in control of Tammany Hall.

It would be erroneous to assume that the whole procedure was orderly: the Ring was an attempt to impose order upon a chaotic city government. At every level of city life smaller rings existed, wherever initiative and private enterprise looked promising. Assemblyman Thomas C. Fields arranged for the legislature to appropriate $460,000 to adjust fire claims in the city. He then organized the submission of false claims for this sum, receiving one third of the total (the rest was split with Henry Genet in the senate). Of the $188,000 Fields received, there was inevitably a cut for Tweed, Connolly, the speaker of the assembly, and another dip of the beak for Genet.[89] For a time the county sheriff, James O'Brien, had a private arrangement with James Hayes on the board of supervisors to have fraudulently inflated bills passed and paid. For this service Hayes received a substantial kickback from O'Brien, and when the ex-sheriff led a rebellion against Tweed, Hayes followed him into the political wilderness.

There were never enough posts available to satisfy the ambitions of every claimant, and seldom enough money coming in to keep everyone smiling. The family was looked after first. President Grant found government appointments for his cousins, brothers-in-law, and other relatives, said to amount to forty persons. On a more modest scale, appropriate for a city government, Boole's brother Leonard was appointed paymaster and bookkeeper in the bureau of sanitary inspection and street cleaning in the city inspector's department (at an annual salary of $2,500). Sweeny's family was unusually well provided for: his uncle, Thomas J. Barr, was police commissioner; one brother-in-law, John J. Bradley, was county treasurer and commissioner of the sinking fund (Bradley's brother George was second auditor of city accounts); and another brother-in-law, William A. Henry, was auditor of accounts; Sweeny's brother James was clerk of the Supreme Court and deputy chamberlain. Tweed's brother Richard was assessor; one of his sons, Alfred, was clerk in the 9th district court; another son, William M. Tweed, Jr., was assistant district attorney; his nephew William H. King had a job in the department of public works. Connolly's son James became auditor of accounts in the comptroller's office (with an annual salary of $6,000) and commissioner of street openings appointed by the Supreme Court. One son-in-law, Robert C. Hutchings, was given a judicial appointment as surrogate. Another, Joel A. Fithian, was appointed assistant receiver of taxes ($6,000 p.a.) and commissioner for the widening of Broadway. Fithian was also a prominent lieutenant in the comptroller's 21st ward machine. A nephew, Richard C. Beamish (president of the Bernard O'Neill Association—O'Neill was an alderman and political ally of "Slippery Dick"), was also provided with a clerkship in the Supreme Court.[90] Little effort was made to hide these relationships: in the *Corporation Manual* of 1868, James Townsend Connolly and Joel A. Fithian are listed as residing at 121 East 34th Street, which was also Connolly's address.

At first the Ring added its own surcharge upon all city and county contracts. So easily did the revenue flow, so well established were the mechanisms of corruption, that pressure soon built up to increase the 10% Ring kickback. The figure shot up to 55%, and by July 1869 it had reached 60%. Four months later the Ring was regularly adding 65% on to city bills. Soon wholly fictitious bills were being hurriedly passed for payment by Connolly's office in the Hall of Records on Centre Street. The possibilities seemed limitless. Bills were submitted for work contracted but not done. Work done privately for members of the Ring, and their friends, was charged at inflated prices to the city. The chaotic system of public administration gave carte blanche for fraud on an heroic scale. The spoils were divided with 10% (rising to 25%) to Tweed, 10% (rising to 20%) to Connolly, 10% to Sweeny, 5% to Mayor Hall, and a further 5% to Woodward and Watson. A sum was also set aside for political bribery in Albany and elsewhere. The office of the comptroller was the key to the organization of corruption, but anyone in that office, at that time, would have struggled to act other than the way Connolly did. He owed much to Tweed, and the "Boss" was unquestionably in control of Tammany Hall; the judiciary was at his feet. Even so prominent a figure as Tilden acted slowly and circumspectly in his relations with the Ring. They were believed to be dishonest crooks, but they were men of power. In any event, Connolly was not a free agent. Watson explained the way the system worked, and largely handled the money. Sweeny kept a careful eye on all of the comptroller's dealings. His relatives and supporters looked forward to a long period of lucrative public employment. Despite his rebellions of 1861 and 1862, Connolly was a creature of Tammany Hall and could not realistically look elsewhere for sustenance.

The Tweed Ring evolved out of a system of corruption that was established in New York during Fernando Wood's second term as mayor from 1856 to 1857. The corruptionists, of whom Wood was the most flagrant, waxed and waned as political fortunes varied, and as new opportunities presented themselves; but the system of corruption "worked" and endured. It was a truth universally accepted that the character of those seeking public office should be beyond suspicion and that the corruption would end when virtuous men could be prevailed upon to return to public life and resume their old responsibilities. By the 1860s it was widely asserted that men of probity and wealth shunned public affairs. "The [Citizens'] Association deeply laments the apathy of respectable and honored citizens which leads them to refuse their names as candidates for office . . ."[91] Wealthy men as ever dominated "society" but the social elite regarded politics with disdain, and when they allowed themselves to enter the arena of public life, neither pursued it as single-mindedly as the corruptionists, nor brought with them virtuous men of the comfortable classes to fill the numerous jobs required to keep a complex city government functioning. When Matthew T. Brennan pulled out of the 1866 race for comptroller, he made this point with characteristic bluntness in a letter to Moses Taylor, Royal Phelps, William B. Astor and other reform-minded men of the business community: ". . . the active, enterprising gentlemen with large schemes behind them which a Comptroller has defeated, or a Comptroller can 'put through,' are more zealous at the polls, more effective at combination, and more ready to spend money to secure a pliable representative than you are to retain a good one."[92] With certain notable exceptions, those who entered politics frankly did so to enrich themselves.

In the collective memory of the city—or more precisely, in the myth of the "fall" which served to explain the degraded state of New York—the colonial era stood for a time when simplicity and virtue pervaded the whole community. The period when merchants lived in modest dwellings near their warehouses and stores, and when artisans worked in the lofts of their own homes and did business with customers who similarly lived nearby, stood in sharp contrast to the present. The wealthy, seduced by the elegant dwellings of La Grange Terrace on Lafayette Street, the brownstone homes surrounding Gramercy Park and the mansions on Fifth Avenue, moved uptown; the taste for luxury and ostentation corrupted the city. The rush uptown emptied the lower wards of fashionable inhabitants. Churches, theaters and stores leap-frogged each other in the desire to maintain their place in the flow of life uptown. Whole districts of tenements housed the city's poor. For the wealthy, Broadway was the center of culture; for the working class and immigrants, life centered on the theaters and saloons of the Bowery. New York was becoming a modern city, in which the rich and the poor knew little of each other. They lived in different parts of the city, sent their children to different schools, worshipped at different churches, read different newspapers, attended different theaters, supported different political parties.

What the tenement-dwellers in New York saw most in the rich was not civic charitableness but a canting morality and a cold determination to keep themselves apart. They seemed to be less distinguished actors on the civic stage than resolutely determined to exclude the city and its threatening democracy from "society." Edith Wharton, who grew up in one of the most aristocratic of old New York families, scarcely ever gives a sense of Tammany's city in her novels of New York life: the curtains are always closed in the carriages which take her characters through the city.[93] New York "society" found its perfect organizer in Ward McAllister, and in Mrs. William Astor its dictatorial leader and incomparable champion of exclusivity and the hierarchical principle. So intense was the competitive individualism in New York that the small number of philanthropists, often of Unitarian, Quaker or Methodist background, who devised schemes of civic improvement and humble Christian charity struggled to be heard. Many rich New Yorkers sincerely believed that help for the destitute was misguided. Only the most unyielding Calvinists argued that if such people could not look after themselves, they might just as well die or go elsewhere, but some such message often underlay the activities of bodies like the Association for Improving the Condition of the Poor. By 1855 the argument had become a commonplace that the social elites of New York had little sense of civic responsibility. "New York was filled with men of all nations," argued Henry Tappan in a discourse before the New York Geographical Society, "and men from every part of the Union, who seemed to congregate here only for one purpose—to make money. They had no time to become the fathers of the city. Totally absorbed in the one purpose, they heard not the voice of the Genius of the place; they formed no strong local attachment. The men who might be supposed capable of giving a right direction to the public counsels, kept aloof, and pursued their own prosperous business." They were unfavorably compared with the Boston elites, noted both for civic pride and charitableness.[94]

Far more than the financiers, merchants, reformers, clergymen or charitable workers, it was the lowly, corrupt Tammany ward bosses who held the city in a semblance of cohesion. Everywhere in the city gangs of laborers and mechanics swarmed over wooden scaffolding on construction sites, tearing down older and smaller buildings, hauling timber, brick and stone through the streets. Long lines of horse railways, heavy omnibuses hauled slowly by teams of horses, carried as many as thirty people at a time on the long journeys north and south through the island. As deputy street commissioner, Tweed reigned supreme over the main source of city patronage. Jobs were the cement that bonded the tenement-dwellers to the city and its political system. Finding jobs, whether for the truly needy or as a matter of political expediency, gave political power to the ward bosses and ultimately to those who provided the money. "Dear Tweed, can you find this man a place?" Connolly would write, dozens of times a week. Every saloon-keeper and member of a ward management committee looked to men like Connolly for places on the public payroll. And not just Tammany hacks did so: during Tweed's appeal in 1876, his counsel, David Dudley Field, produced a highly embarrassing letter from Tilden, written some years before he became governor of New York, asking Tweed to find a "small appointment" in his department for a needy person.[95] The comptroller had within his gift 118 positions in the executive department, and many of these were highly desirable in that they involved the collection of taxes. In turn, favors were translated back into outright payments to politicians, as well as votes and financial "contributions" for Tammany candidates; patronage was at the heart of the mechanism of political power. Tammany ultimately relied upon the immigrant voter, for whom appeals of an abstract public good, or high-minded political philosophy, counted for less than the ability to find work. Reformers denied it, but there was an element of Robin Hood in the Ring's enthusiasm for robbing the rich and, in their own way, aiding the poor.[96]

Sweeny and Tweed were beginning to extend their financial activities and services. Sweeny received a "balm" of $150,000 for brief services rendered as receiver of the Erie rail line. In appreciation of his making Judge Barnard's supply of injunctions available to the Erie predators, Tweed received a bloc of Erie shares from Jay Gould. In October 1868 they were both elected to the Erie board.[97] When the New York Bridge Company was organized in 1869 to build a bridge across the East River, the two men, along with Hugh Smith, received a total of 1,260 shares in the company. It was a nice sweetener: at $100 per share, they were expected to pay only twenty per cent of their value. Their holdings were reduced to 560 each, to enable Connolly to be included in the deal. Tweed, Sweeny, Smith and Connolly were among the largest stockholders in the project, and were effectively in control of the public and private investment made by the city. Connolly appears among the directors of the Viaduct Railroad Company in 1871, a bizarre scam to fund by city bonds an elevated railroad built upon large masonry columns. Big times were on the way.[98]

In January 1870, with the state legislature controlled by the Democrats for the first time in twenty-four years, Tweed introduced a new city charter in the lower house at Albany.[99] The charter's inner political purpose was to enable Tweed to head off yet another attempt by "Prince Hal" Genet (leader of the 12th ward and a Democratic state senator), James O'Brien (the county sheriff), Thomas J. Creamer (landlord of Apollo Hall), Michael Norton, and others under the banner of "Young Democracy" to reform the Ring out of power. The maneuverings of Dana's *Sun* over the insurgency of Young Democracy suggest why opposition to Tweed was so readily thwarted. Early in 1870 the *Sun* encouraged Genet, Creamer and Norton, fiercely attacking the corrupt, dishonest Ring led by Tweed. The Young Democracy, feeling the strength of their position on the Tammany Society General Committee, planned to dislodge Tweed at a meeting to be held on 28 March. On the evening before that meeting, Tweed opened up a line of communication with the *Sun* and offered $11,000 if the paper could be persuaded to "let up" on its attack on the Ring. (He used a similar unsubtle tactic to suborn Nathaniel Sands, leader with Peter Cooper of the Citizens' Association, and he also sought to bribe the *New York Times*.) On the 26th the shift of the paper's coverage was signaled by a long, sympathetic interview with Tweed. With the wind no longer in the sails of Young Democracy, Tweed deftly arranged for the council of sachems to ban the use of Tammany Hall for the meeting of the general committee. For the remainder of the year, the Ring fully controlled the *Sun*.[100]

Although opposed by Bryant in the *Evening Post*, Manton Marble in the *World* and Greeley's *Tribune*, the proposed charter was praised in Dana's *Sun*. Unexpectedly it received the approval of the *New York Times* and the Citizens' Association, which saw in its proposed concentration of power an acknowledgment of long-standing abuses of government due to an excess of democracy and the diffusion of civic responsibility.[101] Tweed proposed to return to the city much of the power stolen by the Republican reforms of 1857. Under his charter it would be the mayor, not the governor, who would appoint virtually all city officials and would, in consultation with the comptroller, have the power to set salary levels. Existing claims upon the city and county were to be submitted to a board of audit, consisting of the mayor (Hall), comptroller (Connolly), commissioner of public works (Tweed) and the president of the board of parks (Sweeny). These four—the central figures in the Ring—would be left unchallengeably in control of the revenues of the city. "Such a concentration of powers over this city," wrote Tilden, "was never before held by any set of men or any party as was thus vested in the 'Ring'".[102]

Stories were soon circulating in New York of vast sums expended on bribes when the Tweed charter was passed by huge majorities in both houses of the state legislature in April. Tweed wrote to Connolly on 16 July 1870 requesting that the comptroller "redeem my word" and authorize payment to Democrats who supported the charter. His note ends in a characteristic vein: "Thank you as a personal favor to me to pay their Bills and when you call on me to reciprocate you will find a sum as ever ready."[103] According to Tilden, the Ring spent as much as a million dollars on bribes. Tweed admitted to the strategic disbursement of $600,000. There was a whip-round among the Ring and its clients to defray these immense costs. When the board of audit met for its first meeting early in May 1870 work began in earnest to recover these sums. Bills were passed amounting to $6,312,000, principally for work that was supposed to have been done on the Court House on Chambers Street. It was estimated that no more than ten per cent of the sum authorized was legitimate.

As things looked in 1870, Connolly's position within the Ring was secure. Late in that year Tweed inserted a minor provision in the Tax

The mayor Oakey Hall, a lawyer and former District Attorney, author of burlesques and skits, was a more cultured individual than the others in the Ring, and moved in a world of exclusive gentlemen's clubs, and elegant Broadway entertainments. Tweed, Connolly and Sweeny found him a useful front for the Ring's serious business of civic corruption.

Levy Bill which gave the mayor authority to appoint the comptroller for a term of two years. The first incumbent would hold office for a period of four years, until New Year's Day 1875, thus remaining in place even if the electoral fortunes of the Ring turned sour. Matthew T. Brennan, the former comptroller, was regarded as a man of integrity who had support among the reformers in the Democratic Union organization. Brennan was also enthusiastically supported by Genet and Norton as someone who might disrupt the Ring if he could be persuaded to run against Connolly.[104] Tweed persuaded Brennan, who in 1868 had been appointed by mayor Hall to be police commissioner, to run instead for sheriff in October 1870. Tweed thus left Connolly a clear run for comptroller: it was a favor which he came bitterly to regret. The pieces slotted neatly into place: Hall was re-elected mayor, Hoffman (who went all out for the white

Among comptroller Connolly's tasks was the sale of city and county bonds to generate revenue in anticipation of the collection of taxes. A six-per cent bond sold to George Quimby was signed by the mayor, John T. Hoffman and Connolly on 18 July 1868.

racist vote in an ugly campaign)[105] was elected governor by a handsome majority, Brennan easily won as sheriff and Connolly was reelected comptroller by some 20,000 votes.

As long as the financial secrets of the Ring were protected, Connolly felt that his position was unchallengeable. Emboldened by the flow of warrants across his desk, and by the Ring's solid political prospects, Connolly dispatched James Watson, the city and county auditor and chief bagman for the Ring, to talk to Tweed:

> He [Watson] said that Connolly said that he had to take all the responsibility and the risk, and the thing couldn't be done without him. I said: "It couldn't be done without either." I asked how he could do it that way anyhow. He said: "The way we can do it is this: These people [the contractors and manufacturers] could be satisfied with less percentage; I think they would take one third, instead of one half, because they are giving nothing for it; I can make that arrangement with them, I know." "Well, very well," I said, "go on, and make the arrangement, if you can, and I am willing."[106]

In effect Tweed, Connolly (and Watson) were arranging a discrete coup against the other members of the Ring. The main victim was the mayor, whose share of the booty was reduced to five per cent without being informed of the change. Since the money arrived in dribs and drabs, and since the sums received were increasing, Hall may not have noticed a sudden change in his payments. Tweed's share was boosted to twenty-five per cent, and Connolly's doubled to twenty per cent. Sweeny's share fluctuated around ten per cent. With this move the Ring ceased to be composed of near equals. When Tweed and Connolly claimed three times the revenue of Hall and Sweeny, they were asserting their mastery of the situation.

Connolly was singled out for praise in *Frank Leslie's Illustrated Newspaper* for having given "general satisfaction" as comptroller, and for having "acquired the confidence of his fellow-citizens of different shades of public opinion."[107] With things looking so sunny, the Connolly family moved house to 42 Park Avenue and began construction of a "magnificent mansion" on the northwest corner of Fifth Avenue and 130th Street.[108] The contractor, Andrew J. Garvey, told the special committee of the board of aldermen investigating the Ring frauds that "it was a large, handsome double house, of 40 or 50 feet frontage, with an extension and a handsome coachhouse in the rear." The construction of Connolly's house was a microcosm of Ring corruption. The total sum illegally warranted for payment was $248,406, of which Garvey received $119,972 for work which the contractor valued at $50,000 or $60,000. The remaining balance of $128,434 was recycled within the Ring—a satisfactory arrangement for everyone involved, not least the comptroller. A row of trees was planted at public expense in front of Connolly's new home.[109] That year, the apogee of the Ring, the funded and bonded indebtedness of the city and county (for which Connolly was responsible) increased from $50,628,830 to $94,485,446.

The men who formed the Tweed Ring were not only ambitious politicians: there was an important social dimension to the position they occupied in New York. Like their social betters who belonged to the New York Yacht Club, the Union League and the American Jockey Club, they created a parallel world of (male) sporting and social institutions. The Tweed Ring was secured by their mastery of the working-class saloons of New York, but their own social milieu was modeled upon the class expectations of men who had done well by themselves and anticipated doing better in the future. There was an internal hierarchy within Tammany, established by social standing, which placed the lawyer Oakey Hall, who had been elected to

"Slippery Dick" at the apogee of his career in 1869.

the aristocratic Union Club in 1861, far above Tweed. John Morrissey, whose career as renowned boxer, thief, gang leader, street brawler and Democratic politican exemplified the rough-and-tumble roots of the party, became the owner of more than a dozen gambling halls in New York. In 1861 he opened the first casino in Saratoga, followed two years later by the opening of the resort's first race-track. His patrons were not drawn from the Five Points, but from the wealthiest men in the city, like August Belmont and Leonard Jerome. The passion for gambling and the turf, and also patronage of the city's more elegant brothels, brought the elites together.

The inner sanctum of exclusivity, like the Union League Club, could not be breached, but there was a similar institution for the wealthiest Democrats, the Manhattan Club, where newspaper proprietors and Wall Street plungers met on familiar terms with Tammany bosses. While wealthy Republicans enjoyed the summer pleasures of Saratoga, leading Democrats in the orbit of Tweed and those who had dealings with him joined the Americus Club at Indian Harbor, Greenwich, Connecticut. The Americus was formed in 1849 as a club for "gentlemen of leisure" who paid a substantial initiation fee and monthly dues to enjoy a large clubhouse with frescoed salon, plush armchairs in the library, billiard room, and a kitchen run by French chefs. Among the members—limited to 100 by club regulation—were a few Republicans (Thurlow Weed), dissident Democrats (Matthew T. Brennan), Wall Street tycoons (Jay Gould, James Fisk, Jr.), judges (George Barnard) and Tweed's minions (Andrew J. Garvey, Joseph Shannon, Charles Cornell, James Watson and Elbert A. Woodward). Tweed became president of the club in 1867. Its annual ball, held at the Academy of Music, was widely reported in the New York press.

The splendor of the Americus Club ball at the height of the social season in early January 1871 exceeded every expectation. Members of the club had no place in Mrs. Astor's "400", but they had good reason to be pleased with what they had done for themselves in New York. Two hundred men were employed for weeks transforming the Academy of Music into a fantasy wonderland. At that time it was the largest opera hall in the world. Food for 10,000 people, conveyed from a nearby hotel, was described in respectful detail in the press. Tweed wore his notorious $15,000 diamond stickpin, which seemed to grow in size each time it appeared in one of Nast's cartoons. The members of the club were handsomely dressed in a uniform of blue swallow-tail coat with gold buttons bearing the Tammany tiger's head, blue pantaloons with broad gold stripe, white vest with gold buttons, white necktie and patent leather pumps. *The Star* described Connolly at the ball as

> . . . one of the old school of Irish gentlemen, who knew the value of social power and the fascinations of good manners. In the boxes he was gracious, on the floor he was gallant, and at the table he was trenchant. When called upon loudly for a speech he held up his fork reprovingly and at once proceeded to discuss his little quail.[110]

Others, with sharper eyes, detected signs of strain within the Ring. A reporter for the *Evening Telegram* overheard a discussion between Connolly and one of the guests:

Comptroller Connolly looked very much troubled and wore a puzzled air during the evening. So much so that Jim Sweeny, Peter's brother, went up and asked him what was the matter. Says Dick, "I don't mind telling you, since you're your brother's brother; but you know how I fixed that six millions deficit in the Treasury." "Yes," says Jim, "Peter told me." "Well," replied Richard, "they are coming down on me for the money now, and I haven't got enough to pay them with. I promised them half the whole amount to swear me out of business, and what would I do if they sued me for it." "All I can say," said Jim, "is go and see the Boss."[111]

Two weeks later the Richard B. Connolly Association held a musical evening, again at the Academy of Music. James O'Brien, chairman of the association, introduced the evening's entertainment. The reconciliation between Young Democracy and the Ring seemed complete. The mayor's handsomely engraved invitation remained unused.

In the winter of 1870–71, feasts and balls confirmed the preeminence of the Ring in New York City. The celebrations which accompanied the marriage of Tweed's daughter Mary Amelie to a gentleman from New Orleans were among the most lavish the city had seen. Mrs. Connolly gave the young couple a silver ice dish. The mayor, belonging to a different social world altogether, did not attend the ceremony but sent a present: even within the Ring New York was still New York.

The comptroller occupied a position of some distinction within the Irish community: he was a Knight of the Order of St. Patrick, and prominently placed at the Order's annual banquet, and he was on a committee of invitation for a banquet to honor John Martin, an Irish patriot who had been exiled to Van Diemen's Land for his part in the revolt of 1848.[112]

Tweed's position seemed secure. But there were visible limits to his power, if not to his ambition. He had financial dealings with leading Wall Street figures (August Belmont was an officer in the company Tweed created to build an elevated railroad in the city) but was ruthlessly excluded from "polite" society. Tilden was a wily and tenacious opponent within the state Democratic Party. Though he forced his own candidates upon the party's convention in September, Tweed was unable to dislodge Tilden from the chairmanship. Nor had he been successful in a scurrilous campaign in 1869 to remove Belmont from his position as chairman of the Democratic National Committee. A wealthy New York banker, correspondent for the Rothschild's banking and investment interests in North America, and a leading figure in society, Belmont could be wounded by Tweed, but

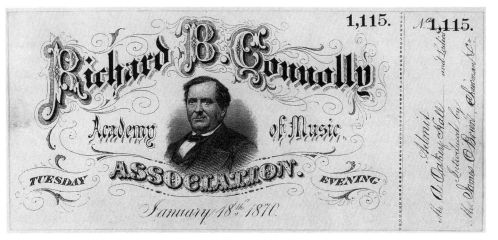

"The mayor's handsomely engraved invitation remained unused."

the "Boss" could not reach high enough to play an influential role on the national stage.[113]

The case of the missing vouchers

The Ring was secure only so long as the truth of their financial affairs was shielded from the public. That was the comptroller's task. There were probably more men in New York than in any other American city who knew how to read a balance sheet, and who understood the full creative potential of accountancy. A trickle of complaints about corruption began to appear in the Republican press. These hints and veiled accusations, taken up and repeated by reformers and rebel Democrats, so threatened to gather momentum that Hall and Connolly wrote to William E. Dodge, president of the Chamber of Commerce, on 4 August 1870 requesting that the chamber appoint a panel to examine the public accounts. With most of the members out of town in August, no such special meeting of the chamber could be arranged. In the meantime, the vice president of the chamber, George Opdyke, demanded a full statement of receipts and expenditures for the period since January 1869 which could then be available for scrutiny. A group of leading Wall Street financiers and industrialists, led by John Jacob Astor Jr., was eventually nominated to examine the comptroller's books. When the Astor Committee's report was finally published on 1 November 1870, on the eve of the election, reformers were astonished to read that the account books had been "faithfully kept" and that the securities and sinking fund were being correctly managed. Everything was scrupulously in order. "It would," wrote Alexander Callow, Jr., "be difficult to find in the annals of American urban history a greater example of political whitewash."[114] The committee was fiercely lampooned by Thomas Nast as the "Three Blind Mice," but the errors of their report were noticed too late to affect the polls. "Slippery Dick" had successfully pulled the wool over the eyes of some of New York's sharpest businessmen. As with the successful deception of Peter Cooper (who was led to believe that Tweed's new city charter was a sign of his desire to run the government in a business-like manner), the bribing of Sands, the attempted bribery of the *Times*, the outwitting of the Three Blind Mice may help to explain some of the sharp outrage which the respectable class felt towards the Ring. They had been easily fooled, and bested, by clever, uneducated rogues, and felt humiliated, angry and vengeful. Male pride was at stake in the events of 1871.

A snow storm hit New York in January 1871. Fog and ice in the river obstructed harbor navigation. Gales raged at sea, and trains were delayed by as much as six hours. On the 24th five inches of snow blanketed the city. "The scenes on Fifth, Madison and other main avenues leading toward Central Park were exceedingly brilliant and animating. The park and environs were alive with sleighs of every description gliding about with kaleidoscopic confusion, the varied colors and tints of furs, dresses, afghans, robes, vehicles and steeds merging into the illusion."[115] Among this throng on 26 January was the county auditor and Ring bagman, James Watson, known throughout the city for his passion for trotting horses. At Eighth Avenue and 130th Street, above the park, a horse pulling the sleigh driven by a man named Charles Clifton veered in front of Watson's team, reared, and struck the auditor with a hoof. Watson died on the 30th. It was a moment in which the Ring's seasonal celebrations were at their peak, but Connolly realized the importance of securing Watson's books. "I did a big day's work yesterday," he boasted to Andrew Garvey. "I got hold of Watson's book containing the list of payments to us. I tell you, I soon put it out of the way."[116] Even with the secure disposal of damaging evidence, the replacement of so central a figure was fraught with difficulty. Tweed proposed to bring in as county auditor Cornelius Corson. Abram Genung was sure that Connolly knew Tweed's man to be "unscrupulous," and that once installed in office Corson would keep Tweed well informed of the inner workings of the comptroller's office.[117] In addition to being an old friend of Tweed's, and a partner with him in the New York

Printing Company, Corson's curriculum vitae was a slice of Ring life. He had been clerk to the commissioners for the building of the 9th district court house, chief of the bureau of elections, clerk to the board of county canvassers, and official reporter to the board of aldermen. He was, in addition, a court stenographer and prepared the proceedings of the board of supervisors. For these services it has been estimated that the busy Corson received $24,500 per year.[118] Connolly resisted the appointment of Corson, but, despite the great security of his position in late 1870, he was unable to prevent it. In the end he and Tweed compromised: the county book-keeper, Stephen C. Lynes, Jr., became the nominal county auditor, while Corson was given charge of certain important appropriations. The appointment of Lynes, a Republican, was confirmed by the ever-pliant mayor Hall. The position thus vacated, that of county bookkeeper, was filled by a newspaperman, Matthew J. O'Rourke, who had met Connolly in April 1870 while they were both in Albany. Upon learning that O'Rourke was working on a book or series of articles "The Representative Men of the Empire State," Connolly, always sensitive to the Ring's need to curry favorable publicity, suggested that a place might be found for O'Rourke in his department.[119]

For the time being, the crisis caused by Watson's death was under control. Not long afterwards ex-county sheriff James O'Brien directly approached Connolly with a request to find employment in his office for a friend, William Copeland. (O'Brien was president of the Richard B. Connolly Association and had warmly supported a plan to erect a statue of Tweed in some suitably prominent place in the city).[120] Nonetheless, Connolly was uncertain about what should be done about O'Brien. He was obviously well fixed politically and was in with Tweed. Despite his efforts to ingratiate himself with the Ring, it was persistently rumored that he was Tilden's man, and that O'Brien's various opportunistic attempts to defeat Tweed at Albany and within Tammany Hall had been coordinated by Tilden. It had not escaped notice that the most enthusiastic supporters of O'Brien's Young Democracy were largely drawn from Tweed's opponents.[121] There was also the question of O'Brien's unsettled claims, of doubtful legality, amounting to some $350,000. They had been blocked by Sweeny in a quiet maneuver which revealed his power within the Ring. Sweeny was an old enemy of the ex-sheriff. O'Brien's new-found enthusiasm for Tweed suggested that a small favor might be appropriate. Connolly had found a job for the roughneck Richard Croker, a young protégé of O'Brien's, after a similar request. No single person could have represented the complex "rowdy element" within Democratic Party politics, as the *New York*

Times suggested of O'Brien.[122] It was sufficient that he *sought* such a leadership role, at a time when the interests of the Ring were devoted to the calm, regular, organization of graft. Even though he was out of office, O'Brien was a man to be feared. Albert Bigelow Paine, writing thirty years afterwards, described the scene as Connolly wrestled with the decision whether or not to appoint Copeland: "[H]e [Connolly] was equally afraid to grant or to refuse O'Brien's request. Perspiration streamed down the fat face of 'Slippery Dick' and he looked pale and old."[123] Connolly weakly chose to avoid another bruising battle; he had much else on his mind. Copeland was appointed clerk in the auditing department. Had Connolly been a little more suspicious, or had his position been a little stronger, neither O'Rourke nor Copeland would have entered the comptroller's office. In less than a year the Ring was destroyed by the revelations of the two.

"[I]t was while discharging those duties" [of county bookkeeper,] wrote O'Rourke, "that my eyes were first opened to the real nature of the business that was being daily transacted . . ."[124] O'Rourke says that he was unaware of the frauds before working in Connolly's office, but there is something basically incredible in his assertion: *every* newspaperman in the city was aware of the frauds. In fact, it would be hard to find anyone who read newspapers in the city over the preceding decade who would not have seen hundreds of articles, many in considerable detail, about the many layers of fraud and corruption in the city government. O'Rourke suggests that it was only with the discovery that a bill submitted by a friend was being deliberately ignored, while large fictitious claims were being paid, that he directly confronted Connolly. On the same day (19 May), he submitted his resignation to Lynes. It was later charged that O'Rourke had been dismissed from his post as clerk in the bureau for dishonesty, and so he was determined to see that the exact sequence of events made its way into the public record. Before his resignation took effect, O'Rourke transcribed financial records concerning payments made for the repair and furnishing of the city's armories. At the same time, Copeland began to examine city warrants for expenditure from 1869 to June 1870. His notes made it clear that the firms of Andrew J. Garvey, James Ingersoll, John Keyser, and others had received vast sums of money for work on city projects. There was unmistakable evidence that fraud had taken place. It did not take long for Copeland's and O'Rourke's information to circulate. Indeed, anyone with access to the comptroller's office could have made similar discoveries. Copeland's notes were sent direct to O'Brien. O'Rourke seems to have made contact with George Jones, publisher of the *New York Times*.

Although lacking the immediate impact of *Harper's Weekly* with its Nast cartoons, the *New York Times* was the most persistent and fierce critic of the Tweed Ring. Its columns bristled with indignation: "There is absolutely nothing—nothing in the city which is beyond the reach of the insatiable gang who have obtained possession of it. They can get a grand jury dismissed at any time and the Legislature is completely at their disposal" (24 February 1871). The rest of the New York press was either bribed or circumspect, while Nast and the *New York Times* were fizzing with delight at the chance to destroy the Ring. When the threat of lawsuits failed to silence Nast, the Ring used the board of education to hit at his publishers, Harper Brothers. There were old scores to settle: James Harper, a fierce opponent of Tammany, had been elected mayor in 1844 on an anti-Catholic, Know-Nothing ticket. It was determined no longer to buy Harper's books for the city schools. This too backfired, and gave their enemies yet another theme for their attacks on the corrupt administration.

More direct approaches were made to Nast, who was offered a large bribe to take a sabbatical year in Europe. Money was the lingua franca of the Ring and they thought they could stuff the mouths of their critics with greenbacks. O'Brien offered to "sell" Copeland's transcriptions to Tweed and received an immediate payment of $20,000, with a promise of $130,000 later if he refrained from using them. It was a classic shakedown. More interested in revenge and power than in cash, O'Brien took Tweed's money and then tried to peddle Copeland's material to one or more of the city newspapers. They declined to touch the story, and then O'Brien went to the proprietor of the *New York Times*. When Tweed heard that George Jones planned to publish a story on the armory frauds, Connolly was dispatched with the offer of an unprecedented bribe for the *New York Times* to forget the matter. Five million dollars were mentioned. One version of the exchange between the two men appears in the official history of the paper:

> JONES: "I don't think that the devil will ever bid higher for me than that."
> CONNOLLY: "Think of what you could do with five million dollars! Why you could go to Europe and live like a prince."[125]

Within weeks it was Connolly, not Jones, who was checking the sailing schedules of transatlantic packets. The *New York Times*, which called Connolly's board of apportionment figures a "sham" on 18 May, and which claimed a month later that there was a prima facie case of fraud and malfeasance against the comptroller, had the bit between its teeth.[126] Jones brusquely rejected Connolly's bribe, and the story broke in July.

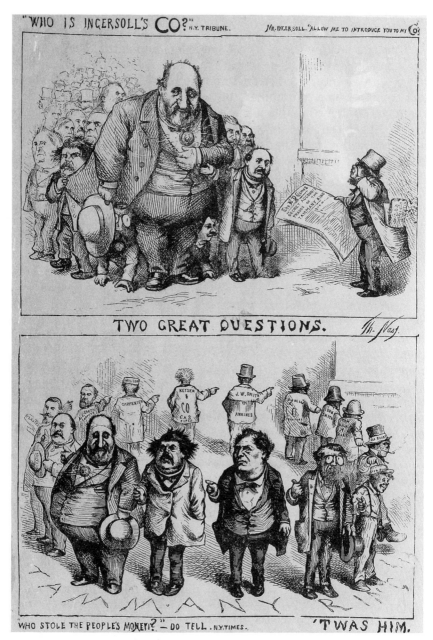

Thomas Nast's prodigious gifts for mockery found a perfect target in the Tweed Ring in 1871. After the revelations of fraud in the *Times*, a reporter for the *Herald* called at Ingersoll's office where he found (from l.) Connolly and Sweeny cowering behind Tweed's enormous figure. Was he planning to flee the city? And who was the "and Co." in his firm's name? In the lower panel (l. to r., front), Tweed, Sweeny, Connolly and Hall pass the blame.

It was the greatest journalistic sensation in the United States since the assassination of President Lincoln. The *New York Times* began to print O'Rourke's records of the armory frauds on 8 July, and followed with Copeland's revelations on the 22nd. The stories were largely written by O'Rourke. A pamphlet listing warrants paid to favorite firms for buildings, offices and for National Guard armories by New York County was widely distributed, and a special supplement summarizing the accusations was published in English and German on the 29th. The *New York Times*, in ready alliance with Oswald Ottendorfer, the reform-minded editor of the *Staats-Zeitung*—the man whom Peter B. Sweeny tried to make Tammany candidate for mayor in 1868 instead of Oakey Hall—sought to stir the generally quiescent German community in New York, and thus to weaken their allegiance to Tammany Democracy.[127] In truth, there was little love lost between the Germans in "Kleindeutschland" (wards 10, 11, 13 and 17 between Division Street and East 14th Street, largely east of the Bowery) and the predominantly Irish ward bosses of the Democratic Party in the city.

Soon after the first revelations began to appear in the press, and at a highly inopportune moment, the Irish question exploded in the face of the Ring. Under pressure from Hibernian patriotic societies, the mayor banned the traditional march by Orangemen celebrating the anniversary of the Battle of the Boyne on 12 July. Connolly took part in the decision, though in the subsequent outcry and recrimination his role was ignored.[128] Governor Hoffman intervened to rescind the ban, but feelings were running so high that when the march took place, Irish mobs attacked the Orangemen and then the ineffectual police and state militia. There were dozens of deaths. Most of the blame fell upon Hall, not least because he had so enthusiastically pandered to Irish nationalism as to appear on the reviewing stand of the annual St. Patrick's Day parade dressed all in green. He was sarcastically renamed "O'Hall" in the press. The violence that day was the worst in the city since the Draft Riot of 1863.

A tense feeling persisted into August. Taking their minds off domestic worries, Sweeny and Tweed, guided by Jay Gould's brokerage partner, completed a takeover of the prosperous Hannibal and St. Joseph rail line.[129] The Richard B. Connolly Association of the 21st ward met early in the month at a saloon on 36th Street and Second Avenue to affirm, despite the so-called revelations in the *Times*, their confidence in the probity of the comptroller. The *Irish Citizen* asserted on the 12th that the mayor and comptroller "have not violated any law; have no need to 'repent.'" On the 14th the Bernard O'Neill Association, also of the 21st ward, made a similar proclamation for Connolly. "This precious collection of loafers," sarcastically noted the *New York Times*, "'declare' that Hon. Richard B. Connolly has never, in the course of his official life, been guilty of one single act to which the citizens of this great metropolis could take exception." As the political crisis deepened, the followers of people like James O'Brien, drawn from the lowest strata of saloons and political clubs, made their presence felt. Ex-Alderman Richard Croker, who as a sign of the rapprochement between O'Brien and Tweed had been appointed by Connolly as super-intendent of market rents and fees, was accused in early September of assaulting a man named Moore. Two weeks later laborers employed by the city angrily demonstrated outside City Hall. They had not been paid since Foley's injunction.[130]

Every politician in the city that September knew the capacity of the slum-dwellers for riot and violent attacks upon property. "Who will ever forget the marvelous rapidity with which the better streets were filled with a ruffianly and desperate multitude," wrote Charles Loring Brace in 1872, recalling the 1863 Draft Riot, "such as in ordinary times we seldom see—creatures who seemed to have crept from their burrows and dens to join in the plunder of the city—how quickly certain houses were marked out for sacking and ruin . . ."[131] Fear of social disorder was a powerful inhibition upon those who clamored for the downfall of Tweed. The prosperous walled them-selves off as best they could from proletarian discontent and the "dangerous classes." *The Nation* reminded its readers on 12 October that "the region over which Tweed rules is as much a 'terra-incognito' as Montenegro or Albania." It was clear to contemporary observers that the relations between rich and poor had changed for the worse, and an imagined version of rural community served to measure the break down of relations between rich and poor in the city:

> In the country rich and poor usually worship in the same church. In the large cities,—notably in New York,—a wealthy congregation usually builds a fine church for itself, and a mission chapel a mile off for the poor its hired or voluntary missionary can gather together. In the country, the sick or destitute are relieved by individual care and benevolence; in the city, a hired distributor of alms investigates the case and doles out assistance. In the country you help a man by finding work for him; in the city, you "give him a dollar and let him go.". . . Not only [do] they live much farther apart in the city, but when they come into contact their attitude towards each other is very different.[132]

Attentive readers of the annual reports of the Association for Improving the Condition of the Poor would have recognized the framework of understanding in the pages of *The Nation*. The 1867 report argued that immigrants no longer seemed to blend easily with the native stock. Rather, they tended to "create for themselves distinct communities," impervious to American sentiments. This process of segregation extended to schools, churches, newspapers. Such communities were living in the midst of New York as though they were still subjects of a foreign power.[133] By common consent, there was a crisis in communications within the city; but when there was communication neither the rich nor the poor, neither Yankee nor immigrant, seemed very happy with what they came to know about each other. Unless a different spirit could be made to infuse the life of the community, these segregating walls would grow more forbidding. What must be done, first and above all, was to remove the main centers of contagion from the body politic. The operation against the Ring was a measure of decontamination, of sanitary reform.

Tilden went upstate to Albany in the torpid heat and humidity of August to consider tactics with the lawyer Francis Kernan. The ex-governor Horatio Seymour agreed with Tilden that there were potential political advantages in a vigorous pursuit of the Tweed frauds:

> When the public mind is turned to the question of frauds, etc., there will be a call for the books at Washington as well as in the city of New York. I think a spasm of virtue will run through the body politic... The corruption in our party is local. In the Republican party it is pervading.[134]

Tilden saw George Jones of the *New York Times* at Saratoga. On his return to the city he held discussions with O'Conor and Ottendorfer. A clear course of action was decided upon.

John Foley, a litigious manufacturer of fine pens with a factory and showroom at 236 Broadway, who was president of the Citizens' Association for the 12th and 19th wards, called a public meeting on 7 August to discuss the accusations. A "gang of roughs" tried to disrupt the meeting, but failed. The resolutions which were passed at Foley's meeting, which were sent to the mayor on the 8th, consisted of a demand that the city and county pay-rolls since 1868 be made available for public inspection. Hall (knowing well that Foley's political ambitions had largely remained unsatisfied during the reign of the Tweed Ring)[135] rejected these demands, and was particularly sharp in his condemnation of the "insulting tone" of the resolutions.[136] In an attempt to seize the initiative, Hall requested on the 16th that a joint committee composed of supervisors, aldermen and a group of prominent citizens investigate the allegations which had appeared in the press. (Connolly had successfully handled a similar committee—"The Three Blind Mice"—before the 1870 elections, and Hall probably felt that he could do the same.) The Joint Investigating Committee met for the first time on 28 August. Within two weeks it began to issue brief reports which established the facts of the city's current financial position. This was clearly a holding operation, designed to keep the process of reform within the sight, and perhaps the control, of the mayor. The committee's final report was issued on 24 October, by which time there was a new comptroller, and a new spirit of reform prevailed in the city. The swift-pace of public events left the mayor's investigation as little more than an irrelevance.[137]

The Citizens' Association, heartened by the revelations in the *Times*, called a protest meeting. But Peter Cooper's support for Tweed's charter had cost the association much credibility with Republicans and reform Democrats, and the meeting was hurriedly canceled.[138] With the association sidelined, the reformers' offensive began in earnest with a carefully planned mass meeting at the Cooper Union on 4 September, held under the auspices of the group of merchants and financiers organized by Havemeyer and Tilden as the Council for Political Reform. Speakers emphasized that it was the money of tax-payers and property-owners which had been grossly misappropriated. It was a message which went down well with the millionaires, bankers and merchants who filled the Cooper Union, as did the call from Ottendorfer for non-partisan government of the city. Their task, plainly, was to define the common interest in such a way as to diminish class conflict, while reasserting their leadership role in public life. The plan which emerged from the meeting on the 4th was for a Committee of Seventy to be appointed, with Havemeyer as chairman, which would investigate the allegations which had appeared in the press, and bring charges against the culprits[139] (see appendix on the membership of the committee, pp. 294–9). A subscription book was opened to defray the expenses of the meeting, and the donors were a clear indication of what and who the Committee of Seventy represented: the donors' list was led by bankers and financiers like August Belmont, who gave $500, and Jay Cooke & Co., who added $100; industrialists were also prominent: Jackson S. Schultz, the millionaire tanner, gave $100, George Jones gave $50 and ex-mayor George Opdyke, who had sabotaged the Metropolitan Health Bill in 1864, gave $100. By comparison to the sums many of these same men gave to Grant's campaign in 1868, the city's financial elite opened their purses to the cause very cautiously.[140]

After the many abuses and corruption of public life during the past decade, many feared that the decay had gone too far, that the city could no longer be saved. Classical and Biblical parallels came easily to mind. As Henry P. Tappan had argued, similar fears dogged earlier efforts to reform the city government: "Public virtue has died out. There is no patriotism to appeal to. . . . What now remains? . . . The state is divided into contending factions. . . . Will reform come by a terrible revolution? . . . Is it Carthage that we are describing?" Perhaps echoing the Sibyl in *Aeneid* VI, Havemeyer ambiguously argued at the Cooper Union meeting that ". . . the remedy is with you; the city will be saved when the people deserve salvation."

"The *New York Times* has succeeded in getting up a notable agitation," Frederick Law Olmsted wrote to a friend outside the city, "but I don't reckon much on the results. It will end in some specious compromise and a more cautious class of speculators in politics will for a time take the lead. But I see no way open to radical improvements. The disease is too strongly seated." Despite the revelations, Lydia Maria Child was uncertain of the outcome: "But *will* justice finally prevail? It is a herculean job to clean out the stables where such beasts have congregated." George Templeton Strong also doubted whether the people truly possessed the "moral virility" to purge corruption from the body politic. He found eminent representatives of the Wall Street financial community unwilling to be "prominent" in the attack on the Ring. Even the civic-minded real estate developer Samuel B. Ruggles "fears these villains might take vengeance on him by stopping certain improvements now in progress to the damage of sundry uptown lots of his. But his conscience is a little uncomfortable." Nevertheless Ruggles became a member of the Committee of Seventy. There were some who found it advisable to avoid taking sides as the civic crisis played itself out, but, as the Cooper Union meeting demonstrated, respectable New Yorkers were united in fulsome denunciation of the "gang of rogues" who had corrupted the city and threatened the rule of law. The solution of the reformers was simple and direct: throw out the malefactors, cleanse the temple, restore our control over the city and its turbulent people.[141]

The Committee of Seventy, truly understanding the nature of the impending struggle, at once hired nine accountants. The balance sheet, the canceled check, the payroll book, and deposit records of dozens of banks across the city, were now the key evidence in a new kind of warfare to be waged against civic corruption. Beyond that, unrelenting publicity was a necessity. The *Herald* noted that "there was very little enthusiasm manifested" at Cooper Union. But these were sober citizens in the business community, with property and investments in the city. Such men had not for a decade—since the founding of the Citizens' Association in 1863—so openly declared their intention to act collectively for civic betterment. Rectitude was their shield, but, by and large, the people of New York remained passive observers as the Ring was destroyed. The Committee of Seventy could not depend upon that passivity, and, on the night after the Cooper Union meeting, in the best San Francisco style, eight men of property met secretly to form a vigilance committee. (Robert B. Roosevelt's influence was visible here: he had toyed with the idea of using O'Brien and his rough-necks against Tweed, suspecting that the Ring, so busy with its graft, no longer retained the emotional loyalty of the Democratic Party of the saloons and "repeaters.") If the Ring tried to raise the immigrants in the slums, as some feared, there might be a need for vigilantes. Havemeyer, dismayed by the persistent "listlessness and apathy" of the "laboring population," acted quickly to establish reform associations in every assembly district in the city.[142]

Within the legal steps taken against the Ring there was a political agenda, and an obvious precedent. In 1863 the Citizens' Association adopted a structure that was designed to dig deep into the political loam of the city: each ward had an executive committee made up of 100 men, and every electoral district and block had its sub-committee. Inevitably the further removed one was from the wealthy bankers, lawyers and merchants who dominated the association, the harder it was to relate their language, and moral absolutes, to the talk in the tenements and streets. So it was for Havemeyer and the Committee of Seventy in 1871. The gap between the social agenda of the reformers and the aspirations of the city's poor had rarely been so wide. Despite the fears of the reformers, the poor remained offstage as the struggle proceeded.

Sensing the momentum, a cautious Mrs. Connolly transferred half a million dollars in bonds to the name of her son-in-law, Joel Fithian (the assistant receiver of taxes), who soon left for Switzerland. She was reported in the *New York Times* to possess an additional $3,500,000 in unregistered bearer bonds. Prudent measures were necessary for the sake of the family.[143]

On 7 September Judge Barnard, previously a trusted performer in the Ring interest, granted John Foley an injunction forbidding the comptroller to collect any taxes or authorize payment upon any further claims on the city and county. This was based upon the "two per cent law" in the 1871 Tax Levy Bill, which provided that the total tax in the city and county for 1871 and 1872 should not exceed two percent on the valuation of 1871, save that the surplus of state taxes over those of 1870 could be added to the sum appropriated. The appropriations made by the board of estimate and apportionment exceeded this sum by eight million dollars. Foley's claim was that the rise in debt ". . . is to a large extent attributable to the wrongful acts of certain of the City and County officials, particularly the defendant Hall as Mayor..." (Townsend is one of the few commentators to point out that Foley's application should have been denied by Judge Barnard. Unless joined in the matter by the Attorney General, Foley had no standing in the case.) Connolly had issued a memorandum to all city and county officers in April, pointing out the limitations imposed by the legislation. He called for revised estimates to be prepared, to enable the city to remain within the spending limit. When asked about the injunction, Connolly told a reporter that he sent the papers over to the office of the corporation counsel without reading them. "That's what I always do with these little things." Barnard's injunction could not casually be shrugged off: it meant that no wages of city employees could be paid. The Ring was angrily blamed by the laborers, and Tweed used some $50,000 of his "own" money to pay their wages. He was mightily annoyed when the reform comptroller, Andrew H. Green, refused to reimburse him for this expenditure.[144]

The tactics of the Committee of Seventy were simple enough: they had to lay their hands on the books, and then to divide the Ring against itself.[145] Two years earlier the *Herald*, long a supporter of the mayor, had published a biographical sketch of Hall entitled the "Brilliant Type of Young America." Now he was alone exempted from a demand that Tweed and Connolly should resign. When Connolly was directly requested by the Committee of Seventy on 9 September to produce the allegedly fraudulent vouchers, it looked as if he was to be the fall guy. He asked for a brief delay in complying with the request. Within twenty-four hours the vouchers were stolen from a locked closet in the office of Stephen C. Lynes. News of the theft stunned the city. City Hall wags added new verses to a popular song:

> Where, oh, where, are all those vouchers gone?
>   There's music in the air,
>   I hear it everywhere—
>
> Where, oh, where are all those vouchers gone?
>   There's music in the air—
> Where are those vouchers gone?
>   Oh! Dickey! Oh! Dickey!
>   Dickey never die!
>   Dickey live forever!
>   But your story's in my eye!
>   Oh! Dickey! Oh! Dickey!
>   Dickey never die!
>   Your story's in my eye—
> Where are those vouchers gone, my boy?[146]

Connolly's repeated denial that he had stolen the vouchers was greeted with profound skepticism. Tweed claimed that it was Hall, believing the prosecution could not proceed without the vouchers, who was behind the theft, and that Connolly knew what was being planned. As Tilden saw it, Judge Barnard's injunction was designed to destroy the nascent combination of Connolly and Tweed, and behind the judge's actions he detected the devious hand of "Brains" Sweeny.[147] The New York press generally assumed that the theft pointed conclusively towards Connolly's guilt. It was also slyly implied that the vouchers had been stolen to protect (unnamed) others, and to deepen the pall of suspicion that inevitably hung over Connolly. But the notion that Connolly was a victim of a criminal conspiracy required a greater leap of imagination than most New Yorkers possessed on 11 September. The truth of the break-in was simpler and more sordid than contemporaries suspected. It was later revealed that Tweed, informed by Hall that the vouchers were unique and crucial evidence, had ordered that Connolly's office be burgled and the vouchers burned. It was a calculated attempt by Tweed to throw Connolly to the wolves.[148]

Skunk vs. Rattlesnake

The theft of the vouchers occasioned a meeting of the Ring principals on Monday 11 September, at which Hall directly asked Connolly to resign. He suggested that Connolly's departure would appease an outraged public opinion and save the others in the Ring. Sweeny agreed that a scapegoat was needed, and that the comptroller was inevitably the logical candidate. The basilisk Tweed watched Hall and Sweeny take the initiative in attacking the comptroller without himself joining in. There was much talk in the city about the need for the respectable members of the Ring to act (both Hall and Sweeny were members of the Union Club, the Democrats' answer to the Republican Union League Club), and Tweed knew he was not "respectable."[149] If Connolly went, Tweed suspected that he, too, might be sacrificed. These thoughts drew him again into a temporary alliance with Connolly. United once in dividing the revenue, now they scrambled on their own to evade the blame. News of this meeting soon reached the ear of George Templeton Strong, who noted in his diary that "It is understood that Hall and Sweeny are in alliance, offensive and defensive, against Tweed and Conn[olly]—skunk vs. rattlesnake."[150]

On the 16th the mayor approached the politically ambitious Gen.

George B. McClellan with an urgent request that he accept the comptrollership. It was only after a close friend pointed out Hall's purpose (self-exoneration) that McClellan was persuaded to decline the offer.[151] Tweed had his own ideas about the future of the Ring. The deputy commissioner of public works, William E. King, approached him with an offer from ex-sheriff O'Brien: if Tweed would buy O'Brien's claim against the city, he would be protected from prosecution. Tweed believed that O'Brien was acting on Tilden's behalf and that his offer was genuine and came with a promise of safety from the Committee of Seventy, which (he believed) had been persuaded to obscure Tweed's personal role in the frauds.[152] O'Brien had denounced the Ring in the presence of Tilden at the Cooper Union meeting on 4 September and was among the numerous respectable men, including Andrew H. Green, William M. Evarts, Robert B. Roosevelt and John Jacob Astor, Jr. who were elected vice presidents of the meeting. It is one of the small puzzles of the story how the hard-headed and realistic Tweed could have bought O'Brien's story. His offer to the "Boss" was as sweet a shake-down as has ever been known in New York politics, for O'Brien had no influence over the Committee of Seventy and was operating wholly in his own interest. Tweed paid his share, and prevailed upon Connolly to pay $75,000 as well; they hoped to save themselves together. This led them profoundly to misinterpret Tilden, who remained tenacious: the prize in national politics for the man who purged the Ring was too high.[153]

While Tweed was secretly opening negotiations with O'Brien (and as he thought Tilden), Hall and Sweeny were themselves attempting to arrange a discreet meeting with the leaders of the Democratic Party, Tilden and Belmont. Persuading themselves that the party could only be damaged by further revelations and scandal, they offered the sacrifice of Tweed and Connolly. Tilden's account of this approach is typically oblique: "The most artful members of the Ring plotted to save themselves—to come in as part of a new system—even as reformers—with added power—upon Connolly's ruin."[154] Matters had gone far beyond such an exercise in damage limitation. The complete downfall of the Ring was demanded by Tilden.

Word of Hall and Sweeny's approach to Tilden no doubt soon reached Connolly. There were very few secrets which stayed out of the press that September. The split in the Ring became highly public on the 12th when the mayor wrote to the comptroller demanding his resignation. (According to the *New York Times*, this letter brought "an almost universal feeling of rejoicing among financial men at the quarrel between the leaders of the Ring.")[155] In reply, Connolly said that resignation would be tantamount to a plea of guilty to the theft of the vouchers, which he did not intend; and that copies of the missing vouchers were safely in hand. He sarcastically reminded the mayor (such letters were strictly for public consumption): "My official acts have been supervised and approved by your superior vigilance. So far as my administration is questioned, equal responsibility attaches to yourself."[156] Despite the threat behind such brave words (the existence of duplicate copies of the vouchers may have come as quite a surprise to the other members of the Ring), Connolly was teetering on the verge of total disaster. He knew better than to depend upon Tweed. Indeed, it seemed as though everyone was busy making deals at his expense. A reporter from the *Times* interviewed Connolly on the 12th: "He was now sixty-two years of age, of failing health, and tired of public life. He would, therefore, in all probability soon retire into privacy, but not until he had been fully vindicated in this matter."[157] Although an unreformed Tammany dominated the Democratic state convention in Rochester in October, and despite sweeping victories by reformers in the city elections in November, Tweed's machine was still capable of effective delaying action and made a vigorous armed retreat from power. His forces blocked the reconstruction of Tammany Hall as late as January 1872.[158] On the inside, however, there was no longer a Ring. All that survived was a cockpit filled with desperate men, each frantically hoping to be the first to betray the others.

Connolly jumped on the 14th. He asked his former employer William F. Havemeyer to arrange a meeting for himself with Tilden the following day. When they met Tilden told Connolly that as a political power he and all the other members of the Ring "had ceased to exist."[159] Connolly was unceremoniously told to resign his public and party offices—but not at once. By a careful scrutiny of Tweed's charter, Tilden had discovered that the comptroller was authorized to appoint a temporary deputy and to confer upon him all his official responsibilities. And he discovered that this could not be legally challenged by the mayor. Connolly's successor was to be Andrew Haswell Green, who had kept the corruptionists at arms reach from Central Park for more than a decade. (He shared with Connolly the early experience of having worked at the auction rooms of Simeon Draper.)[160] This small measure ensured the downfall of the Ring. It was a precaution taken by Tweed when he devised a new charter for the city: if an unfriendly mayor was elected, the Ring could at least preserve the comptroller's office by being able to name a successor. (Mayors were elected for a term of two years, but the comptroller was appointed for four years.) As long as Connolly was in occupation of his office legally, his appointed deputy could function in coordination with Tilden and the Committee of Seventy. The meet-

Twice elected mayor in the 1840s, William Frederick Havemeyer was a respected, though perhaps not a forceful, political figure in the Democratic Party. His large family was prominent in New York commerce and philanthropy. Portrait by T. H. Matteson, 1847.

ing between Tilden and Connolly began with the comptroller being bleakly informed that he must abandon all hopes of political survival. It ended unexpectedly with Tilden telling him that at all costs he must retain his post. By some quirk of fate, Connolly and Tilden momentarily became allies as the Ring was brought down.

A further meeting was arranged for the evening of the 15th, but Connolly did not turn up. Havemeyer was despatched to Park Avenue to find the comptroller. "I found him sick and almost ready to give way under the pressure," Havemeyer told a journalist from the *World*. "He said it was crucifying him."[161] Racked by anxiety and indecision, and fully aware of the posthumous reputation of Judas, the bewildered Connolly asked Havemeyer's advice. The next day a letter arrived which made clear where Connolly's duties lay:

> Even if you are conscious of having done wrong in your trust, you owe it to the community not to commit another wrong, but to make every reparation within your power.
>
> To surrender your office into the hands of a confederate would be a fresh betrayal of your trust; and, while it might damage yourself, would fail of doing justice to the community.[162]

Tilden assured him that by surrendering his office into the hands of the reformers Connolly would have less to fear from the public than from his confederates. Indeed, Tilden said that "the storm would pass him and beat upon the others." Taking such language at face value (and obtaining nothing in writing from the wily lawyer Tilden), Connolly wrote to Havemeyer on the 16th: "In thus acting, I am governed by a warm desire to restore the city department over which I preside to the confidence of the community, and to secure such an examination of the affairs of the city as will satisfy the just demands of the public."[163]

His supporters in the 21st ward, in the St. Patrick's Mutual Alliance, Tammany Hall, the Democratic Party and in city government knew nothing of Connolly's actions. A large crowd, "made up principally of laboring men," assembled on the evening of the 16th at Foley's Hotel on Centre Street, to defend the beleaguered comptroller.[164] Timothy Daly, leader of the 19th ward St. Patrick Mutual Alliance, spoke, as did assistant alderman Garry, William Shields of the 21st ward, the editor of the *Irish People*, ex-coroner "Billy" Grover, and ex-alderman and streetfighter Richard Croker. In their different capacities, these were the people who looked to Connolly for preferment, and they knew, to a man, that he was being singled out for persecution because he was Irish. By placing himself in Tilden's dry hands, Connolly betrayed them every bit as much as he betrayed Tweed, Hall and Sweeny. In doing so, he became a Judas figure. A police guard was posted in the comptroller's office on the 18th. "I should not care to insure his life," noted Strong on the next day. He was not the only one who faced threats of violent reprisal if he broke ranks. Garvey hurriedly transferred his property into his brother's name and fled the city.[165]

Connolly was still in the habit of making a daily appearance at the comptroller's office. On 25 November Sheriff Matthew Brennan, his old rival for the comptrollership, entered the office. Connolly offered his hand to Brennan, who, accepting it, then notified the startled Connolly that he was under arrest. Connolly immediately turned to Tilden, who had been watching the scene:

> "Mr. Tilden, I am arrested."
> "No," said Tilden, looking surprised. "What is the bail, Sheriff?"
> "One million dollars," Brennan replied.
> "Let me look at the papers," Tilden took them and walked to the window as if to examine them, and then returning them to the Sheriff, remarked, "I am surprised at this; the bail is really one million."[166]

O slippery Tilden! Connolly's arrest was based upon a complaint to which the only affidavit attached was Tilden's. He later testified that he did not know that Connolly was to be arrested, but Townsend, for one, did not find that claim credible.[167] Nor should we.

Once he had fallen from power and was under arrest there was a shift in portrayals of the broken man. The pathos of his fate, and journalistic accounts of his distressed and ruined countenance, undermined the righteous indignation of the reformers. But these fleeting and reluctant acknowledgments of the comptroller's humanity were soon replaced by contempt and outrage when Connolly jumped bail and fled to Europe on New Year's Day, 1872. The struggle against the Ring, once begun, went so quickly that Tweed's power seemed chimerical. Indeed, the speed of Tweed's fall seemed to minimize his guilt. He was never written about with the personal loathing and contempt heaped upon Connolly. The legal cases against the Ring lumbered messily on, as the state sought to retrieve the stolen wealth from the guilty men and tried the estates of men such as James Watson. In his successive prosecutions, imprisonments and dramatic recapture in Spain, Tweed kept the story alive for several years. When he appeared at City Hall before the aldermanic committee investigating the Ring frauds, the crowds "pushed and jostled each other in their eagerness to get a glimpse of the ex-Boss."[168] His testimony in 1877 dominated the New York press for two months. Barnum could have made a fortune exhibiting Tweed. His revelations, and the ensuing denials and counter-claims about the behavior of figures like O'Brien (who was in 1877 a leader of anti-Tammany Democrats), provoked a wide-ranging press debate about the bona fides of the reformed Democratic Party. After deposing Tweed as Grand Sachem on 30 December 1871, and expelling Tweed, Hall, Sweeny, and Connolly from membership of the Tammany Society, the newly cleansed Hall over which "Honest John" Kelly presided did its level best to pretend that Tweed had never existed.[169] Mayor Oakey Hall was tried twice, and twice acquitted, but his political career was over. Sweeny successfully settled

Connolly in 1872, after he had fallen from power.

the city's claim against himself by passing blame on to his dead brother James. He returned to New York after a period in Europe and lived quietly well into the next century. The contractors skipped town or turned state's evidence; they never mattered anyway. The precarious alliance between Republicans and former War Democrats on the Committee of Seventy had broken down in October 1873 in a strained debate over whether the committee, now having achieved its primary purpose, should dissolve, or turn itself into a permanent force for reform in the city. Despite mayor Havemeyer's forceful opposition, most of the members seemed willing to declare themselves winners and return to private life. John Foley, interviewed in the *New York Times*, thought that "the jig was up": it no longer mattered what the Committee of Seventy decided.[170]

Connolly's story has a stranger and sadder ending. He was the first of the Ring to be imprisoned. His fate was a source of some "bad feelings" among Tilden's allies. Samuel G. Courtney, who with Havemeyer had implored Connolly to appoint Green as his deputy, wrote to Tilden that "Mr Connolly is still in duress, and I am afraid he cannot get the required bail. What's to be done? I mean to stand by him and sustain him now, for under my advice (together with the urgent appeals of Mr H[avemeyer]) he resigned, and the result is imprisonment . . ."[171] He was betrayed and abandoned by the reformers once his usefulness had passed. On his arrest Connolly was told that the claim against him might be settled for one and a half million dollars. He offered a million. When this was declined, Connolly's wife intervened. This Roman matron's sole words preserved by history were then uttered: "Richard, go to jail." And there he remained, "suffering from physical and mental prostration" according to the *Times*, in lieu of a million dollars' bail until Judge Barnard intervened and released Connolly on a writ of habeas corpus.[172]

After leaving prison he wrote a cautious letter to Tilden denying that he had ever claimed that Tilden "acted unkindly" towards himself, saying that he had never been anything but "fully satisfied" with the advice he received from Tilden and Havemeyer in September 1871:

> Be assured, my dear sir, that while I live I shall remember with gratitude your very kind treatment to me during that eventful period in my life, and I know by my future acts I shall prove worthy of your friendship and esteem.[173]

Connolly, without Tilden's esteem or friendship, fled to Europe with his wife. It was confidently believed, though probably much exaggerated, that he had taken six million dollars—the only one of the Tweed Ring to have gotten away with the loot.[174] He lived at first with his son-in-law in Vevey—the Vevey of Henry James's *Daisy Miller*—and no more picturesque American exile could be imagined. He was said to have a château and a private yacht basin on Lake Geneva and a mansion in Paris. But then many stories circulated in New York about "Slippery Dick" in exile. A tourist claimed to have seen Connolly on the piazza of a hotel, "shunned by everybody, with trembling hands and vacant eyes." Another report described him as "broken down in health, having been afflicted with softening of the brain." He was said to have speculated unwisely in Egyptian bonds and to have lost his fortune. A friend of the family described him as traveling from place to place "in the hope of finding relief from his sufferings, never stopping anywhere." By the 1920s, the process of turning Connolly into a symbol of crime and punishment was complete: "After eighteen [*sic*] years of exile, his hair white, his body bent, his pockets almost empty, Slippery Dick died in Marseilles, an ignoble Lear."[175]

He offered $400,000 to settle the civil liability against him in 1874. The corporation counsel Wheeler H. Peckham and the lawyer Charles O'Conor favored accepting Connolly's offer, which they thought could be raised to $500,000. Peckham's plea to Governor Tilden, complete with pathetic detail ("His property has undoubtedly shrunk, and doubtless he has been blackmailed to a large extent") met with stony hostility.[176] In December 1877, after an abortive attempt in the aftermath of Sweeny's settlement to cut a deal for $500,000, Connolly instructed his lawyer to consent to the full verdict against him of $8,537,170.15 in favor of the city. No money was collected: the verdict was a symbolic act. Fifteen years later, when Fanny Fithian returned to the city for the first time since her parents' flight, there were rumors that the state's claim against her father's estate was to be settled. The rumors were denied by Mrs. Fithian's lawyer, and the story faded from memory.[177]

Americans found exiles like Connolly figures of pathos. The fate of Benedict Arnold, snubbed and ignored in his English exile, and the more recent memory of Edward Everett Hale's *The Man Without a Country* (1865), which retold the story of Philip Nolan, one of Burr's conspirators who was sentenced to exile aboard a U.S. Navy vessel never to hear a word about his native land, harshly warned against betrayal of trust. But his trembling hands and bent body in the accounts of his last years were caused by Bright's disease, not contrition. As late as 1877, Connolly was reported in the New York press as being resolute (some regarded his attitude as being brazen). He was "still very positively opposed to making any restoration of his money to the City."[178] He died in 1880, a widower at the age of seventy. "Many stories have been circulated concerning Connolly's greed," noted the *New York Times* in an unexpectedly sympathetic obituary:

> but these tales may be all traced to men who sought in one way or another, to over-reach him. He was not a popular man—was not even liked by his fellows—and possessed few of the engaging arts of the ordinary politician. He had not even the remarkable skill and cunning as a schemer which characterized Sweeny. But he was a man of sagacity and shrewd common sense. He was not given to vulgar show or extravagance, and his social life was always above reproach. The influence of his

estimable and high-minded wife was felt in his household and was ever exerted in behalf of noble and charitable projects.[179]

Connolly lived long enough to see the reformers at each other's throats: the aggressive John Foley accused comptroller Andrew H. Green of "gross mismanagement of the City finances"; Henry Ward Beecher was accused in 1875 of having sexual relations with Mrs. Theodore Tilton; and in the same year Henry Nicoll, the upstanding lawyer and member of the Committee of Seventy, was caught having embezzled hundreds of thousands of dollars from his clients' trust funds. Tilden was cheated out of the presidency in 1876 by the Republican supporters of Rutherford B. Hayes. The news must have brought some cheer to the old man when he read it in the press.[180]

CHAPTER FOUR

"New York demands a park and will have it, be the cost what it may."[1]

Waste land

I n the late 1840s, the city of New York was largely confined to the densely built area below 14th Street. As one travelled north up the island the number of buildings rapidly declined. An occasional unimproved lot gave way to broad stretches of land awaiting development. *Doggett's New York City Directory* for 1850 listed residents by street and house numbers only from the Battery to 25th Street. On the East Side, there was a built-up area on Third Avenue, between 24th and 28th Streets. On the West Side, Seventh, Eighth and Ninth avenues contained discontinuous rows of properties between 14th and 23rd Street. There were scarcely any buildings at all on fifth Avenue above 25th Street. When William C. Waddell's Gothic villa on fifth Avenue between 37th and 38th streets was built in 1845 it was reached along a dirt road from the northern side of Washington Square. From the tower of the house it was possible to see both the North (as the lower Hudson River was known in this period) and East River. A field in the garden, planted with wheat, yielded an annual crop of one barrel.[2]

To the north there were dirt roads and isolated small clusters of buildings (one between Sixth and Eighth avenues between 28th and 32nd streets, another on either side of Eighth Avenue in the forties). They were called "suburbs," but signs of gentle pastoral scenery were few and far between. The "lower depths" of the densely populated inner-city, which carried such a charge of social anxiety, threatened to re-emerge as a waste land, an outer zone of random residential and commercial development largely created by the increasing number of

Sixth Avenue: "To the north there were dirt roads and isolated small clusters of buildings."

factories located to the north of the built-up areas of the city. "An insanitary cordon of slaughter houses, milk distilleries and bone-boiling establishments, hog-pens and dung heaps," was the significant reality of the suburbs in 1851. "The foulest imagination could not give form and expression to the countless and monstrous shapes of filth, obscenity, and abomination of which they are the home. Golgotha, Gehenna, and the midnight revels of graveyard ghouls at their unnameable feasts, united could not furnish a scene to compare with them."[3] Travellers arriving by train down the Hudson River from Albany passed through ". . . straggling half-built streets, with shabby stores, lumber-yards, heaps of rubbish, petty wooden houses, and a general aspect of disorder."[4] It was not an impressive entrance to the greatest city in the republic. There was a geography of concern in mid-century New York, and the northern reaches constituted an uncertain and troublesome terrain.

The commissioners' 1811 plan set out the future shape of the city by extending a grid of regular streets and avenues over the irregular pattern of old Dutch landgrant farms, orchards and market gardens, as well as random outbuildings, barns, sheds and other structures situated in a miscellaneous, largely characterless landscape which had lost its rural identity (few farms survived into the 1840s), but which had not yet begun to look much like a city.[5] When New York was occupied by the British during the revolutionary war, virtually every tree on the island (except a few fruit orchards) was cut down. Second-growth woods had regrown along the least visited parts of the island (the deep ravines leading down to the East River). Few New Yorkers chose to live in this indeterminate land. Peter Cooper remained a suburbanite until the New York and Harlem Railroad began to leave, overnight, in front of his house cars filled with cattle destined for the glue factory he owned at 28th Street and Fourth Avenue. Horace Greeley rented an old farmhouse, once the summer residence of Isaac Lawrence, formerly the president of the New York branch of the United States Bank, on an eight-acre site overlooking the East River from Turtle Bay on 49th Street. Accustomed to the bustle of downtown life, Greeley found the silence ". . . so sepulchral, unearthly, that I found difficulty in sleeping."[6] The only means of transit to the offices of the *Tribune* was an hourly stage on Third Avenue. He was able to offer accommodation to Margaret Fuller, who arrived from Boston in late 1844 to write for the *Tribune*. Her description of the location of Greeley's home was reassuring to her friends:

> This place is to me entirely charming; it is so completely in the country, and all around is so bold and free. It is two miles or more from the thickly-settled parts of New York, but omnibuses and cars give me constant access to the city, and, while I can readily see what and whom I will, I can command time and retirement. Stopping on the Harlem road, you enter a lane nearly a quarter of a mile long, and going by a small brook and pond that locks in the place, and ascending a slightly rising ground, get sight of the house, which, old fashioned and of mellow tint, fronts on a flower-garden filled with shrubs, large vines, and trim box borders. On both sides of the house are beautiful trees, standing fair, full-grown, and clear.[7]

Fuller soon began to hold court for her many admirers. For some, the journey to visit her was something of an ordeal. "It was an undertaking for *me*, I assure you," wrote Lydia Maria Child to Anna Loring,

> for we live three miles apart, and the roads were one mass of mud. I went out in the Harlem omnibus to *forty-ninth street*, where she told me she lived. But instead of a street, I found a winding, zig-zag cart-track. It was as rural as you can imagine, with moss-covered rocks, scraggly bushes, and a brook that came tumbling over a little dam, and run [*sic*] under the lane. After passing through three great swing-gates, I came to the house, which stands all alone by itself, and is as inaccessible, as if *I* had chosen it, to keep people off. It is a very old house, with a very old porch, and very old vines, and a very old garden, and very old summer-

houses dropping to pieces, and a very old piazza at the back, over-grown with very old rose bushes, which at that season were covered with red berries. The piazza is almost *on* the East river, with Blackwell's Island in full view before it. Margaret's chamber looks out upon a little woody knoll, that runs down into the water, and boats and ships are passing her window all the time. How anything so old and picturesque has been allowed to remain standing near New York so long, I cannot imagine.[8]

The dominant structure above 14th Street was the Croton distrib-uting reservoir at fifth Avenue between 40th and 42nd streets. Built between 1839–42, on a site which had been a potters field since 1823, the reservoir dwarfed virtually every building in the city. Its sheer sloping undecorated walls were, like New York's prison The Tombs, neo-Egyptian in inspiration. A popular walk had been created on its ramparts, affording fine views of the smoke stacks and four- and five-story buildings of the city's industries on the West Side.

To the north of the distributing reservoir lay Yorkville to the east, and just visible along the East River were the tops of the wooded land owned by John Jones, lying between 64th and 66th streets from Third Avenue to the shoreline. Extending northward along the river from Jones's home on 68th Street were the estates and gracious white clapboarded homes of the Riker family at 75th Street and the Schermerhorn family (one branch on 73rd Street, another on 84th).[9] Too far to be visible was the city's first man-made link to the adjacent countryside, the High Bridge (a Roman-style masonry aqueduct with a pedestrian walk) which crossed the Harlem River at West 174th Street and carried Croton water to Manhattan. It was opened in 1848. Bloomingdale Road (now Broadway) ran north seven miles from City Hall to the village of Bloomingdale, with its asylum for the insane and orphan asylum. One mile further north lay Manhattanville, site of the imposing Greek Revival building of the Leake and Watts Orphan House and School, at the end of the Harlem Plains on the Hudson. Like every New York road, the Bloomingdale was "... a mass of mud in wet weather and a desert of dust at other times..."[10] Bloomingdale Road was "opened" (that is, levelled and widened) after much delay and complaint by the landowners who had been charged for the expense, during "Boss" Tweed's regime in 1868, but it was not paved until 1890. Third Avenue led north to Yorkville, five miles from City Hall, and to the old Dutch settlement of Harlem two miles further. The Manhattanville and Bloomingdale stages, meeting the Brooklyn ferry at Fulton Street, were fine, handsome vehicles drawn by two horses, carrying twelve to fourteen passengers. The fare was twelve and a half cents.[11] Dirt roads, avoiding marshes and stone outcroppings, cut convenient routes cross-town.

Land to the east and to the west of the distributing reservoir had already attracted the attention of John Jacob Astor and Samuel B. Ruggles, the city's leading property speculators. In 1831 Ruggles paid $180,000 to level the site of Gramercy Farm (between 19th Street on the south and 22nd Street on the north, between Fourth and Third avenues).[12] Most other investors looked for property (the standard building lot was 100 feet by twenty-five) which required as little filling, levelling or drainage as possible. As the value of land below 14th Street rose, ponds such as the Collect (bisected by Leonard Street and Centre Street east of Broadway) were filled, and streams were enclosed and built over. The property line was extended outward into the Hudson and East rivers, requiring extensive filling. These "water-lots" were sold by the city corporation as a right to reclaim land which was under the high-water mark. There were many complaints that Astor, whose investments in city real estate were funded from the profits of his China ships, was reluctant to fulfill his obligations and complete improvements. (On his death in 1848, his wealth was estimated to be between $20 and $30 million.)[13] The commonest sight in the city in the 1840s must have been horse-drawn wagons, loaded with gravel for landfill, dustily passing through the city streets. Ruggles estimated that three million cart loads of earth would be needed to level the irregular site of his Gramercy Park development.

The construction of Crystal Palace on the site adjacent to the Croton distributing reservoir did much to spur building up both fifth and Sixth avenues. It was uncertain whether wealthy New Yorkers wanted to live in this largely undeveloped area, and development carried significant risks. In 1853 George Higgins erected a row of ornate mansions on fifth Avenue opposite the distributing reservoir. Unable to find purchasers, he sold them to a female college in 1860 and, for years, they were a reminder of the vagaries of uptown development and speculation. The Sixth Avenue surface rail line, to 50th Street, was opened on 10 August 1852; the Eighth Avenue line, running from Chambers Street to 51st Street, was opened on the 31st. By the time the "Exhibition of the Industry of All Nations" at Crystal Palace opened in July 1853, horse-drawn street cars brought visitors in great numbers up fifth Avenue. The fare was five and a quarter cents. An ascent to the top of Latting Observatory, by the first steam-powered elevator, afforded even more spectacular views of the city. With the large number of visitors attracted to the Crystal Palace, the surrounding empty lots were filled with beer tents and grog shops in hastily erected shanties. Patrons of amusements such as cock-fighting and gambling and perhaps much worse were drawn to the site. The concerns of property owners and custodians of public morals at the tendency of uptown development to create bear gardens, and other socially troublesome manifestations of public taste, runs throughout the debate on the park idea in the 1850s.

North of the reservoir, above straggling nurseries and the former site of Dr. Hosack's Elgin Botanic Garden,[14] stretched the ugliest, most commercially useless land in New York. An arsenal, standing at a bleak site at fifth Avenue and 64th Street, held a portion of the state's military explosives. An abandoned mill largely blocked a stream that rose on the West Side at 74th Street and circuitously made its way to the East River. Marshy land was thickly grown with tangled vine, making foot passage virtually impossible. Poison ivy grew rampant. Stone had been quarried for decades on this central strip of the island. A large plot had been laid out for the Croton receiving reservoir between 79th and 86th Streets. Outcroppings of stone, swampy bogs created by blocked watercourses, and an irregular ground level encouraged hard-headed property speculators to look elsewhere. Goats, pigs and dogs roamed at will. Several squatter encampments were located in this waste land, housing perhaps 5,000 people, largely poor, who lived "... in rude huts of their own construction ..." on the site. There were 200 shanties, barns, stables and bone factories. These had mud floors and open fireplaces. When the site was finally cleared for the construction of Central Park, the board of commissioners auctioned off the remaining buildings. $2,200 was raised. The highest price paid for a shanty was seventy dollars.[15] For all its ugliness, the site was more heavily built up and populated than is generally imagined. Topographical maps, such as that which Egbert L. Viele completed for the board of commissioners in 1856, suggested it was land little disturbed by contemporary society. So few trees remained on this land that residents collected driftwood on the deserted banks of the East River. Rag-and-bone pickers, displaced from lower Manhattan by rising real estate values, found space and a congenial environment in the waste land here. Convoys of their small dog carts brimming with city refuse no doubt did much to please the residents of the first of the rich men's mansions which had begun to line fifth Avenue below 25th Street.[16]

There were two distinct settlements in the land made into Central Park: the southernmost was inhabited by the Irish, whose free-range chickens, pigs and ragged children, viewed from carriages of passing travellers, dismayed the tidy classes. "Nigger Village" and its "Ebon inhabitants" to the north, according to the *New York Times*, "present a pleasing contrast in their habits and the appearance of

The site of Central Park was occupied by several squatter encampments. During one of his rambles in Manhattan in 1844, Poe found the bleak scene and tumbledown shanties to be "exceedingly picturesque."

their dwellings to the Celtic inhabitants, in common with hogs and goats, of the shanties in the lower part of the Park."[17] By the standards of "respectable" New York, these were lawless places well beyond the reach of the city's churches and civil society. Inevitably they attracted the interest of a few curious walkers in the expanding city: "I have been roaming far and wide over this island of Mannahatta," wrote Edgar Allan Poe in May 1844.

> Some portions of its interior have a certain air of rocky sterility which may impress some imaginations as simply *dreary*—to me it conveys the sublime. Trees are few; but some of the shrubbery is exceedingly picturesque. Not less so are the prevalent shanties of the Irish squatters. I have one of these *tabernacles* (I use the term primitively) at present in the eye of my mind. It is, perhaps, nine feet by six, with a pigsty applied externally, by way both of portico and support. The whole fabric (which is of mud) has been erected in somewhat too obvious an imitation of the Tower of Pisa. A dozen rough planks, "pitched" together,

form the roof. The door is a barrel on end. There is a garden, too, and this is encircled by a ditch at one point, a large stone at another, a bramble at a third. A dog and a cat are inevitable in these habitations; and apparently there are no dogs and no cats more entirely happy.[18]

Poe's humane curiosity contrasted sharply with the alarm sanitary reformers felt when they looked at the site. Street grading had repeatedly created areas of marshy soil in lower Manhattan. City Inspector John H. Griscom argued in 1842 that overcrowded slums bred the "miasma" which caused typhus, yellow fever and cholera. That "humid miasmatic state of the atmosphere" which produced "poisonous exhalations" threatened infection and disease. Such land was dangerous to health. (The theory of the "miasmatic" diffusion of disease gave sanitary reformers a particular interest in ventilation, and a powerful belief in the healthful benefits of fresh air.) It had been repeatedly argued that the most unhealthy locations in the city were houses built on marshy, undrained soil. If conducted with disregard for the ancient watercourses of the island, rampant development of the land occupied by the Central Park squatters would be as much a threat to the community as the malaria of the Pontine marshes was to the Roman Empire.[19]

The park idea

Between 1830 and 1860 New York City expanded at a break-neck pace.

date	total city population	total state population
1830	202,589	1,918,608
1840	312,710	2,428,921
1850	515,547	3,097,394
1860	805,651	3,880,735

After the final emancipation of slaves in New York in 1827, the total population (white and "free colored") of New York City by decades. Source: *The American Annual Cyclopedia and Register of Important Events of the Year 1861* (New York: D. Appleton & Co., 1868), 525; state population: Jos. C. G. Kennedy, *Preliminary Report on the Eighth Census 1860*, Senate, 37th Cong., 2nd Sess., (Washington: Government Printing Office, 1862), table 1.

Although the voracious development northwards was just beginning in the early 1840s, the demand for real estate, and for unrestricted commercial development, was transforming the physical aspects of the city. In 1843 the population above Canal Street was 278,436. By 1860, it had reached 725,003 and had triggered off a rise in the value of real estate which made millionaires out of modest farmers, and important citizens out of property speculators.[20] Poe was perhaps the only New Yorker in 1844 to find the land above the Croton reservoir "sublime." In the eyes of investors, the empty land to the north meant one thing: the promise of a brilliant return on their investment. Other than Ruggles, few investors actually improved their properties, preferring instead to allow builders to lease the land for housing. The New York property speculator, like the "bulls" on Wall Street, characteristically purchased land with borrowed money, in the hope that rapidly rising real estate values would enable a quick, effortless profit to be realized.

Increasingly given to nostalgic reflections upon the virtuous early years of the city, New Yorkers first became fully conscious of the scale of the changes in the city in the 1840s. Older residents recalled the "quiet little City" of their earlier years:

> New York, as you knew it, was a mere corner of the present huge city and that corner is all changed, pulled to pieces, burnt down and rebuilt—all but our little native nest in William Street, which still retains some of its old features; though those are daily altering. I can hardly realize that within my term of life, this great crowded metropolis, so full of life[,] bustle, noise, shew and splendor, was a quiet little City of some fifty or sixty thousand inhabitants. It is really now one of the most rucketing cities in the world and reminds me of one of the great European cities (Frankfort for instance) in the time of an annual fair—Here it is a Fair almost all the year round. For my part, I dread the noise and turmoil of it, and visit it but now and then, preferring the quiet of my country retreat; which shews that the bustling time of life is over with me, and that I am settling down into a sober, quiet good for nothing old gentleman.[21]

Rapid growth aroused profound social fears of racial swamping by Irish-Catholic immigrants, fears of unrestrained immorality and lawlessness in the city, and of the specter of social disintegration. The city was increasingly coming to be seen as something alien, which could only be represented as a maze, a mysterious terrain in which people no longer knew each other.[22] The new city seemed to be a world of strangers. Anti-urbanism has had a long history in western culture, and for many decades it formed a staple of American social thought. With the growth of the cities in the 1840s, a qualitative change in the struggle to understand them is registered in Edgar Allan Poe's story, "The Man of the Crowd," published in *Gentleman's Magazine* in December 1840. In it we see an urban world of puzzling interactions and mysteries, akin to the Paris of the novels of Eugene Sue. Set in London (though this is the merest of conventions), the narrator, in a mood of the "keenest appetancy," takes a lively interest in the scene before him—the crowded street. He is a skilled observer, one whose evenings sauntering on the Bowery or Broadway have been put to good use. He is one of those who knows how to "read" the passing throng, sharply differentiating between social types as they pass before him. He carefully distinguishes those who seem decently satisfied from the others who are merely restless or gesticulating. The streets are crowded with urban social types: a procession of clerks, pickpockets, gamblers, "dandies," whores, drunkards, "Jew peddlers," street beggers, invalids, modest young girls and military men, who reveal themselves by their dress and looks. The narrator is confident of his grasp of this heavily coded urban world, and he sheds stronger illumination upon the scene than the "fitful and garish lustre" of the city's gas lamps.

When a "decrepid old man" passes before him, the narrator uncomfortably wonders at the "absolute idiosyncrasy" of his expression. The man has a daunting aura of vast mental powers, but also of caution, penuriousness, avarice, coolness, malice and blood thirstiness. This combination of judgments makes no sense, and the narrator is drawn by a "craving desire" to follow the old man. Each of his initial perceptions is qualified as he notes the man's good linen, the diamond he is wearing, the dagger he conceals. The narrator believes he possesses the skills to read the stranger, but as the old man's behavior changes, and as his expression of "intense agony" is followed by uneasiness, vacillation and agitation (classic literary signs of a guilty conscience—but of what?), the narrator's self-confidence drains away. Trailing the man through a "Night Town" world of tenements and gin palaces, he is left with nothing more certain than his own obsession. He remains in pursuit hour after hour, until growing weary "unto death," all the while being ignored by the old man. In the end the narrator concludes that the old man's bizarre behavior reveals him to be "the type and genius of deep crime" which does not permit itself to be read. Such a profusion of signs, and such an elusive or withheld meaning, dismays the narrator. Illegibility in the city seems intolerable. The absence of communication between the two men makes the reader wonder whether the narrator's conclusions are founded upon a reading of the old man, or are puzzling symptoms of a mania which he shares with the subject. In the city an appearance of individuality reigns; but it is no longer a place where certainty can retain its old self-confidence. Poe's city is a profoundly disturbing place. The mystery of the old man is deepened by the growing mysteriousness of the narrator. Who is the real "man of the crowd?"[23]

The most casual of encounters comes freighted with a burden of uncertainty, of epistemological anxiety. Another illustration of the perplexity of city life, which teeters on the brink of humor but which retains its more troubling edge, concerns the search *Evening Post* editor William Cullen Bryant made for Catherine Maria Sedgwick in 1860. "Last evening," he wrote to his wife Frances,

> I went to look for Miss Sedgwick. I went to Harry's, his door plate was gone and nobody would answer the bell. I then went to Rackemann's. He had moved and with his family they said was at the Clarendon Hotel. In going to the Clarendon Hotel I stopped at Dr Bellows's—he knew nothing about Miss Sedgwick's place of sojourn and had been looking for it in vain. At the Clarendon, they told me that Mrs Rackemann was in Berkshire and he was out. I stopped at Mr Valerios door. The girl said Miss Sedgwick was at Mrs Carpenters No 58 in the same street. I went thither, it was Mrs Faulkener's and Mrs Robert Sedgwick came forward. Miss Sedgwick she told me was at Mr Dudley field's. I did not go further.[24]

New Yorkers, least of all those of Bryant's generation, did not understand the new forms of social life and personal mobility that were emerging in the city, and many hoped in some way to adapt urban life to tame some of its uncertainties. Parks, with their civilizing mission, promised to be places to regularize and make visible the interactions which seemed so perplexing on the city streets. They were a response, one of many, to anxieties such as those at the heart of Poe's story.

The city's growth provoked alarm that the whole island would be smothered. In a notebook in which he recorded ideas for stories, Nathaniel Hawthorne wrote: "A sketch—the devouring of the old country residences by the overgrown monster of a city. For instance, Mr Beekman's ancestral residence [at first Avenue and 51st Street] was originally several miles from the city of New-York; but the pavements kept creeping nearer and nearer; till now the house is removed, and a street runs directly through what was once its hall." Bryant observed in 1844 that "[c]ommerce is devouring inch by inch the coast of the island, and if we would rescue any part of it for health and recreation it must be done now." Even more alarming imagery appeared in the *New York Times*: "The huge masses of masonry which are springing up in every direction seem to threaten us with a stifling atmosphere of bricks and mortar." These concerns were sharply magnified by the city's growth after the Civil War: unless the park was built, "the great necessities of commerce would swallow up the whole of Manhattan Island and leave no breathing room for its inhabitants."[25] (Only aggressive verbs seemed appropriate for the process of growth in New York.) Neither the *New York Times* nor the *Evening Post* was remotely hostile to commerce, and both papers proudly anticipated the city's future development. Rather, the park idea in New York emerged out of psychological as well as physical and social anxieties. The city's "stifling atmosphere" was as much a threat to emotional coherence and civic stability as it was to the citizens' need for "pure atmosphere."

Rapid growth raised the question whether there was a duty one generation owed to another in the management of a city. Little thought had been given to this problem in the Jacksonian era. The development of the city in the 1840s forced it into the discourse of politicians, just as the problems raised by the slums and threats to public health and public order pushed clergymen and sanitary reformers to seek a redefinition of community. As it was for Dr. John H. Griscom, who argued that the larger needs of the community required immediate action to improve housing conditions, so it was for the Democratic mayor Fernando Wood, who said that the community required action to preserve unimproved land for a park: "In my opinion, future generations, who are to pay this expense, would have good reasons for reflecting upon the present generation, if we permitted the entire island to be taken possession of by the population, without some spot like this, devoted to rural beauty, healthful recreation, and pure atmosphere."[26]

Mount Auburn Cemetery in Cambridge, Massachusetts, developed in 1831, and Greenwood Cemetery in Brooklyn, laid out in 1839 on a site of 250 acres on Gowanus Heights, were for many years pleasure-grounds enthusiastically visited on Sunday afternoons. "Have you been to Greenwood, sweet reader? If not, we advise you to take the earliest opportunity of achieving a visit there.—The effect were good, truly, if the whole mass of our population—the delver for money, the idler, the votary of fashion, the ambitious man—if *all* could ofttimes, move slowly through that Beautiful Place of Graves, and give room to the thoughts that would naturally arise there."[27] The picturesque effect of a few headstones sited in a landscape of irregular surface, open meadows and leafy glades was a striking vindication of the new ideals of natural landscape design. Although some of the charm was eventually lost as both cemeteries became more heavily planted, and as cast-iron railings were erected around private plots, their evident popular success encouraged the growing appreciation of parks and the picturesque landscape in the next decade.[28] As J. B. Jackson has suggested, the rural cemeteries were not simply another artificial space; they were ". . . an *environment*, a place for new, primarily social, experiences. It represented the rejection of structure, the rejection of classical urbanism with its historical allusions, and the rejection of architectural public space."[29] And with their success came an unexpected problem: people who came to the park to be amused, and thus who behaved as though on a pleasure jaunt, disturbed those who wished quiet contemplation. The bustle and ostentation of carriages changed the cemetery's atmosphere, and before long strict regulations were imposed to control behavior and limit the casual access of visitors. The beneficial effect which the originators expected that nature itself would exert did not produce the hoped-for state of mind among visitors. There were lessons to be learned from Mount Auburn about the need for social controls which the board of commissioners of Central Park seem to have carefully absorbed. Nonetheless, the notion that "Cemeteries are good schools, and Death reads us many a stern lesson from these marble pulpits; but a garden is no less a school . . ." gave powerful impetus to the park movement.[30]

Despite the proximity of open countryside, there were few places in New York of any size for convenient leisurely recreation. To head off proposals in 1833 to relocate the Custom House into the park before City Hall, and build a new city hall at Union Square, Bryant in the *New York Evening Post* attacked "the present rage for speculation" and argued that there was "a deficiency of public squares in the lower part of the city for the purposes of health and refreshment."[31] N. P. Willis complained in 1844 that for a metropolis proud of its wealth and fashion, New York singularly lacked a "driving park." Battery Park, fronting the harbor, consisted of twenty-four acres, half of which had been reclaimed in 1852 from land beyond the waterline, was a favorite location for strolling. Nearby Bowling Green, a small oval enclosure at the foot of Broadway, dated back to the Dutch settlement. The park surrounding City Hall, about ten acres with an attractive fountain, was first fenced in 1792. When New Yorkers mentioned "the Park" before the 1850s, it was City Hall Park they were referring to. In 1807 the commissioners charged with laying out the plan for the island reserved a substantial open space (between Third and Seventh avenues, from 23rd to 34th streets) for a "Parade." As development began to proceed uptown, it was reduced in size in 1814, and was abandoned as a public space in 1829.[32] Washington Square, just under ten acres, originally a potters field and then a parade ground, was laid out as a park in 1828. The park laid out in 1831 by Samuel Ruggles and called Gramercy Park was barely an acre and usually kept under locked restricted access. Ruggles successfully petitioned the city for tax-exempt status for the park, arguing that a better class of homes would be built in the surrounding streets than if the park did not exist. These in turn would yield greater tax revenues. (Like so many uptown speculations in the 1830s and 1840s, the development of Gramercy Park was slow gathering momentum. By 1845 only two houses had been completed, and seven were under construction. The willows, maples and chestnut trees gave the park a charming aspect; it was surrounded on all sides by empty lots and isolated buildings.) Gramercy Park was followed by Tompkins Square, a ten-acre site between Avenues A and B from 7th to 10th Street, laid out in 1833. As late as 1851, Tompkins Square was mainly used as a parade ground. "It is not much frequented, as the trees are young, and the place is not finished." Union Square, at the intersection of Broadway and 14th Street, was only three acres. It was noted in 1853 that Union Square ". . . presents to the wealthy citizen an elegant site for his residence, and to enterprising landlords a favorite position for hotels" (Phelps Stokes, 5, 1851). Madison Square, a six-acre site, was successively a potters field, US government arsenal, and the location of a juvenile asylum before it became a park in 1847. It was named after President James Madison, who died in 1836. Gas lights were installed in 1852. "Elegant mansions are rising rapidly around it, in all the splendor of recent Metropolitan improvements . . ." Larger sites to the north such as Hamilton Square (fifteen acres between Third and Fourth avenues, for three blocks above 65th Street), Bloomingdale Square (between Eighth and Ninth avenues for four blocks above 53rd Street, containing seventeen acres), and Manhattan Square (nineteen acres between Eighth and Ninth avenues for four blocks above 77th Street, described as being "in a rough state" in 1852) remained undeveloped.[33] With the beginning of the construction of Central Park in 1857, Bloomingdale Square was abandoned as a public space.

The modest size of these parks, which with several other small squares amounted only to 170 acres for the whole city, contrasted painfully with the spacious parks American visitors encountered in the great capitals of Europe. The business of making parks, of turning land into locations for public pleasure, had never quite been ignored, but it was clear to many in the 1840s that the existing parks were inadequate for a city growing as rapidly as New York.

While travelling in England in 1845, Bryant lamented the short-sightedness of the city fathers of the "quiet little City" who had attended so little to any needs other than commercial ones:

The population . . . increasing with such prodigious rapidity; your sultry summers, and the corrupt atmosphere generated in hot and crowded streets, make it a cause of regret that in laying out New York, no preparation was made, while it was yet practicable, for a range of parks

Bryant, poet, Democratic Party stalwart and editor of the *New York Evening Post*, had long lamented the lack of provision made in the city for public parks. His sustained support for the park campaign helped to arouse public opinion.

and public gardens along the central part of the island or elsewhere, to remain perpetually for the refreshment and recreation of the citizens during the torrid heats of the warm season.[34]

The provision of public parks was an attractive idea that drew upon many currents of antebellum social thought and culture. The growth of industrial manufacture, and the sharpening division of classes, led sympathetic observers to fear that the poor, pent up in ugly and insanitary cities, were being brutalized. The idea that they might have no share in the enjoyment of nature alarmed Lydia Maria Child, recently moved to New York to edit an abolitionist journal. While walking up Broadway one day in March 1844, she came upon the grand fountain that dominated the park around City Hall. The spray leaped "joyously" in the morning sunlight, and the park was bathed in "a mantle of rainbows." The beauty of the scene made Child gasp with delight and reflect that though the precious possessions of the rich could be hidden away, such a scene could be shared by all:

Undated engraving by J. L. Phillips, 9 Dey St., New York, of the fountain before City Hall which enthralled Lydia Maria Child.

> And this, thought I, *is* a universal gift. . . . For the laborer returning from daily toil to his narrow and crowded home, here is a wayside vision of freedom, of beauty, and of joy. Who can calculate how much it cools and refreshes his fevered soul? There are those who inquire what was the use of expending so much money for something to look at? Alas for them! for they know not "a thing of beauty is a joy forever."[35]

The desire not only to enjoy such a moment, but to wish that it be *shared* by all suggests a powerful democratic motive for those who wished to create parks The appreciation of the beauties of nature was not passive or merely aesthetic, and the beneficial effects of exposure to nature were touchstones of romantic doctrine and antebellum values. The park idea carried with it overtones of proselytism: this is good for you.

In a discourse entitled "Work and Play" delivered in 1848, the Hartford Congregational minister Horace Bushnell argued against the narrow political economy which would define man solely in terms of duty and work:

> Who that considers the ethereal nature of a soul can conceive that the doom of work is any thing more than a temporary expedient, introduced or suffered to perfect our discipline? To imagine a human creature

dragged along, or dragging himself along, under the perpetual friction of work, never to ascend above it; a creature in God's image, aching for God's liberty, beating ever vainly and with crippled wings, that he may lift himself into some freer, more congenial element—this, I say, were no better than to quite despair of man. Nay, it were to confess that all which is most akin to God in his human instincts is only semblance without reality. Do we not all find within us some dim ideal, at least, of a state unrealized, where action is its own impulse; where the struggles of birth are over, and the friction of interest and care is no longer felt; where all that is best and highest is freest, and joyous because it is free; where to be is to be great, because the inspiration of the soul is full, and to do is easy as to conceive; where action is itself sublime, because it is the play of ease and the equilibrium of rest?[36]

The reduction of "friction," the end of "struggle," opens the soul's larger "play of ease." Contemporaries may have heard other notes in this sermon. On 2 August 1848, three weeks before Bushnell spoke, the last U.S. troops left the Mexican port of Vera Cruz. Thus ended a war which added the territories of California and New Mexico to the Union. The occupation of Mexico City by an American army commanded by Gen. Winfield Scott was the culminating moment in a restless war of national expansion and self-assertion. Before the Treaty of Guadeloupe Hidalgo was signed, gold was discovered in the Sacramento Valley in California. Within a year the population of California had grown by 100,000. The war with Mexico was perhaps least popular in New England (it was violently criticized by Thoreau and others as being a slaveowner's plot). Emerson ironically asked of such a moment,

> . . . who is he that prates
> Of the culture of mankind,
> Of better arts and life?[37]

Bushnell was among those who "prates" of aspects of human nature other than the bellicose and the materialistic. Indeed, his praise of the arts of peace carried an endorsement of "activity *as* an end" in itself. He encouraged thoughtful people to regard "improvements" and "beautifications," such as parks, as sustaining the work of "Christian nurture." (The families of Frederick Law Olmsted and Charles Loring Brace were members of Bushnell's congregation.)

Walt Whitman, who spent many an afternoon schmoozing with workmen across the city, records a conversation he had with a Central Park policeman:

Of fine afternoons, along the broad tracks of the Park, for many years, had swept by my friend, as he stood on guard, the carriages, etc., of

American Gentility, not by dozens and scores, but by hundreds and thousands. Lucky brokers, capitalists, contractors, grocery-men, successful political strikers, rich butchers, dry goods' folk, &c. And on a large proportion of these vehicles, on panels or horse-trappings, were conspicuously borne *heraldic family crests.* (Can this really be true?) In wish and willingness (and if that were so, what matter about the reality?) titles of nobility, with a court and spheres fit for the capitalists, the highly educated, and the carriage-riding classes—to fence them off from "the common people"—were the heart's desire of the "good society" of our great cities—aye, of North and South.[38]

Bushnell, born in 1802, cannot really tell us why the park so rapidly became a stage for the ostentation of the city's nouveau riche. But another Congregational minister, Henry Ward Beecher, certainly can. He contributed a regular column to *The Independent,* signed only with a star, collected in 1855 under the title *Star Papers, or, Experiences of Art and Nature.* Beecher's discussion of "Christian Liberty in the Use of the Beautiful" suggests a very comforting doctrine about wealth and its enjoyment:

> . . . if rightly viewed, and rightly used, his ["a Christian man"] very elegances and luxuries will be a contribution to the public good. One may well say, "How can I indulge in such embellishments in my dwelling, when so many thousands are perishing for lack of knowledge about me." This is conclusive against a selfish use of the beautiful. But rightly employed, it becomes itself a contribution to the education of society. It acts upon the lower classes by acting first upon the higher. It is an education of the educators. And the question becomes only this: How much of my wealth given to the public good shall be employed *directly* for the elevation of the ignorant, and how much *indirectly*? How much shall I bring to bear directly upon the masses, and how much indirectly through institutions and remote instrumentalities?
>
> I can not but think that Christian men have not only a right of enjoyment in the beautiful, but a duty, in some measure, of producing it, or propagating it, or diffusing it abroad through the community.[39]

Beecher's formulation of this problem might be reformulated as a trickle-down theory of social benevolence. "[I]n all your labors for the Beautiful," he argued, "remember that its mission is not of corruption, nor of pride, nor of selfishness, but of *benevolence*" (*Star Papers*, 302). The Christian merchant, of which New York had many, was expected to hold his wealth accountably. "We can no more escape an imperious obligation, as we have 'opportunity to do good unto all men,' 'to be rich in good works, ready to distribute,' than we can annihilate ourselves as moral beings."[40] Attending carefully to Beecher at Plymouth Church, he would have heard a message

Henry Ward Beecher reassured wealthy New Yorkers that embellishments and concern for the beautiful need not be accompanied by uncomfortable traces of a guilty conscience. "It acts upon the lower classses by acting first upon the higher." Undated engraving by D. J. Pound from a photograph by Whippel & Black, Boston.

which helped to loosen the bounds of that tradition of American Protestant thought and made ostentatious display increasingly justifiable.[41] At a cost of $15,000,000, Central Park would be, in Beecher's terms, an example of mediated or indirect benevolence. It afforded the wealthy an incomparable stage upon which to act as examples to the "lower classes" while at the same time assuring these same "lower classes" the opportunity to benefit from their example.

Not only did parks promise greatly to improve the quality of life in the city, they hinted at a civic glory awaiting New York and tapped a vein of civic pride and boastfulness: the park will transform the center of the island, wrote Clarence Cook in *Putnam's Monthly*,

> . . . into a pleasure ground around which will spring up terraces, villas, and blocks of dwelling houses, excelling in beauty and magnificence any we can now boast of in the New World, and giving new ideas of the beneficent principle of democracy which permits the mind to expand to its utmost possibilities.[42]

Later in the summer of 1853, such prose became part of the excited publicity campaign in support of the park project in the *New York Journal*:

> The shanties and other disfigurements that are so disgraceful upon the land approach to our city would disappear; cottages and villas would spring up on all sides, and, more particularly, gather round the Park. And, ere long, we should see all the avenues of approach lined with embowered mansions, and Manhattan become one of the most beautiful and distinguished places upon the globe[,] the pride of the city, the honor of the nation![43]

These bold social visions of the role of the park in the beautification of New York contained another subliminal message as well. As read by real estate owners and property speculators, articles like Cook's and that in the *New York Journal* effectively said: this park thing is going to be good for *someone*, and it might as well be me. At a crucial moment in the debates about the park, the coalescing of the idealist arguments with the interest of the property market sealed the project. Few of the narratives telling the story of the park have adequately stressed the lucrative possibilities created by the park idea. Without a sense of the role such interests played in the 1850s (and ever after) we are left without a persuasive explanation for such a massive expenditure of public money.

The early summer of 1853 was also the moment when the Crystal Palace was opened on the site adjacent to the Croton distributing reservoir now occupied by the delightfully reconstructed Bryant Park. The opening ceremony, which included an address by President Pierce on 14 July, was the occasion of an outpouring of proud rhetoric and celebrations. (In Albany, the legislature was discussing the creation of a large park in New York.) The park project, and indeed the whole project of uptown development, was buoyed by the city's newly proclaimed role as competitor and even successor to

London, from whose exhibition in 1851 the idea of the Crystal Palace was copied. The New York site was less than one-fifth the size of the Crystal Palace in Hyde Park, but the project was awash in boosterism. The city's pride was no less at stake in the creation of a park than it had been in the Crystal Palace.[44]

As the promise of the park idea grew vaster, the limitations of the city in the 1840s grew more tangible and irritating. The conductors of the street cars may have been "often rude and sometimes brutal in their treatment of passengers" (who, to one observer, were "rough and dirty and contact with them keeps a person in constant dread of an attack of the itch, or some kindred disease"), but the park idea carried a utopian hope that it would civilize a rough-edged city.[45] The first historian of the Central Park, Clarence Cook, firmly roots the project in the late 1840s, at the moment when Bushnell invited the republic to acknowledge that ". . . all that is highest is freest, and joyous because it is free...":

... about the year 1848 the people of New York began to find that something must be done to supply the want, getting to be felt every day more and more, of space to walk abroad and recreate themselves. There was no place within the city limits in which it was pleasant to walk, or ride, or drive, or stroll; no place for skating, no water in which it was safe to row; no field for base-ball or cricket; no pleasant garden where one could chat with a friend, or watch his children play, or, over a cup of tea or coffee, listen to the music of a good band. Theaters, concerts, and lectures were the only amusements within reach of the mass of the people; the side-walks, the balconies, the back-yards, the only substitutes for the Hyde Park or Tuileries of the Old World, or the ancient freedom and rural beauty of Young New York.[46]

The park idea was, like every significant evolution of social consciousness, enmeshed in the interests and hopes of many different individuals and groups. There will be occasions, as the story is traced, to register the complexity of the process. It should properly be seen as an anonymous tale, a city story without a hero, in which, at different moments, interventions were made (for many different reasons) and contributions offered. Central Park was not created because Bryant thought it was desirable, because Downing agreed, or because Olmsted had an intriguing and clever design for its layout.

Downing

"A Talk about Public Parks and Gardens," published by Andrew Jackson Downing in the *Horticulturist* in October 1848, has long

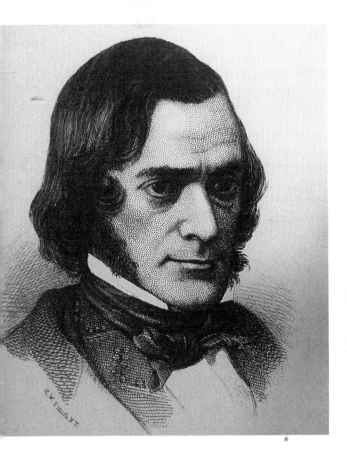

Andrew Jackson Downing, combining a romantic love of the picturesque with a scientific horticulturalism, alerted his fellow-countrymen to the desirability of improving their residential properties. His support for the park idea for New York gave the notion powerful momentum. Undated engraving by H. W. Smith.

been given pride of place in the campaign for a large park in New York. For Clarence Cook, it gave "... the first expression to the want, which everybody at that time felt, of a great Public Park." Olmsted regarded the article as having inaugurated the agitation for a park. Similar arguments were expressed by Edward Hagaman Hall.[47] Forceful advocacy of the importation to the United States of gothic architecture, and enthusiasm for natural or "gardenesque" styles of Loudon, made Downing, through *A Treatise on the Theory and Practice of Landscape Gardening*, published in 1841 when he was twenty-six, and other publications (*Cottage Residences*, 1842; *Architecture of Country Houses*, 1850), someone who alerted his countrymen to the desirability of improving their residential properties. Downing thus had a considerable influence on the American suburban countryside. Henry Ward Beecher was the specialist in these kinds of reassuring doctrines about the uses of wealth. Downing's belief that the man who renders his home more beautiful "not only contributes to the happiness of his own family, but improves the taste, and adds loveliness to the country at large" encouraged a spirit of altruistic self-interest in the American landed gentry that was firmly within the Beecher tradition.[48]

The links which connect Downing to Central Park are clear and often acknowledged. Calvert Vaux, Olmsted's future partner, was brought to the United States in 1850 by Downing to work in his office in Newburgh, New York. Vaux, who married Downing's sister-in-law, designed the bridges and other structures in the park, and defended the legacy of Downing's work.[49] Personally encouraged by Downing, Olmsted repeatedly acknowledged the far-reaching influence of the latter's doctrines. Not perhaps an original thinker about landscape or architecture, Downing made his greatest contribution to the cultural perspectives of the 1840s as a popularizer of European aesthetic doctrines and as an enthusiastic exponent of the cultivated style of the English country gentleman.[50] It is in his social vision of the role of parks that Downing's influence needs its most careful analysis.

"A Talk," set out in the form of a dialogue between the Editor and a Traveller (at the time it was written Downing had not yet made his first visit to Europe), uses the example of "aristocratic" Europe's democratic provision of public parks and gardens to make a point about the tendency of American society.[51] He describes the great European parks as "the pleasant drawing-rooms of the whole population; where they gain health, good spirits, social enjoyment, and a frank and cordial bearing" which he believed was "totally unknown" in the United States (*Rural Essays*, 142). Acknowledging the aristocratic origins of many European parks, the Traveller was particularly interested in the ability of German free towns to create substantial public gardens, thus demonstrating the capacity for self-government. (Similarly, the successful practices of European societies were often cited by sanitary reformers in New York, who felt their own local government was uniquely inept and obstructive.) The European parks were an impressive demonstration of social tolerance and cohesion:

> Every afternoon, in the public grounds of the German towns, you will meet thousands of neatly-dressed men, women, and children. All classes assemble under the shade of the same trees. . . . There they all meet, sip their tea and coffee, ices, or other refreshments, from tables in the open air, talk, walk about, and listen to bands of admirable music, stationed here and there throughout the park. (*Rural Essays*, 141–2)

Downing was writing in the aftermath of the failed revolutions of 1848, and mentions the European tumult in the beginning of the dialogue. It deserves emphasis. Although his vision of a civilized community was thoroughly middle-class, characterized by a clear preference for gracious, orderly behavior we should see Downing as a good son of the democratic spirit of 1848.[52] Wanting to affirm his republican and democratic roots by praising parks as triumphs of practical democracy, he approves when "the people" gained access to what were royal parks. With Lamartine, and with Lamartine's careful qualifications, he would have agreed with the inevitability of the "accession of the masses to political rights, to prepare for their progressive, inoffensive, and regular advancement to justice; that is to say, to equality of standing, intelligence, relative well-being in society."[53] At the same time, the Traveller stresses the requirement that access to parks be strictly controlled and orderly and explains that the great achievement of the parks, their social mission, was to spread the values of civilization. Downing positions himself to play both sides of the issue, though his attention is directed primarily towards the concerns of those who were his clients, the comfortable people whose country seats he so warmly praises in his writings on architecture. Concern for social order, which runs through debates about Central Park in the 1850s, referred naturally to local anxieties, as well as reflecting a generalized apprehension of the dangers of social disorder dramatically revealed in the European revolutions of 1848.

For a democratic society, resistance to democracy was deeply and surprisingly entrenched in New York. The Rev. Chapin observed that "... here, where everybody says that all men are equal, and everybody is afraid they *will* be; where there are no adamantine barriers of birth and caste; people are anxiously exclusive. And though the forms of aristocracy flourish more gorgeously in their native soil, the genuine *virus* can be found in New York almost as readily as in London, or Vienna."[54] Downing's Editor carefully interrogates the Traveller about whether "the more educated of our people," whose preference for "natural exclusiveness" was widely acknowledged, would accept the increased possibility of unplanned and undesired social interactions. "[Y]ou must remember," assured the Traveller, "that there is no *forced* intercourse in the daily reunions in a public garden or park. There is room and space enough for pleasant little groups or circles of all tastes and sizes, and no one is necessarily brought into contact with uncongenial spirits ..." (*Rural Essays*, 143). In other words, the park will not challenge social exclusivity, but rather will assume it to be the basis for a carefully controlled experiment in social proximity.

Downing's vision of the park embodied a clear and utopian social mission: it would "soften and humanize the rude, educate and enlighten the ignorant, and give continual enjoyment to the educated"

(*Rural Essays*, 142). Advocates of the creation of a large park in New York, hoping to use social fears for the cause of social improvement, suggested that it would act as a prophylactic against disorder. Henry P. Tappan put the matter unequivocally in 1855: "The multitude of a city crave excitement and amusement. Provide them with beautiful public gardens and places of culture, and they will generally be content. Leave them without cultivation to provide amusement for themselves, and need we be surprised if intemperance, debauchery, and riot ensue?"[55] The park symbolically became part of the broader cultural arsenal (sanitary reforms, home missions, good government campaigns) with which the middle class surrounded itself against the poor. Appearing so early in the debates, these concerns never quite disappear. They were used as enthusiastically by those who opposed the park as by those who supported it, and they remain part of an ambiguous legacy of the social debates which followed.

After presenting the need for the park, and the means by which it could be made acceptable to the better classes, the Traveller is asked how a park could be paid for. Downing's approach is voluntaristic. After praising the actions of city governments in Germany, the Traveller suggests that "public liberality" can be appealed to for the funds necessary. "Make it praiseworthy and laudable for wealthy men to make bequests of land, properly situated, for this public enjoyment," he suggests, "and commemorate the public spirit of such men by a statue or a beautiful marble vase, with an inscription, telling all succeeding generations to whom they are indebted for the beauty and enjoyment that constitute the chief attraction of the town" (*Rural Essays*, 145). Money could be raised by ladies' fairs and teas; life-memberships could be used to fund particular trees or areas of planting. A "voluntary taxation" on local property would defray other expenses. (By "voluntary," Downing means freely chosen and imposed by the community, not a tax which could be paid or not as individuals preferred.)

Downing returned to the question of money in "Public Cemeteries and Public Gardens," published in the *Horticulturist* in July 1849. Whereas his first instinct was to regard a park as a public institution combining private benevolence with taxation, he here advocates a different approach to the financing of parks. Mount Auburn Cemetery, first proposed as early as 1825, was the creation of the Massachusetts Horticultural Society which regarded the coalescence of a landscape garden and rural cemetery as directly furthering the society's aims: it would raise public taste and demonstrate the improvements possible through horticultural science and landscape art. It was, in David Schuyler's apt phrase, a *didactic* landscape.[56] A park created by a publicly chartered institution suggested one alternative. Another, explored by Downing, would be a park created by a private corporation as a venture organized on capitalist lines. A small admission fee would be charged to generate revenue (the *absence* of an entry fee was an important dimension of the democratic park), but the bulk of the funds necessary for its construction would be raised from shareholders. In return for their investment they would have to be offered special inducements, such as the exclusive privileges to drive horses and carriages in the park. (This reflects a level of subtlety in Downing which is interesting. He knew his wealthy people.) Other fund-raising possibilities suggested themselves: band music and "excellent refreshments" would attract the "better class" to the park; fêtes and annual exhibitions might also serve to attract visitors. It is indicative of Downing's thinking in 1849 that he asks: "Would such a project pay? This is the home question of all the calculating part of the community, who must open their purse-strings to make it a substantial reality" (*Rural Essays*, 158). He concludes the park could succeed in its mission to civilize and make money as well:

> That such a project, carefully planned, and liberally and judiciously carried out, would not only *pay*, in money, but largely civilize and refine the national character, foster the love of rural beauty, and increase of knowledge of and taste for rare and beautiful trees and plants, we cannot entertain a reasonable doubt. (*Rural Essays*, 159)[57]

He did not live long enough to observe the debacle of the Crystal Palace in New York in 1853–4. Funded precisely on the basis suggested by Downing, the failure of the exhibition to be ready for the opening ceremonies in July 1853 kept the crowds away until the fall, by which time it was too late to recoup the costs of building and decorating. The exhibition went into bankruptcy in 1854, and after several years of ignominious use for miscellaneous public functions, the building was destroyed in a fire in October 1858. Everyone lost money on the Crystal Palace, and it was a sobering reminder that despite the promoter's boasts of the superiority of the endeavors of "private individuals," there was little reason to believe that there were plausible private sector alternatives to the involvement of the government.[58]

Downing's thinking changed again during his visit to England in 1850. In "The London Parks," published in the *Horticulturist* in September 1850, he presented the fruits of a detailed examination of the great London parks. They left him enthralled by their size. Regent's Park, he wrote, contains *"three hundred and thirty-six acres of more lawn, ornamental plantations, drives and carriage roads"*

(*Rural Essays*, 553). In the midst of "black and dingy" London, the parks seemed "like districts of open country-meadows and fields, country estates, lakes and streams, gardens and shrubberies" (*Rural Essays*, 548). Their particular charm lay in their contrast with the straight lines of the surrounding streets. Large parks shut out all signs of the city, and he liked the idea that the visitor had the feeling of having "got astray and quite out of reach of the Metropolis." Downing's admiration for the carriage drives in London parks and the equestrianism on Rotten Row is a reminder of his deep-seated anglophilia. The mulberry livery of the Duke of Devonshire's coachman, and the sight of "footmen in gold and silver lace, gaudy liveries, spotless linen and snowy silk stockings," were in his opinion worth commenting on. English women sit more firmly in the saddle, and ride more boldly, than their American counterparts. With London so magnificently provided for, "[i]s New-York really not rich enough, or is there absolutely not land enough in America to give our citizens public parks of more than ten acres?" (*Rural Essays*, 557). In this he was following in the steps of Bryant, who had written during a visit to England in 1845:

> To-day we arrived at Derby, and hastened to see its Arboretum. This is an inclosure of eleven acres, given by the late Mr. Josiah [*sic*] Strutt to the town, and beautifully laid out by Loudon, author of the work on Rural Architecture. It is planted with every kind of tree and shrub which will grow in the open air of this climate, and opened to the public for a perpetual place of resort. Shall we never see an example of the like munificence in New York?[59]

What London added to Downing's thinking about parks was scale: that more than 1,000 acres was devoted to parks in an imperial city was a revelation. It was a benchmark against which all further proposals for a park should be judged. This in turn inevitably led to the problem of whether any group of private individuals, however generously supported by the public, could raise the needed funds for a park on a truly adequate scale. And where was the land to be found, in so central a location as the parks in London, Paris, Munich and Vienna? Downing returned to these problems in 1851, after the first proposals had been made for a park in New York, and his response will be discussed later.

Downing contributed to the park idea, as it stood in the late 1840s, a clarified sense of the complex social mission of parks. He saw parks as operating in a society sharply divided by class, manners and appetites; he hoped that they would please the cultivated, while they tried to "soften and humanize" the populace; that they would heal some of the divisions of class, while raising the general level of civility. He was the first writer on the subject in the United States to grasp that parks function in an ideological context. He strengthened middle-class support by making the management of parks, their safety and acceptability, one of the key terms of the debate. By his repeated attempts to consider the financing of the project, Downing suggests how the idealist arguments for parks could be sold to a class fearful of social disorder, and devoted to private speculation in the property market. It was he who pointed the way towards the coalition of interests which created Central Park.

The decision to build a park

In February 1851 Bryant's *Evening Post* printed the remarkable fact that real estate and other property owned by the city (from parks and public grounds to schools and offices) was valued at $19,505,310.88. The sum expended on the aqueduct and the two Croton reservoirs amounted to $14,327,583.95 (Phelps Stokes, 5, 1832). It was no longer a "quiet little City," In his annual message to the common council on 7 January 1850, Democratic mayor Caleb Woodhull reminded the aldermen of the inadequacy of the city's provision of parks and of their many advantages for a "well governed city." "I have no doubt," he wrote, "of the policy of encouraging public squares, whenever it can be done without involving the city in unreasonable expenditure. It is perhaps not generally considered that all the public squares below Forty-second street comprise only in the aggregate, about sixty-three acres, being less (all together) than one-forth of the size of one of the large parks in the city of London."[60] Thanks to Downing, these arguments had quickly established themselves in public discourse. Comparisons with London became a way to assert a growing consciousness that New York had now entered upon a competition with unquestionably the largest city in the world and the seat of the greatest imperial power. After the war with Mexico, there were many thoughts of empire. And perhaps fewer concerns, all told, about the eventual consequences of this first, fatal step away from the republican simplicity of the city as it had been a generation earlier. What prompted Woodhull? A climate of opinion, encouraged by Bryant and Downing; but also perhaps the intervention of an unnamed "worthy and excellent citizen" who, after being away from the city for two years in Europe, returned to New York anxious to confer the advantages of the parks he had seen in Europe upon his fellow residents. A meeting was held at his residence, at which a committee was appointed which called upon the owners of a tract of land on the East River to inquire whether they would sell the land for use as a park. Several large landowners, including John Jacob Astor, Jr. were also consulted. The committee called upon the mayor, urging that the land be acquired. Few contemporary traces of the identity of these individuals survive.[61] But their activities probably created the link between the idea of a park and mayor Woodhull's address in 1850.

The common council, with a narrow Whig majority on the board of alderman, and an even slenderer majority on the board of assistant aldermen, were unwilling to act. Their behavior was not necessarily prompted by Republican austerity: the corruption of the common council, colloquially known as the "Forty Thieves," was notorious, and inaction on a measure was often a tactic used to flush out potential bribes from interested parties.

In the mayoral election in November 1850, both candidates (Fernando Wood ran as a Democrat, opposed by the Whig merchant Ambrose Kingsland) favored the creation of a city park. In the spring and summer of 1851 the new mayor, Kingsland, and the common council of New York began the process of creating a city park. The reasons put forward by Kingsland[62] in a communication to the common council on 6 May 1851 reflected the wisdom of the preceding decade: the tide of the city's population was headed remorselessly northward up the island, precisely towards the area where there were insufficient places for recreation. The city had to respond to the changing size and location of the population. Below City Hall, New York would soon be wholly devoted to commercial purposes, and the park surrounding City Hall and the Battery would be left far behind the surging movement of population up the island. Kingsland had absorbed something of the arguments put forward by Downing, in which the social mission of a public park was linked to the necessity to offer "inducements" to the affluent:

> There are thousands who pass the day of rest among the idle and dissolute, in porter houses, or in places more objectionable, who would rejoice in being enabled to breathe the air in such a place, while the ride and drive through its avenues, free from the noise, dust, and confusion inseparable from all thoroughfares, would hold out strong inducements for the affluent to make it a place of resort.[63]

Kingsland left the discussion of the location of a new park to the committee on lands and places which considered his proposal, but James Gordon Bennett's *Herald* was quick to support the site examined by the committee of gentlemen: "There is a piece of ground, covered with old forest trees, containing three hundred acres, between the Third avenue and the East River, and north of Fortieth street, that would furnish a most admirable site for such a purpose."

Portrait of Ambrose Kingsland by Charles Loring Elliott, 1853. Kingsland defeated
Fernando Wood in the 1850 mayoral election. A man of great personal integrity,
Kingsland was a merchant from an older mold of public life. He fitted out the first
vessel to sail from New York for sperm oil, and was mayor when Herman Melville
published *Moby-Dick*. Kingsland requested the common council to create a park for
the city.

"Kleindeutschland" at leisure: Jones Wood, proposed in 1851 as a suitable site for a park in New York, was a wooded area running down to the East River between 66th and 75th streets. For several years after a more central site was chosen, Jones Wood remained a favorite spot for excursions by East Side residents.

The report on 3 June recommended the site mentioned in the *Herald*, ninety acres of wooded land owned by John Jones and an adjacent tract owned by the Schermerhorns. In total, the committee recommended that 160 acres along the East River (running north from 66th to 75th streets, and extending as far west as Third Avenue) be taken by right of public domain and made into a public park.[64] It was an unimproved tract, with a good cover of mature trees, which ran dramatically down to the riverbank. The presence of something like a forest in the city was so striking in the early 1850s that it assumed a mythic antiquity. An old resident recalled it as being "... the last fortress of the forest primeval that once covered the rocky shores of the East River, and its wildness was almost savage..." (Phelps Stokes, 5, 1834). That the view largely consisted of Blackwell's Island, site of the city's almshouse, prison and fever hospital, and the two- and three-story clapboarded houses of prosaic Brooklyn beyond, did not seem a decisive argument against Jones Wood. In an editorial on the 5th the editor of the leading commercial paper argued that the city was sufficiently provided with parks, was surrounded by quick-flowing rivers, and that any such reduction in habitable space caused by "turning half the island into a permanent forest" would drive the city's surplus population to adjacent communities. The *New York Journal of Commerce* concluded that "... the grand Park scheme is a humbug; and the ... sooner it is abandoned, the better."[65] There were complaints that the proposed park was too large, too expensive, and too remote from the rest of the city.

Tribunes of the workingman thought the whole thing was for the carriage class. Fears that rowdies would dominate the park were expressed by the refined. But on 6 June the common council, doubtless reflecting the interests of the Jones Wood landowners, tried to speed things up by directing the corporation counsel to petition the state legislature to appoint commissioners to take the site for use as a public park, and authorizing the comptroller and mayor to negotiate for the purchase of the land at any time before commissioners were appointed. The commercial interests of the city, principally located at the southern tip of the island, were not slow to notice that the park would benefit themselves scarcely at all. When proposals to expand the Battery were made in 1821, a merchant recalled that owners of real estate uptown had been exempted from the assessment. "Why should property in the immediate neighborhood of this large contemplated park be exempt from local assessment, when it must be evident to every person of common discretion and discernment that it must be largely benefited?" The proposal lacked basic equity between uptown and downtown property owners. It was angrily asked "Why should those who have already enjoyed such manifestly unfair exemptions, be permitted for their own particular benefit to lay a new tax upon our citizens? Is it equal? Is it just? Is it right?"[66] The potential for conflict between the commercial interests of the city and the owners of large properties uptown was clearly revealed by these letters. They also raised a technical question about the financing of the park, about the extent to which those likely to benefit most from its creation would be assessed a proportion of the cost, which reappeared two years later as a decisive issue in the legal dispute. The requisite act, introduced into the assembly by James Beekman of the 5th district of New York on 17 June, passed through the legislature in July. Its rapid passage provoked a renewed public discussion about the appropriateness of the location of Jones Wood.

Downing wrote in the spring of 1851 that "We only regret that the people of our large cities...cannot see, with their own eyes, the beauty, and realize the advantages of such parks in the midst of towns."[67] The extensive debate which followed in May and June gave him another chance to return to the topic in the August issue of the *Horticulturist*. Obviously thinking about the editorials and correspondence in the *Journal of Commerce* (where it had been argued that the park threatened to become "a perpetual source of expense" and was a "wholly unnecessary" expenditure, reflecting "the greedy desire for display and glitter on the part of [the city's] wealth-seeking inhabitants" in letters to the paper on 20 and 24 June 1851), Downing mocked the "timid tax-payers, and men nervous in their private pockets of the municipal expenditures" for their lack of vision (*Rural Essays*, 148). He was anything but grateful to Kingsland for his proposal. Like the common council decision to face the rear of City Hall with brownstone, as that side of the building would face unin-habited countryside, rather than the good marble used on the front, Downing regarded the proposal as penny-pinching and short-sighted. At least 500 acres were needed for a population over half a million people. A site running north from 39th Street to the Harlem River, encompassing the two Croton reservoirs (a proposal which had first been put forward by Alderman Shaw of the 12th ward, and which had warmly been supported by Nicholas Dean, commissioner of the Croton Water Works, in a widely publicized exchange of letters at the end of June[68]) seemed far more preferable. Downing chided those who expressed alarm about the proposal, and repeated his argument that the parks of Europe demonstrated how the people together can enjoy "... the same music, breathe the same atmos-phere of art, enjoy the same scenery, and grow into social freedom by the very influences of easy intercourse, space and beauty that sur-round them" (*Rural Essays*, 151). In summary form, this en-compassed much of the social vision of American reform. Downing had earlier presented these ideas in a more qualified form, as though excessively willing to grant the fears of the wealthy. Now he emerged boldly prepared to challenge the conventional anxieties:

> The higher social and artistic elements of every man's nature lie dormant within him, and every laborer is a possible gentleman, not by the possession of money or fine clothes—but through the refining influence of intellectual and moral culture. Open wide, therefore, the doors of your libraries and picture galleries, all ye true republicans! Build halls where knowledge shall be freely diffused among men, and not shut up within the narrow walls of narrower institutions. Plant spacious parks in your cities, and unloose their gates as wide as the gates of morning to the whole people. As there are no dark places at noon day, so education and culture—the true sunshine of the soul—will banish the plague spots of democracy; and the dread of the ignorant exclusive who has no faith in the refinement of a republic, will stand abashed in the next century, before a whole people whose system of voluntary education embraces (combined with perfect individual freedom), not only common schools of rudimentary knowledge, but common enjoyments for all classes in the higher realms of art, letters, science, social recreations, and enjoyments. (*Rural Essays*, 152–3)

With this ringing affirmation of republican faith and belief that education and culture, and by implication parks, can banish the "plague spots" of democracy, Downing insured that all future defenses of the park idea would firmly occupy the same ground. Whatever *other* motives were involved in the creation of parks, the utopian case had been set out. It remained a resource of great usefulness in the years ahead. Such an argument manifestly appealed to middle-class reformers like Lydia Maria Child, and thus hinted at the possibility of a cross-class alliance, between reformers and Democratic politicians who soon came to the see the park as a desirable source of employment and/or potential corruption. The link between reformers and machine politicians was a curiously enduring arrangement, for however the struggle against corruption drove them apart, they were united in the Jacksonian commitment to opportunity. Although his death in 1852 denied him the opportunity to design the park, Downing's contributions were clearly decisive.

His vivid advocacy in August 1851 left the aldermen in a quandry. Enemies of the park continued their sniping, and now its most influential advocate (who had been asked to landscape a piece of land between the Capitol and the White House in 1851) rejected both the proposed location and the size of the park. A special committee was hastily appointed to weigh once again the advantages and disadvantages of several alternate sites in the city. The issue had unexpectedly begun to polarize opinion. Supporters of the Jones Wood site, who included property owners who would greatly benefit from an East Side location (how much they would benefit did not become apparent until 1854) as well as those who hoped to sell their property to the city, tried to force the common council to have commissioners of estimate and assessment appointed. These moves were blocked when Judge Edmunds of the Supreme Court, finding material errors in the bill, refused their petition.[69] In effect, this rendered the legislation null and void. Fresh legislation would be required at Albany for the Jones Wood proposal, or any other, to be reconsidered.

After carefully comparing the claims of Jones Wood and a more central site, the aldermanic special committee reported in January 1852 in favor of the latter. It was expected to be a great deal more expensive than Jones Wood, but with 760 acres, it was more than three times the size. The price, per acre, was significantly lower. For the first time the name "Central Park" began to appear in print. This report was received by the common council, but there was no action taken, despite Kingsland's suggestion that the legislature be petitioned to repeal the Jones Wood bill and authorize the purchase of the land for Central Park. He also pointed out that inaction was likely to have undesirable consequences: the contractor opening Second Avenue to Harlem had gone ahead before any political decision was made to block his contract, "thus marring many of the natural beauties of the location." The continued opposition

Portrait of Jacob A. Westervelt by Edward Mooney, 1855. Westervelt succeeded Kingsland as mayor in 1852. He represented downtown mercantile and manufacturing interests, and did not conceal his suspicion that the uptown supporters of Jones Wood were financially 'interested' in the proposal.

to increased city expenditure by commercial interests persuaded the nervous common council to request the legislature to reduce the size of the park. Meanwhile, in April the assembly in Albany re-authorized the taking of Jones Wood, while the senate continued to assess the respective sites. Confusion prevailed on all sides.[70]

Elected in November 1852, the new mayor, Jacob A. Westervelt, took office in the first week in January. His family's roots extended back to the Dutch colonial period, and he had made a fortune as a ship-builder in the heyday of sail. (In partnership with Robert Carnley, he manufactured 200 sea-going vessels at his yard at Corlear's Hook and was said to have made most of the packets which sailed the Le Havre and London routes before 1837.) His home on East Broadway, facing Grand Street, had a representation of a ship's taffrail above the front door. Westervelt had served as assistant alderman for the 13th ward in the common council of 1840–2, but had few debts to Tammany Hall. It was widely believed that he owed his victory in the mayoralty race to Whig votes. He was a reforming mayor who overcame fierce resistance to place New York's police in uniform. Westervelt said nothing about either park proposal in his first message to the common council in January 1853. His many links with the commercial leaders of the city, and in particular with the downtown merchants most closely involved with the city's seaborne trade, made his silence on the subject ominous. Without Kingsland's continued support, the prospect of the various park measures seemed even more uncertain.[71]

The *New York Times*, as it was repeatedly to do throughout the 1850s, rallied support for the park:

> Let us act not only for the present, but for the future. The cleanliness and health of the City is a matter of first necessity. Let us lay, or rather remove the dust, that great bane of New-York. Let us have a *park* that shall correspond with her present growth and prospects, and be a joy to the coming millions which are to dwell upon our island. With honesty, energy, faithfulness and largeness of view in her councils, New-York, while she carries her affluence and numbers up to the greatest city of Europe, may advance the health and comfort of her people, and counter-act many of the evils otherwise incident to such great concentrations of men.[72]

But the paper failed to speak with one mind about the appropriate site. On 13 June 1853 the paper seemed to favor a romantic site on the Hudson. ("A sloping bank to the margin of the silvery Hudson; a thickly wooded background; intervening acres of flowery sward; stately avenues of waving trees, and treasures of grassy knolls and romantic glens, are what we want for a Peoples' Park.") A week later, on the 21st, it supported the idea of reconciling the rival proposals by joining the central and the Jones Wood sites together. On the 23rd it urged the largest site possible—wherever that might be.

Although Bryant's *Evening Post* approved of the extension of the park, the *Journal of Commerce* renewed its opposition. A double park would form a barrier dividing the island into two halves. "Smaller parks would be a blessing . . ."[73] But the paper's case against the park went deeper than the essentially utilitarian question of how to achieve the maximum benefit to the community. In a long editorial on 24 May, the legislative history of the measure was surveyed, with the clear implication that at every stage over the past two years the Jones Wood proposal had been forwarded by an (unnamed) group which had the most to gain from the building of the park. The land in question was worth over a million dollars. The measure had been most aggressively pressed by those who owned adjacent lots. If the city as a whole was to pay for the park, they would directly benefit from a tax on the whole city. "The parties who carve out the park," argued the *Journal*, "fix the lines to suit their ownership, and measure the public convenience by their individual interest." There were other provisions of the bill which seemed unfair and highly objectionable. If the city was to have a park, it would be best if it was to be located around the Croton reservoirs, as had first been suggested in the *Journal of Commerce* in 1851; in the meantime, there were many other urgent public wants which deserved to be addressed first.[74]

Defenders of the park idea returned again and again to the beneficial effects of a park upon the health and well-being of the city's inhabitants. "It is manifest," argued James Gordon Bennett's *Herald*,

> that the sanatory [*sic*] condition of the city would be thereby vastly improved, from the very simple process of an occasional ventilation of the lungs of our industrial classes. How much the crimes engendered in the sinks of vice and dissipation within the city would be diminished by affording to the masses of the people the more wholesome, attractive, and innocent recreations of a park, may partially be conjectured from the ameliorating influences of the parks and public gardens of Paris upon the whole body of its population. Paris would not be Paris without them. It would be more likely, the scene of constant plots, riots, street butcheries, and barricades. Let us have the park![75]

The alternative to the park was poor health and civil disorder. Such beliefs were fervently held by reformers, which made it all the more surprising that the city's leading advocate of sanitary reform, Dr. John H. Griscom, joined in the attacks against the park. Writing to the *Times* to express his objections, he argued that the notion that the insanitary evils of the city could be averted by the creation of parks was simply a fallacy. Repeating arguments made in the *Journal of Commerce*, he pointed out that on an island-city there was an abundance of other resources for recreation and fresh air. By reducing the amount of land available for housing, a large park would exacerbate the city's many problems with crowded tenements and high rents. Jones Wood was an irrelevance to the larger needs of ventilation in the city. The larger central site would make matters worse. He prophetically noted that "[t]he wealthy alone will be able to live near it ..." In any event, he calculated that its beneficial effect would extend no more than 1,000 feet beyond its perimeter. He stated that:

> If we would ... ventilate the City, we must begin by enlarging and ventilating the dwellings; by prohibiting the erection and occupation of the thousand rooms no larger than prison cells, and by prohibiting the occupation as residences, of hundreds of cellars, in which the poor are now compelled to crowd themselves. It will be of no use to make parks, plant trees and flowers, open fountains and make elegant drives, as long as lot owners and landlords are permitted to put up such "cloud capped" tenements, and cram them with people ...[76]

Voicing many of the arguments which would be used by the most radical contributors to *The Sanitary Condition of New York* in 1865, Griscom identified the central contradiction. The merits of a park were largely connected with its role in restoring health (social, psychic, physical). If Griscom was right, the park in itself would achieve little of deep or permanent value. A great deal of money would be spent, and much positive mischief would result in an already over-crowded real estate and housing market. Griscom proposed the creation of eight parks of 100 acres, or sixteen of half that size, dispersed throughout the city. It would, he thought, be a more democratic solution to the city's need for parks. Alternatively, he proposed the creation of low-density housing on the site proposed for Central Park, with wide streets separated by gardens. His arguments about the value of the park for public hygiene were unanswerable, and remained unanswered; but they were narrowly focussed, and failed to address the full range of motives engaged in the debate. Comprehensively overturning the reigning assumptions about the beneficial effects of a park, Griscom's letter provoked little response. He had approached the topic with the rationalism and logic of a scientist, but it was clear, across the range of attitudes towards the park, that the proposal reflected beliefs and aspirations—often utopian—and interests—mostly financial—which did not ultimately require there to be a scientific basis for the effect of parks upon the health of the community. What, if anything, remained to justify the expenditure was a utopian vision of community, civic pride, and property values.

As the day approached when the legislature would act on the select committee report, those who favored one or the other sites accelerated their polemics. Downing's name was invoked for and against Jones Wood. Large petitions for and against each site (one of which had been left for signatures at the busy offices of the *Herald*) arrived in Albany. Over 600 people wrote to the select committee opposing any park as a "mere luxury." In late May and early June, opponents and proponents presented memorials, petitions and remonstrances in the senate, trying to create the impression of an irresistible tide of public opinion. Among these was a memorial from mayor Westervelt against the Jones Wood bill, which did not commit him to support any other proposal.[77] Perhaps increasingly alarmed at the way the issue seemed to be spinning out of control, the *New York Times* wrote bitterly of the avarice and opportunism it encouraged: "The rivalry is ardent and bitter. The projected location of a Park in a given part of the City is too potent a temptation to the avarice of land-owners not to induce all of them to tug at every rope, by which a hope of bringing the improvement to their own boundary lines, is suspended" (21 June 1853).

The select committee report emphasized the advantages of Jones Wood: with a mature tree-cover, it would be available for immediate enjoyment. It would cost less to develop the park at Jones Wood; the central site was unhealthy, and would cost more to buy and improve. five of the seven experts interviewed (the State Botanist, Professor John Torrey; a gardener; a horticulturist; and a nurseryman; and one who indicated no profession) preferred Jones Wood. It is interesting that of three gardeners who gave testimony, two (Benjamin Munn and Samuel J. Gustin) both favored the larger site in the center.[78] The central location nonetheless had received the strong endorsement of the board of aldermen on 9 June, and some of the support for Jones Wood was believed to be "interested": "Those who were so anxious for the Jones Wood Park were those who were to be more or less pecuniarily benefited by it."[79]

But again the question of posterity was raised. The select committee report asked what duty the present generation owed to the next: ". . . [those] whose children fill the bills of mortality, are entitled to ask what has posterity done for us? Why should they be taxed *now* to plant groves, which seventy years hence may shelter those who come after them, when health and pure air, wafted from the breezy river, through ample shades, are within their present grasp?"[80] It is necessary to remind ourselves that the debate over the site was not one-sided, and merits for both locations had been forcefully urged. (The Jones Wood site might have made a very fine park, providing that it was not the only major park created.) If money was to be the primary consideration, Jones Wood was preferable. But there were other reasons to regard it as acceptable: it could be brought into use quickly, and the site was undoubtedly attractive. Rather than come down conclusively on one side or another, the select committee proposed to refer the matter back to New York City, to be decided by the common council formed at the forthcoming election in November.

The authority of the select committee's report was weakened by a powerful minority report submitted by senators Beekman, Cooley and Bartlett, in which they argued vehemently for the superiority of the central site.[81] Legislation to acquire the site of Central Park, which received the enthusiastic backing of Cooley and the other senators who submitted the minority report, was passed on 21 July. For a brief period in 1853, the legislative framework existed for the city to acquire both Jones Wood and Central Park.

Both sites remained available, and proponents sought to turn the strengths of one site or the other into disadvantages. The tree cover of Jones Wood seemed, to the *New York Times*, an invitation to licentiousness: "No one who has given any time to observation, can doubt what scenes would be enacted under the shades of those woods, at that distance from the city . . ."[82] On 12 August the common council passed a resolution which authorized the first step to acquire the land for a central park, but it was a statement of preference, of merely symbolic significance for no action could be taken until the election.[83] In the intervening period, a last-ditch attempt was made in the Supreme Court by rival advocates to halt, or speed up, proceedings. A group of property owners, who stood greatly to benefit from Jones Wood, petitioned the court. Mr. Amery, whose mother owned seventy-five acres between 63rd and 73rd streets; Mr. Tallman, owner of sixty-four acres of land between 57th and 69th streets; and Mr. Harson, owner of 600 lots, requested the court to appoint a commissioner for the purchase of Jones Wood. Another petition, from C. S. Woodhull and J. I. Coddington, sought to block the acquisition of Central Park. Their case depended upon the irregularity of the amount of land to be taken from its owners ". . . chiefly for purposes connected with public pleasures, and the adornment of the City, rather than for the practical usefulness of everyday purposes."[84]

Watching the frenzied efforts of property owners to force the city, against the wishes of the common council, to purchase Jones Wood, Westervelt found the spectacle distasteful. He argued in his message to the common council on 2 January 1854 that the acquisition of both sites would deprive the city of building land it could ill afford (this was Griscom's argument); contracts already let for opening streets might raise the threat of "prolonged and expensive litigation" (Kingsland had warned of this); and he felt that the waterfront on the

East River, with its potential for use as deep-water docks, was "invaluable for commercial purposes." For these reasons, Westervelt argued, the Jones Wood measure threatened to "inflict lasting injury to the commerce of our City."[85]

On 8 January 1854, Judge James I. Roosevelt of the Supreme Court declined to appoint commissioners for the acquisition of Jones Wood.[86] The legislature nonetheless required the corporation counsel, Robert J. Dillon, to request the appointment of commissioners. Despite the opposition of the corporation, as expressed by the common council, he went ahead and appeared before Justice Roosevelt. The corporation hired three lawyers to represent its position, who argued against its own corporation counsel. It was an extraordinary case. Justice Roosevelt stressed a signal difference between the bill to acquire Jones Wood and that for Central Park. The latter provided for nearby property owners, who would greatly benefit from the creation of Central Park, to be assessed a significant sum towards its cost. As the *Journal of Commerce* had repeatedly emphasized, the Jones Wood bill made no such stipulation. It was to be paid for by general taxation revenue of the city, thus greatly benefiting the small number of landowners in the vicinity. "It provides a garden for B's lot," the Judge explained, "in the Nineteenth Ward, quadrupling its value, and takes A's garden in the fifth Ward to pay for it." The passage of the Jones Wood bill also raised some uncertainties about the legislature's procedures. Judge Roosevelt's verdict, which rejected the corporation counsel's petition, had the effect of declaring the Jones Wood legislation null and void. Thus the way was cleared for the decision to be made after the forthcoming election. In 1851 Justice Edmunds blocked Jones Wood, and in 1854 Justice Roosevelt did the same. It would probably be more accurate to say that the commercial interests of the city, as represented in the *Journal of Commerce*, sank Jones Wood, even if Central Park was the price they had to pay to do it. The motive which underlay the dispute was not in truth about the fitness of Jones Wood as the site for a park. Rather, it was a contention between landowners and property speculators: who was to benefit, and by how much?

In the city elections in November 1853, the amended city charter replaced the old board of aldermen and board of assistant aldermen with boards of aldermen and councilmen of twenty each. It did its intended work: the "Forty Thieves," "the most debased, corrupt and disgraceful body of men ever invested with legislative power, at least in this country," were swept away.[87] (Tweed, who entered the council as alderman for the 7th ward in January 1852, took his profits and anticipated the fall of the "Forty Thieves." He won election to Congress for the fifth New York Congressional District in 1853, after only one year as alderman, and walked away from the house-cleaning of the amended charter with a smile on his lips.) The "reform" common council's decision to petition the Supreme Court to appoint commissioners of estimate and apportionment to acquire the lands for Central Park speedily followed. On 17 January Judge William Mitchell in the Supreme Court duly appointed five men, "... all gentlemen well known to the community, and in whom a wide confidence was felt that their difficult task would be performed with fairness and judgment."[88] A decision had been taken, and with the repeal of the Jones Wood act by the state legislature in April 1854, it was clear that if New York was to have a park, it would be Central Park. The process of acquiring the land was complex and likely to prove time-consuming. Central Park was composed of thousands of lots, each of which would have to be examined as to title. A reasonable value for each lot would have to be decided. To the irritation of everyone, this process took nearly three years.

Organizing and reorganizing

While the commissioners toiled, Fernando Wood was elected mayor in November 1854. He had supported the idea of a park for the city in his unsuccessful race for mayor against Kingsland in 1850, and in his inaugural address to the common council in January 1855 he again supported the project. "In my opinion," he explained, "future generations, who are to pay this expense, would have good reasons for reflecting upon the present generation, if we permitted the entire island to be taken possession of by the population, without some spot like this, devoted to rural beauty, healthful recreation, and pure atmosphere."[89] When property-owners, particularly those with holdings at the southern end of the park, successfully persuaded the common council to pass a resolution asking the legislature to make 72nd Street the southern boundary of the park, Wood vigorously vetoed this measure. He reiterated themes in his letter explaining the veto that linked him to Bryant's idea of the park as refuge from the commercialized city:

> We will be derelict, if by any narrow or selfish feeling of present saving, we deprive the teeming millions yet to inhabit and toil upon this island, of one place not given up to mammon, where they can, even if but one day in the year, observe and worship nature, untarnished by conflict with art. To admit the necessity of a great park, and to assert that this will be too large, is, in my opinion, an exceedingly limited view of the question, and entirely unworthy of even the present position of this

metropolis, to say nothing of a destiny now opening so brilliantly before us.[90]

In the summer of 1855 the commissioners returned a report awarding owners of land to be taken for the park over five million dollars, of which sum $1,657,590 was to be assessed upon the owners of adjacent property. This triggered off an additional round of legal challenges, which seemed to receive a sympathetic hearing from Judge Roosevelt. But these challenges were averted, and on 5 February 1856 Judge Harris of the Supreme Court signed the report, thus authorizing the mayor to take the land for a park. Legislation created a Central Park fund to raise the money to pay for the land thus now acquired. A management structure did not exist until May, when the common council gave control of the project to the mayor and street commissioner Joseph Taylor, acting as commissioners of the Central Park on a board of commissioners with full powers to improve the park. Since mayor Wood's dealings in real estate had been a notorious source of accusations of fraud and corruption, a consulting board was appointed to help the city decide what it should do with the park. It was led by Washington Irving and George Bancroft, distinguished men of letters, as well as the ex-editor of *Putnam's Monthly Magazine* (Charles F. Briggs, displaced when the magazine was purchased earlier that year by the firm of Dix & Edwards); Charles A. Dana, a former participant of Brook Farm (the transcendentalist experiment in Massachusetts) who was now Greeley's assistant on the *Tribune*; James Phalen, a merchant, who promptly moved to Paris and played a distant and minor role in the board's deliberations; James A. Cooley, a member of the state senate, who had signed the minority report favoring the central site; and one Stewart Brown. Of these, Irving at seventy-six was clearly an honorably spent force who could preside at meetings of the consulting board, but who would be expected to make few positive contributions. Cooley, Briggs and Bancroft were in their fifties, some two decades older than Dana. They were all busy men, with only Cooley having any sustained interest in the whole subject. Among their first decisions was to employ Egbert L. Viele[91] to do a topographical survey of the site. At thirty-one, he brought to the park a West Point education, military service in the Mexican war, several years' employment by the state of New Jersey as a topographical engineer, and good connections in the Democratic Party. He had been preparing a survey of the site as a private speculation and was clearly an authority on the problems likely to be encountered in the building of a park. With the support of mayor Wood, Viele was appointed engineer-in-chief at a salary of $2,500 per year. He proposed a plan for the drainage of the site, which was adopted, though nothing could be done on the park until money for improvement had been appropriated. Unlike the members of the first park commission, Viele possessed certain technical skills and that was sufficient to allow his design for the park to be tacitly passed or adopted at a meeting on 3 June 1856. It was assumed he knew what should be done.

In the discussions of the park several possible notions of what it should contain had emerged. In his last article on the New York park in 1851 Downing hoped that visitors too could "... have the substantial delights of country roads and country scenery, and forget, for a time the rattle of the pavements and the glare of brick walls." It was clear, as soon as Downing began to discuss the park's cultural and civilizing mission, that it implied not only a didactic landscape, but a space where the city's educational, scientific and cultural transactions could take place. Downing's park was in effect the site of a civic culture, and he proposed to fill it with worthy buildings (including the Crystal Palace) and a permanent luxuriant display of the trees and horticultural wonders of the planet, a zoological garden and exhibits by industrial societies. It would also provide space for statues, monuments and buildings "... commemorative at once of the great men of the nation, of the history of the age and country, the genius of our highest artists" (*Rural Essays*, 150). From the start it seemed that no one, least of all Downing, actually expected that the park would be a piece of wilderness transplanted to the city. Rather, it was widely assumed that the park would naturally host activities and house buildings that removed from serious consideration any further thought that the park would become a true natural alternative to the rigidity, noise and excesses of the city. To the majority of people there seemed little need for vision or artfulness. It was just a space to be filled with attractive embellishments and noble monuments. Everyone brought to the discussion his own wish-list, and the *kitsch* quotient in the various proposals was inevitably fairly high. Architects from Boston writing in early July 1856 argued that the design for Central Park should include popular amusements, military parades, exhibitions, conservatories, aquariums, fish ponds and places of refreshment, as well as dwellings for the commissioners and the laborers:

> ... the work of improving such a tract as this, embracing an area of several miles in extent, and diversified with the greatest variety of natural surface, presents no more tangible or comprehensible idea, than that of the execution of great military operations, embracing the direction of vast bodies of men over widely extended tracts of country.[92]

Viele surveyed the site of Central Park and was appointed by Fernando Wood as engineer-in-chief. When the board of commissioners was reorganized in 1857, Viele's services were dispensed with. He later successfully sued the city for compensation for his work. Undated engraving by J. C. Buttre.

Viele was clearly the man to give leadership to such a project. With four assistant surveyors, and twenty policeman on regular patrol to maintain order on the site, he began work. Surveying the scene, the *New York Times* observed that few New Yorkers knew anything of the location. It was treeless, housed squatters, and from the heights in the north afforded spectacular views on all sides. "The Central Park in its present condition has altogether a most disagreeable aspect."[93] If sufficient care was taken by the commissioners, it had the potential to become the most beautiful park in the western hemisphere. Viele's plan was accompanied by an explanation which forcefully asserted the Republican pedigree of the park idea. He seemed prepared to reject Downing's approach, which based the design for the park upon the best European models:

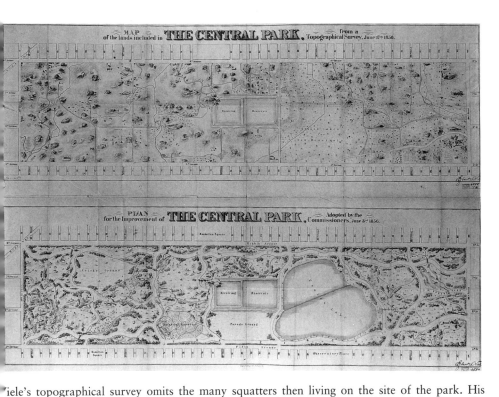

PLAN for the Improvement of THE CENTRAL PARK, Adopted by the Commissioners, June 3d 1856.

Viele's topographical survey omits the many squatters then living on the site of the park. His suggested plan commanded little support, however, and he was soon edged out of the picture by political rivals.

... to seek the parks of Europe for a model for our own would be a reflection upon our national taste, which finds so much food for study in the everchanging scenery which in this country is so remarkable.

Besides, those Parks, in many instances, are but appendages of grandeur to rank, where lavish expenditure, aided by all the appliances of art, give regal effect to scenes which the people enjoy at the discretion of their possessors; while our Park, like the Government, comes from the people, and to them, in all phases of Society, it must necessarily be devoted. Hence at the outset, we should seek to know the peculiar wants of all classes, and to endeavor to gratify them at every step, with a due regard to the principles of art and an economical expenditure of money.[94]

Patriotic sentiments often required the rejection of anything European. A contributor to the *Horticulturist* after Downing's death had argued that "[i]t is the mission of Rural Taste to improve, beautify and adorn the native soil, not to re-produce the scenery and products of foreigners."[95] Viele's text was cast in the political language of the 1840s and 1850s, both of the Native American and

Jacksonian persuasion: "grandeur," "rank," "lavish expenditure" smacked of the aristocratic parks of Europe. A good Democrat, Viele wanted nothing to do with such notions. His plan for Central Park was simple and rather unimaginative. He envisaged a grand road ("The Circuit") which would follow the perimeter of the park. An entrance on Eighth Avenue between 66th and 67th streets gave access to a cricket ground. Running along the fifth Avenue side northwards from 74th to 86th Street, where the "Croton Lake" began, there was to be a botanical garden and a parade ground. The roads were lined with trees, and small ponds were to be allowed to form along the path of watercourses. He followed the existing east-west dirt road for his transverse crossing above the lake. Ground-level bridges would carry visitors over the streams, but there was no provision for pedestrian footpaths. Travelers along The Circuit would repeatedly encounter traffic crossing the park, as well as a stream of vehicles entering or exiting the park at the gates which Viele placed at regular intervals along the outer perimeter. His plan made the least demand upon either his skills as an engineer or whatever skills he possessed as a landscape gardener. Clarence Cook's comment can scarcely be improved upon: "No thought was required to make it, and no other knowledge than a mere acquaintance with the topography of the ground to be worked. There is not a single difficulty overcome, a single advantage improved, a single valuable or striking improvement suggested."[96]

The Viele period in the history of the park was slow to get underway. The legislature was strangely reluctant to pass the bill required to create the financial machinery for the city to borrow the money to start real work. Common council appropriations allowed for little more than a preliminary effort to clear the most marshy land. After the intense public attention and petition-gathering which accompanied the decision to buy the central site in 1853, the long delay in acquiring the land, and the haphazard nature of the first park board, combined to leave the project dead in the water. The commissioners did nothing to stir public opinion behind the project, and Viele seemed to have no vigorous conception of what the park might become. The furious debates of 1853 ceased, and nothing happened.

In April 1857, as part of a larger reorganization of the city government, Fernando Wood was summarily removed from any involvement with the park and its improvement. The park was placed under the control of a non-partisan and independent board of commissioners whose eleven members were named in the legislation. For all of his support for the park, Wood had been able to do little to move the project forward. His fierce struggles with the Republicans at Albany had drained time and money away from the park. He remained mayor, however, and the new board of commissioners would have to raise the money for the park through the common council. No longer in control, local politicians remained important figures nonetheless in the ensuing development of the park. Theirs was more a negative power, to obstruct and annoy. And even that level of involvement worried the *New York Times*. "We have had sorrowful experience of the fact that our municipal administration is conducted wholly in the interest of our leading rowdies and blackguards," the paper argued in an editorial:

> They have our streets, our taxes, our Police and our Courts of Justice in their hands; and why should they not reign over the Central Park as well?
>
> There is no reason why one hundred, or even fifty years hence, people should not seek New-York to enjoy themselves, just as they now seek it to make money in. But under the *regime* of blackguardism this can never be. As long as we are governed by the five Points, our best attempts at elegance and grace will bear some resemblance to jewels in the snouts of swine. Better the Park should never be made at all if it is to become the resort of rapscalions,—if young bloods are allowed to run races in it with trotting horses, and thus place the lives of everybody in danger, and render equestrian exercise impossible,—if no attempt is to be made to keep it clear of the intemperate, the boisterous and disorderly.[97]

These were harsh words from a paper that had fervently supported the project virtually since it began publication in 1851. It was a warning against allowing men from the grog shops, gambling dens and the "young bloods", whose trotting horses made the Manhattanville Road a menace to life and limb, to make the park their own playground. If the new commissioners could meet that challenge, the park would survive, and deserve to do so. The commissioners met on 30 April, with such warnings clearly in mind. The reform Democrat Cooley, continuing from the consulting board, was elected first president. The new board was dominated by merchants (John A. C. Gray, Charles H. Russell, W. K. Strong and John F. Butterworth), lawyers (Robert J. Dillon, Andrew H. Green, Thomas C. fields, and Waldo Hutchins) and manufacturers (Charles W. Elliott). James Hogg, the nurseryman who had testified before the senate select committee in 1853, was included. An attempt was made to conciliate the various factions within the Democratic Party with the inclusion of Cooley and Samuel J. Tilden's friend, the reform Democrat Green; the anti-Wood faction led by John McKeon was represented by Dillon; fields had close contacts with Wood. Among the board's first decisions was to form a committee to report on the necessity of by-laws for the governance of the park. When the first request for funds was made to the board of aldermen, the maintenance of public order was clearly foremost in the commissioners' minds. "To ensure to the largest number the advantages of the Park, the commissioners will see to it that in the regulations for its government, and in the efficiency of those persons to whom will be entrusted the execution of those regulations, the most complete guarantee shall be furnished for the preservation of order and propriety. So that children from their schools, invalid persons of both sexes and all ages, shall at all times feel that their resort to these grounds is attended with entire security and immunity from all that can demoralize or harm."[98]

Viele was reappointed engineer-in-chief in June 1857. The commissioners discussed advertising for fresh submissions for the design and then decided to do so at their meeting on 25 August. George E. Waring, who had been renting Olmsted's Staten Island farm, was appointed superintendent of draining, and by late summer over 500 laborers had begun the work of digging up and carting stone and clearing growth around the many stagnant pools and marshes in the park. Grading had begun on the space which Viele's plan designated as a military parade ground. The treasurer, Andrew H. Green, perhaps the first of the commissioners to appreciate the need for strict centralized control of expenditure, persuaded the board to require the chief engineer to report the names and compensation of all persons employed on the park. Viele was instructed that no further persons could be employed without explicit permission. The owners of shanties on the site were directed to remove their buildings under threat of being sold off by the commissioners. Steps were taken to purchase the grounds and building of the arsenal from the state for $275,000; and as with every such transaction, the slightest delay aroused fears that interested parties were manipulating the transaction for their own benefit. The board acted vigorously, but distrust of government was so pervasive that every act was inspected on all sides for ulterior and partisan motives. Trust had to be earned, and that would come slowly.

Olmsted

In 1861, writing an introduction to a single-volume edition of his three volumes of travels in the south, Frederick Law Olmsted reiterated many of his basic themes: that free labor was more efficient and socially beneficial than slave labor, and that it was slavery which

Frederick Law Olmsted, a most conservative gentleman, was a failed farmer, traveller in the slave south and designer of Central Park. Olmsted feared the unmodulated sway of money, and cheered the reformers ("Hurrah for Peter Cooper and Hurrah for the Reds") who sought to encourage "a democratic condition of society."

impeded the social development and economic growth of the South. During the course of his extensive travels in the 1850s, he repeatedly found examples of the natural resources of the south poorly used. There were white people he met who were living as he thought very meagre and poor lives. The "shabby and half-furnished cottages" he saw along hundreds of southern side roads frankly puzzled him.[99] Why did these people live in conditions which in the north would be reserved for cattle? And why were the southern whites so complacent? Apparently even the most illiterate, idle and depraved southerner was able to enjoy a sense of racial superiority from the sheer existence of slavery. His chapter "The Experience of Virginia" in *A Journey in the Seaboard Slave States* (1856) contains the fruits of Olmsted's interrogation of the history of Virginia from its early settlement. There were many reasons, rooted in the class composition and early development of the colony, to explain its comparative backwardness, but in order to explain the peculiar poverty of the lives of the southern small farmer and laborer he returned again and again (as did so many northerners who gravitated towards the Republican Party) to slavery and its malign effect upon the southern economy and upon the southern worker.

His arguments about the productivity of land, of the relative efficiency of labor, functioned in a political moment. The introductory chapter of *Journeys and Explorations in the Cotton Kingdom* (1861) was titled "The Present Crisis." He hoped that the publication of this distillation of his southern travels in London would strengthen British support for the free-labor north. The book was dedicated to John Stuart Mill. At another level, the poverty of southern life, outside the world of the great plantations, led Olmsted to assert the case for civic culture. The south had a rural culture of islands of so-called civility surrounded by bad roads, inconvenience, grudging and often rather primitive hospitality and little of what he recognized as true evidence of community. He felt the absence of virtually everything in the south that he had come to value in civilization. Norfolk, Virginia, contained "No lyceum or public libraries, no public gardens, no galleries of art ... no public resorts of healthful and refining amusement; no place better than a filthy, tobacco-impregnated bar-room or a licentious dance-cellar ... for the stranger of high or low degree to pass the hours unoccupied by business."[100] Trying to sum up his experience of staying in many homes in the south, Olmsted argued that "I found no garden, no flowers, no fruit, no tea, no cream, no sugar, no bread ... no curtains, no lifting windows ... no couch. ... For all that, the house swarmed with vermin. There was no hay, no straw, no oats ... no discretion, no care, no honesty ..." (*Cotton Kingdom*, 520). The few planters who were living surrounded by servants and material comforts were physically remote from their neighbors. The self-sufficiency and isolation of the plantation economy brought many personal benefits to the wealthy, he argued, "... but it will not bring thither good roads and bridges, it will not bring thither such means of education and of civilized comfort as are to be drawn from libraries, churches, museums, gardens, theatres, and assembly rooms ..." Such "advantages" of civilization "... chiefly come from or connect with acts of co-operation, or exchange of services. ... They grow, in fact, out of employments in which the people of the community are associated, or which they constantly give to and receive from one another, with profit" (*Cotton Kingdom*, 18). As Olmsted envisages it, culture is inextricably the fruit of the inter-relations between free men. The fine arts, letters or intellectual life cannot thrive in a society based upon slavery. Rather, its culture will be materialistic, repressive and philistine. The brutality and poverty of the people seemed to him the logical consequence of the nature of the slaveholding social order.

The south, with its many defects, made the virtues of the north ever more precious to Olmsted. "A man forced to labor under their system," he wrote,

> is morally driven to indolence, carelessness, indifference to the results of skill, heedlessness, inconstancy of purpose, improvidence and extravagance. Precisely the opposite qualities are those which are encouraged, and inevitably developed in a man who has to make his living, and earn all his comfort by his voluntarily-directed labor. These opposite qualities are those which are essentially necessary to the success of an adventurer in commerce. The commercial success of the free states is the offspring of their voluntary labor system. (*Seaboard Slave States*, I, 164–5)

The free laborer, whose efficiency and productivity was vital testimony of the economic and cultural superiority of the north, also gave shape to Olmsted's sense of the moral ascendency of the market economy:

> ... I wonder if it would not be possible to obtain men for the labor of ships, as well as for any other labor, who would always perform the services required of them heartily, promptly, and fully, as an honest return for their wages and rations; who would obey orders, not like whipped curs and cowed slaves, but as free men and brave men, and wise men, with a republican respect for right laws, and a sensible understanding of the fit division of responsibility between them and their officers. I fear not, unless some thorough, comprehensive, and generously-directed educational department shall be adopted as a permanent, and indivisible part of our naval system. (*Seaboard Slave States*, I, 166)

Amidst a blizzard of question marks, Olmsted had similarly argued the same point in the *American Whig Review* in 1851. True discipline in the merchant navy need not solely be enforced by officers of "irritable and violent temper" or subordination produced only by fear:

> Is not a manly acknowledgement of a real "ordainment of good sense" to the management of a ship, the best subordination? Is not a sensible respect for a judgment that always shows itself calm, sufficient and decisive, or an energy that can be patient, and an activity that can be silent and self-possessed, the best discipline? Is it not more reliable in extremity than cringing submission to the despicable power of a bullying braggart, like most of our mates, whom no man, dog, sailor, however they may skulk out of reach, can ever see stamping, braying and kicking

about docks in his lion's skin, without hearty disgust and contempt? Do our officers really doubt if freely combined action is more effective than forced labor? Or that it is so only by regard to duty and by republican submission to law, as the crank of the shaft by which all associated labor, must be brought to operate usefully?[101]

The free labor principles of the north encouraged men and women to work "heartily, prompty, and fully"; but Olmsted repeatedly complained that the common people in the north were "ill-natured." He wrote to Brace that northern workers were "desperately selfish and incapable of friendship of more than words. Not so beastly and stupid as the English but more crafty and hypocritical—yet better according to their light than the rich."[102] Having sailed on an American merchant ship to China, he had no illusions about the kind of man who sailed before the mast. He wrote in a letter to the *New York Times* in 1854 that native American sailors

> . . . so far from being the brave, generous, heroic men they are poetically and romantically described to be, are the very meanest, most reckless, dastardly and despicable class of men ever allowed to be long at liberty in the world. Why? Because the seamen in American ships (I do not mean in American alone) are so treated that it is impossible for them to retain self-respect and decent, orderly, *gentlemanly* habits of mind. . . . I do not believe there is one native seaman in a hundred, who is not a helpless drunkard when on shore, and always shipped in an intoxicated condition when he goes to sea. And there are even a smaller number who do not always fear and hate their officers when at sea, obey them from fear more than from a regard to their contract or from the effect of a decent discipline, and desert them whenever they dare to, if their selfish interests or instincts direct it.[103]

If there were alternatives to the reign of brutality and negligence at sea, Olmsted believed they would begin ashore, with the training of young men in "mercantile naval training schools," which would bring a better-educated and more suitable person into the profession. On this whole subject Olmsted had misgivings. While praising the free-labor system, he expressed significant reservations about labor in general. He did not agitate, as had Melville in *White-Jacket* (1850), to abolish flogging in the navy. Ever the gradualist, he believed in the possibility of changes in the relations between ships' captains and crews, and in naval custom itself. Sailors under the present regime of brutality were compared to chattel slaves. Olmsted wrote that "[f]rom the beginning they have been used at sea to be treated like slaves—far worse than slaves in general—what wonder their character becomes slavish and even diabolical!"[104] ("Who ain't

a slave?" asks Ishmael in *Moby-Dick* [1851], "Tell me that.")
Olmsted also noted the comparison in his discussion of "The Property Aspect of Slavery" in *A Journey in the Back Country* (1860).
Olmsted once asked an overseer about punishing the slaves under his control. The man remarked ". . . it's my business, and I think nothing of it. Why, sir, I wouldn't mind killing a nigger more than I would a dog." "His conversation on this subject," wrote Olmsted, "was exactly like what I have heard said, again and again, by northern shipmasters and officers, with regard to seamen."[105] The master of a ship, like the slaveowner, possessed absolute power over the crew. Short of breaking the absoluteness of that power, and legally limiting its exercise, the reforms he proposed would not directly address the problem of "that brutalizing tyranny."

It is crucial for the understanding of Olmsted to appreciate that he had known, first-hand, the harsh hand of absolute domination. It may also help to explain how difficult he found it to function under the interfering authority of others. Viele and Green in Central Park, Bellows in the Sanitary Commission, and others encountered in a long career, found Olmsted always indignantly gasping for independent breath and resentful of what his superiors or employers believed to be rightful authority. His inner ambivalence about authority made Olmsted an unconvincing conservative; his doubts about American workers and his belief in the need for social order (and his life's work trying to shore up the disintegrating community of American cities) left Olmsted no less uneasy around those who believed in the essential virtue, discipline and sobriety of the urban proletariat.

What unites these disparate comments is Olmsted's respect for the law, "decent discipline" and an acceptance of "the fit division of responsiblity" between those in authority and those subject to that authority. He preferred a ship's crew which accepted discipline "as free men and brave men, and wise men," but no matter how shockingly abused discipline did not cease to be necessary. Like so many "institutional" conservatives in antebellum America, the chaos and disorder of a rapidly expanding society convinced him of the need for coherence and order. "Discipline does not mean forced or frightened obedience, as too many young officers suppose; discipline means *system*" (*Papers*, 2, 327). But when he experienced the infliction of "discipline" by an overseer during his southern travels, we cannot fail to see that Olmsted's response was complex, agonized and humane. With the same overseer who ". . . wouldn't mind killing a nigger more than I would a dog . . ." he encountered a slave girl of about eighteen hiding in the bushes. Unhappy with the evasive answers he received from her, the overseer told her to kneel down and proceded to strike her with his rawhide whip thirty or forty times. "They were well laid on, as a boatswain would thrash a skulking sailor," noted the ex-sailor Olmsted, and without apparent sign of "angry excitement" on the part of the overseer:

> At every stroke the girl winced, and exclaimed, "Yes, sir!" or "Ah, sir!" or "Please, sir!" not groaning or screaming. At length he stopped and said, "Now tell me the truth." The girl repeated the same story. "You have not got enough yet," said he, "pull up your clothes—lie down." The girl without any hesitation, without a word or look of remonstrance or entreaty, drew closely all her garments under her shoulders, and lay down upon the ground with her face toward the overseer, who continued to flog her with the rawhide, across her naked loins and thigh, with as much strength as before. She now shrank away from him, not rising, but writhing, groveling, and screaming, "Oh, don't, sir! oh, please stop, master! please, sir! please, sir! oh, that's enough, master! oh, Lord! oh, master, master! oh, God, master, do stop! oh, God, master! oh, God, master!"

A young "gentleman" of fifteen watched the scene impatiently, waiting for their journey to resume. It was the first time Olmsted had ever seen a woman flogged, and what remained with him (apart from the words of the girl) was the passionless attitude of the overseer whose approach was "grim [and] business-like." Olmsted watched the beating, his emotions reaching a boiling point, but he said nothing. His horse, growing restless, gave him an escape and he angrily rode up a nearby hill. "Choking, sobbing, spasmodic groans only were heard."[106] When the overseer joined Olmsted, he was laughing at how he had prevented the girl from cheating him out of a day's work. Olmsted carefully distanced himself from the abolitionists who would have made such a scene the occasion of a blistering sermon.

What is so striking in Olmsted is the absence of explicit comment. It reflects, in writerly terms, a tact that Henry James alone of his countrymen would have best understood. The power of the scene is to be found precisely in the absence of any expression of Olmsted's indignation. The feelings were there, but the young man watching the scene at Olmsted's side ". . . had evidently not the faintest sympathy with my emotion. . . ." Intervening in the scene, dramatically stopping the beating, perhaps buying the girl's freedom on the spot, would allow the reader in the north a pleasant escape from the reality of slavery. Olmsted does not afford his readers that fantasy. The overseer went about the business with dispatch and a banal business-like demeanor, and resumed his conversation with Olmsted when he rejoined the party. Slaves were being beaten every day, and it is just as well that it be seen for what it was, stripped of lurid, leering melodrama. The terrible normality of the scene remains. No one who could have written these pages could ever use the words "order" and "discipline" abstractly. They meant something very precise. It is taking us to the heart of Olmsted that we understand why he used them at all.

His metaphor for social discipline was a machine functioning by "the crank of the shaft." Four months after his appointment as superintendent of Central Park, Olmsted proudly wrote to his father that "...I have got the park into a capital discipline, a perfect system, working like a machine, 1,000 men now at work" (*Papers*, 3, 113). During the Civil War, Rev. Henry W. Bellows, Olmsted's close colleague on the United States Sanitary Commission, similarly argued that the soldier: ". . . is a man who has not merely a willingness to obey, but a habit of obedience,—one trained and disciplined, not by tactics, but by time and experience, in the character and qualities of mind that make him in his very blood and bones like a machine."[107] The nuanced difference between the discipline rooted in a consenting and republican dignity, appropriate for a peacetime public park, and a rigorous and mechanical military discipline required by a nation at war, explains something of the shift in emphasis between the two men—and also suggests a shared foundation in the need Olmsted and Bellows felt to haul to attention the slouching, quarrelsome American of the 1850s. When Olmsted summed up what was wrong with the south, it was the disorganization of southern life which gave an edge to his criticism. "[T]he constantly-occuring delays, and the waste of time and labor that you encounter everywhere, are most annoying and provoking to a stranger. The utter want of system and order, almost essential, as it would appear, where slaves are your instruments, is amazing—and when you are not in haste, often amusing" (*Seaboard Slave States*, 1, 162).

While concern for order and discipline remains a constant in his social thought, Olmsted's politics of order were in a state of flux. On the first leg of his journey south in 1853, he stopped at Nashville, Tennessee, where he had long conversations with his brother John's classmate from Yale, Samuel Perkins Allison. Writing to Charles Loring Brace on the steamboat which carried him from Nashville to Paducah, Kentucky, on 1 December, he described Allison's frank conversation about the absolute necessity for the expansion of slavery, and of his belief in the superior cultivation of the southern gentleman. "He did not believe there was a gentleman in the whole Northwest. . . . And he evidently thought there were very few, and they but poorly developed, anywhere at the North. There was not a man in Yale College who had anything of the appearance or manners of a gentleman, from the North, except a few sons of professional

Bellows, a New York Unitarian clergyman, shared Olmsted's alarm at the slouching quarrelsome American of the 1850s, and argued, in a defense of Central Park in the *Atlantic Monthly* in April 1861, that the most needed "mission" for the city was "to teach and induce habits of orderly, tranquil, contemplative social amusement, moderate exercises or recreation, soothing to the nerves." Undated engraving by A. H. Ritchie.

and commercial people who had been brought up in the large towns. There were no gentlemen at the North out of the large towns" (*Papers*, 2, 234). This was perhaps more college dormitory conversation than a serious engagement with class and sectional differences. As it continued, the conversation left Olmsted uncomfortably aware that his arguments were no less precarious than Allison's. He was willing to grant considerable substance to what the southerner said:

> I tried to show him that there were compensations in the *general* eleva-
> tion of all classes at the North, but he did not seem to care for it. He is,
> in fact, a thorough Aristocrat, and altogether, the conversation making
> me acknowledge the rowdyism, ruffianism, want of high honorable sen-
> timent & chivalry of the common farming & laboring people of the
> North, as I was obliged to, made me very melancholy. With such low
> material, and selfish aims in statesmanship [*as the best men of
> the South have*] and with such a low, prejudiced, party enslaved and
> material people [*at the North*], what does the success of our Democratic
> nationalist amount to—and what is to become of us? (*Papers*, 2, 234,
> passages in italic deleted by Olmsted)

Considered dispassionately, the condition of "common farming & laboring people" in the north left a great deal to be desired. But when he wrote his account of his southern travels there was an entrenched denial of his doubts and ambiguities. During his conversations with Allison in 1853, there was a sense that commitments were still possible, that his personal position and the future of the nation were still fluid. Despite the profound disappointments of 1848, Olmsted's hopes for an invigorated democratic spirit, manifested through free labor and social order, remained.

> I must be either an Aristocrat or more of a Democrat than I have
> been—a Socialist Democrat. We need institutions that shall more
> directly *assist* the poor and degraded to elevate themselves. Our
> educational principle must be enlarged and made to include more than
> these miserable common schools. The poor & wicked need more than to
> be let alone.
>
> It seemed to me that what had made these Southern gentlemen
> Democrats was the perception that mere Democracy as they understand
> it (no checks or laws upon the country more than can be helped) was the
> best system for their class. It gave capital every advantage in the pursuit
> of wealth—and money gave wisdom & power. They could do what they
> liked. It was only necessary for them, the gentlemen, to settle what they
> wanted. Or if they disagreed, the best *commander* of the people carried
> his way. The people doing nothing but choose between them. He had no
> conception of higher than material interests entering into politics. All that
> these sort of free traders want is protection to capital. Agrarianism would
> suit them better if they could protect that and use what they consider
> their rights.
>
> But I do very much [feel] inclined to believe that Government should
> have in view the encouragement of a democratic condition of society as

well as of government—that the two need to go together as they do at the North in much greater degree than at the South or I suppose anywhere else. But I don't think our state of society is sufficiently Democratic at the North or likely to be by mere *laisser aller*. The poor need an education to refinement and taste and the mental & moral capital of gentlemen.

I have been blundering over this and have not, I think, expressed at all what I wanted to. In a steamboat cabin—dark, shaking, and gamesters and others talking about the table—I can't collect my ideas. But to put some shape to it. Hurrah for Peter Cooper and Hurrah for the Reds."
(*Papers*, 2, 234–5)

Like Downing, Olmsted was a believer in system, discipline and order, and something of a Red Republican, a Socialist Democrat; a critic of laissez faire and a believer in the immense social and economic benefits of free labor. The man who believed in 1853 that there was a need for "institutions that shall more directly *assist* the poor" wrote two years later that there was a need to send them elsewhere, to "scatter the starving laborers throughout the country wherever their labor was needed." A train ticket given to a starving laborer was a form of assistance, but a two-edged one. Its attractions as social policy, as a form of pauper cleansing of the city, could not be denied. But did Olmsted listen to those who doubted the remedy was adequate for the scale of the problem? Did he look carefully enough at who the poor were, and listen to what *they* had to say on the subject? The rich paradoxes of Olmsted (and of Olmsted's America) display themselves before us.[108]

The stubborn failure of his farm on Staten Island to yield a profit, and the ending of his second series of "Yeoman" letters in the *New York Times* in June 1854, persuaded him to transfer the mortgage on the farm to his brother John (who intended to sell it) and to move to New York City in search of a new career. With the financial backing of his father, in May 1855 Olmsted entered into a partnership agreement with publishers Joshua Dix and Arthur T. Edwards, who had acquired *Putnam's Monthly Magazine*. The financial salvation for Olmsted in 1855 ended two years later in near-disaster. The books he assembled from the articles about his southern travels continued to appear: *A Journey in the Seaboard Slave States* in January 1856, and *A Journey Through Texas* a year later. But despite receiving thoughtful praise (and a rewarding hostility to his work in the south) sales were disappointing. A trip to Europe to drum up trade (he represented the firm in London until October 1856) made little difference to business. He joined his father, brother and sister-in-law, and the family travelled together on the Continent. (This too ended in sadness when his brother John, whose health had in part been the reason for the journey, showed no sign of improvement; John Hull Olmsted died in Nice in the fall of 1857.) Relations deteriorated with Edwards, who proved to be rude and thick-skinned. Sales of *Putnam's* fell off. Olmsted's work as a publisher seemed nebulous, and he spent much of his time working on his own books. He was not vigorous in the effort to protect his father's investment and remained a passive and uncomfortable bystander while the firm finally went bankrupt in August 1857.

Living in New York that summer placed Olmsted in the midst of a political storm. The decision of the Supreme Court on the Dred Scott case, published in March 1857, struck down the Missouri Compromise. It was greeted with indignation throughout the North. Olmsted's Free Soil sympathies had kept him closely involved with efforts to revive German settlements in Texas and the anti-slavery political force they potentially represented. In 1855 he had raised money to support a Free Soil paper in Texas, Adolf Douai's *Zeitung*, and he had raised money to buy rifles and a howitzer for the Free Soilers in Lawrence, Kansas, where the pro-slavery legislature, meeting at Lecompton, planned a constitutional convention which would ensure the state went slave-holding. In protest, a Free State convention met in Topeka in July. Despite a Free State majority in the October election, the "Lecompton constitution," supported by the Democratic President Buchanan, would effectively insulate slaveholders from further attack. When President Buchanan appointed Robert J. Walker as governor of the Kansas territory, Olmsted drew upon angry editorials in Greeley's *Tribune* to write his introduction to T. H. Gladstone's *The Englishman in Kansas* in April (*Papers*, 2, 424–8).

While the struggle in Kansas unfolded in the papers every day, the Republican legislature in Albany proceeded, through a new charter, to pass a bill which removed control of the police from the city government, an excise bill which promised to shut thirteen out of fourteen saloons in the city, and a bill which removed control of Central Park from the city—all measures designed to emasculate Fernando Wood and the Democratic political machine over which he ruled. Wood declined to collaborate in this procedure, and launched a campaign of legal resistance, delay, insubordination and defiance in the name of Home Rule. In the streets there were pitched battles between Wood's police force (the "Municipals") and the "Metropolitans," created under the new charter. The *Herald* covered this conflict on 17 June under the prophetic headline "Civil War in the Metropolis." In early July the disorder heightened when rioting broke out between rival gangs, the Dead Rabbits and the Bowery

Boys. It took elements from six regiments of the state militia to end the brawling. On 24 August the New York branch of the Ohio Life Insurance and Trust Company failed, triggering off a financial panic and a near-collapse of the markets, heralding the worst depression in twenty years. By October the New York banks suspended specie payments. "The merchants & bankers [are] horribly blue," Olmsted wrote to his brother, "& bank-riots are almost apprehended. The talk is much worse than you would suppose from the papers" (*Papers*, 3, 81). Unemployed workers filled the streets demanding that somebody do something to help them. Wood's pleas on their behalf earned him the ever-deepening enmity of the "better class" of New York politicians. It became a test of political integrity among Wood's opponents (reform Democrat, Republican, Whig, or Native American) to reject the demands made by such "mobs."

In July Olmsted went to the Morris Cove Inn near New Haven Connecticut to work on the manuscript of *A Journey in the Back Country*. There he encountered an old friend, Charles W. Elliott, manufacturer and author of *Cottages and Cottage Life* (1848) and a contributor to *Putnam's Monthly Magazine* during Olmsted's tenure. Now one of the commissioners on the new board of commissioners of Central Park, Elliott had studied landscape gardening with Downing, and was a friend of Brace's. He was a man of generous sympathies. In the hard winter of 1855, while Olmsted argued for the desirability of sending starving laborers out of New York, Elliott urged support for local "Soup Dispensaries."[109] Elliott told Olmsted that a superintendent was needed. Over the previous five years Olmsted had not engaged in any of the debates about the question of a park in New York. He could hardly have failed to be aware of the issue: a paragraph by Downing on the subject was added to Olmsted's article on the park at Birkenhead in the *Horticulturist* in May 1851. He returned back to his Staten Island farm from his first journey in the south in April, 1853, at the moment when the great debate over the park was underway. Olmsted's twenty-seventh "Yeoman" letter in the *New York Times* appeared on 30 June 1853. The same issue contained Griscom's letter "Public Parks vs. Public Health." In the midst of so many other concerns, Olmsted could hardly have failed to take a close interest in the progress of the debate. This interest, however, does not appear in his few published letters from 1853, and when he was away from New York immediate events of travel preoccupied him. The alacrity with which he sought the post of superintendent reflected a distinct need for a steady income and, perhaps less visibly, an abiding interest in parks and what they might contribute to the making of a civilized society.

The Central Park superintendentship was a politically sensitive position.[110] A candidate who was perceived as being too partisan could readily be blocked by any of the factions represented on the board. In the light of Olmsted's apparent absence of partisan involvement, and his experiences as a farmer and writer, Elliott encouraged him to apply for the position. Olmsted received the support of 200 notables, including publishers (George H. Putnam), journalists (Greeley, Parke Godwin, Whitelaw Reid), writers (Irving, Bayard Taylor), scientists (Asa Gray) and the merchant brother of former mayor William Havemeyer.[111] But, in a series of calls upon his return to New York, Olmsted discovered that Viele rudely preferred a "practical" man for the post, and that for John A. C. Gray, the New York merchant who was vice-president of the board, it was only Washington Irving's support that persuaded him to vote for Olmsted. The other candidates included a surveyor, a house builder, a professor of chemistry, and the son of John James Audubon, but all lacked Olmsted's experience and socially prominent supporters. Among the commissioners, Olmsted was opposed by the Democratic lawyer Thomas C. fields (whose later career culminated in the embezzlement of over a million dollars from the city and flight from justice), but with the determined support of Elliott and Green he was successful. At the 11 September meeting (at which the board of commissioners put aside Viele's plan and decided to hold a public design competition), he was appointed to the post of superintendent with a salary of $1,500 per year. He was subordinate to Viele as engineer-in-chief. "It seems to be generally expected that Viele & I shall quarrel, that he will be jealous of me, & that there will be all sorts of intrigues. I shall try the frank, conscientious & industrious plan, and if it fails, I shall have learned something more & be no worse off."[112]

He remained uncertain *why* he had been appointed, and reasonably doubted whether his experience as a farmer and genuine claims to "practical" ability had played much or any role in the decision. Despite the recommendations of Greeley, Irving and the others, which signified his recognition among the city's literary community, and his respectability in the eyes of the city gentry, when he met the foreman and the laborers whose work he was to direct, Olmsted felt that he lacked appropriate credentials. He knew more about the day-to-day problems of constructing the park than they. But he sensed in their eyes and smiles, in their polite concern for how he coped with muddy fields, in their little comments on his dress and abilities riding a horse on rough terrain, a dismissiveness towards himself. In his relations with Viele and fields, it was never wholly to disappear. He had entered into a different New York, and found its values not his own.

Through those first interviews and early days with the work crews in the park, the meaning of the park changed, perhaps irrevocably, for Olmsted. The park idea for Olmsted was a civilizing one, as it had been for Downing. It offered to citizens of every class an elevating vision of nourishment and civility. As he took up his duties, the practical complications of the superintendent's role seemed less a matter of fulfilling an idealistic mission of nourishing civilized values and winning the plaudits and patronage of the city's elite, than of the challenge presented to his sense of self-respect and dignity by those who were manifestly his inferiors in knowledge and experience. After observing the meetings of the board of commissioners for less than a month, Olmsted regarded it as being "unmanageable, unqualified & liable to permit any absurdity" (*Papers*, 3, 102). In his first letters after his appointment there is a sense of a beleaguered gentleman surrounded by opponents, of being embayed by yapping, selfish hounds against whom he can only shake his stick and express his contempt. The park had come to stand for the struggle of his class for their rightful ascendancy; for the attempt by gentlemen reformers to reclaim the role they formerly occupied in the community; for the battle of honest men against the thieves in City Hall and their political maneuvers; for the "sunshine" against the "shadow" and all of its minions.

He saw, early on, that it was necessary to secure power; power meant entering the political bear-pit. The board, for all its intended nonpartisanship, often voted along party lines, and the internal divisions were closely related to the political situation in the city. From the start of Olmsted's tenure as superintendent he was confronted by the problems raised by the depression, and this quickly became part of the internal politics of the board and of Olmsted's relations to it. With a mayoral election due in early December 1857, the political stakes were high. (In the run-up to the election, the president of the board, James Cooley, served as chairman of a meeting held at the Academy of Music on 24 November in support of Daniel F. Tiemann.[113] This helps us to understand the viciousness of the attacks on the board in November from mayor Wood's supporters.) Large numbers of laboring jobs at the park were the most visible remedy the mayor and the common council could offer to the city's unemployed. The collapse of the financial markets, and the reluctance of capitalists to buy park bonds in the uncertain situation, meant that the city comptroller's office was unable to raise the sums requested by the park board. This forced the commissioners to vote in late September to authorize the dismissal of 700 laborers, most of the park's workforce. They had been hired in expectation that the money to pay them would soon be forthcoming, and had gone without pay in August and September. There was an unexpected bonus in this for Olmsted. It enabled him to get rid of all of the incompetent foremen, and especially those who had been so dismiss-ive of his own role. It was a disaster for the laborers, but a quietly satisfying moment for Olmsted. Andrew H. Green also used the financial crisis as the moment to strengthen his control over the finances of the park. On 8 October the board accepted his proposal to deny to any employee the ability to enter into a contract, debt or liability on behalf of the board.[114] This effectively stripped away from Viele whatever discretion he previously possessed about the management of the park.

On 22 October mayor Wood proposed to help the city's unem-ployed laborers by funding new public works projects. He also called for flour, cornmeal and potatoes to be sold to laborers at cost. Otherwise, he warned, there was a grave danger of assaults on private property. The common council voted $50,000 for macadam-izing Second Avenue and other streets, but this was blocked by litigation in the courts. A further application for $250,000 was made by the board to the common council and on 2 November this sum was borrowed to resume work in Central Park. The board of com-missioners, willing at such a moment to be seen playing a positive role, granted Olmsted the power to hire up to 1,000 laborers, and also gave him the authority to make dismissals. This was, at last, the bonanza the politicians had been waiting for. "All persons applying for work upon the Central Park are directed to the office, Seventy-ninth street and fifth-avenue, where a registry is made."[115] The *New York Times* noted that "There was not a candidate for election or reelection . . . who did not determine to get himself returned by means of the Central Park." Promises were freely made, and tickets calling upon the superintendent to give the bearer employment at sight were printed and distributed before the election.[116] Nonetheless, on the day of the ballot, Olmsted wrote to the board:

> Gentlemen: In reply to the inquiry addressed to me at your meeting, I beg to report that, having regard only to the most economical method of carrying on the required work upon the Park, *no more* laborers are needed than I am at present authorized to employ.
>
> Considering the question of whether the number of laborers might not be employed by working them in sets—one alternatively with the other, strictly in the same manner—I must reply that such an arrangement would be attended by obvious economical disadvantages.
>
> I have the honor to be gentlemen,
>
> FRED. LAW OLMSTED, Superintendent.
> Central Park, New York, December 1, 1857.[117]

Olmsted's letter was written, we must assume, with its rapid public circulation in mind; it was a political statement affirming that he was reluctant to use the park to play traditional politics. As superintendent, Olmsted was not charged with providing welfare to the unemployed. The humanitarianism which he expressed at other times found no place here. His concerns were strictly with the economical execution of the board's instructions. What was at stake behind this letter was the integrity of the park itself. He affirmed that the board would not become the creature of political expediency. To help the unemployed more than the board had done would, he believed, turn the park over to the corrupt interests which would surely destroy it. To save the park for the people, it was necessary to turn his back upon the city's unemployed.

Instead of satisfying the common council, Olmsted's reluctance to pass these laboring jobs over to the aldermen earned him their passionate enmity. They felt betrayed by the way the board had finessed the crisis, and a committee of the common council began an investigation of charges that the board of commissioners had exercised political favoritism in employment and had extracted political levies from the workforce. (The real reason seems to have been that the board of commissioners refused to appoint a member of the common council as their pay-desk clerk. The outraged councilman vowed to make trouble for the board, and did so.) The hearings of 7 December revealed the exasperation of certain of the aldermen, who proposed now to abandon all funding of the park to punish the board of commissioners for trying to create a "political machine." Tiemann had defeated Wood, and the mood of the aldermen was desperate. Olmsted faced the accusation that good Democrats were being discriminated against:

> ... after a great deal of running around [testified Alderman Steers, he] had found Mr [Andrew H.] Green, and received an order for the employment of 50 men. The order was to Mr. Olmsted. He took the order to him and was told to send up 10 men. He sent them. The first that presented himself was accosted with—"Well, I suppose you are a good Republican." The man said no, he was a good Democrat. He was told to stand aside. The others heard it, and he supposed they said they did not belong to any party, for they were employed, and the man who said he was a Democrat was not.[118]

The accusations had the unintended effect of immeasurably strengthening Olmsted's position on the board, and in the eyes of those in the city who despised the corrupt politicians. He regarded the accusations against himself as a badge of integrity. Olmsted had come through his first crisis with great honor. The integrity of the board had been sustained, and control of the park had been kept out of the hands of the councilmen. The aldermanic inquiry established that the park was being run on an explicitly nonpartisan basis, that no extravagances were being allowed in payments, that a tight surveillance was maintained over every expenditure, and that the commissioners had declined to draw upon their personal allowance of $300 for carriage hire. For the aldermen it was an unmitigated failure. The battle over employment in the park, as the *New York Times* observed, was part of the larger campaign for political reform in the city:

> The Central Park is the first public work we have had in this City for many a day, in which an attempt has been made to conduct it honestly, and without reference to political consideration. Everything else we have is more or less daubed over with the slime of corruption. So far, in spite of the desperate efforts of the gang of knaves who rule us in the City Hall, the experiment has been remarkably successful. We call upon the public, as the next step in the great work of City reform, so well inaugurated by Wood's defeat, to strengthen the hands of the Commissioners and the Superintendent in their resistance to the schemes of the factious conspirators, who have so long plundered us.[119]

Specific administrative responsibilities such as the control of the hiring, and the ability to get rid of men who merited dismissal, were crucial tests for Olmsted of his success or failure in the larger social project which the park represented. The fate of the park was not settled by the failure of the aldermanic inquiry (similar efforts were to be repeatedly made), but these events left supporters of the park with greater confidence that it was a battle which might be won. Olmsted learned that his ability to fight against corruption and on behalf of his vision of civil society depended upon his obtaining a measure of control in his day-to-day functioning as superintendent. He was soon aware of the role he was intended to play in the internal politics of the board. As early as 6 October (that is, within three weeks of his appointment) he observed that the commissioners who were doubtful about Viele promoted his own role in the park. He had been requested to make a report on the problem of drainage, which was precisely the area of responsibility of the chief engineer (*Papers*, 3, 94–100, 103–5). The competition to design the park attracted him for financial reasons (the winning design would receive a prize of $2,000), but also, he told his father, it appealed to him because ". . . the whole control of the matter would be given me . . ." (*Papers*, 3, 114). The early months on the park taught Olmsted much about power, and its usefulness. It is perhaps to oversimplify Olmsted's relationship to Viele to say (as does Melvin Kalfus) that he had been gunning for the chief engineer.[120] He was in part responsible for

Calvert Vaux invited Olmsted to join him in preparing the "Greensward" design for the Central Park competition. He had trained in architecture in London, and been brought to America as Downing's architectural assistant. The firm of Olmsted, Vaux & Co. (1865–72) designed Prospect Park in Brooklyn and completed major projects in Chicago, Buffalo, Bridgeport, New Britain and Riverside, Illinois.

undermining Viele, but Green had that task well in hand before Olmsted's appointment. Viele's role in the park would have been limited, and then ended, no matter what Olmsted did.

Calvert Vaux was outraged at the mediocrity of Viele's plan, and had told whoever would listen amongst the commissioners that an alternative was necessary. The lingering doubts about Viele, the lack of progress, and sharply focused criticisms like Vaux's of a plan the board had somehow been stuck with, contributed to the decision to hold a design competition.[121] Vaux, as the custodian of the Downing legacy, was determined to secure the commission, and he approached Olmsted with a suggestion that they collaborate. He possessed a knowledge of the ground that was nearly unique, and for Vaux that was a great advantage. Whether Olmsted possessed any other dis-

The park's success was rooted in the new forms of leisure activity it made available to New Yorkers. Skating in the park captured the imagination of the public. Every day male bystanders crowded around the ladies' skating pond, which became a fashionable attraction.

tinctive ideas about the design of the park was unclear. Viele, who intended to submit his own proposal, told Olmsted he was completely indifferent to whether the superintendent entered the competition. He had seen Olmsted increasingly used by his enemies on the board of commissioners to weaken his authority, and remained contemptuous of the "unpractical" writer.

The competition rules called for an expenditure of no more than $1,500,000, four east-west crossings, a parade ground of twenty to forty acres, three playgrounds of three to ten acres each, a site for an exhibition or concert hall, a site for an ornamental fountain; a site for a prospect tower, a flower garden of two or three acres, and a place which could be flooded for skating in the winter. The Olmsted-Vaux submission, worked on during the evenings throughout January and February, was something of a speculation, requiring many hours' work and an investment of hundreds of dollars. The initial deadline, 1 March 1858, was extended by one month, and their "Greensward" plan was submitted on the last day of the competition. Thirty-five entries were received (two were not formally entered in the competition), most consisting of models, drawings to scale and an accompanying text which was printed at the order of the board. The process of deliberation took a month, and the full range of the submitted designs provides a useful occasion to examine the "park idea" as it was in April 1858.

The design requirements of the competition imposed a straightjacket upon the submissions.[122] Having to accommodate many of the same design elements, it is hardly surprising that variations between the entries attract our attention. The submissions assume that military displays and parades would figure prominently in the way the park was used. Patriotic displays and parades by the state militia, volunteer fire companies, trade unionists, Ulstermen wearing orange sashes, St. Patrick's Day parades by Irish nationalists, and German *turnvereine*, dressed in colorful and manly uniforms, were a popular aspect of city life. The design submissions provided for parade grounds with plentiful space for military maneuvers and for berms or sloping terraces to accommodate the substantial number of spectators who would regularly be gathered to watch.[123] Plan #17, for example, included a heroic parade ground three-quarters of a mile long by 300 feet wide. Entries #4 and #28 proposed a parade ground for military units of division size; the former included a shooting gallery of 1,700 feet which would be adequate for cannons. Adam Gigrich (#7) wanted the parade ground to be equipped for target shooting. H. Noury (#8) omitted the Croton reservoir from the park altogether to provide a military parade ground adequate for a force of 40,000 to 50,000 men. The size of the parade ground in other submissions varied from twenty-two acres to thirty-eight acres. The plan from "D. M." (#12) called for a separate entrance for military use, and for triumphal arches at the entrances. Entry #29 tentatively suggested that parade grounds were unnecessary.

Most of the submissions assumed similarly that parks were didactic landscapes where the lessons of history and culture should be imparted. Few submissions failed to place statuary, columns, towers, and arches in the park. Quotations and citations from classical culture abounded. There was a liberal sprinkling of statuary representing classical deities and figures from mythology. A statue of Apollo, surrounded by figures representing Agriculture, Autumn, Horticulture and Spring opened on to a 100-foot wide avenue of Apollo leading to Flora's fountain, Neptune's cascade and Jupiter's basin (#8). One plan called for a "Park Lane," a one-mile long Appian Way lined with statuary, fountains and monuments (#4). Two submissions included arcades lined by columns of busts of distinguished heroes. The Valhalla created by King Ludwig of

Bavaria at Ratisbonne suggested the usefulness of such a reminder of the achievements of the civilization. "Similar attempts, if carried out on a liberal scale, undoubtedly tend to inspire our mind with gratefulness, and a desire to follow the footsteps of those whom the entire nation may well be proud to consider their own" (#11). "Leander" envisaged a "grove of history" and a "grove of authors" (#24). At the center of his temple, "Manhattan" proposed siting a fountain topped by a sitting figure, the Genius of America (#26). Gigrich placed a fountain atop a twenty-five- to thirty-foot hill which was topped by a symbolic figure the "Déess of Liberty" whose arm bearing a scepter extended forward. Her ". . . beneficial sway is acknowledged by the millions of happy people inhabiting the land." Along with a concert hall, deer park, Corinthian-style temple, 110-foot high weeping fountain, #30 proposed a large monument to President Washington.

The displays of military prowess and the symbolic representation of "culture" suggest not so much alternative versions of the city's destiny, but complementary facets of the larger society. While many contributions are explicitly for an imperial city, others suggest a city expressing at its heart the recollection of the past and acknowledgement of its role as fount of the highest ideals of western culture. Warlike triumphal arches fit for conquering armies and the display of captured booty on the one hand, and contemplative paths and a "grove" with busts of noble poets and philosophers; a war of expansion against Mexico, and a ceremony to unveil a bust of Sir Walter Scott. On that occasion, William Cullen Bryant addressed some remarks to the assembled notables of the city. His words convey a haunting message of what the building of the park ultimately meant: "And now, as the statue of Scott is set up in this beautiful park, which, a few years since, possessed no human associations, historical or poetic, connected with its shades, its lawns, its rocks, and its waters, these grounds became peopled with new memories. Henceforth the silent earth at this spot will be eloquent of old traditions, the airs that stir the branches of the trees will whisper of feats of chivalry to the visitor. All that vast crowd of ideal personages created by the imagination of Scott will enter with his sculptured effigy and remain. . . . They will pass in endless procession around the statue of him in whose prolific brain they had their birth, until the language which we speak shall perish, and the spot on which we stand shall be again a woodland wilderness."[124] Conventional in landscape paintings and park design, the valhallas, temples and groves in so many of the plans also suggest a deeper concern that the past not be obliterated amidst the tumult of marching men and the busy affairs of commerce.

Most of the entries for the design competition conceived of the park from the perspective of carriage passengers.

The way the park was expected to be used, and by whom, was reflected in decisions made about carriageways and paths. The submitted entries conceptually tend to represent the park in terms of how it would be viewed by carriage passengers. The succession of vistas, rocks, groves, lawns and parades was part of an unfolding diorama of pastoral scenery. The procession of scenes was too slow, when viewed on foot; in 1858 the visitor on foot was largely assumed to stroll for a time in just one area of the park. Entry #21 (and others) made no provision for pedestrian paths, assuming that visitors on foot would keep to the lawns. Hepp and Vogel (#11) separated pedestrian traffic from the carriage routes. All of the plans made provision for a wide carriage drive of sixty feet to 120 feet which circled the park. John B. Deutsch (#6) went against the grain as he combined Republican simplicity with sober economy in a proposal to ban riding in the park altogether. "My idea is to bring the public here on a common level; let visitors enjoy themselves on foot. It will also prove less expensive and easier to keep in order."

Fear of the lower classes, and of crime, drunkenness and disorder, repeatedly surfaced in discussions of the park. The *New York Times* editorial warning against allowing the park to slip into the hands of the *"regime* of blackguardism" appeared on 21 April 1857. In June the board of commissioners had stressed their determination that "the most complete guarantee shall be furnished for the preservation of order and propriety."[125] Rumor had it that lager beer sellers and bar-keepers had been secretly buying up valuable corner lots in the vicinity of the park, as they had done around the Crystal Palace in 1853. The *Herald* added its voice to these warnings. In Europe, rank and social distinctions are generally acknowledged, and a simple watchman might suffice to keep the "lower orders" out of an aristocratic park, but in America things were different.

> Here we have no "lower orders"; nobody has any "superiors"; we know no "nobility and gentry": nothing but a public which is all and everything, and in which Sam the five Pointer is as good a man as William B. Astor or Edward Everett. Further, whatever is done by or for Sam, as much as any one else, and he will have his full share in it. Therefore, when we open a public park, Sam will air himself in it. He will take his friends, whether from Church street or elsewhere. He will enjoy himself there, whether by having a muss, or a drink at the corner groggery opposite the great gate. He will run races with his horse in the carriage way. He will knock any better dressed man down who remonstrates with him. He will talk and sing, and fill his share of the bench, and flirt with the nursery girls in his own coarse way. Now, we ask what chance have William B. Astor and Edward Everett against this fellow-citizen of theirs? Can they and he enjoy the same place?[126]

The park was in danger of becoming "a great bear garden," and *Harper's Weekly* urged the "leading capitalists" to prevent the defilement of fifth Avenue by winning the race to purchase the desirable lots near the park.

No mention was made of public safety in the design requirements, but several entries for the Central Park competition reflected contemporary anxieties, and offered a variety of solutions. Gas lighting for the park featured in a number of designs. "D. M." placed a spiked fence around the park which was intended to keep out "improper persons" and trespassers at night (#12). Police stations are included in plan #4. It was self-evident to the designer: "How would it be, when the Central Park should be suddenly opened to its thronging

"Can they and he enjoy the same place?": to friend and foe alike, the park was an overwhelming success. It provided New Yorkers with a new, elegant stage to see and be seen.

masses without the above necessary organization, and with its present system of police? Would it be a safe resort for unprotected ladies; for children and young persons; for the sick and the infirm, and the aged citizen? Could they sit down with their little family groups, beneath the cooling shade without danger of being insulted, run over, knocked down, perhaps robbed, and maybe murdered? I think not." "Arcadia" planned police lodges at major park entrances, with telegraphic communication with the city station houses. He also wanted mounted park police:

> People will be unwilling to trust themselves in any but the most frequented parts, and the beautiful and sequestered walks and nooks will present few temptations to persons of prudence, especially women and children. If, on the contrary, disorderly people find at the outset that the Park is no place for them, that they are marked, followed, and annoyed in every way by the authorities, so long as the disorderly element manifests itself, they will be overawed by the moral influence and example of the well-conducted, and will soon find that the Central Park is a greater boon to them than to their more fortunate fellow-citizens. I can conceive nothing better calculated to humanize the brutal and refine the coarse than the page of the book of nature, which the calm lawns, woods, and lakes of Central Park will present to them . . . (#23).

"Central Park on Music Day": When a gentleman might tip his hat to an atractive lady, as Society looked on.

Only one contributor reiterated the familar belief that "natural beauty" would tame the denizens of the billiard rooms and groggeries (#29). The others were more reliant upon an active police presence. The high-minded arguments that the park would please the cultivated, while it softened and humanized the populace, which had been so often urged by Downing in the previous decade, had not survived the social crisis of 1857.

Olmsted and Vaux's "Description of a Plan for the Improvement of the Central Park"[127] differs at once from the other submissions by beginning with a quote from Emerson. Literary allusions were almost wholly absent in the other practical-minded submissions. And with this quotation, in which Emerson praised the "beautiful gardens" of Italy and Germany in 1844 and the role such gardens might play in encouraging the people's devotion to their land, Olmsted and Vaux were loyal to Downing's belief that American parks should model themselves upon the example of European cities. Viele and others doubted whether Europe afforded an appropriate example, but Olmsted and Vaux boldly asserted their views. Accused of being an "unpractical," literary man, with this quote Olmsted also reminded the board who he was, and whose names had appeared on the letters which secured him the superintendentship. In other words, the quotation from Emerson was not merely a casually decorative text.

Eclectic references to European gardens were common to many of the submissions, but what set "Greensward" apart was a depth of perspective and historical sense. At a time when the land surrounding the park was largely unimproved, Olmsted (for he would actually have written the "Greensward" text) envisaged Central Park surrounded by "... a continuous high wall of brick, stone and marble." He assumed that the shores of the island would soon be completely lined with docks and warehouses, and that the park itself would be surrounded by hotels, theaters, factories and railroad stations. The city had repeatedly been surprised by the pace of urban growth. Every great public building from City Hall, built in 1811, to the Custom House, built in the previous decade, had been outstripped by the growth of the city. What was "out of town" twenty years ago had now been swallowed by the city. With this argument Olmsted tried to suggest that a park should be planned with the future needs of the city in mind. None of the other contributors grasped such a fundamental point. It naturally led to the question of the transverse roads. He suggested a comparison: if one thought about a street running north-south from Chambers Street to Canal Street, at the core of the city's busy commercial center, and with only one street open for crosstown traffic, it was clear that the proposal of Viele, and of so many of the other entries, which assumed that crosstown traffic would move against the planned movement on the circular carriageway, would result in the most monumental chaos. The transverse routes (filled with "... coal carts and butchers' carts, dust carts and dung carts ...."), would soon be clogged with traffic, and thus destroy all pleasure of the refined when encountered eight times during a single circuit of the park. Such roads would also have to be left open to traffic throughout the time when the park was closed at night. It would have to be well lit, and a stout fence erected to keep "... marauders pursued by the police from escaping into the obscurity of the park. ...." The long and narrow shape of the park posed problems like those caused by the wide boulevards of European cities, where transverse streets were carried on high arches. His suggested treatment, sinking the transverse roads below the level of the park, and the decision to carry the paths and carriageways across by ground-level bridges, is the single most widely praised aspect of the design of Central Park. It was an artful solution to the traffic problem in that the disruption of the visual pleasures of the park was kept at a minimum. It also served social ends, by isolating the "coarse" commercial traffic from the carriages carrying those in search of more refined pleasures. The sunken transverse roads preserved the benefits of the park for the carriage-born, while confining pedestrians to the five segments of park created by the transverse roads. Access to adjoining parts of the park would have to be made by the bridges created for the drive, or equestrian ride.

The anticipated extension of housing on all sides of Central Park led to Olmsted's plan to create a tree-lined barrier along the outer wall. This would conceal the city from within the park. This was essentially a question of "effect": the visual impact of the created landscape depended not so much upon the obscuring of the surrounding city, but upon the suggestion that such an outcome was possible. The disguise and concealment of "unsightly" buildings outside the park, and "artificial deformities" within, tasked the talents of Samuel I. Gustin in entry #30. He proposed to ". . . mask them entirely and shut them out of sight, or by breaking up and diversifying their monotony, to modify, if not transform them, for they are not in all cases capable of entire transformation, from deformities into beauties . . ." Olmsted's thinking about the problem of the city was thoroughly within the conventional approach of landscape gardening of his age. The park represented a refreshing break from the harsh gridiron of the city streets, and every effort was made to enhance that sense of difference.

Richard Sennett has argued that the transverse roads and perimeter wall of trees in Central Park represent ". . . the dualities of denial: to build you act as though you live in emptiness; to resist the builder's world you act as though you do not live in a city."[128] What were the alternatives in 1858? Without the sunken transverse roads traffic congestion in the park would have soon destroyed its singular charm; and the option of leaving the existing landscape (polluted, unsightly, overgrown and "unimproved") was effectively no option at all. Both facets of the design of "Greensward" were positive responses to the site, and the city, as it was. Over the next decade the board of commissioners of the park became increasingly involved in planning the environment outside the park, but only one submission, that of Lewis Masquerier (#18), advocated a larger conception of the park and its environment. He suggested the creation of housing in the adjacent streets that would harmonize with the park design. He advocated something akin to the monumental avenues and façades which organized the space of smaller parks in Paris. A fifth Avenue built like the rue de Rivoli, with its elegant terraces of uniform height, lack of ornament and imposing coherence, embodied Masquerier's extension of the park idea. Olmsted and Vaux made no such proposals in "Greensward," contenting themselves with the immediate task of defining the park from within its projected boundaries. In this sense alone they turned away from the city.

Olmsted took his opposition to "artificial structures" much further than the other entries. He objected to cultural clutter, or what he later called "incidents" in the park, and wanted to avoid anything which would obtrude upon the viewer. "The idea of the park itself," he wrote, "should always be uppermost in the mind of the beholder." (In 1866 he proudly noted that "We have headed off, or fought outright and conquered a number of projects for statues and other constructions" in the park, but prophetically feared that "the worst is perhaps before us.")[129] Olmsted's was no less a didactic landscape than that of the other contributors, but made absolute reliance upon landscape in preference to valhallas, shrines, edifying fountains and neo-classical columns to do the work of the park. Vaux's great terrace at the head of the Mall provided a superb vantage point for looking at the lake, but "Greensward" made no provision for viewing terraces for military parades. They planned for two buildings "of moderate dimensions" on the playground (located in the southwest corner of the park) where cricket and other games could be watched. Obliged to leave a site for a music hall, they added a palm-house and conservatory. Places of refreshment were included in designs for the flower garden.

No provision was made for long straight drives, fearing the opportunity such a path would give for trotting matches. Underlying "Greensward" was the belief that design could do much to avert social evils. Olmsted and many of those who most enthusiastically supported the park conceived it as a place for placid, contemplative pleasures acceptable to the city's wealthy. "It will effect a marked change in the habits of our people—bringing out every pleasant day hundreds and thousands of carriages and creating a kind of delightful recreation which thus far has no existence in this City."[130] Olmsted's Central Park has invited an analysis emphasizing its class content. But the boisterous pleasures he wished to avoid were as attractive to the city's wealthy gamblers, devotees of horse racing, frequenters of assignation houses, Saratoga spas, gambling clubs and lavish saloons as to its lower classes with their preference for lager beer, dog fights and dance halls. He clearly wished to exclude the wealthy rake as well as "Sam the five Pointer" from the vision of community defined by Central Park. The distinction between respectable "sunshine" and "gaslight" defines the social barriers he sought to erect. "The popular idea of the park is a beautiful open green space, in which quiet drives, rides, and strolls may be had. This cannot be preserved if a race-course, or a road that can be used as a race-course, is made one of its leading attractions."

Vaux's great terrace provided a place for contemplative and refined pleasure at the heart of the park.

The failure to provide for ". . . the pleasure and benefit of manly and invigorating horsemanship" was one of the grounds upon which two members of the board of commissioners, Robert J. Dillon and August Belmont, attacked Olmsted's design in May and June 1858.[131] The case made by these prominent Democrats, in a series of amendments proposed to the winning "Greensward" design, was in part a reponse to the supercession of the Democrat Viele by Olmsted, and to the position Green had achieved on the board, decisively defeating Dillon for the presidency. Dillon and Belmont wanted a simpler design for the park, in which utility would not be sacrificed for beauty. They also ridiculed any provision of transverse roads, confidently asserting that there would never be enough traffic in the city to warrant four such roads. Modest entrances, and a long, straight carriage route around the perimeter, were what Viele had provided, and which was now overthrown by "Greensward." A comparison between Viele's plan and "Greensward" helps sharpen the issues involved. Where Viele envisaged a wide carriageway which would follow the line of the wall along fifth Avenue, Olmsted wove a sinuous route which gained several attractive vantage points while subtly discouraging carriage races. Where Viele was content to plan for ponds, Olmsted planned bold and extravagant lakes. Viele proposed to line the carriageway with trees; Olmsted envisaged the north of the park as a more heavily planted area, and for the terraced "berceau walks" south of the Croton reservoir (The Ramble) to be yet more richly planted. The effect aimed at was "... of a drive through a thick forest, crammed with tall spindling trees, as though a richly wooded country ..." Where Olmsted planned for a complex linking of Vista Rock to the Mall, terrace and lake, Viele crossed a stream with the Glen Road. Olmsted was fecund with ideas, and Vaux, who designed the structures, roads, bridges and drives imposed upon the whole a harmonious style of ornate, decorative profusion.

When Olmsted won the design competition and was appointed architect-in-chief in 1858, his triumph seemed complete. But the attacks on the park, upon the board of commissioners, and upon his own role did not let up, and he also faced another struggle, against Andrew H. Green, comptroller of the park, for the freedom to implement the plan without oppressive interference. The two struggles were interlinked: to keep the park free from the city's notoriously corrupt politicians, Green exercised petty and draconian control of expenditure. He was an autocrat by temperament and brooked not the least hint of impropriety. This tight rein reduced Olmsted to exasperation and repeated threats to resign. There was little time to create his masterwork calmly. But this is part of another tangled story, of Olmsted's management of the park and its politics. I have tried to suggest how the park was created. It was a glorious victory for the city, as comments during the period of major construction make clear. Olmsted's administration brought discipline to the workforce. As he told his father, it was being run like a machine. Bryant, who had long hoped for a park in the city, intensely admired Olmsted's achievement: he was one who "... selects all his subordinates and agents with an instinctive wisdom, and who does not allow a dollar of the public money to be paid out except for value received, [who] would be an infinitely better President than we have had since Van Buren..."[132] Olmsted's work seemed conclusive proof that "... a really great public work *can* be undertaken and carried out with spirit, economy and success, even in New-York, when the control of it is committed to energetic men, utterly free from party views and political objects."[133] On a visit to the park in September 1859, George Templeton Strong praised the "... system and order and energy ..." of the organization. "Some three thousand men are employed, and there are no idlers. Everybody is earning his pay. Number of visitors quite large. Several bridges are completed and look well."[134] As an antidote to the widespread feeling that the city

upporters of the park were impressed by the design and by the efficiency of Olmsted's manage-
ent of the project. A new park, however, inevitably looked raw, and local wits were not slow
o mock the celebrated "improvements."

was an ungovernable shambles, Olmsted brought administrative
integrity and dynamism which gave new heart to reformers: ". . . the
skill, tact, honesty and energy with which the work is prosecuted
offer us the most comfortable assurance we can anywhere find that
the capacity of carrying on a public improvement efficiently has not
utterly died out among us."[135] In 1859, as the work on the park
progressed, Olmsted, the "unpractical" man, came to stand for a
new kind of figure in public life: a man of absolute integrity and
commitment to the betterment of society who approached the
management of public affairs with "inflexible executive energy":

> In truth, the Park itself is not so much a miracle as that a work of such
> colossal honesty should be achieved amidst the civic corruption in which
> our municipal affairs are lost. And this is owing mainly to the peculiar
> fitness of the chief of the Park, Mr Olmsted, who is a man of the most
> absolute honesty—who will probably come out of the work quite
> as poor as he went in—who is singularly fitted by natural gifts and
> cultivation for the designing so vast an enterprise—and who has that
> inflexible executive energy which gives great successes to military heroes,
> and which in so noble a triumph as this shows that peace hath her

The park was designed as a rustic venue for a gentleman's leisure.

victories no less renowned than war. . . . Who is not proud that, in a day of swindling in politics, and of cast-iron in building, such grand works can be achieved in rugged honesty and solid stone? It silences forever the clatter of skeptics of the democratic principle as inimical to vast public works.[136]

The order which prevailed in the park represented the victory of its fundamental premise: that the disorder, rudeness and criminality which prevailed elsewhere in the city were not necessary aspects of city life. The park seemed to afford

. . . a moral lesson and encouragement, which in the midst of the official corruption and general municipal disarray of the times, is a rich return for all that we have spent and mean to spend in making the Park. It proves how easily all the scandals which now alarm our own thinkers and disgust the rest of mankind, might be made to disappear from American society. Give us at Albany, at the City Hall, at the Federal Capital, the same honest energy and upright discipline which have ruled in the affairs of the Park, and it would soon be found that Americans are no more insensible than other people to the charms of decency and the advantages of order. No monarchy can make so creditable a show of its subjects as this worst-governed of Republican cities makes of its free citizens in the Central Park. The signs which we recognize all over the place, of responsible and respectable authority, attending to the business of the people with scrupulous fidelity, impress themselves at once on the popular mind, and command its respect.[137]

The struggles against abortion, political corruption and against the misery of the city's "lower depths" yielded no such startling victories. It was the park alone which truly represented the achievement of New York in this period, because it most comprehensively embodied the city's contradictions. With its attempt to reconcile class fears and material interests, with the desire to provide "a majestic breathing space for the life of a great city"[138] and recognition of the need for zealous enforcement of its regulations by keepers trained to respond to commands from their superiors with a smart military salute, the park represents the hopes as well as the fears of New York.

The Committee of Seventy[1]

Executive Committee selected at the 4 September 1871 meeting at Cooper Union

Henry G. Stebbins, chairman; William F. Havemeyer, vice-chairman; Emil Sauer, treasurer; Roswell D. Hatch, secretary; Barclay Gallagher, assistant secretary

Committee of Seventy (in alphabetical order, with reported income, 1865)[2]

Samuel D. Babcock
banker, 37 William Street; h. Riverdale[3]

1. *Appeal to the People of the State of New York Adopted by the Executive Committee of Citizens and Taxpayers for the Financial Reform of the City and County of New York* (New York: The "Free Press" Association, 1871).
2. *The Income Record: A List Giving the Taxable Income of Every Resident of New York* (New York: American News Company, 1865). Despite the title, this work is incomplete but suggests at least the beginnings of a financial place for the members of the committee. Other sources give much larger estimates of total wealth.
3. Occupations and addresses: *Trow's New York City Directory*, compiled by H. Wilson, vol. LXXXIII, for the Year Ending May 1, *1870* (New York: N. F. Trow, [1869]). When no address is recorded, there is either no entry, or else there is more than one person listed with the same name.

Henry Clews WD 68[8], $62,748
(1834–1923) banker, 32 Wall St.; h. Union League Club

Edward Cooper AICP 71
(1824–1905) Democrat; manufacturer, 162 South St.; h. 8
Lexington Ave.; mayor 1879

Charles Crary
lawyer, 1476 Third Ave.; h. 109 E. 82nd St.

T. C. Cunningham
unidentified

Christian E. Detmold UL 63
(1810–87) German-American civil engineer; builder of the Crystal
Palace in New York

John Adams Dix UL 63, $4,250
(1798–1879) lawyer; U.S. senator; soldier, politician (Barnburner);
h. 3 W. 21st St.; governor 1872–4

Nathaniel Gano Dunn
lawyer, 76 Nassau St.; h. 111 E. 84th St.

James Emott
(1823–84) lawyer, judge, N.Y. Supreme Court, 20 Nassau St.,
1856–64; h. Poughkeepsie

Wm. M. Evarts UL 63, AICP 71, $22,500
(1818–1901) lawyer, 52 Wall St.; h. 231 Second Ave.; US senator
1884

John Ewen $28,021
merchant, 111 Broadway; h. Spuyten Duyvil

Wm. M. Fleiss
unidentified

John Foley
gold pen manufacturer, 262 Broadway; h. 16 E. 73rd St.

Barclay Gallagher
editor, 154 Nassau St.; h. 62 Sands St., Brooklyn

John Cleve Green UL 63, AICP 71
banker; philanthropist

---

8. Endorsed Grant at mass meeting of War Democrats at Cooper Union, *New
York Times*, 22 October 1868.

Isaac Bailey   UL 63[4],   CH 65[5],   CMR 67[6]
leather trade, 83 Gold Street; h. 23 Gramercy Place

Lewis Ballard
unidentified

Eugene Ballin   AICP 71[7]
banker, 24 Exchange Place; h. 16 W. 45th St.

Francis B. Barlow   AICP 71
lawyer, 5 Beekman Place; h. 118 E. 30th St.

G. C. Barrett   AICP 71
Democrat; lawyer, 20 Nassau St.; judge, Supreme Court; h. 24
W. 38th St.

W. C. Barrett
Apollo Hall then Tammany Democrat; lawyer, 20 Nassau St.;
h. 112 E. 39th St.

H. N. Beers
unidentified

Jos. Blumenthal
importer, 120 Liberty St.; h. 211 W. 34th St.

James M. Brown   AICP 71
(1791–1877) banker, 59 Wall Street; h. 31 E. 36th St.

James M. Bundy
(1835–91) editor, 11 Frankfort St.; h. 26 E. 22nd St.,

Joseph H. Choate
(1832–1917) lawyer, 52 Wall St.; h. 137 W. 21st St.

Samuel Christie
police; h. 16 Gay St.

4. Member of Union League, 1863. Union League Club, *Articles of Association, By-Laws, Officers and Members of the Union League Club*, 1863 (New York, 1863), cited in Iver Bernstein, *The New York City Draft Riots* . . . (New York and Oxford: Oxford University Press, 1990), 272–6.
5. Member, Committee on Health, *Address of the Committee to Promote the Passage of a Metropolitan Health Bill. New-York, December 1865* (New York: John W. Amerman, Printer, for the Committee on Legislation, 1865).
6. Member, Committee on Municipal Reform, Union League, 1867.
7. *The Twenty-Eighth Annual Report of the New York Association for Improving the Condition of the Poor for the Year 1871 . . . With the Constitution and List of Members* (New York: Office of the Association, 1871), 95–102. Business or corporate memberships are included only when identification is sure.

James M. Halsted $6,687
merchant, 48 Wall St.; h. 18 W. 17th St.

Roswell D. Hatch
lawyer, 156 Broadway; h. W. 84th St. near Ninth Ave.

William Frederick Havemeyer WD68, AICP 71, $40,102
(1804–74) sugar merchant; h. 335 W. 14th St.; mayor, 1845,
1858, 1872

James B. Hodgskin
banker, 14 Broad St.; h. 168 Gates Ave., Brooklyn

Robert Hoe $50,486
(1839–1909) printing press manufacturer, 31 Gold St. and 11
Sherriff St.; h. 111 E. 16th St.

Reuben W. Howes
banker, 30 Wall St.; merchant, 342 Broadway; h. Yonkers

Adrien Iselin AICP 71, $88,394
banker, 56 Wall St.; h. 23 E. 26th St.

Daniel Willis James
metals, 13 Cliff St.; h. 38 E. 31st St.

Albert Klamroth
unidentified

Ernest Krackovitzer, MD WD 68
physician; attending surgeon, Mt. Sinai Hospital;
h. 16 W. 12th St.

George W. Lane AICP 71
becomes City Chamberlain; tea merchant, 93 Front St.; h. 8 W.
29th St.

Thos. A. Ledwith
Mozart Hall Democrat; judge, Jefferson Market Court; 111
Nassau St.; h. 219 W. 33rd St.

Thos. McLelland
h. E. 78th near Madison Ave.

William C. Molloy
unidentified

Severn D. Moulton
coal, 802 Third Ave.; h. 153 E. 49th St.

William H. Neilson
broker, 58 Wall St., H. 213 E. 15th St.

Henry Nicoll
lawyer, 30 Pine St.; h. 8 W. 10th St.

Robert B. Nooney
butcher, 361 Fourth Ave.; h. 112 E. 26th St.

Joseph J. O'Donohue
tea merchant, 88 Front St.; h. 125 E. 46th St.

Edwards Pierrepont WD 68
(1817–92) lawyer, 16 Wall St.; U.S. District Attorney, 41
Chambers St.; U.S. Attorney General, 1875–6; h. 103 Fifth Ave.

Thomas W. Piersall
unidentified

William Raddle
unidentified

Edmund Randolph Robinson
lawyer, 69 Wall St.; h. 25 Irving Place

Robert Barnwell Roosevelt UL 63
(1829–1906) editor, congressman, 32 Beekman Place; h. 26
E. 20th St.

Samuel B. Ruggles
(1800–1881), lawyer, 6 Wall St.; h. 24 Union Place

Edward Salomon
unidentified

Emil Sauer
banker, 45 Exchange Place; h. Staten Island

Frederick Schack
drygoods merchant, 54 White St.; h. 42 W. 32nd St.

Jackson S. Schultz UL 63, CH 65, CMR 67
president, Union League Club, 1870; leather merchant, 343 Pearl
St.; h. 231 E. 12th St.

J. Seligman WD 68, $11,674
banker, 59 Exchange Place

Benjamin B. Sherman AICP 71
banker, 96 Wall St., h. 16 W. 20th St.

H. S. Spaulding
unidentified

Henry G. Stebbins WD 68
banker, 44 Broadway; h. 2 W. 16th St.

Theodore Steinway
piano manufacturer, 109 E. 14th St.; h. 123 E. 52nd St.

Simon Sterne
lawyer, 200 Broadway; h. 6 E. 73rd St.

John A. Stewart
banker, 49 Wall St.; h. 59 W. 34th St.

John Stratton
manufacturer of musical instruments and merchant, 63 Maiden
Lane; h. 227 E. 48th St.

Jonathan Sturges   UL 63,   AICP 71, $30,000
(1802–74) merchant, 125 Front St.; h. 5 E. 14th St.

Julius W. Tiemann
paint manufacturer, 240 Pearl St.; h. 125 W. 43rd St.

Edward Townsend   AICP 71
merchant, 9 Franklin St.; h. 71 W. 19th St.

Geo. Van Slyck
unidentified

Geo. W. Varian
h. 30 W. 29th St.

Joseph B. Varnum   UL 63,   CMR 67,   AICP 71
lawyer, 110 Broadway; h. 14 Gramercy Place

Washington R. Vermilye   UL 63,   CH 65, AICP 71, $78,178
banker, 16 & 18 Nassau St.; h. New Jersey

Charles Watrous
lumber merchant, First Ave.; councilman, 45th dist., 1856; h. 113
E. 46th St.

John Wheeler   AICP 71
h. 54 W. 47th St.

William. H. Wickham
diamond merchant, Maiden Lane; Apollo Hall then Tammany
Democrat; h. 338 Lexington Ave.; mayor 1875

Notes

Notes for Introduction

1. See Thomas Bender's magisterial *Community and Social Change in America* (New Brunswick: Rutgers University Press, 1978; reissued Baltimore and London: The Johns Hopkins University Press, 1982). Bender's earlier treatment of this issue, "The Idea of Community & the Problem of Organization in Urban Reform," *Towards an Urban Vision: Ideas and Institutions in Nineteenth Century America* (Lexington: University Press of Kentucky, 1975; reissued Baltimore and London: The Johns Hopkins University Press, 1982), 129–57, concentrates upon Charles Loring Brace and the philanthropic reformers of the 1850s.

2. Matthew Hale Smith, *Sunshine and Shadow in New York* (Hartford: J. B. Burr and Co., 1868), 366.

3. *The Brooklyn Eagle*, 13 September 1871, quoted in Samuel J. Tilden, *The New York City "Ring": Its Origin, Maturity and Fall* (1873; reprinted College Park, MD: McGrath Publishing Co., 1969), appendix, 9.

4. *The Sun*, 2 April 1878, 1.

5. *The Lower Depths of the Great American Metropolis: A Discourse by Rev. Peter Stryker delivered in the Thirty-Fourth Street Reformed Dutch Church, New York City . . . April 29, 1866*, 4.

6. Samuel B. Halliday, *The Lost and Found; or Life Among the Poor* (New York: Blakeman and Mason, 1859).

7. *The Centenary Edition of the Works of Nathaniel Hawthorne*, Vol. 5, *Our Old Home: A Series of English Sketches*, ed. William Charvat *et al.* ([Columbus]: Ohio State University Press, 1970), 283.

8. *Wrecks and Rescues* by an Early Member of the Board of Managers of the A. F. G. S., revised by the Publishing Committee, second ed. (New York: American Female Guardian Society, 1859), 85–106; quotations from 92.

9. See Clifford S. Griffin, "Religious Benevolence as Social Control, 1815–1860," *Mississippi Valley Historical Review*, 44 (1957), 423–44; Clifford S. Griffin, *Their Brothers' Keepers: Moral Stewardship in the United States,*

1800–1865 (New Brunswick, NJ: Rutgers University Press, 1960); Ralph E. Luker, "Religion and Social Control in the Nineteenth-Century American City," *Journal of Urban History*, 2 (May 1976), 363–8; Paul Boyer, *Urban Masses and Moral Order in America, 1820–1920* (Cambridge, MA, and London: Harvard University Press, 1978); Stuart M. Blumin, *The Emergence of the Middle Class: Social Experience in the American City, 1760–1900* (Cambridge: Cambridge University Press, 1989), 192–206.

10. Theodore Roosevelt, *New York* (London and New York: Longmans, Green & Co., 1891), 200.

11. Vice-President Dan Quayle speaking before the Commonwealth Club of California in the aftermath of the riots in Los Angeles, *New York Times*, 20 May 1992, A20.

12. "The Lounger," "The Central Park," *Harper's Weekly*, 3 (1 October 1859), 626.

13. My reading of Olmsted in chapter four differs significantly from Roy Rosenzweig and Elizabeth Blackmar, *The Park and the People* (Ithaca: Cornell University Press, 1992).

Chapter One

1. Lawrance Thompson, *Young Longfellow (1807–1843)* (New York: Macmillan Co., 1938), 312, 263–4; *Life of Henry Wadsworth Longfellow with Extracts from his Journals and Correspondence*, ed. Samuel Longfellow, 2 vols. (London: Kegan Paul, Trench & Co., 1886), 1, 345.

2. Angelina La Piana, *Dante's American Pilgrimage: a Historical Survey of Dante Studies in the United States, 1800–1944* (New Haven: Yale University Press, 1948), 49.

3. Barrett Wendell, *Stelligeri and Other Essays Concerning America* (New York: Charles Scribner's Sons, 1893), 206–7.

4. In "The Prophet Dante," *New York Times*, 21 August 1871, 4, an ingenious attempt was made to apply the *Inferno* to the political scandals of 1871.

5. Dante, *Inferno*, III, 25–30, translation by Longfellow (1867).

6. Virgil, *Aeneid*, translation by Robert Fitzgerald, 2nd ed. (New York: Vintage Books, 1985), VI, 414–34. See on this theme Pierre Brunel, *L'Evocation des morts et la descent aux enfers: Homère-Virgil-Dante-Claudel* (Paris: Société d'édition d'enseignement supérieur, 1974).

7. Junius Henri Browne, *The Great Metropolis; A Mirror of New York* (Hartford: American Publishing Co., 1869), 458–9.

8. Charles Loring Brace to his sister Emma, October 1849, *The Life of Charles Loring Brace, chiefly told in his own letters*, ed. by his daughter (New York: Scribner's Sons, 1894), 82–3.

9. James D. McCabe, Jr., *New York by Sunlight and Gaslight* (Philadelphia: Hubbard Brothers, 1882; reprinted as *New York by Gaslight*, with a new Foreword by Gerard R. Wolfe, [New York: Greenwich House, 1984]), 581. "Martin" was a pseudonym of Edward Winslow Mc Cabe, a native of Richmond who lived in Brooklyn after 1865.

10. Rev. E[dwin]. H[ubbell]. Chapin, D. D., *A Discourse on Shameful Life* (New York: Thatcher & Hutchinson, 1859), 23–4. There is an engraving and a brief biographical sketch of Chapin in the *New York Journal*, n.s. 5

302 Notes to pp. 13-21

(June 1857), 337, and an account of his career in Matthew Hale Smith, *Sunshine and Shadow in New York* (Hartford: J. B. Burr and Co., 1868), 332-5.

11. Smith, *Sunshine and Shadow*, 709. H. F. Cary translated this line—"Lasciate ogni speranzà voi ch'entrate" (*Inf.*, III, 9)—as "All hope abandon, ye who enter here" (1805-7); Longfellow's version: "All hope abandon, ye who enter in!"

12. T. De Witt Talmage, *The Masque Torn Off* (Chicago: J. Fairbanks, 1879), 32.

13. Howe and Hummel, *In Danger; or Life in New York: A True History of a Great City's Wiles and Temptations* (New York: J. S. Ogilvie & Co., 1888), 128.

14. George G. Foster, *New York by Gas-Light and Other Urban Sketches*, ed. and with an Introduction by Stuart M. Blumin (Berkeley: University of California Press, [1990]), 131.

15. "The New York Tombs," *New York Herald*, 30 July 1851, 7; "Torture and Homicide in an American State Prison," *Harper's Weekly*, 2 (18 December 1858), 808-9; F. B. Sanborn, "American Prisons," *North American Review*, 103 (1866), 383-412, and "The Reformation of Prison Discipline," *North American Review*, 105 (1867), 555-91; James D. McCabe, Jr., *Lights and Shadows of New York Life . . .* (Philadelphia: National Publishing Co., [1872]), ch. 13 [see above note 9]; Charles Sutton, *The New York Tombs; its Secrets and its Mysteries. History of Noted Criminals, with Narratives of their Crimes*, ed. James B. Mix and Samuel A. Mackeever (San Francisco: A. Roman & Co., 1874); see also "The Benevolent Institutions of New-York," *Putnam's Monthly Magazine*, 1 (June 1853), 673-86.

16. Herman Melville, *Pierre or The Ambiguities*, ed. Harrison Hayford, Hershel Parker and G. Thomas Tanselle (Evanston and Chicago: Northwestern University Press and the Newberry Library, 1971), 240.

17. Dewey to Bellows, 28 December 1852, *Autobiography and Letters of Orville Dewey, D.D.*, ed. by his daughter, Mary E. Dewey (Boston: Roberts Brothers, 1883), 230-1.

18. Charles Loring Brace to Theodore Parker, 26 July 1853, *Life of Charles Loring Brace*, 181. Among many similar comments, see Rev. Orville Dewey, *A Sermon Preached in the Second Unitarian Church in Mercer-Street, on the Moral Importance of Cities and the Moral Means for their Reformation, particularly on a Ministry for the Poor in Cities* (New York: David Felt & Co., 1836), 16.

19. Quoted in *Ibid.*, 204. Cf. Lydia Maria Child to Sarah Shaw, 31 July 1877, *Lydia Maria Child Selected Letters, 1817-1880*, eds. Milton Meltzer and Patricia G. Holland (Amherst: University of Massachusetts Press, 1982), 543.

20. Sedgwick, *The Poor Rich Man and the Rich Poor Man* (New York: Harper & Brothers, 1837), 39, 154, 60.

21. Quoted in the *Twentieth Annual Report of the American Female Guardian Society and Home for the Friendless, for the Year Ending May, 1854* (New York: American Female Guardian Society, 1854), 9.

22. Rev. E. H. Chapin, *Moral Aspects of City Life: A Series of Lectures* (New York: Henry Lyon, 1853), 145.

23. "The Metropolitan Health Bill. Letter from Dr. Griscom to Hon. D. S. Coddington," *New York Times* (21 April 1865), 5.

24. Homer's contributions to *Harper's Weekly* began in 1858, when he was twenty-two and still living in Boston. He settled in New York in December 1859 and took a studio in Nassau Street, but declined *Harper's* offer to work exclusively for their magazine. *Harper's Weekly* published a number of his New York scenes, with Central Park a popular subject. After war broke out in April, he got an appointment as artist-correspondent for *Harper's*. See William Howe Downes, *The Life and Works of Winslow Homer* (Boston: Houghton, Mifflin, 1911; reprinted New York: Dover, 1989), 29–39. Downes' summary of "The Two Great Classes" is on 38.

25. See Hon. Joel Tyler Headley, *The Great Riots of New York, 1712 to 1873* (New York: E. B. Treat, 1873); Robert Moody, *The Astor Place Riot* (Bloomington: University of Indiana Press, 1958).

26. George G. Foster, "The Needlewomen," *New York in Slices* (1848), reprinted in *New York by Gas-Light and Other Urban Sketches*, 228–34.

27. Talmage, *The Masque Torn Off*, facing pages 89 and 97.

28. Mary E. Dewey, ed., *The Life and Letters of Catherine M. Sedgwick* (New York: Harper & Brothers, 1871), 322.

29. *The Lower Depths of the Great American Metropolis: A Discourse delivered by Rev. Peter Stryker in the Thirty-Fourth Street Reformed Dutch Church, New York City . . . April 29, 1866*, 7–8.

30. John M. Mason, D. D., "Sermon I," *The National Preacher*, 1 (June 1826), 14. Among his parishioners in the 1830s was Andrew Haswell Green.

31. Chapin, *Moral Aspects of City Life*, 146–7.

32. Dewey, *A Sermon . . . on the Moral Importance of Cities*, 11–13. Emphasis added. Dewey had tried to encourage his parishioners personally to work among the poor, but they complained that they did not know what to do and the effort ceased. His sermon, delivered 5 June 1836, was designed to persuade the congregation to support an independent minister to cross the social divide which separated his parish from the city slums. Nearly $3,000 was raised towards this aim. For Dewey's attitude towards the poor, see *Autobiography and Letters*, 91.

33. Stryker, *The Lower Depths*, 10. Emphasis added.

34. C. L. B[race]., "Winter Among the Poor," *New York Times*, 12 February 1855, 2.

35. *Ibid.*, 165–6, 194.

36. "With all this, let imagination paint the surrounding scenery— the filth, the damp, the rottenness, the noisomeness, the stifling air, the moral debasement . . . it will help us think how wide a circle of men and women around us try to live . . ." Chapin, *Moral Aspects of City Life*, 150; see also Chapin, *Humanity in the City* (New York: De Witt & Davenport, [1854]), 127.

37. See Anne Humpherys, *Travels into the Poor Man's Country: The Work of Henry Mayhew* (Athens, GA: The University of Georgia Press, [1977]), 70; Maren Stange, *Symbols of Ideal Life: Social Documentary Photography in America 1890–1950* (New York and Cambridge: Cambridge University Press, [1989]).

38. Michael Denning, *Mechanic Accents: Dime Novels and Working-Class Culture in America* (London and New York: Verso, [1987]) suggests that such works were read in ways which makes

problematic a straightforward reference to the author's intention.

39. Jacob Riis, *How the Other Half Lives: Studies in the Tenements of New York* (New York: Charles Scribner's Sons, 1890), 33.

40. See, for example, Charles Edwards' comic retracing of Dante's journey in the *Inferno* in *The New York Hooroarer or A Visit to the Infernal Regions and Return*, second ed. (New York: Humboldt Publishing Co., [1893]).

41. See *Memoir of John Griscom, LL.D., Compiled from an Autobiography... by John H. Griscom, M. D.* (New York: Robert Carter & Brothers, 1859), 159–61. During the draft riots in 1863, the asylum run by the Magdalen Society on Fifth Avenue and 88th Street was attacked and it was only due to the intervention of inmates, former prostitutes, that it escaped torching. See Adrian Cook, *The Armies of the Streets: The New York City Draft Riots of 1863* ([Lexington:] The University Press of Kentucky, [1974]), 92–3.

42. *Memoir and Select Remains of the late Rev. John R. M'Dowall, The Martyr of the Seventh Commandment in the Nineteenth Century* (New York: Leavitt, Lord & Co., 1838), 239. See also Flora L. Northrup, *The Record of a Century 1834–1934* (New York: American Female Guardian Society and Home for the Homeless, 1934).

43. Chapin, *Humanity in the City*, 23.

44. Charles Dickens, *American Notes for General Circulation* (1842; London: Chapman and Hall, 1913), 75–6. The coachman, Tim, who accompanied John D. Vose on his tour of Five Points in 1852, claimed to have escorted Dickens and Lord Ashburton on their visits a decade earlier. The underground saloon visited by Dickens was renamed the "Dickens's Place" or the "Dickens Hole." See *Life in New York*, by the author of "The Old White Meeting-House," 2nd ed. (New York: Robert Carter, 1847), 172–3; the account written in 1850 by George G. Foster, *New York by Gas-Light and Other Urban Sketches*, 140–46; and John D. Vose, *Seven Nights in Gotham* (New York: Bunnel & Price, 1852), 19. Indeed, the prospect of following in Dickens' footsteps mightily quickened the interest of fashionable New York in the Five Points. Places that Dickens had not visited, such as the Bowery, were identified as such. "What a pity Dickens had not been for a few weeks a Tompkins Market butcher...," etc.: "Bowery, Saturday Night," *Harper's New Monthly Magazine*, 42 (April 1871), 676. When Fredrika Bremer visited the Five Points in 1851, she was accompanied only by a Quaker woman, Mrs. Gibbons, who belonged to the first generation of genteel volunteer social visitors. "We considered it better and safer to go about here alone," Bremer wrote, "than in the company with a gentleman. Neither did we meet any instance of rudeness or even incivility." *America of the Fifties: Letters of Fredrika Bremer*, selected and ed. by Adolph B. Benson (New York: The American-Scandinavian Foundation, 1924), 326. Rev. Talmage of the Brooklyn Tabernacle visited the Five Points in the company of three police officers and two elders of his church. He referred to their party as "Christian explorers" in *The Masque Torn Off*, 74.

45. David Ward, *Poverty, Ethnicity, and the American City, 1840–1925: Changing Conceptions of the Slum and the Ghetto* (Cambridge: Cambridge University Press, 1989), 21.

46. *A Picture of New York in 1846, with a Short Account of Places in its Vicinity, Designed as a Guide to Citizens and Strangers* (New York: C. S. Francis, 1846), 172–3; Joel H. Ross, M.D., *What I Saw in New-York; or A Bird's Eye View of City Life* (Auburn, NY: Derby & Miller, 1851), 88; *Glimpses of New York City by a South Carolinian* (Charleston, SC: J. J. McCarter, 1852), 96. By 1871 visitors to the Five Points were advised to "secure the services of a policeman for the night" and to be sure to bring smelling salts with them. *Redfield's Traveler's Guide to the City of New York* (New York: J. S. Redfield, Publisher, 1871), 75. Pease's impact upon the Five Points led to jocular complaints that "The Five Points is not what it used to be, with its vice its romance has vanished. It has become Peasey and prosaic, and the old leaven of iniquity has nearly died out." See "Vice Underground," *Harper's Weekly*, 1 (24 January 1857), 52. From the extensive contemporary discussions of Pease, see "The Industrial Schools of New-York, and Charities Connected Therewith," *New-York Quarterly*, 3 (January 1855), 559–75; "Our City Charities. III. The Five Points House of Industry," *New York Times*, 22 February 1860, 1–2. On the Protestant missionary work in the slums, see *The Old Brewery and the New Mission House at the Five Points. By the Ladies of the Mission* (New York: Stringer & Townsend, 1854); Carroll S. Rosenberg, "Protestants and Five Pointers: The Five Points House of Industry, 1850–1870," *New York Historical Society Quarterly*, 48 (October 1964), 327–47; Timothy L. Smith, *Revivalism and Social Reform: American Protestantism on the Eve of the Civil War* (New York: Harper Torchbooks, 1965), ch. 11; Keith Melder, "Ladies Bountiful: Organized Women's Benevolence in Early Nineteenth-Century America," *New York History*, 48 (July 1967), 231–54.

47. B[ayard]. T[aylor]., "A Descent into the Depths: Sixth Ward," *The Nation*, 2 (8 March 1866), 302–4. Chapin's *Moral Aspects of City Life* (1853) contains a lecture titled "The Lower Depths."

48. *The Lower Depths of the Great American Metropolis: A Discourse by Rev. Peter Stryker*, 3.

49. Matthew Hale Smith, *Sunshine and Shadow in New York*, 366. Halliday's *The Lost and Found; or Life Among the Poor* (New York: Blakeman & Mason, 1859; reissued 1861 and 1875 as *The Little Street Sweeper; or, Life Among the Poor*) is among the most unwittingly revealing accounts of the sometimes bitter conflicts between the poor and the missionaries over control of children in the slums. Halliday seems to have been the first in New York to use photography to document the condition of children who came to his attention, and the first to have used photographs in court actions against parents for control of the children. Halliday is also a good source for something akin to a trade in orphans by missionary and relief agencies, and for the astoundingly casual procedures by which slum orphans were given to rural families.

50. "The Benevolent Institutions of

New York," *Putnam's Monthly Magazine*, 1 (June 1853), 673–86; logic of starvation: Chapin, *Humanity in the City*, 202–3; John D. Vose, *Seven Nights in Gotham*, 36; Roy Lubove, "The New York Association for Improving the Condition of the Poor: The Formative Years," *New-York Historical Society Quarterly*, 43 (1959), 307–27; and Lubove's *The Progressives and The Slums: Tenement House Reform in New York City 1890–1917* (Pittsburgh: University of Pittsburgh Press, 1962), 7; Carroll Smith Rosenberg, *Religion and the Rise of the American City: The New York City Mission Movement, 1812–1870* (Ithaca and London: Cornell University Press, [1971]), ch. 6; M. J. Heale, "Harbingers of Progressivism: Responses to the Urban Crisis in New York, c. 1845–1860," *Journal of American Studies*, 10 (1976), 17–36.

51. James Fenimore Cooper, *Notions of the Americans Picked Up by a Travelling Bachelor*, with an Introduction by Robert E. Spiller, 2 vols. (New York: Frederick Ungar, [1963]), 1, 142–3; Sedgwick, *The Poor Rich Man and the Rich Poor Man*, 22; M. A. DeWolfe Howe, *Barrett Wendell and His Letters* (Boston: The Atlantic Monthly Press, 1924), 260; "Poor-Laws and the Sources of Poverty Among Us," *New York Quarterly*, 2 (January 1854), 581–605; quotation from 597–8. It would be interesting to know the name of the author of this article, combining as it does so well the diverse elements of misogyny, nativism and complacent moral callousness. In addition to all the other offenses caused by such women, the author notes that they "bear hardly any vestige of woman-

hood in their countenances" and "have lost nearly all resemblance to womankind." And they are thus as guilty of gender-crime as the notorious abortionist Madame Restell.

52. Carroll Smith-Rosenberg, *Religion and the Rise of the American City*, 173.

53. Charles E. Rosenberg and Carroll Smith-Rosenberg, "Pietism and the Origins of the American Public Health Movement: A Note on John H. Griscom and Robert M. Hartley," *Journal of the History of Medicine and Allied Sciences*, 23 (1968), 16–35.

54. Quoted in Lubove, *The Progressives and the Slums*, 10.

55. Robert H. Bremner, *From the Depths: The Discovery of Poverty in the United States* (New York: New York University Press, 1956), 35–8.

56. *Twenty-Ninth Annual Report of the Managers of the Society for the Reformation of Juvenile Delinquents* (New York: James Egbert, Printer, 1854), 25; *Thirty Fifth Annual Report . . .* (New York: Wynkoop, Hallenbeck & Thomas, Printers, 1860), 40.

57. Henry J. Browne, "Archbishop Hughes and Western Colonization," *Catholic Historical Review*, 36 (October 1950), 269–73; the text of Hughes' attack on the Buffalo convention is reprinted in John Tracy Ellis, ed., *Documents of American Catholic History* (Milwaukee: The Bruce Publishing Co., [1956]), 325–9.

58. On the Children's Aid Society see Donald Dale Jackson, "It took trains to put street kids on the right track out of the slums," *Smithsonian*, 17 (August 1986), 94–103; for Cooper's and Greeley's activities see Laura Wood Roper, *FLO: A Biography of Frederick Law Olmsted*

(Baltimore: The Johns Hopkins University Press, 1973), 100–101; trade in paupers: Robert H. Bremner, *The Public Good: Philanthropy and Welfare in the Civil War Era* (New York: Alfred A. Knopf, 1980), 25–6.

59. Attempts to relocate the almshouse are described in Spann, *The New Metropolis*, ch. 4; Thoreau, "Conclusion," *Walden* (1854); an account of the dispensaries appears in Charles E. Rosenberg, "The Practice of Medicine in New York a Century Ago," *Bulletin of the History of Medicine*, 41 (May–June 1967), 236–8; Charles E. Rosenberg, "Social Class and Medical Care in 19th Century America: The Rise and Fall of the Dispensary," *Journal of the History of Medicine*, 29 (1974), 32–54. Figures for 1859 in "Medical Charities—Dispensaries," *American Medical Times*, 1 (17 November 1860), 350. The staff of the dispensaries in 1870 is listed in the *Manual of the Corporation of the City of New York*, 1870, 383–96.

60. *Report of the Council of Hygiene and Public Health upon the Sanitary Condition of the City* (New York: D. Appleton, 1865), lii.

61. On Griscom, see Samuel W. Francis, M.D., *Biographical Sketches of Distinguished Living New York Physicians* (New York: George P. Putnam, 1867), 45–59; Lawrence Veiller, "Tenement House Reform in New York City, 1834–1900" in *The Tenement House Problem . . . by Various Writers*, ed. Robert W. DeForest and Lawrence Veiller, 2 vols. (New York: Macmillan, 1903), 1, 71–5.

62. R. M. Hartley, "Swill-Milk and Infant Mortality" (letter), *New York Times*, 1 June 1858, 2; Norman Shaftel, "A History of

the Purification of Milk in New York, or, 'How Now, Brown Cow,'" *New York State Journal of Medicine*, 58 (1958), 911–28.

63. John H. Griscom to Lemuel Shattuck, 26 April 1843, cited in James H. Cassedy, "The Roots of American Sanitary Reform 1843–47: Seven Letters from John H. Griscom to Lemuel Shattuck," *Journal of the History of Medicine*, 30 (1975), 141.

64. John H. Griscom, *The Sanitary Condition of the Laboring Population of New York, with Suggestions for its Improvement: A Discourse* (New York: Harper & Brothers, 1845), 8–9. Rejected by a committee of the board of aldermen, it was eventually published by private subscription, with James Harper and Peter Cooper as leading supporters. For the acknowledgment of English reformers, see Griscom to Edwin Chadwick, 14 August 1853, Chadwick Papers, University College, London; Harvester Microfilm, reel 13, file 1897; and Stephen Smith, M.D., *The City That Was* (New York: Frank Allaben, 1911), 51. For an account of Chadwick, see Mary Poovey, "Domesticity and Class Formation: Chadwick's 1842 *Sanitary Report*" in *Subject to History: Ideology, Class, Gender*, ed. David Simpson (Ithaca and London: Cornell University Press, 1991), 65–83.

65. Days of fasting and prayer: Charles E. Rosenberg, *The Cholera Years: The United States in 1832, 1849, and 1866* (Chicago: University of Chicago Press, 1962), 48–9; role of environment: *Annual Report of the Interments in the City and County of New York for the year 1842 with Remarks thereon, and a brief View of the Sanitary Condition of the City*. Presented to

the common council by John H. Griscom, M.D., city inspector. Document No. 59. See also Rosenberg, *The Cholera Years*, 102–3; beneficial effects of cleanliness: Griscom, *Sanitary Condition*, 6.

66. *Annual Report*, 1842. Charles Loring Brace's "Walks Among the New York Poor: The Rag and Bone Pickers," *New York Times*, 22 January 1853, 2, gives a more humane and sociologically nuanced account of the largely German rag-and-bone pickers who lived along the East River in the 11th and 17th wards. For Griscom, these people were "the living personification of uncleanness"; to Brace, they were immigrants caught by viciously exploitative landlords (making he estimated annual returns of between twenty-five and thirty-three per cent on their total outlay), and who hoped to make enough money to settle in the west. The tenement committee of the common council visited the same rag-and-bone pickers in 1856, and were shocked and outraged at conditions they observed. ("The Tenement Committee: How the Poor Live," *New York Times*, 7 July 1856, 4.) In open space on Montparnasse, called the villa des chiffoniers, Parisian ragpickers erected their huts. Bohemians like Privat d'Anglemont admired their preference for fresh air and a superb view of Paris. (Jerrold Seigel, *Bohemian Paris: Culture, Politics, and the Boundaries of Bourgeois Life, 1830–1930* [New York: Viking, 1986], 142.) Poe similarly admired the free and easy lives of ragpickers in what became Central Park. The ragpickers of New York deserve further study.

67. Francis, *Biographical Sketches*, 50, quotes a response to

Griscom's report, later published as *The Sanitary Condition of the Laboring Population of New York*, from the board of aldermen: "*Your committee do not profess to be judges of the subject, or in other words, they do not think it proper at this time, to go into such a measure.*" Compare the two-part review of *The Sanitary Condition* in *The Broadway Journal*, 1 (22 February, 1 March 1845), 113–14, 129; and the review of Griscom's *Annual Report* in the *New York Journal of Medicine*, 4 (March 1845), 222–31.

68. *The Journal of Richard Henry Dana, Jr.*, ed. Robert F. Lucid, 3 vols. (Cambridge, MA: Belknap Press of Harvard University Press, 1968), 1, 120–21.

69. *Ibid.*, I, 122.

70. *The Centenary Edition of the Works of Nathaniel Hawthorne*, Vol. 5, *Our Old Home: A Series of English Sketches*, ed. William Charvat et al. ([Columbus]: Ohio State University Press, 1970), 283–4.

71. Stephen Smith, "Woman as Physician," *Doctor in Medicine and other Papers on Professional Subjects* (New York: Wood, 1872), 54–8.

72. Early medical research: F. H. G[arrison], "Dr. Stephen Smith, The Nestor of American Surgery," *Annals of American Medicine*, 1 (October 1917), 318–22; Bellevue: Page Cooper, *The Bellevue Story* (New York: Crowell, 1948), 7–65.

73. Stephen Smith, *The City That Was*, 35–6.

74. *Ibid.*, 36–9. The tactic of publishing the names and addresses of owners and agents of particularly dilapidated properties was being employed later in the decade: see "The Tenement Committee: How the Poor Live," *New York Times*, 7 July 1856, 4.

75. *Ibid.*, 88.

76. Michel Foucault, *The Birth of the Clinic: An Archaeology of Medical Perception*, trans. A. M. Sheridan Smith (New York: Pantheon, 1973), 33. *Naissance de la Clinique* was first published in 1963.

77. Quoted in Edward K. Spann, *The New Metropolis: New York City 1840–1857* (New York: Columbia University Press, 1981), 137.

78. [William Osborn Stoddard,] *The Royal Decrees of Scandaroon. Dedicated by the Author to the Sachems of Tammany and to the other Grand Magnorums of Manhattan* (New York: Russell's American Steam Printing House, 1869), 31.

79. See James C. Mohr, *Abortion in America: The Origins and Evolution of National Policy, 1800–1900* (New York: Oxford University Press, 1978).

80. My account of health reform in New York follows Howard D. Kramer, "Early Municipal and State Boards of Health," *Bulletin of the History of Medicine*, 24 (November–December 1950), 503–17; Gert H. Brieger, "Sanitary Reform in New York City: Stephen Smith and the Passage of the Metropolitan Health Bill," *Bulletin of the History of Medicine*, 40 (September–October 1966), 407–29; and John Duffy, *A History of Public Health in New York City 1625–1866* (New York: Russell Sage Foundation, 1968); ch. 24.

81. Robert H. Bremner, "The Big Flat: History of a New York Tenement House," *American Historical Review*, 64 (October 1958), 54–62.

82. "Health Laws," *American Medical Times*, 1 (15 December 1860), 423–4.

83. For a sample of the Sanitary Association's publications, see *Public Health of the City of New York: Remarks of Rev. F. C. Ewer before the Sanitary Association, November 21, 1861* (New York: Edmund Jones & Co., Printers, 1861).

84. "The Public Health," *New York Times*, 9 March 1860, 4. It is an interesting aspect of the close relations between medical reformers and the press that a toned-down version of this paragraph appears in *Disease and Death in New-York City and Its Vicinity; Being a Report of Physicians and Citizens upon the Value and Necessity of Sanitary Improvements and Well-Administered Health Laws* (New York: Citizens' Association of New York, 1864), 15–16.

85. John H. Griscom, *Sanitary Legislation, Past and Future: The Value of Sanitary Reform, and the True Principles for its Attainment read before the New York Sanitary Association, October 3rd and November 14th, 1861* (New York: Edmund Jones & Co., Printers, 1861), 6.

86. "Health Laws," *American Medical Times*, 1 (15 December 1860), 423–4.

87. "Health of New York in 1860," *American Medical Times*, 3 (26 January 1861), 63–4.

88. Griscom, *Sanitary Legislation, Past and Future*, 3.

89. Bremner, *The Public Good*, 43.

90. *Ibid.*, 37–53; George M. Frederickson, *The Inner Civil War: Northern Intellectuals and the Crisis of the Union* (New York: Harper & Row, 1965), 98–112; on the fate of post-bellum reform, see John G. Sproat, *"The Best Men": Liberal Reformers in the Gilded Age* (New York: Oxford University Press, 1968). For Olmsted's role, see Roper, *FLO*, 164.

91. Cooper, *The Bellevue Story*, 77.

92. Philip Van Ingen, *The New York*

Academy of Medicine: Its First Hundred Years (New York: Columbia University Press, 1949), 115. See also Howard D. Kramer, "Effect of the Civil War on the Public Health Movement," *Mississippi Valley Historical Review*, 35 (December 1848), 449–62; Richard Shryock, "A Medical Perspective on the Civil War," *American Quarterly*, 14 (Summer 1962), 161–73.

93. "Sanitary Legislation," *American Medical Times*, 4 (11 January 1862), 28–9.

94. "Failure of the Health Bill," *American Medical Times*, 4 (3 May 1862), 250–51; Bryant to Lincoln, 4 January 1861, *The Letters of William Cullen Bryant*, 4 vols., eds. William Cullen Bryant, II, and Thomas G. Voss (New York: Fordham University Press, 1977–84), 4, 198; Opdyke's role in Republican inner-party maneuvers may be traced in Harry J. Carman and Reinhard Luthin, *Lincoln and the Patronage* (New York: Columbia University Press, 1943), 21, 37, 61, 243–4, 297.

95. Godkin to Olmsted, 25 December 1864, *The Gilded Age: Letters of E. L. Godkin*, ed. William M. Armstrong (Albany: State University of New York Press, 1974), 17. They differed about the correct response to the draft riots, with Godkin favoring aggressive military intervention and the declaration of martial law, while Opdyke, as Iver Bernstein has shown, brokered a settlement with the city's traditional conservative elites in the Democratic leadership. See Iver Bernstein, *The New York City Draft Riots*, ch. 4.

96. Christopher Dell, *Lincoln and the War Democrats: The Grand Erosion of Conservative Tradition* (Rutherford and London:

Fairleigh Dickinson University Press/Associated University Press, [1975]), 260.

97. "The Prospect of Health-Reform in New York," *American Medical Times*, 5 (15 November 1862), 276–7.

98. Dana, *Journal*, 1, 121.

99. C. M. Sedgwick to Mrs. K. S. Minot, 11 January 1852, in *The Life and Letters of Catherine Maria Sedgwick*, 335. See also Sedgwick's didactic tale *Home* (Boston: J. Munroe, 1835).

100. See Daniel Walker Howe, "The Social Science of Horace Bushnell," *Journal of American History*, 70 (September 1983), 305–27.

101. David Handlin, *The American Home: Architecture and Society, 1815–1860* (Boston: Little, Brown, 1979); Chapin, *Humanity in the City*, 131–54; Downing, *Cottage Residences* (1842), quoted in Neil Harris, *The Artist in American Society: The Formative Years 1790–1860* (New York: George Braziller, [1966]), 209. See also George Tatum, ed., *Prophet with Honor: The Career of Andrew Jackson Downing 1815–1852* (Philadelphia: The Athenaeum/Washington, DC: Dumbarton Oaks Research Library and Collection, 1989).

102. *The Poor and Criminal Classes of the Fifth and Eighth Wards of New York. A Sermon Preached by the Rev. Alvah Wiswall, in St. John's Chapel, Trinity Parish, October 20, 1872* (New York: Chatterton & Parker, 1872), 4–5.

103. Charles Loring Brace to John Hull Olmsted, [1851], *Life of Charles Loring Brace*, 113. The family life of "the majority in our country," on the other hand, left a great deal to be desired. After Brace returned home from his European travels he noted "the

want exhibited throughout family life here of healthy cheerfulness, of sociality, geniality, and the more tender and kindly expressions of affection" (*Life*, 151). Brace's *Home Life in Germany*, based on his visit in 1851–2, was published in 1853.

104. Ruskin, *Sesame and Lilies* (1865) quoted in Richard Sennett, *The Conscience of the Eye: The Design and Social Life of Cities* (New York: Alfred A. Knopf, 1990), 20; Nancy F. Cott, *The Bonds of Womanhood: "Woman's Sphere" in New England, 1780–1835* (New Haven and London: Yale University Press, 1977), 96.

105. "Our Big Thing on Ice," *Poetical Works of Charles G. Halpine (Miles O'Reilly)*, 261.

106. On Boole's early years, see "The Election To-morrow," *New York Times*, 5 December 1859, 2. Accusations of fraud against Boole appeared in the *New York Herald*, 25, 28 July 1860.

107. Denis Tilden Lynch, *"Boss" Tweed: The Story of a Grim Generation* (New York: Boni & Liveright, 1927), 267.

108. Cook, *The Armies of the Night*, 33.

109. Gustavus Myers, *The History of Tammany Hall*, second ed. (New York: Boni & Liveright, 1917), 205. Boole's appeal for the Black vote appears in *New York Tribune*, 30 November 1863, and McKay, *The Civil War and New York City*, 232–3. McKeon's tactic in 1864 of raising nativist fears, unforgivable in the aftermath of the murderous Draft Riots, was used against him by Fernando Wood in an angrily contested congressional election in 1842. It was an old standby of New York politics. See Mushkat, *Fernando Wood*, 19.

110. Gunther 29,121, Boole 22,597, Blunt 19,383 (*Manual of the Corporation of the City of New York*, 1870, 763).

111. Dell, *Lincoln and the War Democrats*, 260–61.

112. Hon. William C. Gover, *The Tammany Hall Democracy of the City of New York and the General Committee for 1875* (New York: Martin B. Brown, 1875), 51–2; see also *The Autobiography of Andrew Dickson White*, 1, 125–6, for a similar perception of Boole's mental state.

113. *Speech of Thomas N. Carr in Support of Charges Against Francis I. A. Boole, City Inspector, before His Excellency Horatio Seymour, June 3, 1864* (New York: George F. Nesbitt & Co., Printers, 1864). The case against Boole was summed up in *The Application to His Excellency Gov. Seymour, for the Removal of Francis I. A. Boole, City Inspector. Argument of Robert B. Roosevelt in Behalf of the Citizens' Association, June 3, 1864* (New York: The Citizens' Association, 1864). The quantity of ashes produced during a typical winter created an expensive burden upon the city inspector's modest street cleaning budget.

114. Cited by Myers, *History of Tammany Hall*, 206–7.

115. Henry Ward Beecher, "Moral Theory of Civil Liberty," *The Plymouth Pulpit: Sermons, Preached in Plymouth Church, Brooklyn, New York*, second series (London: D. Dickinson, 1870), 431–2. This sermon was preached on the Fourth of July 1869. On Beecher's parish see the striking analysis in Altina L. Waller, *Reverend Beecher and Mrs. Tilton: Sex and Class in Victorian America* (Amherst: The University of Massachusetts Press, [1982]), 104–11.

116. *Address of the Committee to Promote the Passage of A Metro-*

politan Health Board . . . (New York: John W. Amerman, Printer, 1865), 8; Alexander B. Callow, Jr., *The Tweed Ring* (New York: Oxford University Press, 1965), 31–2.

117. See *The Report of the Committee on Municipal Reform, Especially in the City of New-York* (New York: The Union League Club, 1867). This report was largely written by Dorman Eaton, of whose activities see below.

118. *Disease and Death in New-York City and Its Vicinity; Being a Report of Physicians and Citizens upon the Value and Necessity of Sanitary Improvements and Well-Administered Health Laws* (New York: Citizens' Association, 1864) was presented to Mayor Gunther at the December 1863 meeting and subsequently was widely distributed in the city; the "alarming abuses" and "systematic plunder" were briefly summarized in *Our City Government* (New York: Citizens' Association, 1864), which announced the formation of the committee. See also *An Appeal to the Iron Trade of New York* (New York: Citizens' Association, [1864]) which made the call by foremen at thirteen printing establishments for a mass meeting on 18 July, which was followed by *An Appeal to the Book Trade* (New York: Citizens' Association, [1864]), which called for a mass meeting at sixteen printing establishments on 8 August; role of Sands: Stephen Smith, "Address," *Dorman B. Eaton. 1823–1899: Memorial Service . . . Held in the Church of All Souls, New York, January 21, 1900*, 14–15. He was later accused of having fallen under the influence of Tweed.

119. He had sought the position of counsel to the corporation as a Republican in December 1868, but was heavily defeated by Richard O'Gorman by 74,803 votes to 20,864. There is a biographical note on Eaton in *Prominent Families of New York*, [ed. L. H. Weeks] (New York: The Historical Company, 1898), 200.

120. *Address of the Committee to Promote the Passage of a Metropolitan Health Bill* gives an account of the activities of the various Citizens' Association committees active in this reform movement.

121. Professor Charles F. Chandler, "As Commissioner of Health," *Stephen Smith, M. D., LL. D., Vice-President of the New York State Board of Charities. Addresses in Recognition of his Public Services on the Occasion of his Eighty-Eighth Birthday, February Nineteenth, Nineteen Hundred Eleven*, 19.

122. *Report of the Council of Hygiene upon the Sanitary Condition of the City* (New York: D. Appleton, 1865), cxxxiii. Further references in the text.

123. John Bell, M.D., *Report on the Importance and Economy of Sanitary Measures to Cities*. Doc. no. 20, Board of Councilmen, November 28, 1859. (New York: Edmund Jones & Co., 1860), 33. Similar arguments were made by defenders of public parks. See John H. Rauch, M.D., *Public Parks: Their Effects upon the Moral, Physical and Sanitary Condition of the Inhabitants of Large Cities* (Chicago: S. C. Griggs & Co., 1869), 83–4.

124. Chapin, *Humanity in the City*, 177–8.

125. William Chambers, *Things as They Are in America* (New York: P. D. Orvis, 1854), 68.

126. *Disease and Death in New-York*, 1864, 18.

127. William E. Dodge, *Old New York: A Lecture* (New York: Dodd, Mead, 1880), 19.

128. Similar symptoms were observed by Frederick Law Olmsted of the passengers on emigrant ships in 1850: "... as any one may see, from a dozen ships a day often in New York, they come ashore with no disease but want of energy, but emaciated, enfeebled, infected, and covered with vermin. When we observe the listessness, even cheerfulness, with which they accept the precarious and dog-like subsistence which, while in this condition, the already crowded city affords them, we see the misery and degradation to which they must have been habituated in their native land." Frederick Law Olmsted, *Walks and Talks of an American Farmer in England* (New York: G. P. Putnam, 1852; reissued with an Introduction by Alex L. Murray (Ann Arbor: University of Michigan Press, n.d.), 13. The same conditions were described in the decade after the *Report* in *The Poor and Criminal Classes of the Fifth and Eighth Wards of New York. A Sermon Preached by the Rev. Alvah Wiswall . . .*, 4–5.

129. Smith in *Dorman B. Eaton*; Smith, *The City That Was*, 44–5.

130. White, *Autobiography*, 1, 110.

131. Smith in *Dorman B. Eaton*, 18.

132. Smith, *The City That Was*, 124. Further references in the text. The figures cited by Smith were drawn from the report by William F. Thoms, M.D., on the 6th sanitary district, which encompassed the 6th ward, in *The Sanitary Condition of New York*, 73–5. There were fluctuating death rates in this district: 36 per 1,000 in 1860, 40 in 1861, 36 in 1862 and 43 in 1863.

133. *New York Times*, 16 March 1865.

134. On the tactical delay, see Brieger, "Sanitary Reform in New York City," 425. The Sayre amendment is scathingly analyzed in *Address of the Committee to Promote the Passage of A Metropolitan Health Board*, 47–50. His pay increase appears in corporation of the city of New York, *Communication of the Comptroller Transmitting his Financial Estimates or Budget for the Year 1866 Document 2, Documents of the Board of Councilmen, January 8, 1866* (New York: Edmund Jones & Co., Printers to the Corporation, 1866), 118. Dr. Sayre was another of those who seemingly had made their devil's pact with the corruptionists. During the Civil War he had been a member of the executive committee of the New York Surgical Aid Association and had done stalwart work in January 1864 indicting the conditions under which deserters were being held in the "Pen" in the Park Row army barracks. It is worth recalling however that attacks on the army treatment of soldiers were highly partisan in New York: *New York Times*, 21 April 1862, 5; Ernest A. McKay, *The Civil War and New York City* (Syracuse: Syracuse University Press, [1990]), 185–6.

135. *Poetical Works of Charles G. Halpine (Miles O'Reilly)*, 256–7. Stanza 3: Acton was president of the Metropolitan Board of Police; Lyman Tremaine was Attorney General. Stanza 4: "Lord Horace" was Horace Greeley, the editor of the *Tribune*. See John D. Hayes and Doris D. Maguire, "Charles Graham Halpine: Life and Adventures of Miles O'Reilly," *New York Historical Society Quarterly*, 51 (October 1967), 326–44, and William Hanchett, *IRISH: Charles G. Halpine in Civil War America*, with a Foreword by Allan Nevins (Syracuse: Syracuse University Press, [1970]).

136. *New York Times*, 1 July 1865, 1; [E. L. Godkin,] "The Sanitary Condition of New York," *The Nation*, 1 (24 August 1865), 250.

137. Strong entry for 5 November 1865, *Diary*, 4, 44; Jacques M. May, M.D., *The Ecology of Human Disease* (New York: MD Publications, [1958]), 53.

138. Rosenberg, *The Cholera Years*, 185.

139. New York State. *An Act to Create a Metropolitan Sanitary District, and Board of Health Therein for the Preservation of Life and Health, and to Prevent the Spread of Disease* (New York: Bergen & Tripp, Printers, 1866). The passage of the Metropolitan health bill in the state legislature is described in detail in James C. Mohr, *The Radical Republicans and Reform in New York during Reconstruction* (Ithaca: Cornell University Press, 1973), 61–114.

140. *Valentine's Manual*, 1866, 286–7.

141. Edward B. Dalton, M.D., "The Metropolitan Board of Health of New York," *North American Review*, 219 (April 1986), 353–75; passage quoted 363.

142. *The Public Health. The Basis of Sanitary Reform. The Metropolitan Board of Health. Sketch of the Organization and Powers of the Board From the New-York Tribune, August 13, 1866* (New York: re-published by the Citizens' Association of New-York, 1866), 24. If the activities of the reformed health department are measured, day by day, against the deterioration of conditions in the rapidly growing city, it is clear that battles, indeed even whole campaigns, were won, while the war was gradually being lost. Further reforms were soon needed. For the characteristic operations of the Sanitary

Committee of the Board of Health under Smith's leadership, see "The Health Department," *New York Times*, 3 September 1873, 1–2.

143. Olmsted to Kingsbury, 20 April 1871, *The Papers of Frederick Law Olmsted*. Vol. 6, *The Years of Olmsted, Vaux & Company 1865–1874*, eds. David Schuyler and Jane Turner Censer (Baltimore and London: Johns Hopkins University Press, [1992]).

Chapter Two

1. The name was well chosen: François Mauriceau was an eighteenth-century French physician who wrote on midwifery and womens' maladies. "A. M. Mauriceau" was identified as Charles Lohman as early as 1849 in [George Thompson,] *The Countess, or, Memoirs of Women of Leisure, Being a Series of Intrigues with the Bloods, and a Faithful Delineation of the Private Frailties of our First Men* (Boston: Berry & Wright, [1849]), 42; in the *New York Times*, 23 August 1871, and by Edward Crapsey, *The Nether Side of New York; or, The Vice, Crime and Poverty of the Great Metropolis* (New York: Sheldon & Co., 1872), 150.

2. Michael A. LaSorte, "Nineteenth Century Family Planning Practices," *Journal of Psychohistory*, 4 (Fall 1976), 163–83. Norman E. Himes, *Medical History of Contraception*, with a New Preface by Christopher Tietze, M.D. (Baltimore: Williams & Wilkins, 1936; New York: Schocken, 1970), 262, concluded from "internal evidence" that Mauriceau lived in France, and is not the only one to be deceived by

pseudepigraphic evidence. The reputation of the French in such matters in the 1840s was high, and a veneer of French experience was a useful marketing tool. Hence the tale recounted in Charles Sutton, *The New York Tombs*, eds. James B. Mix and Samuel A. Mackever (San Francisco: A. Roman & Co., 1874), 363: "Accompanying a family to Paris as governess, she became intoxicated with the gaieties of the French capital and was loth to return to America. While there she became acquainted with a woman who was quite successful in the sale of certain nostrums, of which she alone possessed the secret of their ingredients. Restell induced her to come to this city, and they soon reaped a harvest."

3. A. M. Mauriceau, *The Married Woman's Private Medical Companion* (New York; n.p., 1847; reprinted New York: Arno Press, 1974), 15. The gin alone, taken in such quantities, would do powerful things to the stomach. The author not having tried the recipe, this is merely speculation.

4. Himes, *Medical History of Contraception*, 262–4, identifies the source of Mauriceau's plagiarism without realizing who "Mauriceau" actually was.

5. Carroll Smith-Rosenberg, *Disorderly Conduct: Visions of Gender in Victorian America* (New York: Alfred A. Knopf, 1985), 226.

6. The ladies' physician's advertisement is reprinted in James D. McCabe, Jr., *Lights and Shadows of New York Life* (Philadelphia: National Publishing Co., [1872]), 619–20. "Martin" was a pseudonym of Edward Winslow Mc Cabe, a native of Richmond who lived in Brooklyn after 1865. Restell's appears in Meade Minnegerode, *The Fabulous Forties 1840–1859: A Presentation of Private Life* (New York: G. P. Putnam's Sons, 1924), 103–4. Another sample of Lohman's handiwork, from the *New York Sun* of 18 March 1839, appears in Clifford Browder, *The Wickedest Woman in New York: Madame Restell, the Abortionist* (Hamden, CT: Archon Books, 1988), 9.

7. Catherine M. Scholten, *Childbearing in American Society: 1650–1850* (New York: New York University Press, 1985), 13–14.

8. *Ibid.*, 19.

9. La Sorte, 167.

10. Characteristic medical literature on abortifacients: Horace Green, M.D., "On the Effects of Ergota in Parturition, with Cases," *New-York Journal of Medicine and Surgery*, 7 (January 1841), 21–32, and John C. Peters, M.D., "On the Action and Uses of Aloes," *New York Journal of Medicine and Collateral Sciences*, 4 (1845), 161–7; LaSorte, 169. The *New York Times*, 6 April 1853, reports the death of a pregnant woman, mother of three, abandoned by her husband, who died after drinking six-pence worth of oil of tansy.

11. Richard Harrison Shryock, *Medicine and Society in America: 1660–1860* (Ithaca: Cornell University Press, 1962), gives a vivid account of the "regulars" in this period.

12. William G. Rothstein, *American Physicians in the Nineteenth Century: From Sects to Science* (Baltimore: Johns Hopkins University Press, 1972), 46–52.

13. For a view of hydropathy as seen by an educated leader of feminine opinion, see Kathryn Kish Sklar, *Catherine Beecher: A Study in American Domesticity* (New York: W. W. Norton, 1976), 185–6, 204–6.

14. [E. L. Godkin], "Orthopathy and Heteropathy," *The Nation*, 5 (24 October 1867), 335–6.

15. *American Medical Intelligencer*, 1 (15 April 1837), 33; quoted in Robert E. Riegel, *Young America 1830–1840* (Norman: University of Oklahoma Press, [1949]), 310.

16. Richard W. Wertz and Dorothy C. Wertz, *Lying-In: A History of Childbirth in America* (New York: Schocken Books, 1979), ch. 3; John S. Haller, Jr., *American Medicine in Transition 1840–1910* (Urbana: University of Illinois Press, 1981), 157. On the eroticized and gendered nature of medical knowledge in this period, see Ludmilla Jordanova, *Sexual Visions: Images of Gender in Science and Medicine between the 18th and 20th Centuries* (Hemel Hempstead: Harvester, 1989).

17. John T. Noonan, Jr., "Abortion and the Catholic Church: A Summary History," *Natural Law Forum*, 12 (1967), 85–131; Daniel Callaghan, *Abortion: Law, Choice and Morality* (New York: Macmillan, 1970), 411–27.

18. Mohr, *Abortion in America*, 34–5; Sauer, "Attitudes to Abortion in America," 56.

19. Browder, *Ibid.*, 17–18.

20. "Medical Malpractice," *New York Times*, 10 April 1873, 5.

21. 2 September 1857, reprinted in *I Sit and Look Out: Editorials from The Brooklyn Daily Times by Walt Whitman*, selected and edited by Emory Holloway and Vernolian Schwarz (New York: Columbia University Press, 1937), 113–14.

22. Whitman, *I Sit and Look Out*, 115–16.

23. Crapsey, *The Nether Side of New York*, 153.

24. Stephen Smith, M.D., *Doctor in Medicine and other Papers on Professional Subjects* (New York: Wood, 1872), 211.

25. Browder, *Ibid*, 15–16, discusses the efficacy of Restell's potions.

26. Charles Dickens, *American Notes for General Circulation* (1842; London: Chapman and Hall, 1913), 70.

27. *The Trial of Madame Restell for Abortion* (New York, 1841). This pamphlet was quickly published by George Dixon, editor of the *Polyanthos*, after the Purdy trial. The interview with Purdy is quoted from the testimony of a friend of Mrs. Purdy, 18.

28. Gunning S. Bedford, M.D., "Vaginal Hysterotomy," *New York Journal of Medicine and the Collateral Sciences*, 2 (March 1844), 201.

29. *Ibid.*

30. It is scarcely necessary to puzzle over the personal hostility of Bedford, who had trained at the leading "Maternité" hospital in Paris, towards Restell. In his eyes she was, like so many midwives of the day, an ignorant and dangerous person whose activities threatened the lives of women. His attitude towards the fetus was equally clear: "Be not deceived, gentlemen," he warned obstetrics students at New York University, "by supposing that the child, while in its mother's womb, enjoys only an inferior life, and that, therefore, its destruction is a matter of secondary consideration. Ask the physiologist, and he will tell you that although its existence is a dependent one, yet the human foetus possesses all the attributes of life, and has an inherent vitality during the earliest periods of conception. Ask the moralist and he will tell you that the foetus is a living being in the broadest acceptation of the term, and that the unjustifiable taking of its life is, in the eye of Heaven,

murder." New York University, Department of Medicine. *Introductory Lecture delivered by Gunning S. Bedford, A.M., M.A.,* Session MDCCCXVI–XLVI (New York: Printed for the Medical Class of the University, 1845–6). Bedford's denunciation of many current obstetric practices, which he regarded as little less than butchery, rings clearly throughout this lecture.

31. *National Police Gazette,* 8 November 1845, 21 February 1846. See also William K. Wimsatt, Jr., "Poe and the Mystery of Mary Rogers," *PMLA,* 56 (1941), 230–48; Samuel Worthen, "Poe and the Beautiful Cigar Girl," *American Literature,* 20 (November 1948), 305–12; John Walsh, *Poe the Detective: The Curious Circumstances Behind "The Mystery of Marie Rôget"* (New Brunswick: Rutgers University Press, 1968); Raymond Paul, *Who Murdered Mary Rogers?* (Englewood Cliffs, NJ: Prentice-Hall, Inc., [1971]).

32. *Madame Restell: An Account of her Life and Horrible Practices,* by a Physician of New York (New York: Published by the Proprietor, 1847), 18.

33. [George Thompson,] *The Countess, or, Memoirs of Women of Leisure,* 42; *Madame Restell,* 19; Junius Henri Browne, *The Great Metropolis,* 584.

34. Paul Boyer, *Urban Masses and Moral Order in America, 1820–1920* (Cambridge, MA and London: Harvard University Press, 1978), 19.

35. John M'Dowell, D.D., "Human Depravity and Its Remedy," *The National Preacher,* 5 (November 1830), 85.

36. "Another Death from Abortion," *National Police Gazette,* 6 February 1864, 3.

37. Abortionists in New York: Crapsey, *Nether Side of New York,* 149; the price of abortions: Mohr, *Abortion in America,* 97; "The Evil of the Age," *New York Times,* 23 August 1871, 6; "More About the Abortionists," *New York Times,* 2 September 1871, 2; Grindle's rates in Crapsey, *Nether Side of New York,* 152; figures on average daily wages in Gordon Atkins, "Health, Housing and Poverty in New York City 1865–1898" (Ph.D., Columbia University, 1947), 67; Grindle's establishment: *New York Times,* 23 August 1871, 6; 2 September 1871, 2; branch offices: reproduced in Mohr, *Abortion in America,* 52.

38. Mohr provides the most comprehensive discussion of the changing public attitudes towards abortion, and the development of legislative control which endured for nearly a century.

39. Quoted in *Madame Restell! Her Secret Life-History,* 9.

40. Applegate's deposition quoted in "Madame Restell and some of Her Dupes," *New York Medical and Surgical Reporter,* 1 (21 February 1846), 158–65. This unsigned article was probably written by the editor, Clarkson T. Collins. This account of the Applegate case was drawn from *A Practical Treatise on Midwifery* by M. Chailly, translated from the French and ed. by Gunning S. Bedford, M. D. (New York: Harper & Brothers, 1844), 303–5; baby farming: James D. McCabe, *The Secrets of the Great City* (Philadelphia: Jones Brothers & Co., [1868]), 431–8 [on McCabe see above note 6]; John H. Warren, Jr., *Thirty Years' Battle with Crime, or The Crying Shame of New York, as seen under the Broad Glare of an Old Detective's Lantern* (Poughkeepsie, NY: A. J. White, 1875), 168; Jacob Riis, *How the*

Other Half Lives: Studies Among the Tenements of New York (New York: Charles Scribner's Sons, 1890), ch. 16.

41. Material from the unsigned piece in the *Medical and Surgical Reporter* ("Madame Restell and Some of Her Dupes") was cited in the *Gazette*. The attack on Restell was carefully coordinated. See Leonard L. Richards, *"Gentlemen of Property and Standing": Anti-Abolition Mobs in Jacksonian America* (New York: Oxford University Press, 1970), 115–20, for an account of the mechanism and procedures of the 1834 attacks. At least fifty such attacks are recorded in the period between 1825 and 1857. The recourse to vigilante attacks is situated in the changing place of vice in the city in Timothy J. Gilfoyle, "Strumpets and Misogynists: Brothel 'Roits' and the Transformation of Prostitution in Antebellum New York City," *New York History*, 68 (January 1987), 45–65, and "The Urban Georgraphy of Commercial Sex: Prostitution in New York City, 1790–1860," *Journal of Urban History*, 13 (August 1987), 371–93.

42. *New York Tribune*, 26 August 1847.

43. "Madame Restell," *New York Times*, 3 September 1871, 8.

44. See the entry on McKeon in *American Biography: Containing Sketches of Prominent Americans of the Present Century*, by Eminent Authors (New York: For sale by the News Companies, n.d.).

45. Marian Gouverneur, *As I Remember: Recollections of American Society in the Nineteenth Century* (New York and London: D. Appleton & Co., 1911), 43–4.

46. *Wonderful Trial of Caroline Lohman, Alias Restell, with Speeches of Counsel, Charge of Court and Verdict of Jury*. Reported in full for the *National Police Gazette*. (New York, 1847), 5. Extensive passages from this pamphlet are quoted in an unsigned review in the *New York Journal of Medicine and the Collateral Sciences*, 10 (January 1848), 92–104.

47. Barbara Welter, "The Cult of True Womanhood: 1820–1860," *American Quarterly*, 18 (Summer 1966), 151–74.

48. *Wonderful Trial*, 19.

49. Imprisonment: "Madame Restell," *New York Times*, 3 September 1871, 8; Whitman's response: *Brooklyn Daily Eagle*, 11 November 1847, quoted in Thomas L. Brasher, *Whitman as Editor of the Brooklyn Daily Eagle* (Detroit: Wayne State University Press, 1970), 145–6; reaction to her imprisonment: John D. Vose, *Seven Nights in Gotham* (New York: Bunnel & Price, 1852), 98.

50. "Ned Buntline," *The Mysteries and Miseries of New York: A Story of Real Life*, second ed. (New York: Berford & Co., 1848), 101.

51. Browne, *The Great Metropolis*, 584.

52. Smith, *Doctor in Medicine*, 104–8; Michel Foucault, *The History of Sexuality: An Introduction* (London: Allen Lane, 1979), 116–19.

53. *Madame Restell*, 12–13.

54. *Trial of Madame Restell. for Abortion* (New York, 1841), 6.

55. Rev. Orville Dewey, *A Sermon Preached in the Second Unitarian Church in Mercer-Street, on the Moral Importance of Cities and the Moral Means for their Reformation, particularly on a Ministry for the Poor in Cities* (New York: David Felt & Co., 1836), 19.

56. The imprisoning of women was

uncommon in antebellum New York. Those who were sent to prison were regarded as hardened and vicious, beyond the reach of repentance or reform. In New York State prisons women prisoners were isolated and given few facilities. The "Auburn System," under which male prisoners were forced to work in rigid discipline and absolute silence during the day and kept in solitary confinement at night, was held to be inappropriate for the small number of women prisoners. Restell's favorable treatment on Blackwell's Island would have been regarded as an important indication that she was unrepentant. The condition of female criminals, and of released convicts, attracted some of the most dedicated of female reformers: see Mrs. C[aroline]. M[atilda]. Kirkland, *The Helping Hand: Comprising an Account of the Home for Discharged Female Convicts, and an Appeal in Behalf of that Institution* (New York: Charles Scribner, 1853). The novelist Catherine Maria Sedgwick was on the executive committee of the home. For her sustained involvement with these neglected women, see Mrs. James S. Gibbons, "Sketches of Miss Sedgwick's Connection with the Women's Prison Association of New York" in Mary E. Dewey, ed., *The Life and Letters of Catherine M. Sedgwick* (New York: Harper & Brothers, 1871), 419–25. See also W. David Lewis, "The Female Criminal and the Prisons of New York, 1825–1845," *New York History*, 42 (July 1961), 215–36.

57. *Madame Restell! Her Secret Life History*, 11.

58. Sergeant Taft interviewed in the *Sun*, 2 April 1878, 1.

59. George W. Matsell, the 300-lb. chief of police from 1845 until the force was reorganized in 1857 and a well known Democrat, was accused by political enemies on the board of aldermen in 1855 of being on Restell's payroll virtually from the beginning of his tenure of office. He was also accused of blackmailing about 100 of Restell's clients. The accusation appears in Gustavus Myers, *The History of Tammany Hall*, with a New Introduction by Alexander B. Callow, Jr., second ed. (New York, 1917; reissued New York: Dover Publications, [1971]), 170–71, Edward C. Mack, *Peter Cooper: Citizen of New York* (New York: Duell, Sloan and Pearce, [1949]), 153 and Browder, *The Wickedest Woman*, 106; see also "Obituary: Death of George W. Matsell," *New York Times*, 26 July 1877, 3. While chief of police Matsell was also part-owner of the *National Police Gazette* (which seldom failed to boost his activities); the *Gazette* throughout this period violently denounced Restell; the accusation that he was bribed by Restell, on that evidence, suggests it was money ill spent, or not spent at all. Or were the attacks regarded by Restell as part of her public image of notoriety, and thus good for trade?

60. Medinger case in *Madame Restell! Her Secret Life-History*, 12; for the changed climate towards abortion in the early 1850s, see Browder, *The Wickedest Woman*, 105–6.

61. [George Thompson,] *The Countess, or, Memoirs of Women of Leisure*, 42.

62. Church attendance: *Sun*, 2 April 1878, 1; Thorstein Veblen, *The Theory of the Leisure Class* (1899; New York: Modern Library ed., 1934), ch. 4.

63. There is a list of residents on Fifth Avenue in *Reuben Vose's Wealth*

of the World Displayed (New York: Reuben Vose, 1859), 115–18. See also Theodore James, Jr., *Fifth Avenue* (New York: Walker and Co., [1971]). Millionaires abounded.

64. *Sun*, 2 April 1878, 1. For the purchase of the lots on Fifth Avenue, and the subsequent public outcry, see William F. Howe, *In Danger; or Life in New York* (New York: J. S. Ogilvie & Co., 1888), 165–6.

65. Edward Van Every, *Sins of New York "Exposed" by the Police Gazette* (New York: Frederick A. Stokes, 1930), 91–104; Browne, *The Great Metropolis*, 585.

66. Howe and Hummel, *In Danger*, 166; *New York Times*, 2 April 1878, 1.

67. McCabe, *New York by Sunlight and Gaslight* (Philadelphia: Hubbard Brothers, 1882), 495. Reissued as *New York by Gaslight* (New York: Greenwich House, 1984) [on McCabe, see above note 6].

68. "Mme. Restell Arrested," *New York Times*, 12 February 1878, 8.

69. *Madame Restell! Her Secret Life-History*, 11; Lloyd Morris, *Incredible New York: High Life and Low Life of the Last Hundred Years* (New York: Random House, 1951), 55.

70. Browne, *The Great Metropolis*, 586.

71. Ellington, *The Women of New York*, 406.

72. Longchamp, *Asmodeus in New York*, 15.

73. Stewart's income: Ernest A. McKay, *The Civil War and New York City* (Syracuse: Syracuse University Press, 1990), 220. There is an engraving of the house in John Grafton, *New York in the Nineteenth Century: 317 Engravings from "Harper's Weekly" and Other Contemporary Sources*, second ed. (New

York: Dover Publications, Inc., 1980), 78.

74. *Sun*, 2 April 1878, 1: "The city has no more magnificent mansion than that in which she dwelt." Lloyd Morris, *Incredible New York*, 55, includes an engraving of "the palace" in all its glory. The existence of such an engraving, and the assumption that there was a market for it, is one of the most striking facts concerning Restell's reputation in this period. There are photographs of the Vanderbilt mansions in Nathan Silver, *Lost New York* (Boston: Houghton Mifflin, 1967), 121–2.

75. Longchamp, *Asmodeus in New York*, 16.

76. Ellington, *The Women of New York*, 408–9.

77. The cost of the frescoed ceilings: Howe & Hummel, *In Danger*, 166; comment on the window shades in Ellington, *The Women of New York*, 408–9.

78. Browne, *The Great Metropolis*, 587.

79. *Madame Restell! Her Secret Life-History*, 4.

80. Purdy's denial: "Absurd Stories About Mme. Restell," *New York Times*, 4 April 1878, 8; Westervelt: Browder, *The Wickedest Woman*, 107.

81. "Mme. Restell's Funeral," *New York Herald*, 3 April 1878, 4.

82. *New York Times*, 2 April 1878, 1; "Her Last Appeal," *New York Herald*, 2 April 1878, 4.

83. "Ann Lohman's Will," *New York Times*, 5 April 1878, 8.

84. Edward Van Every, *Sins of New York*, 103–4.

85. Asbury, *The Gangs of New York*, 103.

86. *New York Times*, 23 August 1871, 6.

87. *Sun*, 2 April 1878, 1.

88. Quoted by Bennett, *The Champions of the Church*, 1073.

89. McCabe, *New York by Sunlight and Gaslight*, 495. Of later

accounts of Restell, only Broun and Leech, *Anthony Comstock*, 159, have noticed this change.

90. Paul Boyer, *Urban Masses and Moral Order in America 1820–1920* (Cambridge, MA, and London: Harvard University Press, 1978), ch. 7.

91. *New York Times*, 14 November 1868, 4. The estimated return on investments in tenements appears in C. L. B[race], "Walks Among the New York Poor: The Rag and Bone Pickers," *New York Times*, 22 January 1853, 2.

92. *New York Times*, 20 April 1853; Claudia D. Johnson, "That Guilty Third Tier: Prostitution in Nineteenth Century American Theaters," *American Quarterly*, 27 (December 1975), 575–84.

93. "The Hideous Vice," *New York Times*, 27 January 1871, 3.

94. This account of Comstock follows Broun and Leech, *Anthony Comstock*, passim. See also Milton Rugoff, *Prudery & Passion* (London: Rupert Hart-Davis, 1972), 123–31; "Sunday Rum," *New York Times*, 3 July 1871, 1.

95. "I confess that the ordinances that close all grog-shops and lager-bier saloons on Sunday seem to me a severe strain on the endurance of the *hoi polloi*, and not the less so because they are ancient laws now enforced for the first time." George Templeton Strong, *Diary*, eds. Allan Nevins and Milton Halsey Thomas, 4 vols. (New York: Macmillan, 1952), entry for 9 May 1867. See also entry for 9 October.

96. H. L. Mencken, "Comstockery," *Prejudices: Fifth Series* (London: Jonathan Cape, n.d.), 17; Broun and Leech, *Anthony Comstock*, 16; Stanley Coben, "The Assault on Victorianism in the Twentieth Century," *American Quarterly*, 27 (December 1975), 604–28.

97. Broun and Leech, *Anthony Comstock*, 72.

98. *Ibid.*, 93.

99. "Arrests for Malpractice," *New York Times*, 31 August 1872, 5.

100. *New York Times* reports: 26 July 1872 (Taft); 28 August 1872 (Smith); 2 October 1872 (Hersland); 7 October 1872 (Bristol); 4 December 1872 (Hill); 14 February 1873 (Rosenzweig); 19 April 1873 (Brown); 24 April 1873 (Wright); 10 April 1873 (Hall).

101. LaSorte, "Nineteenth Century Family Planning Practices," 171.

102. Mohr, *Abortion in America*, 197; Broun and Leech, *Anthony Comstock*, 160.

103. Bennett, *The Champions of the Church*, 1069.

104. Melville, "Bartleby the Scrivener."

105. "Mme. Restell's Arrest," *New York Times*, 14 February 1878, 8.

106. "The Case of Mme. Restell," *New York Times*, 16 February 1878, 3.

107. *Sun*, 2 April 1878, 1.

108. *Ibid.*

109. *New York Times*, 4 April 1878, 8; *ibid.*, 23 May 1878, 8.

110. Whitman to Talcott Williams, 19 June [1882], Walt Whitman, *The Correspondence*, ed. Edwin Haviland Miller, 5 vols. (New York: New York University Press, 1969), 5, 316.

111. Obituaries in *New York Times*: 13 April (Tweed); 2 May (Morrissey); 13 June (Bryant); 19 June (Vermilye); 15 August (Duyckinck); 26 September (Van Buren); 15 October 1878 (Kingsland).

Chapter Three

1. *The Faber Book of Irish Verse*, ed. John Montagn (London: Faber and Faber, 1974), 225.

2. Obituary, *New York Herald* and

New York Times, 1 June 1880, 4.

3. Is this what is alluded to in a gnomic passage about Connolly in *The Book of Daniel Drew: A Glimpse of the Fisk-Gould-Tweed Regime from the Inside*, ed. Bouck White (New York: Doubleday, Page, 1910) "That woman of his whom he picked up from the Turkish Bath where she had been an attendant, used to play him all kinds of tricks, and he wasn't any the wiser. If it had been a man, Dick would have seen through him at once." (169).

4. A sketch of Draper appears in *The Aristocracy of New York: Who They Are and What They Were, Being a Social and Business History of the City by an Old Resident* (New York: New York Publishing Co., 1848), 19. The April 1834 mayoral election was the first to be decided by a popular ballot. Democratic mobs attacked Whig voters in the 6th ward on the first day of the ballot. On the second, the newspaper editor James Watson Webb, Draper, and other Whig leaders organized their own mobs to even the odds. See James L. Crouthamel, *James Watson Webb: A Biography* (Middletown, CT: Wesleyan University Press, [1969]), 50–51. Philip Hone's account of the election in his diary recounts the events as seen by a Whig grandee. See *The Diary of Philip Hone*, ed. with an Introduction by Allan Nevins, 2 vols. (New York: Dodd, Mead and Co., 1927), I, 122–4.

5. See "The Mock Auctions" in George G. Foster, *New York by Gas-Light and Other Urban Sketches*, ed. and with an Introduction by Stuart M. Blumin (Berkeley: University of California Press, [1990]), 208–13. The fourth scene of Benjamin Baker's *A Glance at New York*, first performed 1848, is set in a mock auction, where the two-fisted intervention of Mose the Bowery b'hoy saves Harry the Greenhorn from being cheated by the auctioneers.

6. *Irish Citizen*, 30 September 1871, 404.

7. Horatio Alger, Jr., *Ragged Dick and Struggling Upward*, ed. with an Introduction by Carl Bode (New York: Penguin Books, [1985]), 15.

8. *Ibid.*, 26–7; 102–15.

9. John W. Pratt, "Boss Tweed's Public Welfare Program," *New York Historical Society Quarterly*, 45 (October 1961), 396–411. Walter L. Hawley, "What New York Owes to Tweed," *Munsey's Magazine*, 46 (1907), 616–20, develops a similar argument.

10. *New York Herald*, 20 September 1871, 3. Our sense of the appearance of the Tweed Ring, and of the exciting events of 1871, is overwhelmingly dominated by the cartoons of Thomas Nast in *Harper's Weekly*. Virtually all of the important cartoons are collected in Albert Bigelow Paine, *Th. Nast: His Period and His Pictures* (New York: Macmillan, 1904) and Morton Keller, *The Art and Politics of Thomas Nast* (New York: Oxford University Press, 1968). Perhaps the best alternative source of images of 1871 is *Frank Leslie's Illustrated Newspaper*, which contained a profusion of engravings on topical issues. See the issues of 23 September 1871 (Cooper Union meeting of 4 September), 30 September (John Foley and the stolen vouchers), 7 October (Andrew H. Green), 11 November (Brennan arrests Tweed), 18 November (Oakey Hall), 25 November (Tweed), 30 December (Tweed in court).

11. *New York Times*, 1859, quoted

by Alfred Connable and Edward Silberfarb, *Tigers of Tammany: Nine Men Who Ran New York* (New York: Holt, Rinehart & Winston, 1967), 150; "The Charter Election—Who Shall be City Comptroller?" *New York Herald*, 27 November 1866, 6.

12. Opinions of Connolly: [Abram Polhemus Genung], *The Frauds of the New York City Government Exposed* (New York: Published by the Author, 1871), 31–2; Charles F. Wingate [i.e., Charles Francis Adams, Jr.], "An Episode in Municipal Government. 1. The Ring," *North American Review*, 245 (October 1874), 376–7; Theodore P. Cook, *The Life and Public Services of the Hon. Samuel J. Tilden* (New York: D. Appleton & Co., 1876), 93, 96; Matthew Patrick Breen, *Thirty Years of New York Politics up-to-date* (New York: The Author, 1899), 328; Hon. John D. Townsend, *New York in Bondage* (New York: Issued for Subscribers, 1901), 95; Albert Bigelow Paine, *Th. Nast*, 143; De Alva Stanwood Alexander, *A Political History of the State of New York*, 3 vols. (New York: Henry Holt, 1909), 3, 177; Allan Nevins, *The Evening Post: A Century of Journalism* (New York: Boni & Liveright, 1922), 377; M. R. Werner, *Tammany Hall* (Garden City, NY: Doubleday, Doran, 1928), 124; Croswell Bowen, *The Elegant Oakey* (New York: Oxford University Press, 1956), 40; Seymour J. Mandelbaum, *Boss Tweed's New York* (New York: John Wiley, 1965), 66–7. Notable exceptions to this consensus are Edwin Platt Tanner in *History of the State of New York*, ed. A. C. Flick, 10 vols. (New York: Columbia University Press, 1935), 7, 47–8, and Leo Hershkowitz, *Tweed's New York: Another Look* (Garden City, New York: Anchor Press/Doubleday, 1977).

13. Alger, *Ragged Dick*, 34–7, 55–7.

14. Union League Club of New York, *The Report of the Committee on Municipal Reform* (New York: Union League Club, 1867), 93.

15. See Stuart M. Blumin, "Explaining the New Metropolis: Perception, Depiction, and Analysis in Mid-Nineteenth Century New York City," *Journal of Urban History*, 11 (November 1984), 9–38.

16. O'Conor's disadvantages: John Bigelow, "Some Recollections of Charles O'Conor," *The Century*, 29 (March 1885), 732.

17. John Higham, *Strangers in the Land: Patterns of American Nativism 1860–1925*, corrected and with a new Preface (New York: Atheneum, 1971), 26. See also Dale T. Knobel, *Paddy and the Republic: Ethnicity and Nationality in Antebellum America* (Middletown, CT: Wesleyan University Press, 1986), *passim*; and Robert H. Wiebe, *The Opening of American Society: From the Adoption of the Constitution to the Eve of Disunion* (New York: Alfred A. Knopf, 1984), 335–6. Catholic disadvantages take on a different meaning from other points of view. Matthew Hale Smith describes Catholicism in 1868 as "the State religion" of New York which threatened to carry the city at every election. Priests controlled the large charitable institutions, and the politicians sought to aid the Catholic Church whenever possible. See Smith, *Sunshine and Shadow in New York* (Hartford: J. B. Burr, 1868), 688–93.

18. Alexander B. Callow, Jr., *The Tweed Ring* (New York: Oxford University Press, 1965), 46.

19. Biographical details are based upon the obituaries in the *New York Herald* and *New York Times*, 1 June 1880, and the obituary of Mrs. Connolly in the *Times*, 13 April 1879; on Wood's role in the intra-party maneuvres of the late 1830s, see Jerome Mushkat, *Fernando Wood: A Political Biography* (Kent, OH, and London: The Kent State University Press, [1990]), 8–10.

20. George Templeton Strong, *Diary*, eds. Allan Nevins and Milton Halsey Thomas, 4 vols. (New York: Macmillan, 1952), entry 5 December 1859.

21. Samuel Augustus Pleasants, *Fernando Wood of New York* (New York: Columbia University Press, 1948); Smith, *Sunshine and Shadow*, 268–76. His major speeches in Congress are reprinted in a campaign biography prepared for Wood's bid for re-election as mayor in 1856, Donald MacLeod, *Biography of Hon. Fernando Wood* (New York: O. F. Parsons, 1856).

22. Mushkat, *Fernando Wood*, 15.

23. Pleasants, *Fernando Wood*, 62, and Denis Tilden Lynch, *"Boss" Tweed: The Story of a Grim Generation* (New York: Boni & Liveright, 1927), 150.

24. The first entry for Connolly in the *Trow's New York City Directory* appeared in 1840–41, where he was described as "accountant." His addresses were noted until 1872–3.

25. Edith Wharton, *A Backward Glance* (New York: D. Appleton-Century, 1934), 2, 11.

26. M. J. Heale, "From City Fathers to Social Critics: Humanitarianism and Government in New York, 1790–1860," *Journal of American History*, 63 (June 1976), 21–41.

27. See Edwin Lawrence Godkin, *Unforeseen Tendencies of Democracy* (London: Archibald Constable & Co., 1903), esp. 149, where he writes: "The habit of considering conspicuous inhabitants as entitled to leading municipal places must be regarded as lost." This theme frequently appears in the reform literature of the Tweed era: see Union League Club of New York, *The Report of the Committee on Municipal Reform*, 5, and *Address of the Committee on Legislative Corruption* (New York: The Club House, Union Square, 1867), 11. Jackson S. Schultz, Peter Cooper, Dorman B. Eaton, Francis Leiber and William E. Dodge were among the members of this committee. The Union League Club in its first decade represented that displaced elite in the political life of the city.

28. [James Parton,] "The Government of the City of New York," *North American Review*, 103 (October 1866), 415–16.

29. "Our City Government," *Harper's Weekly*, 1 (17 January 1857), 34.

30. *New York Times*, 5 January 1853, 4; See also Dixon Ryan Fox, *The Decline of Aristocracy in the Politics of New York 1801–1840* (New York: Columbia University Press, 1919).

31. William J. Hartman, "Politics and Patronage: The New York Custom House, 1852–1902," Ph.D., Columbia University, 1952.

32. Tilden to J. L. Sullivan, 31 May 1845, *Letters and Literary Memorials of Samuel J. Tilden*, ed. John Bigelow, 2 vols. (1908; Port Washington, NY: Kennikat Press, 1971), 1, 35.

33. Norman Graebner, "James K. Polk: A Study in Federal Patronage," *Mississippi Valley Historical Review*, 38 (March 1952), 613–32; Charles Sellers, *James K. Polk, Continentalist 1843–1846*

(Princeton, NJ: Princeton University Press, 1966), 286–92; Jerome Mushkat, *Tammany: The Evolution of a Political Machine 1789–1865* (New York: Syracuse University Press, [1971]), 223–5.

34. There is an account of the dismissal of Hawthorne, as seen by the Whigs, in Holman Hamilton, *Zachary Taylor: Soldier in the White House* (Hamden, CT: Archon Books, 1966); see also Stephen Nissenbaum, "The Firing of Nathaniel Hawthorne," *Essex Institute Historical Collections*, 114 (April 1978), 57–86.

35. *New York Tribune*, 29 July 1871, 1–2. On Havemeyer, see Howard B. Furer, *William Frederick Havemeyer: A Political Biography* (New York: The American Press, 1965).

36. *New York Tribune*, 29 July 1871, 1–2.

37. His personal wealth was listed at $100,000 in *Wealth and Wealthy Citizens of New York City* (New York: Compiled with much care and Published at the Sun Office, 1842).

38. *New York Times* quoted in Wm. D. Murphy, *Biographical Sketches of the State Officers and Members of the Legislature of the State of New York in 1862 and '63* (New York: Printed for the Author, 1863), 56.

39. R. B. Connolly to President Franklin Pierce, 3 October 1853, NYHS.

40. The tortuous course of Democratic Party politics in the 1840s and 1850s is traced in Jerome Mushkat, *Tammany: The Evolution of a Political Machine 1789–1865*, and Edward K. Spann, *The New Metropolis: New York City, 1840–1857* (New York: Columbia University Press, 1981), ch. 13. On the Barnburners, see Herbert Donovan, *The Barnburners: A Study of the Internal Movements in the Political History of New York and of the Resulting Changes in Political Affiliations* (New York: New York University Press, 1925) and Frederick J. Blue, *The Free Soilers: Third Party Politics 1848–54* (Urbana: University of Illinois Press, [1973]).

41. Fourth of July: *New York Herald*, 6 July 1851, 1: election of sachems: *New York Times*, 19 April 1853, 8; Gustavus Myers, *The History of Tammany Hall*, second ed., enlarged (New York: Boni & Liveright, 1917), 152, 165; Jerome Mushkat, *Tammany*, ch. 10; reform meeting: "City Reform," *New York Herald*, 7 June 1853, 1. See also the *Evening Post*, 10 November 1857, quoted Pleasants, *Fernando Wood*, 62. On the hostility towards Wood in the Democratic Party, and the lessons learned from his campaigns, see Amy Bridges, *A City in the Republic: Antebellum New York and the Origins of Machine Politics* (Cambridge: Cambridge University Press, 1984), 117–21.

42. Richard E. Foglesong, *Planning the Capitalist City: The Colonial Era to the 1920s* (Princeton, NJ: Princeton University Press, [1986]), ch. 4, attributes to Olmsted the elitist and anti-democratic tradition of American park creation and management by independent boards of commissioners. Olmsted had good reason to defend the independence of commission management, but he came on the scene after the decision had been taken, for partisan reasons, to remove local (i.e., corrupt) politicians from control.

43. Donald MacLeod, *Biography of Hon. Fernando Wood*, 164–5.

44. Press reaction to the 1857 workingmen's demands in Bridges, *A City in the Republic*, 118.

45. Strong, *Diary*, 3, 373.

46. Connolly's role: "City Politics," *New York Herald*, 6 September 1857, 4–5. The complex struggles within Tammany Hall against Wood in 1856–7 are best described in Mushkat, *Fernando Wood*, 62–85. Both candidates held large rallies at the Academy of Music (for Tiemann's see *New York Times*, 25 November 1857, 1; for Wood's see the issue of 28 November 1857, 1), but the long lists of distinguished citizens elected vice-president of the meeting contained in Wood's case an artful confection of figures such as ex-mayor Westervelt, Anson G. Phelps and Francis B. Cutting, who had neither attended the meeting nor planned to support Wood, and who wrote indignantly to the paper on 30 November denouncing the hijacking of their names.

47. Strong, *Diary*, 2, 385, entry for 5 February 1858.

48. *New York Times*, 23 November 1859, 4. See also the issue for 1 December 1859, 3, for the use of political advertisements in the campaign against Wood, and the issue of 7 December 1859, 1, for a description of the scene at Mozart Hall when the result was announced.

49. Dewey to Mrs. David Lane, winter 1859, in Dewey, *Autobiography and Letters*, 252; Tilden, *Letters*, 1, 127. Bryant blamed the fiasco on the "shilly shallying" of Havemeyer, who delayed accepting the nomination long enough for the support of Republicans to be lost. William Cullen Bryant to John Bigelow, 14 December 1859, *The Letters of William Cullen Bryant*, eds. William Cullen Bryant, II and Thomas G. Voss, 4 vols. (New, York: Fordham University Press, 1984), 4, 129–30.

50. See Tyler G. Anbinder, "Fernando Wood and New York City's Secession from the Union: A Political Reappraisal," *New York History* 68 (January 1987), 67–92.

51. See *A Condensed Biography of Fernando Wood, compiled from the Original Documents, by a Veteran Democrat* (New York: n.p., 1866); Mushkat, *Fernando Wood*, 35.

52. Lynch, *"Boss" Tweed*, 151; *New York Evening Post*, 6 September 1877. Dishonest supervisors and aldermen in New York became so blatant in the 1860s that in the opinion of Olmsted they needed "to be fought quite as much as Lee and Typhoid." Olmsted to Henry W. Bellows, 3 October 1862, cited in *The Papers of Frederick Law Olmsted, 4. Defending the Union*, ed. Jane Turner Censer (Baltimore and London: The Johns Hopkins University Press, [1986]), 440.

53. Brown had twice lectured to sympathetic audiences at Concord Town Hall. Reactions to his death appear in Ralph L. Rusk, *The Life of Ralph Waldo Emerson* (New York: Columbia University Press, [1949]), 401–2 (who also notes Hawthorne's indignation at Emerson's praise for Brown: "Nobody was ever more justly hanged.") and Gilman M. Ostrander, "Emerson, Thoreau and John Brown," *Mississippi Valley Historical Review*, 39 (March 1953), 713–26; Havemeyer meeting reported in the *New York Times*, 5 December 1859, 3 and Supplement; Lincoln's address of 27 February 1860 appears in the issue of the following morning; the text of the Cooper Union address is reprinted in Abraham Lincoln, *Speeches and Writings, 1859–1865*, ed. Don E. Fehren-

bacher (New York: The Library of America, [1989]), 111–30; see also Avery Craven, *The Coming of the Civil War* (New York: Charles Scribner's Sons, 1942), 407–8; and George M. Frederickson, *The Inner Civil War: Northern Intellectuals and the Crisis of the Union* (New York: Harper & Row, 1965), ch. 3, for responses to the Harper's Ferry raid.

54. Quoted in Wm. D. Murphy, *Biographical Sketches of the Legislature of New York in 1862 and '63*, 57–8.

55. *New York Times*, 6 November 1861; *New York Herald*, 1 June 1880; Florence Gibson, *The Attitudes of New York's Irish Towards National Affairs, 1848–1898* (New York: Columbia University Press, 1954), 132; Ernest A. McKay, *The Civil War and New York City* (Syracuse: Syracuse University Press, 1990), chs. 1–3.

56. *The Life and Letters of E. L. Godkin*, ed. Rollo Ogden, 2 vols. (New York: Macmillan, 1907), 1, 213. His comment on Wood was written on 29 April 1863. There is an engraving of the dashing Ben Wood in the Copperhead journal *The Old Guard*, 1 (October–December 1862), facing 241. His novel is discussed by Jerome Mushkat, "Ben Wood's 'Fort Lafayette,'" *Civil War History*, 21 (1975), 160–71.

57. Stewart Mitchell, *Horatio Seymour of New York* (Cambridge: Harvard University Press, 1938), 226–7; McKay, *The Civil War and New York City*, 40–41.

58. "First O Songs for a Prelude," *Drum-Taps* (1865), Walt Whitman, *Complete Poetry and Collected Prose*, ed. Justin Kaplan (New York: The Library of America, [1982]), 417.

59. Rev. H. W. Bellows to Russell Bellows, 19 April 1861, Bellows Papers, Massachusetts Historical Society; McKay, *The Civil War and New York City*, 58–9, adds several bystanders' accounts to this swing of sentiment in the city.

60. Tyler G. Anbinder, "Fernando Wood and New York City's Secession from the Union: A Political Reappraisal," *New York History*, 68 (January 1987), 67–92; Mushkat, *Fernando Wood*, 111–13; a photograph of the Union Square meeting appears in McKay, *The Civil War and New York City*, 63.

61. Iver Bernstein, *The New York City Draft Riots* (New York: Oxford University Press, 1990), 19.

62. Among its executive committee were Tweed, Peter B. Sweeny, and "Prince Hal" Genet (grandson of the freebooting "Citizen" Genet, first French ambassador to the United States). See Christopher Dell, *Lincoln and the War Democrats: The Grand Erosion of the Conservative Tradition* (Rutherford and London: Fairleigh Dickinson Press/ Associated University Press, [1975]), 121; Hershkowitz, *Tweed's New York*, 82.

63. State of New York, *Presentation of Flags of New York Volunteer Regiments to His Excellency, Governor Fenton July 4, 1865* (Albany: Chief of Bureau of Military Record, Weed, Parsons & Co., Printers, 1865), 87.

64. This complex period may be reconstructed through Eric Foner, *Politics and Ideology in the Age of the Civil War* (New York: Oxford University Press, 1980); Mushkat, *Tammany Hall*; Lynch, *"Boss" Tweed*; Werner, *Tammany Hall*; and Hershkowitz, *Tweed's New York*.

65. On the 1861 election in New

York, see Hershkowitz, *Tweed's New York*, 83–5.

66. Quoted in Wm. D. Murphy, *Biographical Sketches 1862 and '63*, 57; and (to suggest the political usefulness of the record of 1861) in "Hon. Richard B. Connolly," *Frank Leslie's Illustrated Newspaper*, 29 (9 October 1869), 69.

67. The speech calling for an end to party was made in the senate on 15 April and is quoted in Murphy, *Biographical Sketches 1862 and '63*, 58. The Mozart Hall nomination was reputedly sold to the highest bidder by Wood, who had a reputation for being "purchasable." He was accused of bleeding Charlick white, and then turning around and secretly selling his support to Connolly: "Mr Charlick's tickets were burnt in the presence of Fernando Wood, and on election day the Mozart machine worked openly and actively for Connolly." See *A Condensed Biography of Fernando Wood by a Veteran Democrat*, 15. Connolly's defection to the Republicans was attacked in the *Irish American*, which supported Wood's man. After the election the *Irish American* attributed Connolly's victory to electoral fraud. Their hostility was a chink in Connolly's role as an Irish New York politician. See Gibson, *The Attitude of the New York Irish*, 132.

68. See *Narrative of Privations and Sufferings of United States Officers & Soldiers while Prisoners of War in the Hands of the Rebel Authorities: Being the Report of a Commission of Inquiry Appointed by the United States Sanitary Commission* (Boston: Published at the office of "Littel's Living Age," [1864]), 6–10; see also James J. Heslin, ed., "The Diary of a Union Soldier in Con-

federate Prisons," *NYHSQ*, 41 (July 1957), 232–78.

69. *Repeal of the Church Property Bill: Speech of the Hon. Richard B. Connolly . . . March 14, 1862* (Albany: Printed by C. Van Benthuysen, 1862). By a law passed in 1784, control of all church property in New York was vested in a board of lay trustees chosen by the congregation. A dispute between the Catholic Church of St. Louis in Buffalo and Bishop John Timon, led the parish to be placed under interdict in 1851. The Putnam Bill in 1855, strongly supported by State Senator Erastus Brooks, made clerical ownership of church property illegal. It passed but was never enforced. The issue stirred up strong anti-Catholic sentiment, and it was cleverly chosen by Connolly at a moment when it would do himself, the Church, and the Irish immigrant community the maximum benefit. All was negated, however, by the Draft Riots in July. See *The Controversy between Senator Brooks and "†John," Archbishop of New York. Growing Out of the Speech of Senator Brooks on the Church Property Bill in the New York State Senate, March 6, 1855*. Arranged for publication with an Introductory Preface by W. S. Tisdale (New York: De Witt & Davenport, [1855]).

70. Mushkat says little about Connolly in his biography of Wood, but this maneuver in 1862 helps explain a supposition, voiced later in the decade, that Connolly remained under Wood's influence. See [Frederick Beecher Perkins,] *The Ermine in the Ring: A History of the Wood Lease Case* (New York: G. P. Putnam, [1868]), 7.

71. Hershkowitz, *Tweed's New York*, 88.

72. *New York Times*, 23 November 1862.

73. *New York Tribune*, 9 June 1880.

74. [Genung], *The Frauds of the City Exposed*, 32.

75. The deposing of Waterbury and his replacement in 1863 by Purdy as Grand Sachem was in part due to the waning fortunes of the pro-southern element within Tammany. See *Address of Nelson Waterbury upon his Installation as Grand Sachem of the Tammany Society, March 3, 1862* (New York: Wynkoop, Hallenbeck & Thomas, [1862]), where he praised Lincoln for his resistance to those seeking to turn the war into one of conquest and the destruction of slavery.

76. See Byrdsall's *The History of the Loco-Foco, or Equal Rights Party, its Movements, Conventions and Proceedings* (New York: Clement & Packard, 1842); Leo Hershkowitz, "The Loco-Foco Party of New York: Its Origins and Career, 1835–1837," *NYHSQ*, 46 (July 1962), 305–29.

77. Mushkat, *Tammany Hall*, 358; Lynch, *"Boss" Tweed*, 267; electoral results in *Manual of the Corporation of the City of New York* (New York: John Hardy, Clerk of the Common Council, 1870), 736.

78. See the account of Smythe in *American Biography: Containing Sketches of Prominent Americans of the Present Century, by Eminent Authors* (New York: For Sale by the News Companies, n.d.); William J. Hartman, "Politics and Patronage," ch. 5.

79. "The Collector," *New York Times*, 18 April 1866, 4.

80. *New York Times*, 1 June 1880, 4. Hershkowitz, *Tweed's New York*, 115, attributes Smythe's appointment to Connolly's influence, but Connolly's alleged role does not appear in Hartman's account. The importance of the appointment of Smythe is suggested in John and LaWanda Cox, *Politics, Principle and Prejudice, 1865–1866: Dilemma of Reconstruction America* (New York: Free Press, 1963), 107–28, and Edward L. Gambill, *Conservative Ordeal: Northern Democrats and Reconstruction, 1865–1868* (Ames, Iowa: The Iowa State University Press, 1981), 57–8. The role of Manton Marble and Tilden in the appointment of Smythe is suggested in letters from each to Montgomery Blair, 10 March 1866, Blair Mss, Library of Congress, quoted George T. McJimsey, *Genteel Partisan: Manton Marble, 1834–1917* (Ames, Iowa: Iowa State University Press, 1971), 69. Gideon Welles, secretary of the navy under Lincoln and Johnson, commented on Smythe's appointment on 16 April 1866: "Smythe, from what I hear of him, is better than some of the candidates, perhaps better than any," but wondered if such an appointment would be in the best interests of the administration. His further doubts were noted in his diary on 20 July 1866, *Diary of Gideon Welles*, eds. Howard K. Beale *et al.*, 2 vols. (New York: W. W. Norton, 1960), 2, 484, 558. On Smythe's subsequent behavior in office, which drew the Olympian disapproval of E. L. Godkin, see "The Week," *The Nation*, 8 (4 February 1869), 83. Jerome Mushkat in *The Reconstruction of the New York Democracy, 1861–1874* (Rutherford, NJ: Fairleigh Dickinson University Press, [1981]), 95, suggests that Smythe was a disappointment mainly because he insisted on making appointments on merit. Herman Melville met Smythe on 19 April 1857 and travelled with him for

several days in Switzerland and Germany. See Jay Leyda, *The Melville Log: A Documentary Life of Herman Melville 1819–1891*, 2 vols. (New York: Harcourt, Brace and Company, 1951), 2, 573–4. The story of Melville's attempts to secure public employment is told in considerable detail by Harrison Hayford and Merrell R. Davis, "Herman Melville as Office-Seeker," *Modern Language Quarterly*, 10 (1949), 168–83, 377–88.

81. Electoral results in *Manual of the Corporation of the City of New York*, 1870, 733–8.

82. The 21st ward comprised the 22nd and 23rd sanitary districts for the Citizens' Association sanitary survey: see *The Sanitary Condition of New York*, 268–90; tenements: *The Tenement House Problem*, eds. Robert W. DeForest and Lawrence Veiller, 2 vols. (New York: Macmillan, 1903), 1, 216–17; Robert Ernst, *Immigrant Life in New York City, 1825–1863* (New York: King's Crown Press, 1949), 197; Tweed on Connolly: Lynch, *"Boss" Tweed*, 282; suit by Felter: *New York Tribune*, 25 October 1871, quoted in James D. McCabe, Jr., *Lights and Shadows of New York Life* (Philadelphia: National Publishing Co., 1872), 106. "McCabe" was a pseudonym of Edward Winslow Martin, a native of Richmond who lived in Brooklyn after 1865.

83. The best account of the real estate fraud is [Frederick Beecher Perkins], *The Ermine in the Ring*; Sweeny on Brennan in "Secret Ring History," *New York Tribune*, 9 June 1880, 7. The role of Brennan in the case against Boole appears in a deposition by Bernard Kelly and others in *Speech of Thomas N. Carr in Support of Charges Against Francis I. A. Boole, City Inspector, before His Excellency Horatio Seymour, June 3, 1864* (New York: George F. Nesbitt & Co., 1864), 23–6. See also the encomiastic entry on Brennan in *Americian Biography: Containing Sketches of Prominent Americans of the Present Century, by Eminent Authors* (New York: For sale by the News Companies, n.d.).

84. "Rupture of the 'Ring,'" *New York Herald*, 17 November 1866, 7.

85. "City Politics," *New York Herald*, 25 November 1866, 5; 2 December 1866, 5.

86. "Slippery Dick" received 27,179, Kelly received 25,119, and Michael Connolly 19,148. Results by ward in *New York Herald*, 5 December 1866, 3. The *Irish American* supported Michael Connolly, and, as it had done in the 1861 race, blamed the result on fraud. See Gibson, *Attitude of the New York Irish*, 214.

87. *New York Herald*, 10 October 1877.

88. *Report of the Special Committee of the Board of Aldermen appointed to Investigate the "Ring" Frauds*, board of aldermen, Doc. No. 8, 4 January 1878, 692. In 1877 Tweed recalled Woodward and Watson as "young men noted for their fidelity and discretion," *New York Daily News*, 15 September 1877.

89. "Thomas C. Fields Dead," *New York Times*, 26 January 1885, 1. For these transactions he was arrested on 9 November 1871 for fraud to the sum of $563,651.80. Two years later he jumped bail and fled to Havana. He settled in Canada where he eventually died.

90. Grant's nepotism: Milton Rugoff, *America's Gilded Age* (New York: Henry Holt, 1989), 29; Sweeny's and Tweed's family

arrangements appear in *New York Times*, 21 October 1871, 6. Details of Connolly's family appear in *New York Times*, 18 September 1870, 5; 17 August 1871, 4; 14 September 1871, 5; 13 April 1879, 10; [Genung], *The Frauds of the City Exposed*, 34; McCabe, *Lights and Shadows*, 106. The riches accruing to commissioners appointed for street openings are usefully explained in [James Parton,] "The Government of the City of New York," *North American Review*, 103 (October 1866), 440–43.

91. *Report of the Citizens' Association: Our Taxes, Markets, Streets and Sanitary Condition. What New-York might be with a Good Government: Reading for Every Citizen* (New York: George F. Nesbitt & Co., 1865), 13.

92. "Rupture of the 'Ring,'" *New York Herald*, 17 November 1866, 7.

93. The attractive historical texture of works like Wharton's *The Age of Innocence* and *Old New York* was based upon precise recollection and some careful research conducted for the author who was then living in France. When a stage adaptation of *The Age of Innocence* was planned in 1921, Wharton wrote a detailed letter of advice concerning the dress, manners and language of New York society as it was in her youth. See Wharton to Mary Cadwalader Jones, 17 February 1921, *The Letters of Edith Wharton*, eds. R. W. B. Lewis and Nancy Lewis (New York: Charles Scribner's Sons, [1988]), 439–40.

94. Henry P. Tappan, D.D., LL.D., *The Growth of Cities: A Discourse Delivered before the New York Geographical Society on the Evening of March 15th, 1855* (New York: R. Craighead, 1855), 34; Spann, *The New Metropolis*, 67–91; Frederic C. Jaher, "Nineteenth Century Elites in Boston and New York," *Journal of Social History*, 6 (Fall 1972), 32–77.

95. Supreme Court, State of New York. *People vs. Tweed: Case on Appeal made by Defendant*, 2 vols. (New York: National Printing Co., 1876), 1208–9 (continuous pagination).

96. Gordon Atkins, "Health, Housing and Poverty in New York City 1865–1898," 13, attributes this perception of the Tweed Ring to "the people."

97. Julius Grodinsky, *Jay Gould: His Business Career 1867–1892* (Philadelphia: University of Pennsylvania Press, [1957]), 47; John Steele Gordon, *The Scarlet Woman of Wall Street: Jay Gould, Jim Fisk, Cornelius Vanderbilt, the Erie Railway Wars, and the Birth of Wall Street* (New York: Grove Weidenfeld, 1992), 196.

98. David McCullough, *The Great Bridge* (New York: Simon & Schuster, 1972), 134–6; Viaduct Railroad: *New York Times*, 2 August 1871, 4.

99. On the struggle over the charter see Callow, *The Tweed Ring*, 222–35, and Bowen, *The Elegant Oakey*, 61. Nevins surveys press opinion in the *Evening Post*, 380–82.

100. Tweed's suborning of the *Sun* is told in detail in James B. Mix, *The Biter Bit; or The Robert Macaire of Journalism. Being a Narrative of Some of the Black-Mailing Operations of Charles A. Dana's "Sun"* (Washington: n.p., 1870). ("Robert Macaire" was a cartoon figure created by Honoré Daumier in 1836 to represent the archetypal swindling bourgeois of the "liberal" Orleanist régime which came to power in France in 1830.) The bribery of Nathaniel

Sands was part of a clever strategy in 1870 to discredit the Citizens' Association: see *New York Times*, 27 January 1871, 4, where Sands was described as "one of the most crafty and unscrupulous of all the paid agents of Tammany." The story is told in Edward C. Mack, *Peter Cooper, Citizen of New York* (New York: Duell, Sloan and Pearce, [1949]), ch. 19. "Young Democracy" also received the support of other anti-Tammany Democrats, particularly the Democratic Union Organization led by Robert B. Roosevelt, whose regular political commentaries in the *New York Citizen and Round Table* provide an interesting perspective on political maneuverings in the Democracy. See the issue of 12 February 1870. Roosevelt briefly considered running a joint ticket with "Young Democracy" in the city elections (issue of 23 April 1870), but after their defeat by Tweed, O'Brien and the others made their peace with the "Ring."

101. The arguments in favor of the charter appear in *Reform in New-York City. Address to the People of the City of New-York by the Citizens' Association of New-York* (New York: The Citizens' Association, 1870).

102. Tilden's account of the struggle against Tweed's charter in his *The New York City "Ring": Its Origin, Maturity and Fall* (1873; reprinted College Park, MD: McGrath Publishing Co., 1969), 16–22. His comments upon the charter's "concentration of powers over this city" appear on 21. Tilden was everywhere busy secretly orchestrating opposition to the Tweed charter. He tried to alert loyal party supporters, such as William Cullen Bryant and the *Evening Post*, to its dangers. See Charles H. Brown, *William Cullen Bryant* (New York: Charles Scribner's Sons, 1971), 492. The *New York Times* and many less august Republican sources remained skeptical of Tilden's self-serving account of his fight against the Ring. See Benjamin E. Buckman, *Samuel Tilden Unmasked* (New York: Published for the Author, 1876), 61–3; and Townsend, *New York in Bondage*, 71–2.

103. Tweed to Connolly, 16 July 1870, NYHS.

104 "Political," *New York Citizen and Round Table*, 6 (12 February 1870), 648.

105. Thus Hoffman, speaking at Morisania, 30 October 1867: "Our Radical friends, in Congress and out of it, have asserted that the negro is the equal of the white man; and accordingly they have conferred upon him the right of suffrage; and the Freedman's Bureau is to see that he votes correctly. Now, if he needs to be taught how to vote, he cannot be fit to vote. Why, you white men of the North, you don't need to be fed, and clothed, and taught how to vote for the Government. (Cheers.)" Quoted in Hiram Calkins and De Witt Van Buren, *Biographical Sketches of John T. Hoffman and Allen C. Beach, the Democratic Nominees for Governor and Lieutenant-Governor of the State of New York* (New York: The New York Printing Co., 1868), 69.

106. Lynch, *"Boss" Tweed*, 340.

107. *Frank Leslie's Illustrated Newspaper*, 29 (9 October 1869), 61.

108. *Trow's New York City Directory*, 1871; Breen, *Thirty Years*, 373; Callow, *The Tweed Ring*, 194–5.

109. *Report of the Board of Aldermen*, 1878, 552; and *New York Times*, 21 March 1871, 2.

110. *The Star*, 6 January 1871.

111. *Evening Telegram*, 6 January 1871.
112. *Irish Citizen*, 1 January 1870, 93; 25 March 1871, 191.
113. "Belmont and Tweed," *New York Citizen and Round Table*, 6, No. 267 (25 September 1869), 156; Irving Katz, *August Belmont: A Political Biography* (New York: Columbia University Press, 1968), 188–9. Belmont's involvement in the New York Railway Company appears in David Black, *The King of Fifth Avenue: The Fortunes of August Belmont* (New York: Dial Press, 1981), 375–6; see also Harry James Carman, *The Street Surface Railway Franchises of New York City* (New York: Columbia University, 1919).
114. The text of their commendation of the comptroller is reprinted in John Foord, *The Life and Public Service of Andrew Haswell Green* (Garden City, NY: Doubleday, Page & Co., 1913), 165. Callow's comment in *The Tweed Ring*, 241, 243. But is the term "white-wash" appropriate? Why would Astor and his colleagues agree to exonerate a Democratic politician of low repute? They were presented with doctored books, and naively accepted the fiction as an account of the actual state of the city's finances. It was later claimed that in return for their liberal co-operation, certain "wealthy citizens" had their taxes moderated, or not collected at all, for the period from 1868 to 1870—a rumor which utterly lacks credibility. For the claim see Jacob Knickerbocker, *Then and Now* (Boston: Bruce Humphries, [1939]), 213.
115. "Milder Weather", *New York Times*, 25 January 1871, 1.
116. Garvey, in a sworn affidavit, quoted by Wingate [i.e., Charles Francis Adams, Jr.], "An Episode in Municipal Government. 3. The Ring Charter," *North American Review*, 121 (July 1875), 143n, and *Evening Express*, 21 November 1877 (clipping in William C. Whitney's scrapbooks of press clippings about Tweed at NYHS).
117. [Genung], *The Frauds of the City Exposed*, 35.
118. *Manual of the Corporation of the City of New York*, 1866, 50; Callow, *The Tweed Ring*, 120–21; Werner, *Tammany Hall*, 169.
119. O'Rourke was appointed 24 January 1871, and resigned at the end of May largely to write the *New York Times* articles which appeared in July. His role in the downfall of the Ring was obviously crucial, but is recorded in very few sources. There are a few letters from him to Tilden, from October and November 1871, in Box 22, Tilden Papers, New York Public Library. O'Rourke's role is emphasized in Townsend, *New York in Bondage*, 72–3. Achieving the rank of captain in the Civil War, he published two books (1866, 1872) on sword exercises for soldiers. A three-page leaflet held in the Boston Public Library, *Tilden and Tammany. The Secret History of the Operations and Overthrow of the Ring by Matthew J. O'Rourke (formerly of the Comptroller's Office), author of the New York "Times" Exposure of the Ring Frauds*, dating from the mid-1870s announces a pamphlet that was supposed to be in the press. No trace of this pamphlet has been found. The gist of O'Rourke's case was that those who boasted of having played large roles in the fall of the Ring had, in fact, been trimmers or actual accomplices of the criminals.
120. The idea of a statue of Tweed apparently emerged as a practical

joke played by "Joe" Tooker and his cronies at the Oriental Club. To their delight, the idea quickly got out of hand. Justice Shandley formed the Tweed Monument Association, an appeal (signed by O'Brien, Creamer, Genet, Michael Norton, as well as Hall, Sweeny and Connolly) was issued and the sum of $7,973 was collected. Tweed, at first indifferent to the proposal, was eventually observed taking an active interest in its success. Questions were asked about who had and who had not made donations to the fund. Sweeny eventually called matters to a halt, and Tweed was forced to reject the suggestion in March 1871. See *New York Times*, 27 January and 14, 15, 17 March 1871; Breen, *Thirty Years*, 220–27. The proposal was used in anti-Tweed polemics and was wittily recalled after the fall of the Ring, when it was suggested that a statue, with the leading members of the Ring "chained together, two by two, and guarded by city police," be erected in front of the County Court House. See Willoughby Jones, *The Life of James Fisk, Jr.* (New York: Union Publishing Co., 1872), 238.

121. There is a brief sketch of O'Brien's background and, while sheriff of the county of New York, of his direct involvement in electoral fraud, in [Eugene Post Jerome], *The Wig and the Jimmy, or, A Leaf in the Political History of New York* (New York: Published by the Author, 1869), 31. Wingate's articles (written by Charles Francis Adams, Jr.), in the *North American Review*, 1874–6, describe O'Brien as a devious, ambitious, greedy man who longed to displace Tweed in Tammany Hall. His enmity with Peter B. Sweeny was well known. Lynch (*"Boss" Tweed*, 322–3)

and many other authorities believe that Tilden was behind O'Brien's actions in 1871.

122. *New York Times*, 16 July 1869.

123. Paine, *Th. Nast*, 167. Copeland later explained his actions in Connolly's office: "I am a friend of Mr. O'Brien and of course when the troubles arose between Mr. O'Brien and Mr. Connolly I was amongst those that were discharged." Quoted in Bowen, *The Elegant Oakey*, 120.

124. [Genung,] *The Frauds of the New York City Government Exposed*, 11–12, quoting a letter from O'Rourke to the *New York Globe*, 3 August 1871.

125. Paine, *Th. Nast*, 181–2; Davis, *History of the New York Times*, 103.

126. Much of the groundwork for the *Times* revelations had been prepared by the Citizens' Association in a series of reports between 1867 and 1869 in which Connolly's budgets for the city and county of New York were subjected to line-by-line analysis. What is so striking about these reports, however, is that the compilers had not yet concluded that fraud was the central issue. The revelations of 1871 pushed the reformers towards that understanding. See *The City Finances. Letter from the Citizens' Association to Comptroller Connolly* (New York: Citizen's Association, December 30, 1867); *Letter from the Citizens' Association to the Comptroller of the City and County of New York* (New York: Published by the Citizens' Association, 1868); *An Analysis of the Comptroller's County Budget for 1868* (New York: The Citizens' Association, [1868]); *An Analysis of the Comptroller's County Budget for 1869, Made by the Citizens' Association and Presented with Arguments by Counsel to the Senate*

Committee on Municipal Affairs (New York: George F. Nesbitt, Printer, 1869).

127. *How New York is Governed: Frauds of the Tammany Democrats* (New York: Published by the *New York Daily Times*, 1871); Ottendorfer declined the Tammany nomination for mayor in November 1868 "...on account of ill-health and his fear that he would be unable to fulfill the duties of the office," *New York Times*, 24 November 1868, 5; but he was one of those who signed the appeal for funds to erect a statue of Tweed in 1871. For an interpretation of the politics of the disclosures, from a decidedly interested party, see Peter B. Sweeny, *On the "Ring Frauds" and other Public Questions* (New York: J. Y. Savage, 1894), 53–6. There is a biographical note on Ottendorfer in *Prominent Families of New York*, [ed. L. H. Weeks.] (New York: The Historical Company, 1898), 437, and an appraisal of his political role in this period in Stanley Nadel, *Little Germany: Ethnicity, Religion, and Class in New York City, 1845–80* (Urbana and Chicago: University of Illinois Press, [1990]), 150–3.

128. Bowen, *The Elegant Oakey*, 90–95, who lays responsibility for the mayor's actions upon Tweed and Connolly.

129. Groddinsky, *Jay Gould*, 81.

130. *New York Times*, 9 August 1871, 4; *Irish Citizen*, 12 August 1871, 348; *New York Times*, 17 August 1871, 4; *New York Times*, 8 September 1871; quoted in Werner, *Tammany Hall*, 307; and Callow, *The Tweed Ring*, 192. Croker, while a leader of the Fourth Avenue Tunnel Gang, became a protégé of James O'Brien. When O'Brien became sheriff, Croker took his vacant seat as alderman and followed an anti-Tweed line. When the O'Brienites were reconciled with Tweed in 1870, ex-alderman Croker was given a job by Connolly, but when O'Brien went over to the reformers Croker remained loyal to the comptroller, and was a leading figure in the St. Patrick's Mutual Alliance in the 21st ward. He was afterwards a loyal follower of "Honest John" Kelly until he was able to seize control of Tammany Hall in his own right. See Townsend, *New York in Bondage*, 156–68; Lothrop Stoddard, *Master of Manhattan: The Life of Richard Croker* (New York: Longmans, Green, 1931), and Mark D. Hirsch, "Richard Croker: An Interim Report on the Early Career of a Boss of Tammany Hall" in *Essays in the History of New York City: A Memorial to Sidney Pomerantz*, ed. Irwin Yellowitz (Port Washington, NY: Kennikat Press, 1978), 101–31.

131. Charles Loring Brace, *The Dangerous Classes of New York, and Twenty Years' Work Among Them* (New York: Wynkoop and Hallenbeck, 1872), 30. The homes of Republican supporters of the war, and those known to be occupied by African-Americans, were singled out for looting and arson.

132. "Terra incognito:" [Anon. ?E. L. Godkin], "The 'Boss's' Dominions," *The Nation*, 13 (12 October 1871), 236. "In the country": Charles Nordhoff, "The Misgovernment of New York—A Remedy Suggested," *North American Review*, 233 (October 1871), 323. This observation is put with typical vigor in Lydia Maria Child to Sarah Shaw, 32 July 1877, *Lydia Maria Child Selected Letters, 1817–1880*, eds. Milton Meltzer and Patricia G. Holland (Amherst: University of Massachusetts

Press, 1982), 543. See also Spann, *The New Metropolis*, 211–17. Nordhoff resigned as managing editor of the *New York Evening Post* in April 1871 when the largest share-owner of the paper, Isaac Henderson, improperly requested that the attacks upon the Tammany Ring be toned down. His successor, Charlton Lewis, was more cautious in his treatment of the Ring, and thus allowed the initiative to be taken by the *New York Times*, a paper which had been intransigently hostile to the city Democrats since its first appearance in 1851. Throughout this period Bryant was translating Homer, and even appeals from Tilden at the height of the struggle against the Ring in September 1871 could not draw him back to the editorship. See Nevins, *The Evening Post*, 385, and Brown, *William Cullen Bryant*, 492–3.

133. *Twenty-Fourth Annual Report*, New York Association for Improving the Condition of the Poor (New York, 1867), 43.

134. Horatio Seymour to Tilden, 12 August 1871, *Letters and Literary Memorials of Samuel J. Tilden*, 1, 274. See also Mark W. Summers, *The Plundering Generation: Corruption and the Crisis of the Union, 1849–1861* (New York: Oxford University Press, 1987).

135. The NYHS has a scrapbook of material recording Foley's activities with the Reform Association in the 1870s.

136. The text of Foley's letter to Hall, and the mayor's reply, appear in [Genung,] *The Frauds of the New York City Government Exposed*, 12–15.

137. *Proceedings of the Joint Investigating Committee of [the Board of] Supervisors, Aldermen and Associated Citizens, Appointed to Examine the Public Accounts*

of the City and County of New York (New York: Evening Post Steam Presses, 1872). Of the eighteen "citizens" who served on the committee, or who were proposed for membership, only two, James Brown of Brown Brothers & Co. and Thomas W. Piersall, became members of the Committee of Seventy (see Appendix).

138. Mack, *Peter Cooper*, 354.

139. There is an interesting account of the Committee of Seventy, and of the role played by a little-heralded figure in John Foord, *The Life and Public Services of Simon Sterne* (New York: Macmillan, 1903), ch. 8. The announcement of the formation of the committee was made in *Appeal to the People of the State of New York adopted by the Executive Committee of Citizens and Taxpayers for the Financial Reform of the City and County of New York* (New York: The "Free Press" Association, 1871). The main political speech of the evening, by Robert Barnwell Roosevelt, appeared as a separate pamphlet: *Is Democracy dishonesty? Are four men to rule New York with a rod of iron? Speech delivered at the municipal reform meeting held at Cooper Union September 4, 1871.* (New York: Journeymen Printers, 1871). See Appendix for a list of the members of the Committee of Seventy. For Ottendorfer's role and the *Staats-Zeitung* coverage of the meeting, see Nadel, *Little Germany*, 151–2.

140. "Subscription Book of the Executive Committee of Citizens and Tax-Payers for the Financial Reform of the City and County of New York," NYHS; for Belmont's donation see Black, *The King of Fifth Avenue*, 376. Opdyke, Jay Cooke & Co. and William E. Dodge each con-

tributed $5,000 to the Grant campaign. A. T. Stewart gave $15,000. See Richard Lowitt, *A Merchant Prince of the Nineteenth Century: William E. Dodge* (New York: Columbia University Press, 1954), 321. On the civic-minded Schultz, see Gordon Atkins, "Health, Housing and Poverty in New York City 1865–1898" (Ph.D., Columbia University, 1947), 35–7.

141. Tappan, *The Growth of Cities*, 15; Havemeyer, quoted in Jones, *Life of Fisk*, 225; Olmsted to F. J. Kingsbury, 8 October 1871, *The Papers of Frederick Law Olmsted*. vol. 6, *The Years of Olmsted, Vaux & Company 1865–1874*, eds. David Schuyler and Jane Turner Censer (Baltimore and London: Johns Hopkins University Press, [1992]), 471; Child to Francis Shaw, 21 October 1871, *Lydia Maria Child Selected Letters, 1817–1880*, eds. Milton Meltzer and Patricia G. Holland (Amherst: University of Massachusetts Press, 1982), 502; Strong, *Diary*, 4, 382. Samuel B. Ruggles, creator of Gramercy Park, had spent a fortune levelling hills, filling in swamps, and developing property uptown. He was a defender of open spaces in the city, and was one of the most far-seeing property developers in the city. See D. G. Brinton Thompson, *Ruggles of New York: A Life of Samuel B. Ruggles* (New York: Columbia University Press, 1946) and Spann, *The New Metropolis*, 104–5.

142. *New York Herald*, 5 September 1871, 3; Roosevelt: "Murder as a Civilizer," *New York Citizen and Round Table*, 6, No. 304 (23 April 1870), 808; vigilantes: Breen, *Thirty Years*, 353–4; Havemeyer, quoted in Jones, *Life of Fisk*, 225.

143. *New York Times*, 11 September 1871, 4. The bank statements and records of financial transactions obtained by the state in its civil suit against Connolly and his wife are in Box 24, Tilden Papers, New York Public Library. As one might expect, there is a marked increase in transactions in the period from July to September 1871. His accounts in city banks were debited with sums as large as $105,000 in this period. The $75,000 paid to O'Brien would appear to have been debited against Connolly's account at the Bulls Head Bank on 11 September 1871.

144. Foley, Robert B. Roosevelt's enthusiastic lieutenant in the anti-Tammany Democratic Union Organization, had been defeated in campaigns for the board of aldermen, the state assembly, and was only declared winner in the 1869 election to the board of supervisors after bringing a lawsuit to disqualify the police commissioner, Henry Smith, who achieved a higher vote but had failed to resign his post as state law required. He received the support of Roosevelt's *New York Citizen and Round Table*, and the compromised backing of the *Sun*. This story is told in Mix, *The Biter Bit* (1870); New York (State) Courts: Supreme Court, City and County of New York. *John Foley, Plaintiff, against the Board of Supervisors of the County of New York et al. Defendants. Summons, Complaint, Affidavit and Injunction* (New York: Rogers and Sherwood, Printers, 1871). At a brief thirty-one pages, this makes for interesting reading. See also Edward Dana Durand, *The Finances of New York City* (New York: Macmillan, 1898), ch. 5. This clearly outlines the basis of the Ring's financial man-

agement: low taxes, and lots of bonds issued to fund revenue. Townsend on Foley: *New York in Bondage*, 89–90. Connolly's reaction: "Economy in the City Government—Circular from the Controller," *New York Times*, 30 April 1871, 1; Breen, *Thirty Years*, 360; Tweed and Green: *Report of the Board of Aldermen*, 1878, 375. See also Foord, *Andrew Haswell Green*, 165–7, for the new comptroller's attitude towards the continuance of municipal business.

145. Breen, *Thirty Years*, 362; Furer, *William Frederick Havemeyer*, 133. Townsend argues that the Committee of Seventy accomplished "practically nothing" in the effort to catch the thieves. See *New York in Bondage*, 87.

146. *New York Herald*, 13 September 1871, 3.

147. *New York Tribune*, 11 October 1877.

148. Tweed in his "Supplementary Statement," published in the *New York Herald*, 10 October 1877, implicated Connolly in the theft. McCabe, *Lights and Shadows*, 91–9, prints a witness's account and pointedly observes that the theft was designed to throw suspicion upon Connolly.

149. [Entry for December 2, 1872:] "Oakey Hall and Sweeny have been invited to resign as members of the Union Club. Sweeny accepted the invitation; Oakey Hall declined it, and there is a movement to expel him. The question comes up next Wednesday, and its result is doubtful, for a two-thirds vote is needed. . . ." Strong, *Diary*, 4, 402.

150. *Ibid.*, 4, 385. There must have been several panicky meetings of the Ring, mainly designed to ease Connolly's path towards the role of scapegoat.

See the *New York Tribune*, 9 June 1880.

151. Stephen W. Sears, *George B. McClellan: The Young Napoleon* (New York: Ticknor & Fields, 1988), 392–3, 456n.9.

152. *New York Herald*, 10 October 1871, 6. In his testimony in 1877, Tweed explained the transaction with O'Brien in these tortuous words: "King . . . told me that O'Brien said that . . . Tilden, who was then persecuting a great many people, wanted to be a candidate for the Assembly in his (O'Brien's) district, and that he (O'Brien) would get Tilden to let up upon me." See the *Evening Express*, 12 September 1877. O'Brien thus appealed directly to the Ring's suspicion of his link with Tilden, which in all probability was completely fictitious.

153. The intricacies of O'Brien's relations with Tweed and the Ring virtually defy explanation. His apparent alliance with Tilden suggests that he had begun to think about a post-Tweed Tammany Hall, where a selective forgetting of past accommodation and an emphatic record of being on the side of the victors when it counted would be the foundation for subsequent political advancement. O'Brien's supporters offered him as a type of the new, honest Democratic hopeful to cleanse Tammany Hall: "During the time of his official career as Sheriff he won the respect of all good citizens, irrespective of party, by his personal fitness for the office, his eminent integrity and entire incorruptibility. Whatever great temptations have been placed before him, he has never, in the slightest degree, become involved with the corrupt magnates of the 'Ring.' . . . Clearly the 'coming man,' the future great leader of the New

York Democracy, the man worthy and able to hold that proud position, is Senator James O'Brien." "The Coming Man," *The New Varieties*, 16 December 1871, 10. See also *New York Times*, 19 September 1877.

154. Tilden, *The New York "Ring,"* 42. Belmont did not know that Tilden was simultaneously negotiating with Connolly. See Black, *The King of Fifth Avenue*, 377.

155. *New York Times*, 13 September 1871, 1.

156. The correspondence is reprinted in Werner, *Tammany Hall*, 223–6.

157. *New York Times*, 13 September 1871, 1.

158. Mark D. Hirsch, *William C. Whitney: Modern Warwick* (New York: Dodd, Mead & Co., 1948), 57–62.

159. Tilden, *The New York "Ring,"* Appendix, 9. First published in the *Brooklyn Eagle*, 21 September 1871. Hall's contempt for Havemeyer's role in 1871 appears in "Recollections of Men, Women and Things," embedded in his memoir of his early years in New York. *Truth*, 3 June 1883.

160. Foord, *Green*, 19.

161. *Ibid.*, appendix, 8.

162. Havemeyer to Connolly, 16 September 1871, *Letters and Literary Memorials of Samuel J. Tilden*, 1, 279.

163. Tilden, *The New York "Ring,"* 43; Foord, *Green*, 98.

164. *New York Herald*, 17 September 1871.

165. Furer, *Havemeyer*, 137; Strong, *Diary*, 4, 386; *Daily Graphic*, 21 November 1877 (clipping in William C. Whitney's scrapbooks of press clippings about Tweed at the NYHS).

166. Townsend, *New York in Bondage*, 96.

167. Supreme Court, State of New York. *People vs. Tweed: Case on Appeal made by Defendant*, 1231–2. Tweed's lawyer David Dudley Field gave Governor Tilden some uncomfortable moments in cross-examination, of which the account of the arrest of Connolly was among the best.

168. *New York Star*, 4 September 1877.

169. See the *New York Tribune*, 6 October 1877, and *Evening Post*, 8 October 1877; J. Fairfax McLoughlin, *The Life and Times of John Kelly, Tribune of the People* (New York: The American News Company, 1885), 274–85; Hershkowitz, *Tweed's New York*, 207.

170. See reports in *New York Times*, 8, 9, 22, 23 October 1873.

171. Samuel. G. Courtney to Tilden, undated, in Tilden, *Letters and Literary Memorials*, 1, 270–71.

172. *New York Tribune*, 9 June 1880, 7; *New York Times*, 23 December 1871, 10.

173. Richard B. Connolly to Tilden, 1 June 1872, in Tilden, *Letters and Literary Memorials*, 1, 305.

174. Myers, *The History of Tammany Hall*, 248.

175. Views of Connolly in exile: Werner, *Tammany Hall*, 269; *New York Tribune*, 13 October 1877; *The World*, 5 December 1877 (clipping in William C. Whitney's scrapbooks of press clippings about Tweed at the NYHS); *New York Times*, 1 June 1880, 4 (based on Waterbury's comments on Connolly at the consent hearing in 1877); Denis Tilden Lynch, *The Wild Seventies* (New York: Appleton-Century, 1941), 93. Similar stories were circulated about Oakey Hall. ("His wife and daughter in Europe are driven from one hotel to another by people who point at them as the family of one of the Great American Swindlers." Strong, *Diary*, 4, 403, entry dated 2 December 1872.)

176. Wheeler H. Peckham to Tilden, 9 March 1874, *Letters and Literary Memorials*, 1, 329–30. See also Peckham to the Attorney-General Charles Fairchild, 17 April 1877, Peckham Papers, NYHS.

177. *New York Times*, 9, 13, 14, 16 June 1877; *Evening Post*, 4 December 1877 (clipping in William C. Whitney's scrapbooks of press clippings about Tweed at the NYHS). The report on the return to the city of Connolly's daughter appeared as "Mrs. Fithian's Errand," *New York Times*, 30 July 1892, 5.

178. *New York Times*, 14 June 1877, 5.

179. *New York Times*, 1 June 1880, 4.

180. On Nicoll see Strong's *Diary* for 23 January 1875; "Controller Green and John Foley," *New York Times*, 9 October 1873, 8.

Chapter Four

1. "The Central Park Plans" (editorial), *New York Times*, 30 April 1858, 4.

2. Theodore James, Jr., *Fifth Avenue*, with Photographs by Elizabeth Baker (New York: Walker and Co., 1971), 39. The house was designed by Alexander Jackson Davis.

3. "The Suburbs of New York," *New York Times*, 20 July 1851, 2.

4. William Chambers, *Things as They Are in America* (New York: P. D. Orvis, 1854), 62. The Hudson River Railroad which connected Greenbush (on the east bank of the Hudson, opposite Albany) with New York was first opened in 1851. It reduced by half the seven or eight hours' steamboat journey between the two cities.

5. *Map of the City of New York Extending Northward to Fiftieth Street*, surveyed and drawn by

John F. Harrison. Published by M. Dripps, 1851, in I. N. Phelps Stokes, *The Iconography of Manhattan Island 1498–1909* (New York: Robert H. Dodd, 1915–28; reissued New York: Arno Press, 1967), 3, plate 138.

6. Horace Greeley, *Recollections of a Busy Life* (New York: J. B. Ford & Co., 1868), 176–7.

7. Quoted in J[ames]. *Parton The Life of Horace Greeley* (New York: Mason Brothers, 1855), 255.

8. Lydia Maria Child to Anna Loring, 6 February 1845, *Lydia Maria Child Selected Letters, 1817–1880*, ed. Milton Meltzer *et al.* (Amherst: The University of Massachusetts Press, 1982), 217–78. See also Paula Blanchard, *Margaret Fuller: From Transcendentalism to Revolution* (New York: Delacorte Press, 1978), ch. 13.

9. The graceful two- and three-story white clapboarded homes of Jones, Riker and the Schermerhorns appear in lithographs in D. T. Valentine's *Manual of the Corporation of the City of New York* (New York: Edmund Jones & Co., Printers, 1866).

10. Reginald Pelham Bolton, *The Path of Progress* (New York: Central Savings Bank, [1928]), 31, 33.

11. *Phelps' New York City Guide* (New York: T. C. Fanning, 1852); Edward Winslow Martin, *The Secrets of the Great City* (Philadelphia: Jones, Brothers & Co., [1868]), 119.

12. D. G. Brinton Thompson, *Ruggles of New York: A Life of Samuel B. Ruggles* (New York: Columbia University Press, 1946), 57; Carole Klein, *Gramercy Park: An American Bloomsbury* (Boston: Houghton Mifflin Co., 1987), ch. 1.

13. Kenneth Wiggin, *John Jacob Astor: Business Man*, 2 vols.

(Cambridge, MA: Harvard University Press, 1931), 2, 918–19, 939.

14. The gardens were on land which Dr. Hosack originally purchased from the city in 1801 for an average price of $180 per lot. They contained examples of some 2,000 species of plants, as well as a greenhouse and two hothouses. The site was purchased from Dr. Hosack by the state legislature in 1814, and deeded to Columbia College in compensation for real estate lost by the college when Vermont achieved independent statehood. See Henry Collins Brown, *Fifth Avenue 1824–1924* (New York: Fifth Avenue Association, [1924]), 92.

15. "Sale of Buildings in the Central Park," *New York Times*, 16 September 1857, 1.

16. Egbert L. Viele, "Topography of New York and its Park System" in *The Memorial History of the City of New York*, ed. James Grant Watson, 4 vols. (New York: New-York History Co., 1893), 4, 551–60. Quote from 556. Further details from Edward Hagaman Hall, "Central Park in the City of New York," *American Scenic and Historic Preservation Society. Sixteenth Annual Report* (Albany: J. B. Lyon Co., State Printers, 1911), 438–41."Hoovervilles"—shanties built by homeless and unemployed squatters—occasionally reappeared in the park. The most extensive settlement since the great depression of the 1850s occurred in 1930–31. See Henry Hope Reed and Sophia Duckworth, *Central Park: A History and a Guide*, rev. ed. (New York: Clarkson N. Potter, Inc., 1972), 49–50.

17. "The Present Look of our Great Central Park," *New York Times*, 9 July 1856, 3.

18. Letter I, May 14, 1844, Edgar Allan Poe, *Doings of Gotham: Poe's Contributions to "The Columbia Spy*," now first collected by Jacob E. Spannuth, with Preface, Introduction and Comments by Thomas Ollive Mabbott (Pottsville, PA: Jacob E. Spannuth, Publisher, 1929), 25. There is a drawing of a squatter settlement in the present site of Central Park, based upon a painting by Edwin Deakin, in Bolton, *The Path of Progress*, 32. In October 1843 Nathaniel Hawthorne encountered a squatter settlement at Walden Pond which was inhabited by Irish railway workers. The high embankment carrying the railroad seemed much more obtrusive to him than the "picturesque little hamlet" of the squatters. *The Centenary Edition of the Works of Nathaniel Hawthorne*, vol. 8, *The American Notebooks* ed. Claude M. Simpson (Columbus: Ohio State University Press, [1972]), 395–6.

19. Egbert L. Viele, "Topography and Hydrology of New York," a paper delivered at a meeting of the Sanitary Association, 13 June 1859, reprinted in *Public Health of the City of New York: Remarks of Rev. F. C. Ewer* (New York: Edmund Jones & Co., Printers, 1861), 24–33.

20. *American Annual Cyclopedia*, 1861, 526.

21. Washington Irving to his sister Sarah Van Wart, 29 August 1847, in Washington Irving, *Letters*, eds. Ralph M. Aderman, Herbert L. Kleinfeld and Jenifer S. Banks, 4 vols. (Boston: Twayne, 1982), 4, 148.

22. Eugene Sue's *Mysteries of Paris* (1842–3) did much to popularize this way of looking at the city. It was soon followed by George Lippard's bestselling *The Quaker City; or, The Monks of Monk*

Hall (1844–5), a melodramatic tale about the secret corruption of respectable citizens of a city modeled on Philadelphia, and by George Thompson's *Mysteries and Miseries of Philadelphia* (1853). See on this literature Stuart M. Blumin, "Explaining the New Metropolis: Perception, Depiction, and Analysis in Mid-Nineteenth-Century New York," *Journal of Urban History*, 11 (November 1984), 9–38; and Alan Trachtenberg, "The Mysteries of the City," focusing in the post-bellum period, in *The Incorporation of America: Culture and Society in the Gilded Age* (New York: Hill & Wang, 1982), 101–39.

23. This story has received an increasingly sophisticated attention in recent cricism: Robert H. Byers, "Mysteries of the City: A Reading of Poe's 'The Man of the Crowd'" in *Ideology and Classic American Literature*, eds. Sacvan Bercovitch and Myra Jehlen (Cambridge: Cambridge University Press, 1986), 221–46; John F. Kasson, *Rudeness & Civility: Manners in Nineteenth-Century Urban America* (New York: Hill and Wang, [1990]), 83–6; and Dana Brand, *The Spectator and the City in Nineteenth-Century American Literature* (Cambridge: Cambridge University Press, 1991), 83–90, attend to the treacherous difficulty of legibility. A bolder reading of this tale, seeing it as the place where for the first time in Poe's works the father figure fills the stage in all his tragic grandeur, appears in Marie Bonaparte, *The Life and Works of Edgar Allan Poe: A Psycho-Analytic Interpretation* (London: Imago Publishing Co., [1949]), 413–26. Having decided that the crime-tormented old man was John Allan, Poe's step-father, all else falls into place: the

narrator's unconscious intent is to re-enact the Oedipus legend.

24. W. C. Bryant to Frances F. Bryant, 9 May 1860, *The Letters of William Cullen Bryant*, eds. William Cullen Bryants, II and Thomas G. Voss, 4 vols. (New York: Fordham University Press, 1977–84), 4, 153–4.

25. Nathaniel Hawthorne, *The American Notebooks*, 239; William Cullen Bryant, "A New Public Park," *Evening Post*, 3 July 1844, reprinted in Bryant, *Representative Selections*, ed. Tremaine McDowell (New York: American Book Co., 1935), 319–20; "The New Park" (editorial), *New York Times*, 13 June 1853, 4; "A Ramble in Central Park," *Harper's New Monthly Magazine*, 59 (October 1879), 690, quoted in Galen Cranz, *The Politics of Park Design: A History of Urban Parks in America* (Cambridge, MA, and London: The MIT Press, 1982), 5.

26. Donald MacLeod, *Biography of Hon. Fernando Wood* (New York: G. F. Parsons, 1856), 189 This was a note which Olmsted reiterated: "The architecture, stone-cutting [in the park] is as faithful as the most religious of the Middle Ages.... We shall have some things which will glorify our epoch in the after-ages, when the Vandals try to knock them to pieces." Quoted by "The Lounger," "The Central Park," *Harper's Weekly*, 3, (1 October 1859), 626.

27. "City Intelligence. An Afternoon at Greenwood," *Brooklyn Daily Eagle*, 13 June 1846, 2.

28. Andrew Jackson Downing used their success as an argument in favor of the building of public parks in "A Talk About Public Parks and Gardens," *The Horticulturist*, October 1848; *Rural Essays*, ed. George William Curtis (New York: Putnam, 1853; re-

issued New York: Da Capo Press, 1974), 144. Further references in the text.

29. J. B. Jackson, "The American Public Space," *The Public Interest*, Winter 1984, reprinted in *The Public Face of Architecture: Civic Culture and Public Spaces*, eds. Nathan Glazer and Mark Lilla (New York: The Free Press, [1987]), 282–3.

30. [Clarence Cook,] "Central Park. Part 2," *Scribner's Monthly*, 6 (October 1873), 674. See Blanche Linden-Ward, "Strange but Genteel Pleasure Grounds: Tourist and Leisure Uses of Nineteenth-Century Rural Cemeteries," *Cemeteries and Gravemakers: Voices of American Culture*, ed. Richard E. Meyer, with a Foreword by James Deetz (Ann Arbor and London: UMI Research Press, [1989]), 293–328.

31. *New York Evening Post*, 9–10 May 1833, cited Phelps Stokes, *Iconography*, 5, 1720.

32. Hall, "Central Park in the City of New York," 448.

33. Willis quoted in Henry Hope Reed and Sophia Duckworth, *Central Park: A History and a Guide*, rev. ed. (New York: Clarkson N. Potter, Inc., 1972) 16; *Phelps' New York City Guide* (1852); D. T. Valentine, *Manual of the Corporation of the City of New York for 1858* (New York: Common Council, 1858), 363; Gherardi Davis, *The Establishment of Public Parks in the City of New York. Read before the New-York Historical Society, April 6, 1897* (New York: New-York Historical Society, 1897), with additional details from Klein, *Gramercy Park* and Paul Goldberger, *The City Observed: New York. A Guide to the Architecture of Manhattan* (New York: Random House, 1979). Comments on the sites from Phelps Stokes, 5, *passim*.

34. Bryant, letter dated 24 June 1845, published *Evening Post*, 22 July 1845; *Letters of a Traveller, or Notes on Things Seen in Europe and America* (New York: Putnam, 1850), 168–73; *Letters*, 2, 330–32.

35. Lydia Maria Child, Letter IX, 15 March 1844, *Letters from New York*, second series. (New York: C. S. Francis & Co., 1845), 97.

36. Horace Bushnell, *Work and Play; or Literary Varieties* (New York: Charles Scribner, 1864), 17–18.

37. Emerson, "Ode Inscribed to W. H. Channing."

38. Walt Whitman, *Prose Works 1892*, 2 vols. *Collect and Other Prose*, ed. Floyd Stovall (New York: New York University Press, 1964), 2, 582.

39. (New York: J. C. Derby, 1855), 299. Beecher also possessed a strikingly hierarchical sense of society as an organic whole: "It is not the sun upon the *root* that begins growth in a tree, but the sun upon its *top*. . . . And thus, with striking analogy, is it in society. The great mass are producing gross material that rises up to refinement and power, that, in turn, send back the influence of refinement and power upon all the successive degrees, to the bottom!" (*Star Papers*, 295).

40. Rev. Lorenzo White, *The Great Question; or, How Shall I Meet the Claims of God upon my Property?* (New York: Carlton & Phillips, 1856), 36; Lewis Tappan, *Is it Right to be Rich?* (New York: A. D. F. Randolph, 1869).

41. Although he does not refer to Beecher, Clifford S. Griffin in "Religious Benevolence as Social Control, 1815–1860," *Mississippi Valley Historical Review*, 44 (December 1957), 423–44, could easily have done so.

42. [Cook,] "New York Daguerreotyped. Group First: Business

Streets, Mercantile Blocks, Stores and Banks," *Putnam's Monthly*, 1 (February 1853), 121–3. This passage is quoted in a highly relevant discussion in David Schuyler, "The Washington Park and Downing's Legacy to Public Landscape Design" in *Prophet with Honor: The Career of Andrew Jackson Downing 1815–1852*, ed. George Tatum (Philadelphia: The Athenaeum; Washington, DC: Dumbarton Oaks Research Library and Collection, 1989), 306.

43. "A New Park," *New York Journal*, 1 (August 1853), 20.

44. Christopher Hobhouse, *1851 and the Crystal Palace* (London, John Murray, 1937).

45. Martin, *Secrets of the Great City*, 119–20.

46. Clarence C. Cook, *A Description of the New York Central Park* (New York, 1869; reprinted New York: Benjamin Blom, Inc., 1972), 13.

47. Ibid., 14; *The Papers of Frederick Law Olmsted*, ed. in chief Charles Capen McLaughlin, vol. 3, *Creating Central Park*, eds. Charles E. Beveridge and David Schuyler (Baltimore and London: The Johns Hopkins University Press, [1983]), 84. Further references in the text as *Papers*. Edward Hagaman Hall, "Central Park in the City of New York," 449.

48. Norman T. Newton, *Design on the Land: The Development of Landscape Architecture* (Cambridge, MA: Belknap Press of Harvard University Press, 1971), 266, 261. Andrew Jackson Downing, *Landscape Gardening and Rural Architecture* (New York: Dover Publications, Inc., 1991), 9, a reprint of the revised sixth edition of Downing's *Treatise*.

49. Vaux's articles in *The Horticulturist* are of some interest: see his

"Should A Republic Encourage the Arts," 7 (1 February 1852), 73–7; and "American Architecture," 8 (1 April 1853), 168–72. See also Francis R. Kowsky, "The Architectural Legacy of Andrew Jackson Downing" and David Schuyler, "The Washington Park and Downing's Legacy" in Tatum, *Prophet with Honor*, 259–90, 291–312. The absence of originality in Downing's work is emphasized in Tatum's introduction to Downing's *Landscape Gardening and Rural Architecture*, xiii.

50. Neil Harris in *The Artist in American Society: The Formative Years, 1790–1860* (New York: Simon & Schuster, 1966), 210, 213–14, stresses the conservative nature of Downing's architecture.

51. The mild irony of such comparisons was also evident to Olmsted, writing of his visit to New Park, Birkenhead: ". . . I was ready to admit that in democratic America there was nothing to be thought of as comparable with this People's Garden." Olmsted, *Walks and Talks of An American Farmer in England* (New York: G. P. Putnam, 1852; reissued with an Introduction by Alex L. Murray, Ann Arbor: University of Michigan Press, n.d.), 52–3.

52. See Larry J. Reynolds, *European Revolutions and the American Literary Renaissance* (New Haven and London: Yale University Press, 1988).

53. Alphonse de Lamartine, *History of the French Revolution of 1848*, trans. Francis A. Durivage and William S. Chase, 2 vols. in one (Boston: Phillips, Sampson & Co., 1859), 1, 43.

54. Rev. E. H. Chapin, *Humanity in the City* (New York: De Witt & Davenport, [1854]), 71.

55. Henry P. Tappan, D.D., LL.D.,

The Growth of Cities: A Discourse Delivered before the New York Geographical Society on the Evening of March 15th, 1855 (New York: R. Craighead, Printer, 1855), 35–6.

56. David Schuyler, *The New Urban Landscape: The Redefinition of City Form in Nineteenth-Century America* (Baltimore and London: The Johns Hopkins University Press, [1986]), 42–3.

57. On the subject of the financing of parks, and their impact on taxation policy, see Cranz, *The Politics of Park Design*, 75–81.

58. Charles Hirschfield, "America on Exhibition: The New York Crystal Palace," *American Quarterly*, 9 (Summer 1957), 101–16. Charles Sedgwick, a New York lawyer and brother of the novelist Catherine Maria Sedgwick, was president of the association.

59. Bryant's letter to the *Evening Post*, Derby, England, 3 June 1845, Bryant, *Letters*, 2, 320.

60. *New York Journal of Commerce*, 8 January 1850, 1; Phelps Stokes, 5, 1826.

61. A. A., "The East River Park" (letter), *New York Journal of Commerce*, 24 June 1851, 2. Edward Hagaman Hall ("Central Park in the City of New York," 449) says that Fernando Wood, who had been abroad, made the park an issue in his campaign against Kingsland in the mayoral election in 1850. But he was never a "worthy and excellent citizen" and cannot be the person meant. Roy Rosenzweig and Elizabeth Blackmar conclusively identify this gentleman as R. B. Minturn in *The Park and the People: A History of Central Park* (Ithaca, NY: Cornell University Press, [1992]), ch. 1. It is one of the curious aspects of the creation of Central Park that the significant role of such a prominent businessman remained virtually unknown for a century and a half. It was Ruggles, who conceived of the development of Gramercy Park and the surrounding streets as an integrated experiment in planning, who was the more interesting figure.

62. Why Kingsland? He was born in New York in 1804, and formed a partnership with his brother to go into the grocery business as D. & A. Kingsland. The business expanded into a general importing and shipping concern which prospered on the sperm-oil trade. Kingsland fitted out the first vessel to cruise from New York for sperm oil. He was elected mayor on the Whig ticket in 1850, and he was the first to serve for a two-year term. He was thus mayor when that epic of sperm whaling, *Moby-Dick*, was published in 1851. Kingsland was known as a man of integrity and wealth, "but possessed no political experience whatever" before his election. He was a more determined and cleverer man than he was given credit for, which is seen in his repeated vetoes of manifestly corrupt attempts by aldermen to grant "sweet-heart" deals for street railway charters. Two days before he left office the board of aldermen, known universally as the "Forty Thieves," overrode his veto for a contract for the Broadway rail line (see Phelps Stokes, 5, 1843–4). A similar vote in the common council overturned Kingsland's veto of the sale of Gansevoort Market for less than half of its true market value. Denis Tilden Lynch regards Kingsland as an "active participant" in the corruption of the "Forty Thieves," but does not document the accusation. There is no indication in his public life of any previous

interest in parks, connection with Downing, etc. He died in 1878. See "Obituary: Ex-Mayor Ambrose C. Kingsland," *New York Times*, 15 October 1878, 5; George Wilson, ed., *Portrait Gallery of the Chamber of Commerce of the State of New York* (New York: Press of the Chamber of Commerce, 1890), 114–16; *A Condensed Biography of Fernando Wood, compiled from the Original Documents*, by a Veteran Democrat (New York: n.p., 1866), 9; Denis Tilden Lynch, *"Boss" Tweed: The Story of a Grim Generation* (New York: Boni & Liveright, 1927), 70.

63. "Mayor Kingsland's Proposal for a Park," *New York Journal of Commerce*, 7 May 1851, 2.

64. "A New Park," *New York Herald*, 8 May 1851, 4; "The Proposed Public Park," *New York Journal of Commerce*, 4 June 1851, 2. The accompanying editorial comment by the *Journal's* editor Gerard Hallock was doubtful about the proposal, which soon deepened into outright hostility. These doubts were directly addressed in a ringing defense of the proposal: "The New Park of the Metropolis," *New York Herald*, 6 June 1851, 2.

65. "The Proposed Great Park," *New York Journal of Commerce*, 5 June 1851, 2. Complaints are summarized in Allan Nevins, *The Evening Post: A Century of Journalism* (New York: Boni & Liveright, 1922), 192–201; Ian R. Stewart, "Politics and the Park: The Fight for Central Park," *New-York Historical Society Quarterly*, 61 (1977), 124–55.

66. "Manhattan," "Public Parks and the Enlargement of the Battery" (letter), *New York Journal of Commerce*, 13 June 1851, 2;

and, from the same correspondent, "The Large Park Out of Town" (letter), *ibid.*, 16 June 1851, 2.

67. Editorial note appended to "Wayfarer" [Frederick Law Olmsted], "The People's Park at Birkenhead, Near Liverpool," *The Horticulturist*, 6 (1 May 1851), 224–8.

68. "Correspondence in Relation to a Public Park," *New York Journal of Commerce*, 28 June 1851, 2, with accompanying (hostile) editorial comment. See also favorable letters on the Shaw-Dean proposal in the issues of 2, 3 and 24 July 1851 of the same paper.

69. "The New Park," *New York Times*, 2 December 1851, 1. See on this Cook, *Description of Central Park*, 20.

70. "The Mayor's Message," *New York Times*, 6 January 1852, 1. Action was again delayed within the common council on 2 May (Stewart, "Politics and the Park," 141); Donald MacLeod, *Biography of Hon. Fernando Wood* (New York: O. F. Parsons, 1856), 307; Stewart, "Politics and the Park," 142; the text of the second Jones Wood bill is printed in full in the *New York Journal of Commerce*, 8 April 1853, 2.

71. "Death of an Ex-Mayor: Career of Jacob A. Westervelt," *New York Times*, 22 February 1879, 2; G. W. Sheldon, "The Old Ship-Builders of New York," *Harper's New Monthly Magazine*, 65 (1882), 221–41.

72. "The City of New-York—Its Growth and Destiny," *New York Times*, 26 April 1853, 4.

73. Stewart, "The Politics of the Park," 146–7; Nevins, *Evening Post*, 199.

74. "The Jones Wood Park" (editorial), *New York Journal of Commerce*, 24 May 1853, 2.

75. "The Proposed City Park," *New York Herald*, 1 April 1853, 4.

76. J. H. G[riscom], "Public Parks vs. Public Health" (letter), *New York Times*, 30 June 1853, 4.

77. Downing's legacy: "A Workingman," "An Uptown Park," *New York Times*, 5 May 1853, 4; "The New Park" (unsigned letter), *New York Times*, 7 July 1853, 3; petition: "The New Park," *New York Herald*, 11 June 1853, 4; *Journal of the Senate of the State of New-York, at the Seventy-Sixth Session* (Albany: Charles Van Benthuysen, 1853), 722. This memorial was presented by Senator Morgan, a leading proponent of the central site, on 30 May.

78. See Andrew Denny Rodgers, III, *John Torrey: A Story of North American Botany* (Princeton, NJ: Princeton University Press, 1942). Munn was also a contributor to *The Horticulturist*. See his "Of What use is Rural Taste?" in vol. 7 (1 November 1852), 539–40.

79. "Report of the Select Committee on the Bill Relative to a Public Park in New-York," Document 82, *Documents of the Senate of the State of New-York, Seventy-Sixth Session, 1853*, 3 vols. (Albany: C. Van Benthuysen, 1853); senate business on the 22nd, reported in full in *New York Times*, 23 June 1853, 1.

80. "Public Parks: Report of the Select Committee," *New York Times*, 24 June 1853, 1.

81. "Report of the Minority of the Select Committee on the Bill Relative to a Public Park in New-York," Document 83, *Documents of the Senate of the State of New-York, Seventy-Sixth Session. 1853*. 3 vols. (Albany: C. Van Benthuysen, 1853).

82. "The New Park" (unsigned letter), *New York Times*, 7 July 1853, 3.

83. John Foord, *The Life and Public Services of Andrew Haswell Green* (Garden City, NY: Doubleday, Page & Co., 1913), 46.

84. "Law Courts. The Central Park," *New York Times*, 3 October 1853, 3.

85. "Message of the Mayor," *New York Times*, 4 January 1854, 3.

86. "Law Courts. Supreme Court—Special Term before Justice Roosevelt," *New York Times*, 9 January 1854, 3.

87. *New York Tribune*, 1 June 1853, quoted in Edward K. Spann, *The New Metropolis: New York: New York City 1840–57* (New York: Columbia University Press, [1981]), 305.

88. Cook, *Description of Central Park*, 20.

89. Donald MacLeod, *Biography of Hon. Fernando Wood* (New York: G. F. Parsons, 1856), 189.

90. The full text is reprinted in *ibid.*, 308–12.

91. There is a biographical note on Viele in *The Papers of Frederick Law Olmsted, 3, Creating Central Park 1857–1861*, ed. Charles E. Beveridge *et al.* (Baltimore and London: The Johns Hopkins University Press, [1983]), 69–71.

92. *A Few Words on the Central Park by Copeland & Cleveland* (Boston, n.p., 1856), 5.

93. "The Present Look of Our Great Central Park," *New York Times*, 9 July 1856, 3.

94. Quoted in *New York Times*, 29 May 1856.

95. "Rural Taste and its Mission," *The Horticulturist*, 7 (1 October 1852), 441–3.

96. Cook, *Description of Central Park*, 25.

97. "Central Park Misgivings," *New York Times*, 21 April 1857, 4.

98. "The Board of Aldermen," *New York Times*, 4 June 1857, 5.

99. Frederick Law Olmsted, *The Cotton Kingdom: A Traveller's Observations on Cotton and*

Slavery in the American Slave States, ed. Arthur M. Schlesinger, Sr., with an Introduction by Lawrence N. Powell (New York: Random House: The Modern Library, [1984]), 11. Further references to this edition will appear in the text.

100. Frederick Law Olmsted, *A Journey in the Seaboard Slave States in the Years 1853–1854. With Remarks on Their Economy*, with a Biographical Sketch by Frederick Law Olmsted, Jr., and with an Introduction by William P. Trent, 2 vols. (New York and London: G. P. Putnam's Sons, 1904), 1, 151. Further references in the text.

101. [Frederick Law Olmsted], "A Voice from the Sea," *American Whig Review*, 14 (December 1851), 527–8. Virtually the whole of Olmsted's argument fits easily within the developing Republican critique of the south. See Eric Foner, *Free Soil, Free Labor, Free Men: The Ideology of the Republican Party before the Civil War* (London: Oxford University Press, 1970), chs. 1, 2, and 9.

102. Olmsted to Brace, 12 November 1850, *The Papers of Frederick Law Olmsted*, 1; *The Formative Years 1822 to 1852*, ed. Charles Capen McLaughlin *et al.* (Baltimore, MD: The Johns Hopkins University Press, [1977]), 1, 358–9. Further references in the text as *Papers*.

103. *Papers*, 2, 328.

104. F. L. O., "The Arctic: Lessons Concerning Means of Security on Ocean Steamers," *New York Times*, 18 October 1854, 2. The second half alone of this sentence from the original source is included in the text as printed in *Papers*, 2, 322–9.

105. Frederick Law Olmsted, *A Journey in the Back Country*

(New York: Mason Brothers, 1860; reprinted Williamstown, MA: Corner House Publishers, 1972), 83. This passage appears in *The Cotton Kingdom*, 453.

106. *A Journey in the Back Country*, 84–7; *The Cotton Kingdom*, 454–6.

107. *Speech of the Rev. Dr. Bellows, President of the United States Sanitary Commission, made at the Academy of Music, Philadelphia. Thursday evening, Feb. 24, 1863* (Philadelphia: Sherman, Son & Co., 1863), 10.

108. F. L. Olmsted, "Labor: The Famine in New-York.—How to Relieve It.—Laborers Wanted," *New York Times*, 19 February 1855, 2. He made similar arguments on this subject in the issues of 29 January and 8 February 1855. See also the memorable editorial, "Get Them Out of Town," 15 June 1855, 4. Olmsted's belief in the efficacy of sending "starving laborers" to the rural hinterland ignored the fact that the preponderant numbers of such people were illiterate Irish, with neither the skills needed for farm labor nor any wish to be transported so far from their fellow Catholic immigrants into the Protestant hinterland. There was continued demand in the working class for such transportation, but funding was seldom adequate. See on this point Carl N. Degler, "The West as a Solution to Urban Unemployment," *New York History*, 36 (January 1955), 63–84.

109. Charles W. Elliott, "What is to be Done to keep the Poor?" (letter), *New York Times*, 9 February 1855, 3. Olmsted and Brace were also contributing to the *New York Times* in the winter of 1855 on this problem.

110. The story of Olmsted's campaign for the superintendentship has

been often told, and may be traced in *Papers*, 3, ch. 1.

111. Elizabeth Stevenson, *Park Maker: A Life of Frederick Law Olmsted* (New York: Macmillan; [1977]), 156–7.

112. Laura Wood Roper, *FLO: A Biography of Frederick Law Olmsted* (Baltimore, MD: The Johns Hopkins University Press, [1973]), 128. He waited at nearby offices of a lawyer for news from the meeting on the 11th and announced the result in a footnote to a letter to his brother in which he noted the anticipated jealousy of Viele (*Papers*, 2, 79–81).

113. "The Mayoralty," *New York Times*, 25 November 1857, 1.

114. Foord, *Andrew Haswell Green*, 52. See also Benjamin J. Klebaner, "Poor Relief and Public Works During the Depression of 1857," *The Historian*, 22 (May 1960), 264–79.

115. "Central Park," *New York Times*, 13 November 1857, 1.

116. "The Central Park and the Aldermanic Inquiry," *New York Times*, 14 December 1857, 4.

117. "Board of Commissioners of the Central Park," *New York Times*, 2 December 1857, 8.

118. "The Board of Aldermen," *New York Times*, 8 December 1857, 5.

119. "The Central Park and the Aldermanic Inquiry," *op. cit.*, 4.

120. Melvin Kalfus, *Frederick Law Olmsted: The Passion of a Public Artist* (New York: New York University Press, 1990), 191.

121. Henry Hope Reed, Robert M. McGee and Esther Mipaas, *Bridges of Central Park* (New York: Greensward Foundation, Inc., 1990), 12.

122. What follows is based upon the Central Park Commission, *Descriptions of Plans for Improvement of the Central Park* (New York: Board of Commissioners of Central Park, [1858]), 34 numbers.

123. Gustave Le Gray's striking photographs in 1857 of Napoleon III's camp on a vast 29,640-acre plateau at Châlons-sur-Marne—with colorful Zouave regiments, artillery encampments and cavalry formations—encouraged a new sense of the scale and spectacle of military maneuvers.

124. William Cullen Bryant, "Sir Walter Scott: Address on the Unveiling of the Statue of Sir Walter Scott, in Central Park, November 4, 1872," *Orations and Addresses* (New York: G. P. Putnam's Sons, 1873), 392–3.

125. "The Board of Aldermen," *New York Times*, 4 June 1857, 5.

126. "The Central Park and other City Improvements," *New York Herald*, 6 September 1857, 4.

127. Olmsted, *Papers*, 3, 117–87. It is conveniently reprinted in *Landscape into Cityscape: Frederick Law Olmsted's Plans for a Greater New York City*, ed. Albert Fein (New York: Van Nostrand Reinhold Co., [1981]), 63–88.

128. Richard Sennett, *The Conscience of the Eye: The Design and Social Life of Cities* (New York: Alfred A. Knopf, 1990), 56.

129. Olmsted to Richard Grant White, 23 July 1866, *The Papers of Frederick Law Olmsted*, ed. in chief Charles Capen McLaughlin, vol. 6, *The Years of Olmsted, Vaux & Company*, eds. David Schuyler and Jane Turner Censer (Baltimore and London: The Johns Hopkins University Press, [1992]), 101.

130. "Northern Boundary of the Central Park," *New York Times*, 14 January 1858, 4.

131. This may be traced in *New York Times*, 29 May to 11 June 1858.

132. Bryant to John Howard Bryant, c. February 1859, *Letters of William Cullen Bryant*, 4, 99.

133. "The Central Park," *New York Times*, 26 April 1859, 4.

134. Strong, *Diary*, 2, 458.

135. "Central Park Affairs," *New York Times*, 3 September 1859, 8.

136. "The Lounger," "The Central Park," *Harper's Weekly*, III, no. 144 (1 October 1859), 626.

137. "May in the Central Park," *New York Times*, 9 May 1860, 4.

138. *New York Times*, 3 September 1859, 4.

Illustration sources

The author and publisher would like to acknowledge the sources below for photographs appearing on the following pages:

Lights and Shadows of New York Life; or the Sights and Sensations of the Great City by James D. McCabe, Jr. (Philadelphia: National Publishing Co. [1872], frontispiece, pp. 35, 54, 176, 183, 289. *The New York Tombs: Its Secrets and Its Mysteries...*, ed. James B. Mix and Samuel Mackeever (San Francisco: A Roman & Co., 1874) pp. 14, 15, 17, 18. *Harper's Weekly*, 1 December 1860, p. 22. Matthew Hale Smith *Sunshine and Shadow in New York* (Hartford: J. G. Burr and Company, 1868), pp. 26, 284. Horatio Alger, Jr., *Phil the Fiddler; or, The Story of a Young Street Musician* (Boston: Loring, 1872), pp. 24. George Ellington *The Women of New York of The Under-World of the Great City* (New York: The New York Book Co., 1869), pp. 27, 96, 285. Joseph Shannon, *Manual of the Corporation of the City of New York* (New York, 1868), pp. 33, 174. D. T. Valentine *Manual of the Corporation of the City of New York* (New York, 1866), pp. 34, 142, 148, 213, 292. Charles Loring Brace, *The Dangerous Classes of New York, and Twenty Years' Work Among Them* (New York: Wynkop & Hallenbeck, 1872), p. 41. Walter Graeme Eliot, *Portraits of the Noted Physicians of New York 1750–1900*, collected and arranged (New York: American Biographical Society, 1900), p. 51. Gotham Court entrance: an unidentified engraving reproduced in James Ford, ed., et al, *Slums and Housing*, 2 vols. (Cambridge, MA: Harvard University Press, 1936), I, 157, p. 78. A. M. Mauriceau *Married Women's Private Medical Companion* (New York: N. P.), p. 88. J. P. Maygrier, *Nouvelles démonstrations d'accouchements...* (Paris, Béchat, librarie, 1822), plate 29, p. 93. *National Police Gazette*, 21 February, 1846, p. 107. *Wonderful Trial of Caroline Lohman* (New York: [no publisher], 1847), 114. *J. Clarence Davies Collection*, Museum of the City of New York, p. 122. *The Masses*, October-November 1915, p. 130. John Hardy, *Manual of the Corporation of the City of New York* (New York, 1870), p. 146. *Vanity Fair*, VI (July 19, 1862), 25, p. 164. *Frank Leslie's Illlustrated Newspaper*, 9 October, 1869 New York Historical Society, p. 186. New York Public Library, p. 189. *Harper's Weekly*, 19 August, 1871, Museum of the City of New York, p. 194. Art Commission of the City of New York, p. 205. *Harper's Monthly Magazine*, XLIV (May 1872), 845, p. 208. Rev. J. F. Richmond, *New York and Its Institutions 1609–1871* (New York: E. B. Treat, 1871), p. 218. *The Empire State in Three Centuries*, ed. Gen. Dwight H. Bruce, 3 vols. (New York: The Century History Co., n. d.), p. 226. Mayor's Office, City Hall, New York courtesy of the Art Commission of the City of New York, 1853, p. 241. Tinted photograph printed by John Bachmann, 1867 Museum of the City of New York, p. 242. Art Commission of New York, p. 246. Harvard University Art Museums p. 257. [Clarence Cook], *A Description of the New York Central Park* (New York: F. J. Huntington & Co., 1869), pp. 261, 278, 279, 282. *Yankee Notions*, VII (1859), 27, p. 291.

The illustrations on the following pages come from the author's private collection: pp. 140, 173, 184, 227, 230, 233, 256, 268.

Index

References to illustrations are in bold.